Beginning iPhone and iPad Web Apps

Scripting with HTML5, CSS3, and JavaScript

Chris Apers

Daniel Paterson

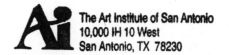

Apress®

Beginning iPhone and iPad Web Apps: Scripting with HTML5, CSS3, and JavaScript

ISBN-13 (pbk): 978-1-4302-3045-8

ISBN-13 (electronic): 978-1-4302-3046-5

Printed and bound in the United States of America 9 8 7 6 5 4 3 2 1

President and Publisher: Paul Manning
Lead Editor: Steve Anglin
Technical Reviewer: Paul Haine
Editorial Board: Steve Anglin, Mark Beckner, Ewan Buckingham, Gary Cornell, Jonathan Gennick, Jonathan Hassell, Michelle Lowman, Matthew Moodie, Duncan Parkes, Jeffrey Pepper, Frank Pohlmann, Douglas Pundick, Ben Renow-Clarke, Dominic Shakeshaft, Matt Wade, Tom Welsh
Coordinating Editor: Adam Heath
Copy Editor: Kim Wimpsett
Compositor: MacPS, LLC
Indexer: BIM Indexing & Proofreading Services
Cover Designer: Anna Ishchenko

Distributed to the book trade worldwide by Springer Science+Business Media, LLC., 233 Spring Street, 6th Floor, New York, NY 10013. Phone 1-800-SPRINGER, fax (201) 348-4505, e-mail orders-ny@springer-sbm.com, or visit www.springeronline.com.

For information on translations, please e-mail rights@apress.com, or visit www.apress.com.

Apress and friends of ED books may be purchased in bulk for academic, corporate, or promotional use. eBook versions and licenses are also available for most titles. For more information, reference our Special Bulk Sales–eBook Licensing web page at www.apress.com/info/bulksales.

The source code for this book is available to readers at www.apress.com.

To Aoï, who had to put up with my moods for so long.
A thousand thanks. With love.

—*Chris*

To Alice, for I can never thank you enough
for the inspiration your love and brilliance provide.

—*Daniel*

Contents at a Glance

▦ Contents v

▦ About the Authors xv

▦ About the Technical Reviewer xvi

▦ Acknowledgments xvii

▦ Introduction xviii

Part I: Getting Started with Web App Development 1

▦ Chapter 1: Development Tools 3

▦ Chapter 2: Development Environment 13

▦ Chapter 3: Introducing Developer and Debugging Tools 29

Part II: Web App Design with HTML5 and CSS3 65

▦ Chapter 4: The Anatomy of a Web Application 67

▦ Chapter 5: User Experience and Interface Guidelines 89

▦ Chapter 6: Interesting CSS Features for Your Web Application
User Interface 117

▦ Chapter 7: Bitmap and Vector Graphics and Downloadable Fonts
with Canvas and SVG 165

▦ Chapter 8: Embedding Audio and Video Content in
Your Web Application 219

▦ Chapter 9: Handling Transformations, Animations,
and Special Effects with CSS 257

Part III: Going Futher with JavaScript and Web Standards 299

▦ Chapter 10: An Object-Oriented JavaScript Programming Primer 301

▦ Chapter 11: Cross-Document Communication 321

▦ Chapter 12: Ajax and Dynamic Content 343

▦ Chapter 13: Using Touch and Gesture Events 367

▦ Chapter 14: Location-Aware Web Applications 397

▦ Chapter 15: A Better Handling of Client-Side Data Storage 431

▦ Index 467

Contents

■ Contents at a Glance iv

■ About the Authors xv

■ About the Technical Reviewer xvi

■ Acknowledgments xvii

■ Introduction xviii

Part I: Getting Started with Web App Development 1

■ Chapter 1: Development Tools 3

The Source Editor 3

    Varanus Komodoensis 3

    Make Yourself Comfortable 4

What About Dashcode? 5

Using the Right Browser 6

    The WebKit 6

    The Gecko and the Fox 7

    Opera 7

    Internet Explorer, Lost at Sea 7

Developing Web-Wise 8

    Acid...Acid...Acid 8

    HTML5 Conformance 8

    A Satellite in Your Browser 8

Developing for iOS 9

    Using the iPhone and iPad Simulator 9

    Using a Real Device Anyway 10

    The ADC Is Your Friend 10

Summary 11

■ Chapter 2: Development Environment 13

Serving the Web Application 13

Mac OS, Making Things Easy 14

An Apache in Your Mac 14

The Script Engine 15

Windows, Choose Your Weapons 16

An All-in-One Installation Process 17

Security Settings 20

Linux, Take Control 22

Handling Multiple Hosts 23

Unix-Based System 23

Windows-Based System 24

Configuring Multiple Web Sites 24

Apache 2: Get Carried Away 24

The Windows Case 26

Have You Made It? 27

Bet You Have! 28

■ **Chapter 3: Introducing Developer and Debugging Tools 29**

Making Friends with WebKit's Developer Tools 29

Enabling the Develop Menu 30

The Develop Menu Exposed 30

Developing on Mobile Safari 32

Overview of the Web Inspector 34

The Developer Tools Window 35

Error Notifications 36

Master Your Code 37

Make the Document Yours 37

Dig Your Style 38

Editing Styles 40

Metrics 40

Advanced Search 43

The Resources Viewer 44

Debugging JavaScript 46

Logging to the Console 46

Using the Interactive Shell 48

Let the Debugger Do the Job 49

The Life Cycle of Your Page 55

Profiling Your Scripts 57

Understanding the Profiles 58

Filtering with the Search Field 59

Client-Side Data Storage 60

Database Storage 61

Cookies 61

Other Storage Features 61

Auditing Your Page 61

Still Unsure? 63

Summary 63

Part II: Web App Design with HTML5 and CSS3 65

■ **Chapter 4: The Anatomy of a Web Application 67**

The iPhone Revolution 67

Belief in Web Apps 68

But What is a Web App Exactly? 70

Planet of the Apps: Who Rules 71

Cross-Platform Master 71

Hardware Access Is No Forbidden Weapon Anymore 72

Free Your Content 72

Release Model 73

Web Apps: Not the Little Brother Anymore 73

Web Apps on Mobile Safari 73

Master the Browser 73

Browser Metrics 74

Think "Web App" 75

Configuring the Viewport 75

Seriously Appy: Using Stand-Alone Mode 77

Showcasing a Proper Icon 77

Running Your Application Full-Screen 79

An Awesome Startup 79

Tweaking the Status Bar 80

Staying in Stand-Alone Mode 80

Build Your First Web App Base Project 81

Your Document Template in Komodo Edit 82

Hiding Mobile Safari's Address Bar 85

Handling Screen Orientation Changes 86

Final Touch 87

Ready to Go 88

■ Chapter 5: User Experience and Interface Guidelines 89

From the Web on the Desktop to the Mobile Web 90

Forget the Desktop 91

Change Navigation Habits 91

Show Ads Thoughtfully 92

Let Users Decide by Themselves 95

Simplicity and Ease of Use 96

Avoid Clutter 96

User Interface 97

Avoid Unnecessary Interaction 99

Make Use of New Input Types Capabilities 100

Ponder Upon User-Supplied Information 101

Avoid Multiplying Steps 102

The Spirit: Be Focused 102

Make Things Responsive 103

Make Your Web App Responsive 103

Make Your Web App Reactive 105

iOS Interface Design Good Practices 105

Adaptability 105

List vs. Icon Approach 106

Considering UI Alternatives 109

Mimicking the iOS UI 109

Building the iPad Experience 110

Be Creative and Innovative 115

Summary 116

■Chapter 6: Interesting CSS Features for Your Web Application User Interface 117

Improving the User Experience with CSS 117

User Feedback 118

Disabling Copy/Paste Functionalities 119

Control Over Callout 120

Selectors 121

Overview of Available CSS Selectors 121

Position in Suite Selectors: Structural Pseudoclasses 122

Advanced Handling of Backgrounds 124

Origin of the Background 125

Global Background Clipping 126

Text-Based Background Clipping 128

Sizing the Background 128

Developing a Photos-Like Gallery 130

Multilayer Backgrounds 134

Colors 135

The Alpha Channel 135

New Color Definitions 136

Using Gradients 137

Basic Syntax 137

Changing the Size of the Gradient 139

Complete Gradient Syntax 139

Advanced Color Handling 140

Boxes and Borders 142

Box Sizing 142

Rounded Box Corners 143

Borders Drawn with Images 145

Shadows 147

Box Shadows 148

Text Shadows 149

Text Effect with Shadows and Outline 150

Adding a Button to Your Header 150

Columns Layout 152

CSS Column Properties 152

Porting Press Content to the Web 155

The Flexible Box Model 158

A Clean and Flexible Way to Handle Column Layouts 158

Ordering Boxes 159

Flexibility 160

Packing and Alignment 161

Targeting WebKit Specifically 162

Summary 163

■Chapter 7: Bitmap and Vector Graphics and Downloadable Fonts with Canvas and SVG **165**

Working with the Canvas Area 165
  The Drawing Context 167
  Drawing Simple Shapes 172
  Colors, Gradients, and Patterns 174
  More Complex Shapes with Paths 175
  Applying Transformations 181
  Simplifying Drawing State Modifications 183
  Using Text 183
  Shadows 187
  Clipping and Compositing 188
  Working with Canvas Pixels 191
Using Vector Graphics 195
  Inserting SVG into Your Documents 196
  Understanding the Coordinates System 196
  Drawing Shapes 200
  Interoperability 201
  Communication 205
  Animation with and Without Scripting 207
  Coping with Temporary Bugs 210
Preinstalled and Downloadable Fonts 211
Summary 218

■Chapter 8: Embedding Audio and Video Content in Your Web Application **219**

Embedding Video Content 220
  Getting Information About the Video 221
  The Video Placeholder 222
  Playing the Video 223
Embedding Audio Content 224
Keep Things Reasonable 225
Take Control Over Your Content 226
  Understanding and Using Ranges 227
  A Number of Supported Events 232
Adding Subtitles and Chapters to Your Media 233
  Creating Your Own Custom Subtitles 234
  Easier Media Browsing with Chapters 243
Workarounds...Let's Go 247
Media Content for the iPhone and iPad 248
  Understanding Video Formats 248
  Dealing with Supported Audio Formats 250
  Encoding for the Web 251
Summary 256

■Chapter 9: Handling Transformations, Animations, and Special Effects with CSS **257**

Transform Your Elements 257
  Checking Transform Support 258

Applying Rotations 259

Translating Element Coordinates 260

Scaling Page Contents 260

Distorting Elements..261

Custom Transformations with Matrices 261

The Origin of the Transformation 262

Working in a Three-Dimensional Environment 262

New Transform Functions...263

Setting the Perspective..263

Preserving the 3D Aspect 265

Back Face Visibility 266

Combining Styles with JavaScript 268

Accessing Current Styles 268

A Native Object to Compute Matrices 268

Transitions 270

The transition CSS Property...271

Initiating a Transition 271

Timing Function Curve 272

Telling When the Transition Is Completed 274

Getting Ready for a Cover Flow–Like Experience 274

The Main Document..275

The Cover Flow Animation 278

Flipping the Current Cover 280

Final Touch to the Animation 280

Double-Check: Preventing Unexpected Behavior 281

Advanced Animations and Key Frames...282

Key Frames 282

Starting and Timing the Animation 283

Animation Properties 283

The Evolution Curve 284

Working with Events 285

Special Effects with CSS..285

Creating Reflections...286

Using Real Masks 287

Create an iOS-Like Tab Bar Using Masks 288

Getting the Initial Tab Bar Ready 289

A Placeholder for Icons 291

Icons Management 292

Creating Icons 294

Custom Icons Using an Image 297

Summary 298

Part III: Going Futher with JavaScript and Web Standards 299

■ Chapter 10: An Object-Oriented JavaScript Programming Primer.............. 301

From the Procedural Model... 301

...to Object-Oriented Programming..302

A First Custom Object 302

Using a Proper Constructor..303

Better Performance with Prototype 304

Implementing Inheritance 305

Prototype-Based Inheritance 305

Shared Properties 306

The Prototype Chain 307

The Execution Context 308

Using the call() and apply() Methods 308

Taking Care of the Execution Context 310

Setting the Proper Context with Handlers and Callbacks 310

Accessing Properties and Methods 312

Defining Getters and Setters...313

Code Isolation and Libraries 314

Isolating Your Code 315

Creating a Library 316

Enhancing Your Spinner Animation 317

Summary 318

Chapter 11: Cross-Document Communication 321

Cross-Document Communication Limitations 322

Communication, the HTML5 Way 323

The Cross-Document Messaging API...323

Data Type Support and Handling 324

Security Considerations 325

Case Study 325

The Main Document...325

The Hosted Document..327

Let's Send a Message 328

Handling the Response 329

Specific Mobile Safari Behavior with <iframe> 330

Working with Proper Windows..332

Notify the Page Is Loaded 333

Properties of the Window Object 334

Encapsulating the API to Ease Communication 335

An Object for the Host Document...335

An Object for the Widget 337

The Host Document and the Widgets..338

Relaxing Subdomain Communication 340

Changing the Domain...340

Security 341

The Last Message 341

Chapter 12: Ajax and Dynamic Content 343

Building an HTTP Request...343

Requests Using the XMLHttpRequest Object 344

The open() Method..344

Sending Requests Using GET or POST 344

Handling the Request State 345

Handling Progress Events 346

Checking the Response 347

Handling Return Formats 348
    Most Common Return Formats 348
    Parsing XML for Use in HTML Documents 349
    Specificities When Parsing JSON 352
    JSON Security Considerations 353
Client-Side Rendering Using Returned Data 354
    Handling Template Variables 354
    Formatting Variables 355
Cross-Origin Communication 356
    Using Proxies 356
    The JSONP Way 357
    The Cross-Origin Resource Sharing 359
Real-Life Example: Display Twitter Trends 360
    The Twitter Trends Feed 360
    Fetching and Rendering Data 360
Be Kind to the Waiting User 363
    Adding Visual Feedback 363
    Handling Excessive Waiting Times 364
Summary 365

■ **Chapter 13: Using Touch and Gesture Events 367**
How to Handle Events 367
    Calling Priority of Handlers 367
    The Capture Stage 369
    Control Over Event Propagation 370
    Preventing Default Behavior 370
    Handlers and Object Methods 371
Classic Events with Mobile Safari 372
    Behavior of Mouse Events 372
    Scrolling Information 372
Multi-Touch Events 373
    New Interaction Processes 373
    Handling Multi-Touch Events 373
    Unlimited Touch Points 374
    Cancelled Touch Events 376
A Page View Built with Touch and Transform 377
    What We Are Going to Do 377
    The Container 378
    Bring Elements and Interaction 379
    Creating Custom Events 382
    Handling Custom Events 384
Working with Precomputed Gestures 385
Create Your Own Gestures 387
    One Code, Many Strokes 387
    The Bounding Box Object 389
    Registering User Strokes 390
    Using the Recognizer Object 392
    Improve Accuracy 394

Summary 395

■ **Chapter 14: Location-Aware Web Applications** **397**

The Geolocation API 398
    Privacy Considerations 398
    Setup Considerations 398
Getting the Current Position 399
    Longitude, Latitude, and More 399
    Handling Errors from Requests 401
    Accuracy, Timeout, and Cached Location 402
Putting the User on a Map with Google Maps 403
    Showing the Map 403
    Centering the Map on the Location of the User 405
    Marking the Position of the User 407
    Showing Accuracy 409
Tracking the User's Position 410
    Registering for Updates 410
    Specific Behavior of the Watcher 411
    Watching Position on Google Maps 412
From Data to Math 413
    Distance Between Two Points 413
    Sharper Distance Between Two Points...414
    The Direction to Take 415
Building a Compass Web App 416
    Create the Mobile Elements 416
    The Graduations..418
    The Needles 420
    The Dial Shine 421
    Render the Compass..422
    Add Elements to the Document 424
    Prepare the Document to Receive Location Data 425
    Use Location Data..426
    Animate the Compass 427
    Prevent Staggering Needles 429
Summary 430

■ **Chapter 15: A Better Handling of Client-Side Data Storage**........................ **431**

Different Storage Areas 431
    How to Use New Storage Capabilities..432
    Specific Behavior of sessionStorage 433
    Being Notified of Storage Area Modification..434
    Security and Privacy Considerations 435
    Caching Ajax Requests 435
    Sending Client Data to the Server 441
SQL Local Database 442
    Opening the Database..443
    Creating Tables..444
    Adding Data to Tables..446
    Querying Data from the Tables 448

Updating Data 449

Using Database in Place of Storage 451

Handling Transaction and Query Errors 452

Maintaining Coherent Access with Versioning 454

Deleting the Database 456

Security Again 457

Offline Web Application Cache 458

How Does It Work? 458

The Manifest File 459

Controlling the Cache with JavaScript 462

Reacting to Events Sent by the Application Cache 464

Deleting Cache 465

Is the User Online? 466

Summary 466

■ **Index** **467**

About the Authors

 **Chris Apers** has more than 13 years experience in web technologies and mobile development, including the PalmOS, webOS, and iPhone. He is a technical manager and architect at Newsweb/Lagardère Active and participates in open source projects such as porting development libraries and software to mobile devices. With the creation of the open source framework WebApp.Net, he provides an easy way to create mobile content targeting WebKit browsers. For more, visit www.webapp-net.com and www.chrilith.com.

 **Daniel Paterson** has a master's degree in comparative literature, and he penned a memoir on integrating literary theory into fictional works, taking novels by Umberto Eco, Milan Kundera, and David Lodge as examples. After his university years, Daniel entered web development and joined Newsweb/Lagardère Active in April 2009. Passionate about the Web as about many other things, he enjoys every opportunity to work on interesting projects and to develop his skills.

About the Technical Reviewer

Paul Haine is a client-side developer currently working in London for the *Guardian* newspaper. He is the author of *HTML Mastery: Semantics, Standards, and Styling* (friends of ED, 2006) and runs a personal web site at www.joeblade.com.

Acknowledgments

We would like to thank the people from Apress, especially Steve Anglin, for giving us the opportunity to take part in this project, and Clay Andres, for his greatly helpful participation in the early stages of the writing. We also send thanks to our editors, Douglas Pundick and Brian MacDonald, for their valuable comments; Paul Haine for his close reading and testing of every chapter and example in this book; and Kim Wimpsett, for helping us make our explanations more straightforward when they became too complicated. Finally, this book probably never would have been published without the close following of its evolution by Kelly Moritz and Adam Heath.

Thanks also go to those who have helped, in one way or another, to bring this book together, among whom are Hans Shumacker, Ivan Mitrovic, Roy Sinclair, Adam Dachis, David Ljung Madison, and Kris Merckx. As for those whom we (may) have forgotten here, we acknowledge your precious help.

Finally and most importantly, our thoughts go to Alice and Aoï who lived with us every day during the past months, putting up with us and our changing moods and late nights of work. Without their patience and support, this book wouldn't be.

Introduction

Although most iOS development is currently focused on native applications using Apple's Software Development Kit, this proves less and less relevant as the number of different mobile devices and OS versions grows. Gathering resources to make web applications that will work cross-platform is far more cost-effective than hiring a team to build specific version-applications. In this sense, it is probable that web applications have only just begun to fight.

Indeed, web browser performance and features make possibilities regarding user experience and provided services ever greater, and web browsers create an exciting field for web developers to play in. With the arrival and implementation of new standards, the boundaries between native applications and web applications have never been so thin; geolocation and Multi-Touch control, for instance, are no longer just a dream. HTML5, on the other side, is not only a new version of the markup language; the new specification comes with a full range of new APIs that will make you forget heavy use of presentational images and let you richly integrate multimedia elements. Because most of these new features originate in recognized specifications, they are not only implemented in the Mobile Safari layout engine but are also widely available on other mobiles devices and desktop browsers.

Web browsers are everywhere; they're the widest distribution platform ever, available on all platforms and, increasingly, on all devices. This makes web development the field where developers can reach the widest audience using minimal resources. This may well turn building web applications into the new El Dorado in the years to come.

Who This Book Is For

This book is especially fit for developers who have strong experience in front-end web development and are looking to turn to mobile development, primarily web application development for WebKit-based browsers. Although the examples and explanations in this book are meant to work on iPhone, iPad, and iPod touch, you should find them quite equally useful for developing for webOS, Android, or the browser from the latest BlackBerry devices, as well as for any modern desktop browser.

This book will be useful also to native application developers because resorting to the `UIWebView` from the iOS SDK is often necessary to gain more control over the interface of your applications, and getting a firm grasp on the latest advances of the technologies presented in this book can be of great help.

What You Need to Know

This book assumes you already have solid knowledge of the Web and its underlying technologies, including a firm grasp of JavaScript development. Not only has JavaScript become essential to enhance the user experience in modern web applications, it is also necessary in order to use the latest APIs brought by HTML5 and other World Wide Web Consortium (W3C) or Web Hypertext Application Technology Working Group (WHATWG) specifications. To build efficient applications, you will also need to have a good understanding of object-oriented programming and JavaScript-specific related mechanisms.

What's in This Book

This book is divided into three main sections. They will in turn bring you the necessary background to build web applications and efficiently develop for mobile devices; take you through a number of new exciting features of CSS3, HTML5, and Mobile Safari; and get you going with more advanced uses of web standards. Here is a short description of each part:

- **Part I, Getting Started with Web App Development:** The first part of this book goes through useful tools to develop web applications. Of course, chances are you have your own habits, with a fully functional and ready-to-use development environment. However, digging into the specific development tools of WebKit browsers will help you build better web applications faster.

- **Part II, Web App Design with HTML5 and CSS3:** This second part will let you get into further detail about what a web application looks like and the rules that you should be aware of to build successful web applications. Following specific guidelines on user interface and user experience—they should be your two primary concerns—we will go through the latest technologies that will allow you to efficiently meet your style, content, and interaction goals.

- **Part III, Going Further with JavaScript and Web Standards:** The final part will take you even further into client-side development, with topics such as Ajax and HTML templates, advanced handling of Apple's Multi-Touch API, and location-aware web applications. The last chapter from this part will bring the ultimate touch to building web applications that behave like native applications by introducing you to ways you can make your pages available and functional offline.

Are You Ready?

Thanks to the incredible iOS platform found on the iPhone, iPad, and iPod touch and to the implementation of the latest web standards in the Mobile Safari, not only will you find that the limit for your web applications practically is the sky, you will also notice that your development process and the options available to you will be more fluid and open to creativity.

Some examples from this book may seem more technical and advanced than others. However, don't be afraid because everything is explained step-by-step. Also, don't forget that testing code yourself and playing around with it is the best way to learn and understand. So, don't hesitate to modify the examples in this book and change them to fit your needs.

Reading this book, you should master the main tools to build advanced web applications that have major assets to be appealing to users. So come, turn the page, and jump into this exciting area of creation!

Getting Started with
Web App Development

## Chapter 1

Development Tools

Unlike native iPhone application development, web application development doesn't require a specific integrated development environment (IDE). As long as you have an editor that can save to plain text, you're OK. Likewise, the primary front-end web developer's tool, the web browser, exists in all shapes, is well known, and is easily available.

Being free doesn't necessarily mean being reckless, and in your development process, you'll want all the software usefulness you can get. This first chapter aims to help you build an efficient working environment while assuring we have a common background from the beginning of our iOS adventure.

The Source Editor

There are plenty fabulous editors out there—open source and proprietary, free or pay, jukebox-like beautiful or running directly from a terminal. From our point of view, a really useful editor should at least support syntax coloring, autocompletion, and some kind of snippet utility.

Varanus Komodoensis

If you're already involved in web development, you've probably already settled with your perfect code pal. If you're not, we suggest you download and install Komodo Edit, a cross-platform, free, and feature-rich open source editor built on the Mozilla code base, which is going to be used throughout all our examples.

> **NOTE:** You can download Komodo Edit for Mac OS X, Windows, and Linux from the ActiveState web site at www.activestate.com/komodo-edit/.

Like Mozilla, Komodo Edit is an open web and open standards initiative. The open web aims to encourage a community-driven development of open and non proprietary web technologies to ensure the viability and open evolution of the Web.

Starting with version 6.0, Komodo Edit noticeably features support for HTML5 and CSS3 syntax out of the box, including support for the -webkit- proprietary prefix. These will all become very useful throughout this book.

Make Yourself Comfortable

Komodo Edit is so feature rich that it almost seems like a lightweight IDE by itself.

When you launch Komodo Edit, it greets you with an offer to restore your previous session; answering "no" will take you to the Start Page (always accessible as a special tab), as shown in Figure 1–1. There, you will find quick links to open files and perform various actions, and ActivateState has even added samples for each option to help you get started. You can access these samples from a built-in Toolbox panel, made visible by selecting the **View ➤ Tabs & Sidebars** menu and then selecting **Toolbox**. You will also notice one of Komodo Edit's interesting assets: project management, which will let you orderly group all the elements of your projects. In Chapter 4, we are going to create a web application template that will be used throughout this book, and using Komodo Edit is an easy way to create, store, and reuse this template.

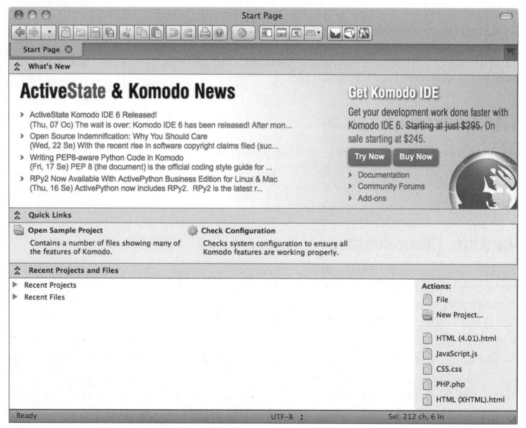

Figure 1–1. *Komodo Edit's Start Page*

Another aspect that can seriously enhance productivity is Komodo Edit's ability to boost code and file reuse though the handling of snippets, templates, and even macros. You can create snippets and templates directly by right-clicking a piece of code and selecting **Add as Snippet in Toolbox** in the contextual menu, so go ahead—save some time.

Also, as stated earlier, Komodo Edit is based on Mozilla, which means it can be extended with add-ons. The add-ons management window is available from the menu **Tools ➤ Add-ons**.

You can also check out the community web site and the extensions section at http://community.activestate.com/. Chances are the one thing you were missing will be there. We're not going to get into thorough detail about Komodo Edit, but it is definitely worth trying. If you haven't settled on a source editor or if you like a change in your working habits from time to time, do check it out. Further documentation is available on the web site.

What About Dashcode?

You may be thinking, "OK, when I installed Snow Leopard, it shipped with Xcode and Dashcode, so why not just use that?" You'd be right, because Apple developed this piece of software specially for this purpose (Figure 1–2).

Figure 1–2. *The new project window in Dashcode 3.0*

Dashcode is a good tool that generates small but nifty web applications with nice transitions between views. What's more, Dashcode makes intensive use of the Model-View-Controller (MVC) paradigm to rationalize and simplify interactions between application layers. Nonetheless, it simply doesn't fit our needs.

First, it is available only on a computer running Mac OS X, limiting its use to developers owning a Mac; today these still make up a small proportion of coders.

Next, it is visual programming software. You very well could build applications with Dashcode without ever touching a single line of code. This can be handy, but it is not our point here. As the reader of this book and a professional web developer, you're going to need full control over your code, and you want to know what is happening at every stage of the developing process to ensure the quality of your web application.

Finally, just like Dreamweaver and other graphical tools, it tends to produce many framework-specific attributes, making the whole code a chore to alter and maintain, and it generates too much unnecessary markup and JavaScript. When developing for the Web, especially for low-memory devices such as mobile browsers, lightweight code should be a primary concern.

Using the Right Browser

To develop for the Web is to develop mainly for a web browser. Although we are going to specifically target Mobile Safari (the browser used on the iPhone, the iPod touch, and the iPad), it can be helpful to have a clear idea of what's going on in this field. Moreover, if you already are a web developer, you're probably used to going through the development process using primarily one specific browser, and developing on a desktop browser rather than a mobile device often proves more efficient.

The WebKit

Developing for Apple devices, you'll have Mobile Safari specifically in mind all the time. Of course, you can strive to make your applications cross-browser compatible, but this would mean more code if not less functionality. Moreover, as you're about to see, Mobile Safari isn't as limited a target as it may at first seem.

Mobile Safari and Desktop Safari are based on the WebKit layout engine. The engine was designed from the beginning to be lightweight and standards compliant. Not only does WebKit implement the latest W3C candidate recommendations, but it also implements draft-stage features with the -webkit- prefix.

The WebKit engine also comes with a full set of tools for developers. We will detail WebKit's Web Inspector in Chapter 3, and you will soon see that it can be of great help in your web application development process.

NOTE: The best option to develop iPhone (or iPod touch or iPad) web applications is to work on an Apple platform. However, you can easily install Safari on Windows, be it XP, Vista, or 7. As an alternative to Safari, we recommend browsers based on the Chromium project, such as Google Chrome, Chromium, or Iron. All three are available for Mac OS, Windows, and Linux.

WebKit is used by many browsers on all platforms, including mobile devices. Among others, you may be interested in SymbianOS, Google's Android, ChromeOS, BlackBerry, and the recent webOS from Palm. Most web applications you build for Apple's browser should work on other mobile devices.

The Gecko and the Fox

Another big actor in the browser market is Firefox, an open source project based on the Gecko engine. Its compliance with standards is very good, and you might appreciate one of Firefox's strongest points: its community. It is infinitely extensible with rich add-ons, such as Firebug, which is a thorough and usable development and debugging tool. This makes Firefox an excellent companion when developing for the Web with features similar to those of WebKit.

Opera

Opera is also available for all operating systems. The Opera team has always put priority on speed and the respect for standards, and although its browser doesn't have a major market share, it is an excellent alternative to the browsers introduced earlier and a good choice for developers too. Indeed, Opera comes with its own set of developer tools, Dragonfly. Opera is also available for mobile devices (Opera Mini), which, unlike Mobile Safari, is a drastically lightened version of the browser and therefore will not let you benefit from all the standards supported by the desktop browser.

Internet Explorer, Lost at Sea

If you are a Windows user wondering about Internet Explorer, we're afraid we couldn't less recommend this browser for web development purposes. Although it definitely was an advanced web browser from versions 3 to 5 (the first major browser to implement CSS support and the first browser to provide then-unnamed Ajax features), it has followed a path away from standards and as of version 8 still lacks support for many features such as CSS selectors and properties (CSS2 selectors and properties, that is), scoring 20/100 at the Acid3 test. It appears that Internet Explorer 9 should mark great evolution in this regard, but for now, the Trident-based browser isn't an option.

Developing Web-Wise

The Web has standards, the first of which are the World Wide Web Consortium (W3C) specifications. These give you, the developer, tools to build brilliant web-based applications. That's why the first concern you'll have about a web browser when developing web applications is its W3C compliance. The more compliant the browser you choose as your first target is, the more your pages will be functional on other platforms and the less extra work you will have to do.

Acid...Acid...Acid

The Web Standards Project is an organization dedicated to promoting and encouraging the respect and adoption of web specifications. Because not all browsers are equal at this task, it provides a tool to easily check how well a layout engine is keeping up. The latest version of the test is called Acid3.

> **TIP:** To know what score a browser achieves at this test, just go to http://acid3.acidtests.org/, and you will get the result within a few seconds.

Mobile Safari passes the test with 100 percent compliance, which is good because it means many possibilities to enhance your applications. If you're using another browser for development purposes, you should have in mind that you could find yourself thoughtlessly discarding very interesting features of HTML, CSS, and JavaScript.

HTML5 Conformance

Although the Acid3 test is a good way to evaluate CSS standards compliance of a browser, it doesn't indicate exactly what is supported. However, you can check the support for HTML5 features available in a browser using the test page at http://html5test.com/ and get a detailed table of supported and unsupported standards.

This test page will list all new APIs, extensions, and HTML5 specificities, indicating the level of support for them in the used browser. Mobile Safari scores 125 (and 7 bonus points) out of 300. Though this may seem low, it actually indicates excellent support of new standards, especially for a mobile browser.

To get more detail about each feature implemented, every element from the list is a link that will take you directly to the relevant page from the specification.

A Satellite in Your Browser

Another central part of modern front-end development—and especially of web application development—is JavaScript. We will heavily resort to JavaScript in most of our chapters and will introduce object-oriented JavaScript programming in Chapter 10.

The compliance of the scripting engine of a browser to the ECMA-262 specification (up to version 3) can be evaluated using the Sputnik test, built by Google and available from `http://sputnik.googlelabs.com/`. It is an open source test gathering more than 5,000 points. Safari obtains a very good score, coming second right behind Opera.

Developing for iOS

Although we have introduced cross-platform options for all the tools you may need, you are going to develop for iOS, and the following software, however useful, is available only on Macintosh systems. If you don't have a Mac, do read on anyway; although you won't benefit from the applications described in the following sections, we will be presenting useful resources for your developing adventure.

Using the iPhone and iPad Simulator

There are many reasons why you wouldn't want to use an iPhone device while developing your web applications. The good news is that Apple provides a free tool that does just what you need as soon as you've become a registered Apple developer. Just sign up at `http://developer.apple.com/ios/`. Then, download and install the free iOS Software Development Kit (SDK), and specifically its simulator, shown in Figure 1–3.

> **NOTE:** Before downloading, do fetch some tea. You'll be on for a near-to-3GB download. Once the installation is complete, the iPhone and iPad Simulator application will be hiding in the folder */Developer/Platforms/iPhoneSimulator.platform/Developer/Applications/*. If you don't want to go mad looking for it before each work session, drag a shortcut to the Dock or your desktop!

The main benefit of the simulator is that you don't have to actually have a proper device to do your testing and drain your battery by loading pages again and again. What's more, not only does it support iPhone simulation, but it now also simulates the iPad, using a real version of Mobile Safari. It also allows you to run tests on different versions of the OS without going through the long and annoying process of reinitializing the device.

Figure 1–3. *The simulator offers only a minimal set of applications fit for development purposes*

This is the closest you'll get to an iPhone living on your desktop. As for non-Mac users, we can only recommend you double-test all your code on a proper iPhone, iPod touch, or iPad to get a proper grasp of how the actual devices behave.

Using a Real Device Anyway

Using the simulator, you'll get less functionality, the bare minimum for development. Take into account that performance may be better on the simulator, which uses your desktop computer for resources, than on the device. Thus, transitions and advanced visual effects or multimedia content, covered in Chapters 8 and 9, should systematically be tested on the targeted product.

Also, because screen size does make a difference, you should always check that all your text and elements (such as buttons) are readable and usable in order not to harm the user experience of your web applications.

The ADC Is Your Friend

Whether you have a Mac to install the simulator on or not, it always is a good idea to register. The Apple Developer Connection (ADC) is resourceful place to browse through and find help. Being a registered developer will gain you access to tips, screencasts, interviews, and much more. If you make your way through information irrelevant to you (that is, information about native iOS applications development), you'll find how hugely beneficial Apple's own information can be. The best place to start is the Safari development page (`http://developer.apple.com/safari/`), where interesting information about supported features is available.

Summary

By now, you should have a functional development environment. Whether you have chosen Komodo Edit or another great editor; whether you've picked Safari, another WebKit browser, or even Firefox; and whether you've been able to install the simulator or not—you have what it takes to make your developing process easier and more efficient. You've also built up some background to comfortably work your way through this book.

In the next two chapters, you're going to begin getting your hands dirty. So that you have a perfect development environment, we'll help through the process of installing a server on your computer where you can host your projects. Then you'll sharpen your development tools by becoming intimate with an absolute time- and hair-saver, the debugging tools.

Chapter 2

Development Environment

You now have tools to create and tools to test. In Chapter 1, we recommended that in order to properly evaluate your application, you should always test it thoroughly on a proper device, whichever it is you are targeting. Likewise, the most reliable way to know how your pages are going to behave on the user's side is to use them in close to real conditions right from the development process.

Once you have your application ready and shining, you will have to host it on a server so it can be served throughout the World Wide Web. Legitimately yet, you may not want to host your web site on a production platform while still in the development stage. Because some restrictions and shortcomings apply only when a site is hosted—along with some welcome conveniences—we're going to guide you through the not-as-hard-as-you-thought process of installing a local server on your working machine.

Your new server will provide all you need to develop web applications and follow the examples in this book. Consider it primarily another working tool. Following just the steps from this chapter, you will not get into advanced functionalities or fancy configuration. You will have a ready server, whatever your platform, that will host your pages and make them available to external devices that share the same wireless network.

Serving the Web Application

We mentioned there are some restrictions when developing your web applications directly on local files. Here's an example before you undertake installing your local web server: you've built a search application with a suggestion feature; when a user starts typing a word—pow!—that very word he was going to type comes up before him! To achieve this, you check words from a list on some remote site. You've tested your application thoroughly from local files, and it's working like a charm. Yet, when you put it online, no more magic—no more suggestions appear. This is because Ajax, the underlying technology for such functionality, works only if requests occur on the same origin. This "cross-domain" restriction didn't happen when you were testing because local files don't have a domain and because, using the file:// URL scheme, the execution context is different. That's why you had never noticed this problem—until it was a little too late.

Another shortcoming if you're using the iPhone Simulator or a proper device in your developing process—which you should—is that neither can access files on your local file system. Hosting your pages is a necessary step to use the simulator as well as your targeted device—iPhone, iPod touch, or iPad.

Mac OS, Making Things Easy

The latest versions of Mac OS X ship with all the components needed to set up a working server. Although site hosting is useful to developers (among others), it usually isn't their primary field of knowledge. Luckily, the configuration process has been made extremely straightforward. Just follow the steps in the next sections.

An Apache in Your Mac

Open **System Preferences …** from the menu, and from the window that appears, open the Internet & Wireless section. Click the Sharing icon, and select the Web Sharing check box (see Figure 2–1). Managed that? Well, good news—your server is set up!

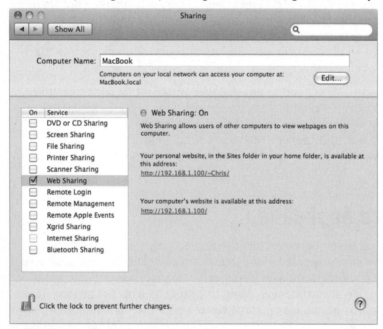

Figure 2–1. *The Mac OS X Sharing panel*

Clicking the personal web site link, Safari, or whatever your default web browser is will open a window using the default files from your new personal site, shown in Figure 2–2. You can modify and add files for this site in your */Users/username/Sites/* folder, where *username* is your session user name.

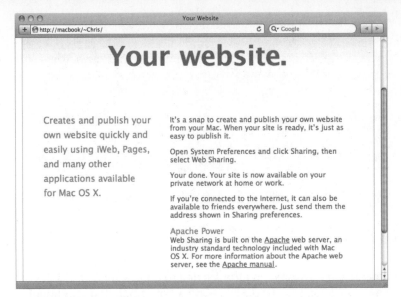

Figure 2–2. *The default web site*

The second link will lead you to the computer's web site. Accessing this URL will give you the common "It works!" message found on the Apache default installation. The files for this web site are located in the */Library/Webserver/Documents/* folder.

If you just can't remember URLs like 192.168.1.100 or can't be bothered to type them, you can also access your site using the computer name. The URL would look something like http://computername.local/~username/.

These simple steps allow you to build a web site with your primary languages—HTML, CSS, and JavaScript. This is the minimal configuration you need to start making hosted web applications, but for building a modern web site, you will probably want to use some brand of server-side scripting language to add more interaction between your site and the user. We'll be using PHP for some examples in this book, so we recommend you follow these steps. It isn't as "click-and-go" as the first part of the install, because you'll be modifying a configuration file with administrative privileges. Still, don't worry: it isn't as difficult as it is impressive.

The Script Engine

Open a Terminal window, and type the following command:

```
sudo vi /private/etc/apache2/httpd.conf
```

You'll be asked for an administrator password. You probably are the administrator for your computer, in which case the password is your session password. However, if you are using a company machine, you'll may have to ask someone to type one for you. The apache2 configuration file should open in Vi, within the Terminal window.

> **NOTE:** We won't be using command-line tools to edit files often in this book. Nonetheless, when we will, we'll use the well-known Vi. If you're not familiar with command-line text editors, you may find them a little frightening. They do often have a steep learning curve. However, because some are popular and truly feature rich, we thought we might introduce one here.
>
> If, on the contrary, you're not a Vi fan and you've installed Komodo Edit, check out the option to enable Vi-type behavior in the **Komodo ➤ Preferences…** menu item; select **Editor ➤ Key Bindings**, and choose Enable Vi emulation, the second option from the top.

Once the file is open, move your cursor down until you reach the lines that look like this:

```
...
#LoadModule php5_module            libexec/apache2/libphp5.so
#LoadModule fastcgi_module         libexec/apache2/mod_fastcgi.so
...
```

You want to uncomment these lines by removing the # signs to enable these modules and allow PHP scripts to execute properly. To do this, type a (for append), uncomment the lines as you would do in any editor, save your changes by typing esc to exit editing mode, and then type :wq (for write and quit).

For your configuration changes to take effect, restart the server by deselecting and reselecting the Web Sharing option in System Preferences or, right from your Terminal window, by typing this:

```
sudo apachectl restart
```

You may be wondering what you have just done. The first line tells the server to load the PHP5 module, allowing you to run PHP scripts on the server side. PHP is a popular, open source, and very powerful general-purpose scripting language. In its latest version, it features object-oriented programming and many functions to make a developer's life easier.

The second line allows separation of script execution and other server tasks. To put it simply, the server and the PHP module—or any other module implementing the FastCGI protocol—run as independent applications, with distinct resources and processes. This accordingly means that if a script crashes PHP, the server won't need to be restarted.

So, without even noticing, you've made it: you've set up a server with PHP5 on your working machine to make the developing process both easier and more professional. If you're the curious kind, we bet you've even modified a few things on your new site (that is, if you're a Mac user, of course). Next is the guide to achieve similar results on a Windows machine.

Windows, Choose Your Weapons

To install a server on your Windows machine, your first move is to get Internet Information Services (IIS) and the components to run PHP. Microsoft has made great efforts lately to make this task much easier than it used to be. http://php.iis.net/, shown in Figure 2–3, is a site specially dedicated to server installation. Go there, and click the Install PHP button.

Figure 2–3. *PHP for IIS by Microsoft*

Of course, you can use any web browser to access this site and proceed, but we recommend you use Internet Explorer for the following operations to ensure everything goes as planned.

An All-in-One Installation Process

Follow the on-screen instructions. You'll be asked to download the Web Platform Installer (Web PI), a lightweight tool that will help you deploy a complete web-serving platform on your machine with stunning ease.

NOTE: The Web Platform Installer needs the .NET Framework version 2.0. If surprisingly your .NET version was outdated or not available on Windows XP, it will guide you through the upgrade before resuming the regular server installation.

Also, the installer won't work with more basic versions of Windows, including Windows Vista Home Basic and Windows 7 Starter Edition.

Once the download is complete, run the application. If you are using Vista or 7, your system will ask your permission to run the Web PI add-on in your browser. Click the bar under the browser tabs (Figure 2–4) and approve by selecting **Run ActiveX Control** (for Vista) or **Run Add-on** (for 7). If you're suspicious, you can get details about what is going to happen from the drop-down menu. Yet, this is Windows software, so you can trust it... On 7 only, you will be asked for allowance again before the program is run. This is the regular process, so just click Allow to continue.

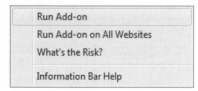

Figure 2–4. *Click Run Add-on to launch the installer*

At this stage, a window should appear with an Install PHP check box selected, as shown in Figure 2–5. You may appreciate that, from tabs on the left, you can choose to install popular components along with the base server. These include open source content management systems (CMSs), e-business solutions, and wiki engines. If any from this software selection trigger your interest, just select the boxes, as shown in Figure 2–6, and the installation will be added seamlessly.

Figure 2–5. *The Web Platform Installer*

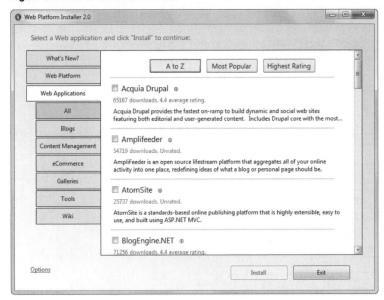

Figure 2–6. *Easy to set up*

Whether you've chosen to add extra treats to your server or not, accept the license contract, and watch the install complete. This should all be fast enough, unless you're on dial-up. You can now return to your browser and type `http://localhost/`. This is your local web site!

Now, you can take control over your web site and—why not?—add more web sites using the dedicated Internet Information Services (IIS) Manager administrative tool you'll find in the Control Panel.

However, you have one final step to go through to make this site available to external devices, which is to make the Windows Firewall allow access to the web service. This is done similarly on both XP and Vista. You'll see that adding an exception to the Windows 7 Firewall is a slightly different story.

Security Settings

On Windows XP, open the Start menu, and choose Security Center from the Control Panel window. Select "Manage security settings for: Windows firewall" at the bottom of the window. Clicking the Exceptions button, you will see the "Add port…" option. Click this button, and add an entry for port 80 through TCP to make your site available.

> **WARNING:** If you have installed some kind of security software, it is possible that the firewall in use on your system is not that of Windows. We cannot cover all configurations in this regard, so we recommend you look into the documentation for your software.

On Vista, from the Control Panel, click "Allow a program through Windows Firewall" under the Security section, as shown in Figure 2–7. From there continue as in XP.

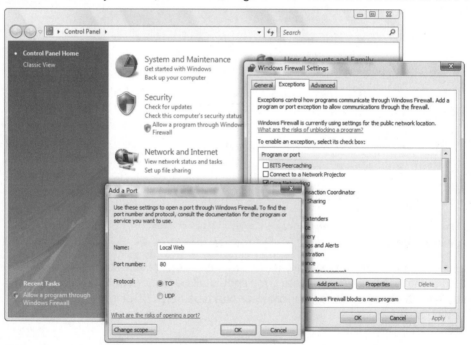

Figure 2–7. *Steps are easy on Windows Vista*

The latest Windows system has added a lot of configuration functionality, losing some of the simplicity you could experience with XP or Vista. Still, the operation remains fairly straightforward as long as you know where you are going.

Once you've opened the Control Panel, at the bottom of the "View and create firewall rules" section, choose the Inbound Rules option, as shown in Figure 2–8. Then, in the new appearing screen, click New Rule from the top of the right pane. A wizard will guide you through the subsequent process.

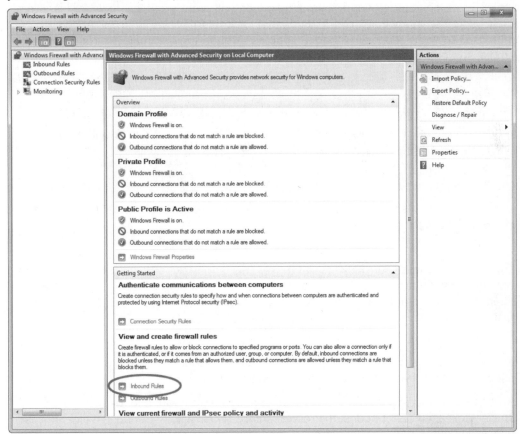

Figure 2–8. *Windows Firewall with Advanced Security on 7*

Choose to add a port rule, and click Next. From there, select the TCP protocol and specify 80 as the local port. On the two following screens, leave all selections unchanged. Then give a name to your new rule, and click the Finish button to save it.

There you are, pretty much ready to build your web applications on your Windows server! You can start adding files to the default site location, in the *C:\Inetpub\wwwroot* directory.

Yet, there is one restriction in using your working machine to serve pages to an Apple device. Because Microsoft and Apple use different communication protocols, you can access your site only using the IP address. To find out what IP your Windows OS is using, simply run `ipconfig` at the command prompt. This will return the IP currently in use.

Linux, Take Control

For the Linux install process, we're going to take you the command-line way. There are two main reasons for this. First, we believe it is the easiest way to install an Apache server on a Linux box. Second, there are so many different graphical tools for installing packages on so many Linux distributions that we couldn't cover them all. Anyway, setting up an Apache server with PHP enabled through the command line is pretty simple, so don't worry.

> **NOTE:** We're using `apt-get` in our examples, which is the front end to the widespread Advanced Packaging Tool (APT) that is used notably in the Debian and Ubuntu distributions. The package names will be the same whatever your flavor of the kernel, and they most likely are in the distribution's repositories. Just check whether you should use yum (yum `install ...`), pacman (pacman `-S ...`), or something else.

As promised, the install begins by opening a Terminal window, and your first command will be as follows:

```
sudo apt-get update
```

The shell will update your package database. This is to make sure you get a clean install, that versions don't mixed up, and that there are no dependency issues. Next is the actual install command. You then use `apt-get` again, but with the `install` option. On one line, type this:

```
sudo apt-get install apache2 libapache2-mod-php5 php5-mysql
```

Output will appear in the Terminal window for a few seconds while the packages are installed, and then you will see the prompt again. That's it!

Depending on your distribution, your server files will not be found in the same directory. On Debian-based distributions, the root directory is */var/www/*. Because we cannot list all possible cases here, we recommend you visit Apache's wiki at http://wiki.apache.org/httpd/DistrosDefaultLayout. This page references all the information you need to get about where the most important Apache files are located on your system. Whatever your flavor of Unix, you can see your site in a browser at http://localhost.

The final touch to your server install is to make the server your own, that is, to change its ownership from root to you. This is easily done on the command line with the chown command (CHange OWNership):

```
sudo chown -R username /var/www
```

Now, you can modify all files and directories on the web site without using the sudo command you used to install it. That wasn't difficult, was it?

Handling Multiple Hosts

Whatever your developing platform, you have a server set up to host all your upcoming web applications. If you want to test your web applications in real-life conditions, there is still one thing to set up, though.

This is necessary for at least one reason: when using Ajax, the so-called cross-domain limitation, of course, wouldn't apply if you were hosting all your pages on the localhost domain.

To remedy this, you have to create a different local host on your computer. You do this by modifying the *hosts* file on your system to define new domains that should point to your local server. This will in turn allow you to test pages on these domains as if they were on the World Wide Web.

> **NOTE:** Please note that although you can use any URL with any top-level domain (TLD), we recommend you don't use existing TLDs to avoid conflicting with existing web sites. Naming your local site apple.com would mean you couldn't go to the actual Apple site anymore!

Unix-Based System

The hosts file is generally nested in the */etc/* directory, the same as your Apache configuration file. On most Unix and BSD systems, it should be at the root of this folder, with other system-wide configuration files. Because root privileges are needed to edit such files, we are going to open it in the terminal with Vi, running the following:

```
sudo vi /etc/hosts
```

A rather short file appears on-screen, looking something like this:

```
##
# Host Database
#
# localhost is used to configure the loopback interface
# when the system is booting.  Do not change this entry.
##

127.0.0.1    localhost
```

After this line, add another rule to the file following the same scheme, with 127.0.0.1 and your site name.

```
127.0.0.1    localhost
127.0.0.1    www.example.local
```

You can now save your file and test this newly created domain in your browser. You should see the same page as the one previously configured with your web server.

Windows-Based System

On Windows systems, this file can be edited with any text editor, without special privileges. You can, for instance, use Komodo Edit here. The /etc/ directory is located in C:\Windows\System32\drivers\, and there you will find your hosts file.

Its contents will look a lot like those of Unix and BSD systems. You should apply the same changes as in the previous section. Your changes will be automatically taken into account.

Configuring Multiple Web Sites

Now, as a treat, there is one last thing we will go through. This step is not necessary; we just thought it might be desirable to some of you. Specifically, we will explain how to create multiple sites on your server. Thus, working on several projects, instead of using subfolders, you can make your browser understand proper addresses.

In addition to the organization benefit of using different site names in different folders, you will benefit from some notion of a "root directory," be it with PHP, HTML, or CSS.

Practically, in PHP, you will access this information using the $_SERVER['DOCUMENT_ROOT'] environment variable. Writing HTML and CSS, if you start an URL with a slash (/) character, the browser will understand that the path you are calling will start from the top of the directory structure down. On the site http://localhost/example/, /images/hey.png means http://localhost/images/hey.png.

Apache 2: Get Carried Away

The following steps apply to Apache servers, in other words, the server type you installed on Mac OS X and Linux platforms. As a lucky Unix user, you will yet have to adapt a little, because, as you've experienced earlier, all platforms don't install Apache in the same way. You have to find Apache's main configuration file, which you are going to modify. There are other ways to manage virtual hosts, but this one is closest to platform independent.

Checking the Configuration

As in the install part, you are again going to edit the file with Vi in the terminal. Open a Terminal window, and type in one of the following two commands depending on your system:

```
sudo vi /private/etc/apache2/httpd.conf      # On MacOSX
sudo vi /etc/apache2/apache2.conf            # On Debian
```

A file will be open with variable content depending on your system. The first thing you want to do is to check for these two lines:

```
# Ensure that Apache listens on port 80
Listen 80

# Listen for virtual host requests on all IP addresses
NameVirtualHost *:80
```

If they exist, very well, you can go to the next step. If they don't, you should add them at the end of the file. To do this in Vi, move your cursor to the end of the file, and again type a (for Append) to enter edition mode. These rules ensure your Apache server will listen for HTTP requests on port 80, whatever the IP (which is the reason for the *).

Configuring Your First Virtual Host

Next is creating the actual virtual host. At the very least, you need to give a name to your site (an URL) and the path to the document root (where your files will go). At the end of your configuration file, add the following code using the names and paths you want:

```
<VirtualHost *:80>
    DocumentRoot /var/www/example
    ServerName www.example.local
</VirtualHost>
```

> **WARNING:** Adding a virtual host using this directive will override the main host that was initially installed. To prevent this, you should create a virtual host using the global server name and document root from that host prior to adding new ones. You will find the information you need within the main Apache config file you are editing.

Once you have performed all the changes you needed, you can save the file and quit Vi by typing Esc key and then :wq (write and quit). Then, restart your server. If you are a Mac user and you have followed the Apache install process, you already know how to do this. For Debian users, run the following command:

```
sudo /etc/init.d/apache2 restart
```

Apache now knows your site exists, but the rest of your system doesn't as long as you haven't added it to your *hosts* file. To fix this, you should follow the steps explained earlier to modify this file.

You now can check your new site in a browser, typing the server name you've chosen. A rather empty page should appear, because your document root holds no files. Nevertheless, it is functional, so we'll be meeting you in the next chapters to fill it with exciting homemade web applications.

The Windows Case

If you're a Windows user, whether you can set up a virtual host depends on which operating system you have installed. Before Vista, it wasn't possible to configure multiple sites on a workstation machine. XP users can only simulate multiple sites by editing their hosts file, as explained earlier.

For Vista and 7 users, however, you can access such features changing the Internet Information Services configuration from **Control Panel ➤ Administrative Tools ➤ Computer Management**. Then, from the window that appears, unfold the Services and Applications section in the left pane, and choose Internet Information Service Manager.

> **NOTE:** If the relevant menu doesn't appear under Windows 7, change the display mode for the Control Panel window to small or large icons from the top-right pop-up menu.

At this stage, your window should look like Figure 2–9.

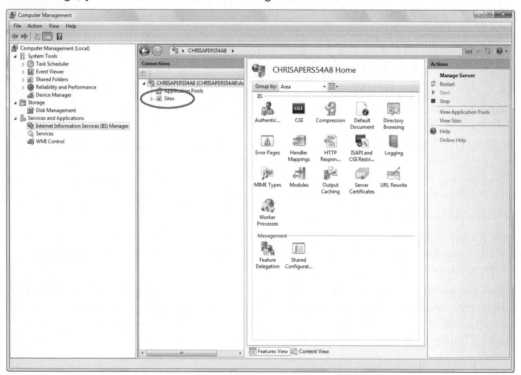

Figure 2–9. *The IIS Manager view*

Next, right-click the Sites directory in the second pane from the left, and choose **Add web site** from the contextual menu. The form that appears is quite simple, as shown in Figure 2–10. Just fill it in with the listing name you want for your site, its root directory path, and the URL you want to access it by.

Figure 2–10. *The web site configuration panel*

Your site is now ready to fly! If you seem not to be able to access the desired URL from a web browser, check that it has been added to your *hosts* file. Otherwise, your machine would not know that this address should be looked for locally.

Have You Made It?

Wasn't that easier than you expected? Setting up a basic server isn't necessarily a complicated task, especially since the two major OS companies have been through great efforts to make it even more accessible. If you're the believe-it-when-I-see-it type, here's the perfect test for you. Create a PHP file in your server root directory. In Komodo Edit, this is done by going to the menu item **File ➤ New ➤ New file...** and choosing the PHP file template. In the newly created file, type the following code:

```php
<?php
    phpinfo();
?>
```

Save the file to your server root directory under the name *index.php*. Now open your local site in a browser: you should see tables with details about your server configuration. This means two things. For one, you've run a PHP script, which means everything is OK; then, you can check all the options available on your new server.

> **WARNING:** if your browser offers to download the file, something has gone wrong during the installation. Check the steps described earlier to find out what has been forgotten.

At this stage, you can even open this page in your favorite Apple device. There are just a couple of conditions you need to check: for all systems, you need your computer and device to use the same Wi-Fi connection. This is always the case using the SDK simulator, because the server and simulator share the same computer. On a Windows system, as we explained earlier, you will have to type the IP address, not the computer name.

In all cases, if you choose the IP address solution, be aware that most Wi-Fi connections use Dynamic Host Configuration Protocol (DHCP). This means the IP address will be attributed dynamically and thus will be likely to change: whereas you may be able to access your server with the same IP any time at your home or office, switching from one to the other—or establishing a connection at Starbuck's—will probably require you make a change.

Bet You Have!

Well, you've begun doing exciting things here. Perhaps for the first time, you've set up a functional server to host and serve your work in progress before showing it to the world. It is also possible that you now have a better understanding of how web sites work, which is also a good point. Now, the last, but definitely not least, thing we have to do to make this setup part complete is to introduce the tools you'll be extensively using all the way through your web app developer's life: the debugging tools.

## Chapter 3

Introducing Developer and Debugging Tools

It isn't obvious that developing for the Web would require specific debugging tools or that such tools would even exist. Not so long ago, front-end development was seriously lacking good tools to analyze and debug page components. But the Web has evolved tremendously: front-end debugging tools have flourished, and most major browsers nowadays come with built-in debugging tools or easily added extensions.

The proliferation of such solutions is recent but by no means surprising. Building a web site generally means tightly combining a markup language, a styling language, and a scripting language. As sites get more and more complex, it can get ever more complicated to keep track of all the elements of these building blocks.

Because we are going to be working specifically with Mobile Safari, which is a WebKit-based browser, and because WebKit's debugging tools for Desktop Safari are extremely well designed, let's get started with Safari's developer tools. You're one step away from handling real-life code now, and we assure you that mastering these tools will save you a lot of time and hassle.

In this chapter, we will talk about the developer tools in Safari. The features we introduce are mostly available using other WebKit browsers, yet we cannot guarantee that all the features will be found in the same place or using the same process.

Making Friends with WebKit's Developer Tools

Not only does WebKit come with excellent support of web standards, but it also provides advanced tools such as a great live document and styles editor and a full-featured JavaScript debugger to make the life of front-end developers easier. These will help you considerably speed up your development process throughout its different stages. From simple control of your HTML markup to database management following the latest HTML5 standards, we are going to help you activate and use these tools at their best.

NOTE: At the time of this writing, we are talking about the latest nightly build of the developer tools. You may be using an older version of these tools. If you are missing some functionalities, you can always get the latest build from WebKit's site at http://nightly.webkit.org/.

Enabling the Develop Menu

Naturally, the first step to use these tools on Safari is to start Safari. From the Preferences window (**File > Preferences...**), choose the Advanced tab. In this section, you want to select the "Show Develop menu in menu bar" option (see Figure 3–1). You now have an extra menu entry in your browser's menu called **Develop**. You can also add an "i" button to your toolbar, and you can always access the tools by right-clicking any element on a web page and choosing **Inspect Element** from the contextual menu.

Figure 3–1. *You can enable the Develop menu from the Advanced preferences*

The Develop Menu Exposed

Let's now explore the Develop menu, shown in Figure 3–2. Your first option allows you to open the current page in any other browser you have available on your computer. Because we are targeting Safari, you probably won't use this option a lot.

Figure 3–2. *Many options are available directly from the new Develop menu*

The second option, however, may come in handy more often. With WebKit's developer tools enabled, you can change the user agent for Safari, which technically means changing the string the browser sends to the distant server to identify itself as such or the engine, engine version, and so on. If you're going through your developing process on Desktop Safari but you want to implement browser- or platform-sniffing capabilities (instead of relying on features detection) to enable specific features for some users or you want to access a site blocked to browsers other than Mobile Safari, this is going to help. Changing the user agent header sent by your desktop browser through this menu will make websites recognize your client as Mobile Safari on iPhone, iPod touch, or iPad.

The **Show Web Inspector** and **Show Error Console** items will both open the Web Inspector, respectively focusing the Elements Inspector and Console sections, which we will cover in further detail soon.

The **Snippet Editor** menu item will open a different window. This idea behind the snippet editor is that building or tweaking a web page can be a cumbersome process. Creating files, modifying, saving, reloading in a browser window, and starting again can be a long process and require switching between many windows and applications. The snippet editor handles all this from the same dual-pane window. We've used it extensively to test code examples for this book, so we believe that it can be a great help to you too.

The upper part of the window is for you to write your code. It handles HTML, CSS, and JavaScript, and it can manage huge amounts of it. The lower part updates as you type to show you the code as it would appear in a proper browser window. In prototyping stage, this can allow you to easily test your code and try plenty of alternatives.

The next entries give you direct access to advanced JavaScript debugging tools inside the Web Inspector window. These will let you quickly debug scripts by providing tools to selectively study your code's behavior and components. Again, we will get deeper into these soon.

The last group of options allows you to modify the browser's behavior. Obviously, cases where your end user would diminish the capabilities of the browser are quite unlikely, because all these characteristics, especially the graphical interface and JavaScript functionalities, are at the heart of a web application's identity. Accessing the richness of the Web nowadays with JavaScript disabled has become an almost impossible task, and it is likely you wouldn't want to develop an application without client-side scripts. Still, you should take into account that some of your users may not enable script execution and therefore should serve understandable content all the same.

Nevertheless, the **Disable Caches** option will come to some avail, because not only is it the best way to test first-visit loading times, but it will also let you test your page when the advanced HTML5 caching abilities are not available.

Developing on Mobile Safari

Let's take a minute to talk about Mobile Safari. The functionalities available on the iPhoneOS browser are limited compared to what we are about to cover, because you can use a console only. You can open the console by tapping **Settings ➤ Safari ➤ Developer** (at the far bottom) and switching the Debug Console option to ON (see Figure 3–3). Also note that you will be able to disable JavaScript or cookies and empty the browser cache to simulate specific browsing conditions.

Figure 3–3. *You can switch the console on from the iPhone settings*

After that, the Debug Console will show right under the address bar in your Mobile Safari windows, displaying the number of HTML, CSS, and JavaScript errors in the page or displaying "No errors" if no errors have occurred (Figure 3–4). Tips and custom messages can also be displayed using the Console API that we will explore later in this chapter.

Figure 3–4. *The Debug Console appears under the address bar*

Tapping the error count will open a list of errors with the line where each occurred and the option to filter them by type—HTML, CSS, JavaScript, or All (see Figure 3–5).

Figure 3–5. *The console shows all the messages*

Be careful, though: the console truncates log entries when they get too long. Try not to generate logs that would span beyond two or three lines, and always focus on the core information you need. To make this less limiting, you can still turn the device to make line longer, which would make your two lines hold a little more content.

Overview of the Web Inspector

Before going through each separate function of WebKit's Web Inspector, the best approach is to get to know the tool as a whole. Invoking the Develop window for the first time will launch a new window by default. Once you have used it once, your last choice—a proper window or a docked one—will apply automatically.

> **NOTE:** From now on, we will designate the Web Inspector as *window*, regardless of its being in window or docked state. Likewise, we will refer to the inspector as related to a browser window, although obviously you can open an instance of the Web Inspector for any browser tab.

The Developer Tools Window

At the top of the window (Figure 3–6), you will find the main series of icons that will act as tabs, giving you access to the various debugging tools. They represent, in order of appearance, the elements inspector, the resources tracker, the script debugger, a timeline inspector, a script profiler, a client-side storage manager, audits, and the console.

Still on the upper part of the Web Inspector, on the right side, is a search field. This field is contextual: it allows you to perform an advanced search within the main area of your current view. For instance, if you are working on your HTML markup, performing a search in this field will search elements within the document; running a query while on the Profiles tab will return the query element in all the profile data.

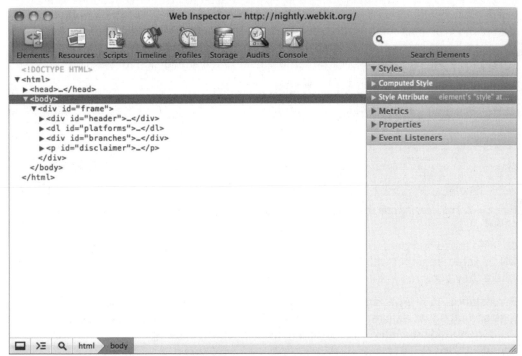

Figure 3–6. *The developer tools window focused on the Elements Inspector*

At the bottom of the window, you have several icons that will be different depending on which tool you are using. In all sections of the debugging tool, though, you will find a window icon and a icon showing a line preceded by an arrow. The first icon lets you dock the Web Inspector window to its parent window, which is very useful if you are working with several pages and a debugger instance for each. It also can prevent you from looking up and editing code from the wrong window by mistake!

The second icon will fire up a console. The console is available regardless of the tool you are currently using. It can be triggered by pressing the Esc key. Next to these icons, if you are inspecting an HTML element in the page, the path to this element in the document tree will be presented in a "breadcrumbs" manner ("html > body" in Figure 3–6) to help you easily navigate the document.

A strong asset of the inspection window is that it is closely related to the page on which you are working. Data in this window will update as the page is modified. If you click a link and land on a different page, the inspector will entirely change its content too. As a consequence, you can inspect only one window with one debugger instance. This shouldn't be an issue, because you can open as many inspector windows as you need, whatever number of pages you have open.

Error Notifications

If something is going wrong in your page—a fair reason to inspect your code—one of the first places you should be looking within the inspector would be at the bottom-right side of the Web Inspector window (Figure 3–7). There, if the WebKit interpreter has identified errors in the code, you will see a red number preceded by a white-on-red cross for errors, and another yellow number next to a warning sign for warnings.

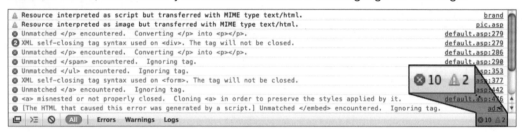

Figure 3–7. *Two icons indicate errors and warnings thrown for the current page; these will be described in the console*

Clicking these numbers will open a console area where the reported errors and warnings will be listed, together with the operations run by WebKit in order to fix them and the line where they occurred in the file.

For instance, in XHTML documents, it is common to get mixed up between self-closing tags and tags that require full closing. If you use a `<link>` tag that you have closed using the corresponding `</link>`, you would get the following message:

```
Unmatched </link> encountered. Ignoring tag. YourPage.html:14
```

This lets you search the element in the source code using the indicated line number, which also is a link that will take you directly to the relevant line using the Resources viewer that we will soon introduce.

"Ignoring tag" here doesn't mean that your link will be dropped altogether; it simply means that the unexpected closing tag will be ignored and won't appear in the DOM tree. This is the way WebKit interprets your code to render your pages. Be attentive to these errors, because they can cause side effects; for instance, not closing tags such as `<script>` or `<canvas>` would result in the elements following them being considered as script or canvas content—and not being displayed.

Master Your Code

Perhaps the most obvious way to get started with WebKit's Web Inspector is with the base of your web application: the HTML markup. It probably is the easiest way too. The Elements Inspector is accessible through different actions. All have their pros, which we will cover now.

Make the Document Yours

The primary way to inspect page components is by selecting the first tab on the top bar, named Elements. It will open a well-presented, syntax-colored tree for your page that occupies most of the Web Inspector window (see Figure 3–8). On the right, you can see a sidebar holding several collapsible panes. By default the <body> tag is highlighted, but you can always invoke the Elements tab by right-clicking any area in the page and choosing **Inspect Element** from the contextual menu.

> **INFO:** Because the debugging tools are built with HTML, CSS, and JavaScript, you may mistakenly begin inspecting the debugger window instead of the code you intended to. Although this may seem to be a limitation of the inspector, it can be useful for those willing to extend the tools. The inspector's evolutions are widely community-driven. We encourage you, if you have the skills and time, to join in and help improve them yourself.

The major asset of this method is that when debugging a page, you generally know roughly where the problem is. By invoking the inspector from a specific area in the page, the document tree will be unfolded down to the node you want to analyze.

What's more, when hovering over an element in your page, the element will be highlighted, with a translucent light blue showing its inner boundaries and a darker blue showing its padding and margins. This means that without even getting your mind into the document tree, you can get a grasp of the layout of your page constituents.

Figure 3–8. *Visual feedback inspecting the code under the book cover image*

Because getting a visual idea of the layout of your page can be an attractive tool, you'll be satisfied to learn that the latter functionality is available from most sections of the debugging tools by clicking the magnifying glass icon in the bottom status bar.

Of course, getting a representation of your element's layout generally won't be enough to seriously analyze what's going on in your code. Let's take a closer look at the Elements Inspector.

No matter how the code you wrote was presented, the inspector's document tree will be appropriately indented with a new line for each new node start. Also, the code will be clearly colored to make it more readable: violet for tags, orange for attribute names, and blue for attribute values. You will even see your inline comments in green. Clicking the disclosure triangle on the left of any node start will toggle its state so you don't end up with endless line feeds to scroll through.

Dig Your Style

In the first pane you have several categories, representing all the styles that are applied to your element, shown in Figure 3–9.

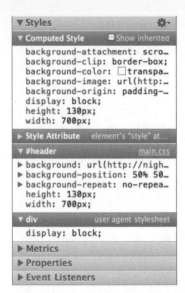

Figure 3–9. *The Elements Inspector sidebar*

The first category of styles from the top is very useful; "Computed Style" is the style the WebKit renderer has taken into account, calculated, and applied. This is handy because it lets you, at a glance, see all the styles that your element effectively has. For several reasons, the computed style also comes in use with rules resorting to numerical values, such as width and height in Figure 3–9. CSS makes extensive use of relative values using units such as ems or percentages. Because all computed sizes are expressed in pixels, comparison is easier.

But the computed style is nothing when debugging your page if you cannot determine what the style has been computed from. This is where the subsequent subpanes come into the picture. Each subpane represents a separate manner in which styles are applied, ordered from the latest applied to the earliest. Style rule specificity in CSS is considered in the following order: styles applied with the style attribute (*inline* styles) are applied first; then, from <link> and <style> tags, id and class selectors; then document tree selectors (more selector specificity meaning more precedence—note that the "weight" of the parent, whether it is evoked with an id, a class, or a tag name, counts); and finally tag names.

> **TIP:** By default, all color-related rules are expressed using RGB or color names (if available). If you prefer to use other color formats in your code, you can switch between hexadecimal, RGB, and HSL either by clicking the colored square next to the rule (this will change the format only for the current rule) or by changing the format by using the gears icon on the top-left side of the sidebar.

All rules will be listed. However, because not all rules will be finally applied, you will notice in the other sections of the sidebar that some are ruled out, showing which style is overloaded by another rule. Again, this presentation gives you precise insight into how your page styles are working.

Editing Styles

Understanding is good, but to be able to modify your style rules directly from the sidebar is even better. You can do this in three ways. First, to deactivate a rule, you would simply deselect the box on the right side of the rule. Your page will immediately act as if this rule had never existed, and style inheritance will be updated accordingly.

To go further, you can edit rules by double-clicking any value, as Figure 3–10 shows. This will show you the rule as editable and let you enter whatever you like. Press Return or click outside the editing area to save and apply the new rule.

Finally, in the latest versions of the inspector, you can create new selectors from scratch to apply styles on several elements at a time. This is done from the option menu, represented by a gear in the top-right corner of the sidebar. Again, a new field will appear, but you will be able to enter both a style rule and the selector to which it applies. As previously, press Return or click outside the editing area for changes to take effect.

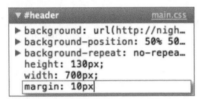

Figure 3–10. *CSS properties are easy to edit*

Not only does the Web Inspector allow you to get a firm understanding of your page, but it also gives you tools to get into serious prototyping without going through the hassle of inspecting, modifying your file, saving, reloading the page, and so on.

Metrics

The second pane from the top, Metrics, offers a visual representation of the size-related rules applying to the page element, namely, margins, padding, borders, widths, and heights, all shown in Figure 3–11. These rules together are referred to as the *box model*. The latest version of the inspector also adds position information for elements with a position property set to relative, absolute, or fixed. This representation, of course, is much faster to use than the CSS rules list found on the Styles pane, and just as you can modify rules inside the latter, you can modify dimensions from the former by double-clicking the value you want to change. You may note that, as within the computed style category, values here are processed to all be given in pixels regardless of the initial definition.

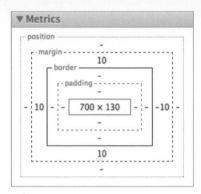

Figure 3–11. *The Metrics pane*

> **TIP:** On both the Styles and Metrics panes, you can modify numerical values by double-clicking them and using the up and down arrows on your keyboard to increment or decrement by 1 (default), 10 (combined with Shift), or 0.1 (with Alt).

The two lower panes in the elements inspector may seem a little more cryptic. They are no less useful.

Properties

Each element in your page is accessible using an instance of a DOM object, which allows you to work with this element from within your JavaScript code. As such, each element has properties of its own and inherited properties. For instance, an <h1> tag is a DOM HTMLHeadingElement instance with HTMLHeadingElement properties but also inherited HTMLElement object properties and methods, and so on, up to the Object object properties.

The different collapsible categories in the Properties pane show an alphabetical list of all the properties and methods of the currently selected object (Figure 3–12). Of course, a DOM element doesn't have only fixed property values. The innerHTML property, for example, will be different depending on the page it is used in; the Properties pane lists all these variable values at the time of inspection.

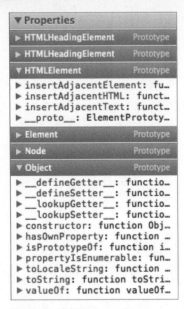

Figure 3–12. *The Properties pane*

Knowing all this probably won't be of any help when editing HTML or CSS, but it definitely can be when writing JavaScript. It brings you a whole range of information to build with or upon that represents the DOM with all the dynamic potential it has. We say not only "build with" but "build upon," because scripting with JavaScript, you probably will be adding properties to your elements. The Properties pane will update as you type or execute scripts, so you can always get a relevant picture of your document and object state.

Event Listeners

The last trick to complete your vision of the DOM through the inspector is, precisely, to see where in the page objects are likely to change. Now, by switching to the last sidebar pane, Event Listeners, shown in Figure 3–13, you can see whether any JavaScript event—like a `click` or `load` event—is attached to it.

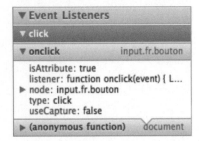

Figure 3–13. *The Events Listeners pane showing listeners hierarchy*

Events are grouped by type, and each event can be unfolded to reveal the functions related to it in the order they are called. This would let you see, for instance, why your listener might never be called—because it is possible to stop propagation from a listener. It would also let you discover memory leaks due to the unexpected stacking of listeners based on anonymous functions, which are more complicated to stop than regular listeners.

Having a list of nodes to which an event is attached is useful when you want to know whether an element is related to a script, but what is especially useful is to have a list of all dynamic elements as a new way to inspect the DOM and to find bug causes such as JavaScript conflicts.

Advanced Search

In addition to the collapsible representation of the document tree and the magnifying glass tool that allows you to select elements directly where they are shown, there is another, more advanced tool available to you when inspecting your HTML document. It's the search field at the top-right corner of the Web Inspector window. We are talking about this tool now because its most nifty uses are those regarding HTML searching, but the search field is always available to the debugging tool currently in use and will yield results from and related to what you have before your eyes.

Searching the HTML markup can be done using advanced options. If your search returns any results, the number of items will be reported on the left side of the search field, as shown in Figure 3–14. All matching occurrences will be highlighted in the document tree, and the first one will be selected.

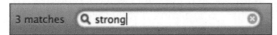

Figure 3–14. *The number of matches is shown at the left of the search field*

The most obvious search option is to simply look up plain text. This is done against the document content (taking case into account) and against tag and attribute names (case-insensitive). Although this may not seem very efficient for large or poorly known documents, it at least is easily understood and used, and because the results are clearly displayed, it should prove altogether useful.

You can also use CSS syntax and selectors to find tags in your document. Selectors are pattern matching rules that allow both simple tag targeting searches and complex contextual selections. This of course is attractive to front-end developers, because it is a language you should know well. Just be careful—searching tag names will trigger a case-insensitive search, but IDs and class names are just as case sensitive in the search field as they are in an XHTML document.

Although we will be covering selectors in more depth in the following chapters, here is a simple example, just to make things clear:

```
<h1>A Big Title</h1>
<p>
    <span>The strong and quick brown <strong>fox</strong>
        jumps over the lazy<strong>dog</strong>.</span>
</p>
```

If you perform a simple text search for *strong* on this document, three occurrences will be found. Of course, you could have expected five, but the search engine recognizes that two of the occurrences actually are closing tags that work with opening tags and so only consider the latter. This is the simplest case.

If this document were larger, you might want to find all second <strong> tags that have as ancestor a <p> immediately following an <h1> heading. Getting somewhat trickier? This is typically where CSS selectors can be of great help. Try typing the following into the search field:

```
h1 + p strong:nth-child(2)
```

This should seem familiar to front-end developers. For readers less familiar with these kind of selectors, there are not so many selectors to remember, so it definitely is worth digging this.

Finally, you have the option to perform XPath searches on your document. The XPath language was specifically designed to perform searches on XML. HTML shares many similarities with XML. The XPath syntax allows advanced structure queries. Applied to the former example, your search query would be as follows:

```
//h1/following-sibling::p//strong[2]
```

Without getting into too much detail about XPath, we simply want to stress that both methods have strengths and limitations. For instance, in our examples, you should notice that CSS selectors express the fact that the <p> tag immediately follows the heading with the + sign, which cannot be translated to XPath. On the other side, CSS selectors have no way to perform backward searches (find an element that has another element as parent), which XPath has.

The Resources Viewer

The Resources viewer gives a graphical overview of the elements downloaded for the current page (see Figure 3–15). You can choose between two graphs from the top area of the left sidebar: Time and Size.

The first view, Time, shows the timeline for all elements that have to be downloaded, together with the total retrieval time. The light area represents the latency period, that is, the time elapsed from the moment the request is sent to the moment the server sends a response. The darker area gives the actual download time. Each element type is represented in a different color, so they are easily identified by reading the legend in the top graph bar. You can filter categories, depending on your needs, using the buttons at the top of the Web Inspector window, and you can choose by which criteria your data should be ordered. The blue and red vertical lines, respectively, indicate when the

DOMContentLoaded and load events are fired, which should help you understand how your page is loaded and from there optimize its design.

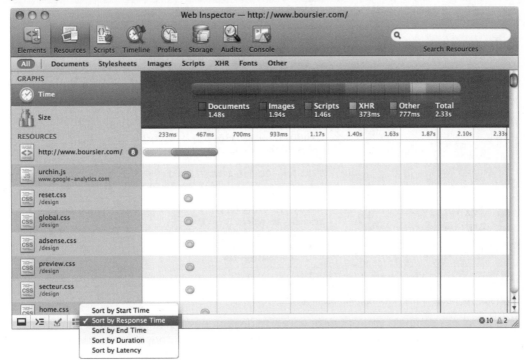

Figure 3–15. *The Resources viewer*

The second view, Size, simply displays the weight of all the elements downloaded for your page ordered by importance, from the heaviest to the lightest. The graph bars with their two areas are still there to make things easier to understand. Here, the first bar represents the weight of the actually transferred file, while the second bar is relevant when HTTP Compress is used to represent the weight of the actually downloaded file. Hence, images will have only a darker bar.

You can differentiate actual file size from transfer size for the filtering. If you choose transfer size, the fact that some elements may be cached is taken into account, so the files taking the most time to be fetched may not be the heaviest. To know whether a resource is available from the cache, simply hover over the relevant bar from the graph; if the file has been cached, a tooltip will appear displaying a file size of 0 bytes. Naturally, because cached elements do not weigh anything, they will all be displayed together, by default at the end of the list.

To get more information about a resource, you may click any element in the left sidebar. This will display images and text files in the main area, as shown in Figure 3–16, with details on the content, and the related headers sent by the client and server (using the tabs above the main view) will appear in the main view. Double-clicking a resource in the sidebar will open it in a new browser window.

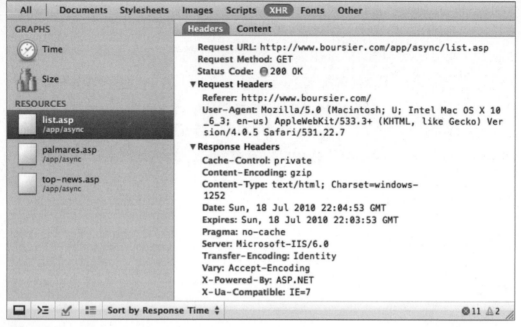

Figure 3–16. *Detail of the headers for a resource*

This of course can help you optimize your site design, by checking the caching process and seeing which elements might slow down the page rendering, but it is also very useful to follow Ajax actions by letting you see the files loaded with their HTTP headers and content.

Debugging JavaScript

Like most scripting languages, JavaScript comes with its share of hair pulling, and it can be hard putting your finger on why exactly your script isn't working. The Web Inspector makes several very handy tools available to you in this task, from the most straightforward script execution timeline to the more complex observation helpers such as breakpoints. We'll now cover how your developing tools can help you get out of scripting chaos faster and with less guessing.

Before you start, please note that, unlike the Elements Inspector, in which the HTML code was clearly displayed as a structured tree, the JavaScript code will appear as it was originally written. Therefore, we would obviously not recommend that you work with these tools on minified code—code from which unnecessary spaces and line feeds have been removed in order to make file size smaller.

Logging to the Console

If you've already coded in JavaScript, it's likely that you've already used an alert() method to get the value of an object or a variable at some precise point of your developing process. Because this has quite a few drawbacks (don't try this with loops, for instance!), you may have gotten further by using some tracing options, which is generally more natural and efficient. The good news is that there is a full Console API that you can use with the Web Inspector.

Table 3–1. *Logging Functions*

Function	Description

`console.log(format, ...);`
`console.info(format, ...);`
`console.debug(format, ...);`
`console.warn(format, ...);`
`console.error(format, ...);`
	Logs a message or object properties to the console. These five functions only differ in the icon shown on the left of the message. On Safari Mobile, only these commands are available; moreover, the formatting options listed in the next table are not available.

`console.assert(condition, format, ...);`	Logs to the console only if the condition is not met.
`console.group(format, ...);` `console.groupEnd();`	Starts and ends a group of logs. Each new group will be indented relative to the other logs.
`console.time(name);` `console.timeEnd(name);`	Respectively starts and ends a timer, supposedly to track code execution times. The name is to identify the timer so that is can be stopped.
`console.count(name);`	Sets a function-call counter. name is used to identify the counter. Counter logs an incremented number for each new call of a function.
`console.dir(object);`	Logs all properties of an object to the console.
`console.dirxml(node);`	Logs an HTML node with all its child nodes as a collapsible tree. In the latest versions of the inspector, `console.log()` acts similarly with HTML elements.
`console.trace();`	Logs the current functions call stack with the values of the passed arguments.
`inspect(object);`	Opens the appropriate inspector tab based on the passed object. Triggered tabs are Element, Database, or Storage inspector.
`console.profile(name);` `console.profileEnd(name);`	Starts and ends profiling script execution.

Several of the listed expressions can take in patterns similarly to C's `printf()` function, with a number of variables. Thus, you can notably use %s to insert a string or %o to add a collapsible object structure. This can help you keep your logs organized and consistent throughout your developing process.

Table 3–2. *Formatting Options*

Format	Description
%s	String.
%d or %i	Integer. Numeric formatting such as %02d is not supported.
%f	Floating-point number. Numeric formatting such as %4.2f is not supported.
%o	Object. With ability to see object details using a disclosure triangle.

Here are two examples of how to use the console log:

```
console.log("My %s is great!", "iPhone");
console.log("My", "iPhone",  "is great!");
```

To make reading easier, the console will automatically add spaces where necessary, and objects will be represented in tree format. These two commands will result in the same output to the console, with a link to the line where they were run. Clicking the link will focus and highlight the relevant line.

Using the Interactive Shell

Sometimes it can be tedious to go through repetitive logging actions to find out the value of an object or variable. Editing a file, saving, reloading the page, and so on, is time-consuming and overall inefficient. Well, some of this work can be done, thanks to the inspector's interactive nature, by typing your commands directly in the console prompt at the bottom of the window. The return value of the command will be printed to the console immediately. There is a lot you can do with this functionality.

The shortest way to a result is to use the logging commands we listed earlier, but you can also run scripts that exist in your page. This will allow you to evaluate the variables in your code, see how they behave, and tweak your page, because all changes as a result of what you execute will be applied directly to the affected elements, if any. Pressing the up arrow will open the history of commands you've already entered, from most to least recent.

The inspector's interactive console even supports code completion: begin typing a command, and suggestions will complete the word. Accept them by pressing the right arrow or the Tab key. Also, when inside a terminal, typing `clear()` will clear all output on the screen, though this functionality is available by clicking the further-right icon at the bottom-left side of the window.

Let the Debugger Do the Job

In everything we have introduced up to now, you are the one typing the commands, determining what to do where, and determining how to do it. If this was not enough, you can take advantage of the advanced debugger implemented in the Web Inspector. We will use the following code to illustrate the various tools of the debugger:

```html
<html>
<head>
    <title>Testing Scripts</title>
    <script>
        var counter = 0;
        var timerID = window.setInterval(myTimer, 10000);

        function myTimer() {
            var span = document.getElementById("count");
            span.textContent = incrementCounter();

            for (var n = 0; n < 100000; n++) {
                new Object().toString();
            }

            if (counter > 1) {
                errorGenerator();
            }
        }

        function incrementCounter() {
            return ++counter;
        }
    </script>
</head>

<body>
    Timer executions: <span id="count">0</span>
</body>
</html>
```

What this code does is launch a timer that calls another function, myTimer(), every ten seconds. The function in turn increments a counter displayed in the browser, then runs through an important loop, and finally generates an exception by calling an undefined function.

Once your page has loaded, you can activate the debugger either from the menu or, if the Web Inspector window is already open, by clicking the Scripts tab.

The window you have just opened has two main parts, shown in Figure 3–17. On the left is the current script as it is written in the file, with line numbering; if the script is directly in a <script> tag in your HTML document, as in our example, you will see this file. On the right, you will find various information about the current script. For the moment, this part is empty.

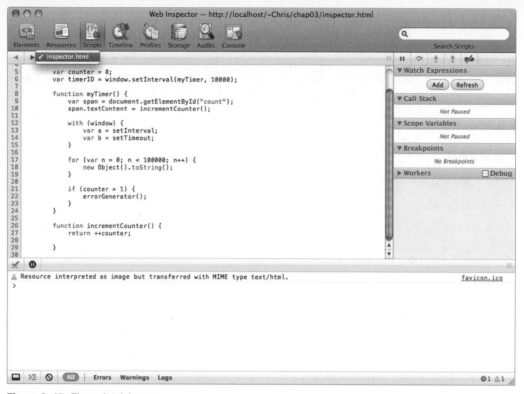

Figure 3–17. *The script debugger*

Each part of the window has dedicated buttons. On the top left, you can choose all available scripts from a drop-down menu. From above the right sidebar, you have the possibility to pause script execution, step to the next function call, step into next function call or out of the current function, and disable breakpoints using the stepping buttons.

Breakpoints

Even when you more or less know at which stage your script stops working, knowing what is going wrong can be trickier. This is where breakpoints can help you.

> **WARNING:** You cannot use the debugger by running scripts from the console. Whatever breakpoints you have placed or exceptions are generated, the execution in this case will not pause. Therefore, you must also think of useful log functions to follow your scripts.

Clicking the line gutter on the left side of the window will toggle a blue breakpoint for the part of the script on that line. Using the previous code, you can, for instance, add a breakpoint on the line where the myTimer() function is defined. When the script is run, it will interrupt at this point (Figure 3–18), and the current state of all variables and functions will be listed in the sidebar.

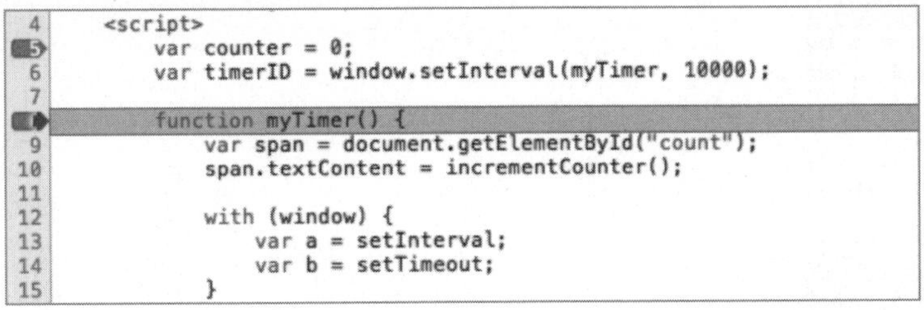

```
 4      <script>
 5          var counter = 0;
 6          var timerID = window.setInterval(myTimer, 10000);
 7
 8          function myTimer() {
 9              var span = document.getElementById("count");
10              span.textContent = incrementCounter();
11
12              with (window) {
13                  var a = setInterval;
14                  var b = setTimeout;
15              }
```

Figure 3–18. *Two breakpoints are placed on the line gutter; the debugger stops on the second one*

You can also fine-tune your script watching with conditional breakpoints. If you want to know what a variable value is if it isn't "foo", right-click any line, and choose **Edit Breakpoint...** from the contextual menu. A text field will pop up for you to enter your expression, as shown in Figure 3–19. The breakpoint in this case will turn orange. If the expression is true, the script will be stopped; otherwise, its execution will resume automatically.

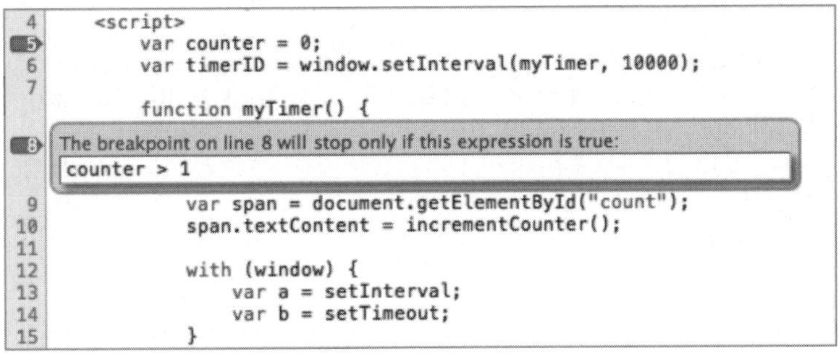

```
 4      <script>
 5          var counter = 0;
 6          var timerID = window.setInterval(myTimer, 10000);
 7
        function myTimer() {

 8    The breakpoint on line 8 will stop only if this expression is true:
      counter > 1

 9              var span = document.getElementById("count");
10              span.textContent = incrementCounter();
11
12              with (window) {
13                  var a = setInterval;
14                  var b = setTimeout;
15              }
```

Figure 3–19. *Setting a conditional breakpoint*

In a debugging process, it can be cumbersome to set a breakpoint, see what's happening, remove it, look for another line, come back to the previous one, and so on. The bottom pane in the sidebar, Breakpoints, is your friend for this. It holds a list of all breakpoints, which instead of deleting, you can deactivate by clicking their respective check boxes. You can also deactivate them all at once using the breakpoint icon at the top right of the sidebar.

Once you have changed options, you will have to reload the page. Scripts will run until a breakpoint is reached. Then, all execution is paused, and contextual information about the execution is shown on the right, as shown in Figure 3–20.

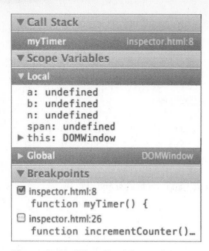

Figure 3–20. *When the debugger stops on a breakpoint, the sidebar is updated with information related to the current execution context*

Stepping

Watching just one part of a script before going through the entire process over again isn't very efficient or natural. To work around this, let's take a closer look at the stepping buttons at the top of the sidebar, shown in Figure 3–21.

Figure 3–21. *The script debugger with stepping buttons*

You can use the first button to pause the execution of the current script before refreshing, allowing you to see the script in action without installing breakpoints, but it will also let you navigate between breakpoints during the debug session. Clicking the second icon will simply run the next instruction. The third icon will let you step into the function under the execution cursor if its code can be seen (this is not the case for functions that belong to the script engine). The last icon reversely lets you step out of the currently inspected function and up one level.

Watch Expressions

In the sidebar, another pane can help you inspect specific elements in your scripts: the Watch Expressions section. The expressions you watch can be quite anything, such as variables, test expressions, instances, and more. The information you will gather can be both local or global and will be updated as scripts are executed.

Continuing with the same example, click the Add button (Figure 3–22), and type `counter` to observe its evolution. Refreshing is not automatic, so you will have to click the Refresh button to update data when a breakpoint is reached.

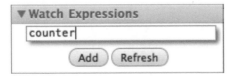

Figure 3–22. *To watch an expression, click the Add button, and enter the expression to evaluate*

Call Stack

The second pane from the top is labeled Call Stack. Here, all the functions that have been called but haven't returned yet are listed, with the most recent call on top.

You can add a second breakpoint on the `incrementCounter()` declaration and start the debug up to this function; this would result in what is shown on Figure 3–23. From there, you can move up the stack by clicking the entries from the pane.

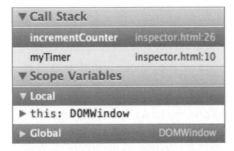

Figure 3–23. *The call stack is displayed in the sidebar in the relevant pane*

> **TIP:** If you want your function's name in the call stack to be more readable in some manner, you can easily assign it a specific name in the debugger with the `displayName` property. Thus, the function `myTimer()`, extended with `myTimer.displayName = "Main Loop"`, will appear as `"Main Loop"` in the call stack. This will also work in the profiler, soon to be introduced.

This of course can be a great time-saver when watching the execution of consecutive scripts or scripts that are nested inside one another.

Scope Variables

The last and arguably richest section in the scripts sidebar is the one under the Scope Variables pane. At any time, the values of all the elements in the scope of the current execution context or used by the current script will be listed here. Stopping at the first breakpoint in our example, the data should look like Figure 3–24, displaying all the variables available to the myTimer() function, regardless of whether they have been initialized.

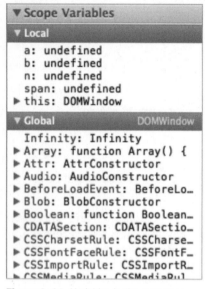

Figure 3–24. *Variables in the current scope, initialized or not, with the huge Global list*

For ease of reading, these elements are classified based on their types and their use in the current scope: Local, Global, and With Block or Closure when available. This view not only makes it easier to find and use the elements available to your script, but it can also help you understand what's going on and how to change it. As with CSS and HTML values, you can alter values in the Scope Variables pane by double-clicking them. The Global pane will notably give a list of classes available at the scripting engine level with their complete prototype.

Exceptions

You've learned how to find errors and how to look at your script behavior. However, you may have noticed that both the JavaScript console and the Scripts section only notify about exceptions—a log in the console, a colored line directly in the script—they do not stop the execution. To make the execution of functions automatically halt on exceptions (Figure 3–25), you can click the Pause icon in the bottom-left corner of the Web Inspector window.

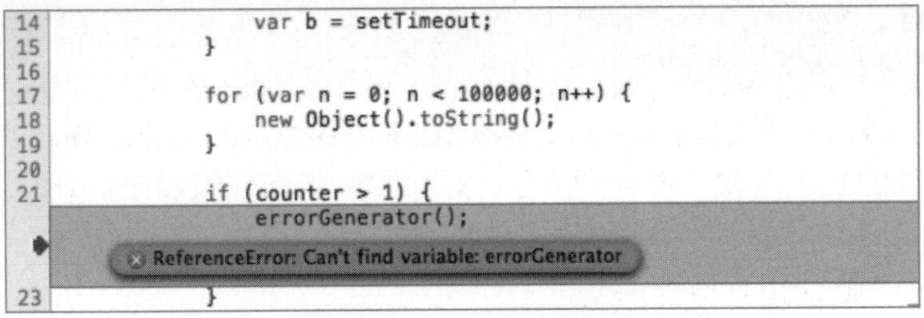

```
14                var b = setTimeout;
15            }
16
17            for (var n = 0; n < 100000; n++) {
18                new Object().toString();
19            }
20
21            if (counter > 1) {
                  errorGenerator();
    ⊗ ReferenceError: Can't find variable: errorGenerator
23            }
```

Figure 3–25. *Click the Pause button will halt the debugger on exceptions*

Clicking once will color the icon blue, meaning that all exceptions will cause the script to pause, so you can check the information available at that stage, as shown in Figure 3–25. Clicking twice will cause the script to halt only on uncaught exceptions—not those caught by a `try...catch` statement.

These tools brought together should make your development process hugely easier and faster. Not only is the JavaScript debugger useful to identify exactly where your script may be going wrong, but as you get used to it, it should also help you in your optimization stages to build overall better web applications.

The Life Cycle of Your Page

It is always interesting to get an overview of what's going on in your page all the way through its life. Which scripts are executed, how long to they take to complete, what amount of code, markup or images are loaded and in which order...this information is important when developing for the Web. The Timeline tab shows you all this information in an orderly and clear manner (see Figure 3–26).

The recording is triggered by clicking the round icon on the bottom-left side of the Web Inspector window. If you click this button and reload your page, you will see that everything is recorded, including what happens after the initial page load and expressed at the top of the drawing area using three parallel timelines—Loading, for elements loaded for the page; Scripting, for script evaluation and events triggered on page load for instance; and Rendering, for all that is done to draw to the screen, what is redrawn, and how it can harm performance.

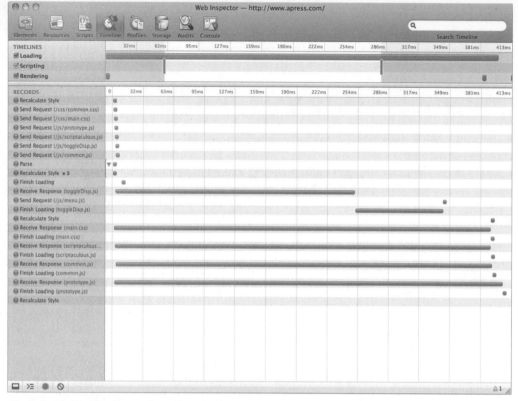

Figure 3–26. *The Timeline section with control buttons on the bottom*

> **WARNING:** You have to be cautious with this inspector tool and always remember that the device you are targeting will not share the same specs as your desktop system and browser, notably regarding connection speeds. That is to say, use this tool, get information from it, but, most importantly, interpret this information while keeping in mind that you are not developing for the device you are debugging on.

For ease of use, although all operations are recorded, you can easily show only some types of events by deselecting categories from the left sidebar opposite the timeline. This will make the events in the timeline change from blue (loading), yellow (scripting), and purple (rendering) to gray.

The timeline width is limited to the width of your screen, meaning the timescale will change depending on its contents. You can refine your inspection target by pulling the handles from the left and right edges of the top timeline area. This will stress the relevant section of the event tree. This will prove especially useful if your page contains animated content or JavaScript timers, because in this case, the timelines will continue drawing changes to the screen, showing newly rendered browser areas and timer iterations.

Hovering over an event in the timeline or the tree view will trigger a pop-up with information about the event, such as the time it took to take effect, its type, or the files requested in a loading operation. Clicking elements in this pop-up will take you to the Resources section of the Web Inspector to get additional information about the event (see Figure 3–27).

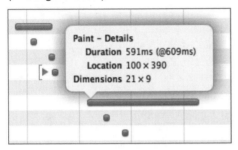

Figure 3–27. *A pop-up showing information about the bar being hovered over*

As with the JavaScript debugger, if you want a fresh start at some point, you can clear the view by clicking the struck circle icon near the bottom-left side of the window.

Profiling Your Scripts

Together with a timeline for all that is happening in your page, you can get a profile of the scripts being run and CPU usage. This feature is available by clicking the Profiles icon (see Figure 3–28).

This section will only hold instructions when you first open it. These instructions invite you to click the Record button, found in the bottom-left area of the window, as with the Timeline section, to show the scripting activity over time. Clicking once will start the recording, and you will have to click a second time to stop the recording and see evaluated data written to the screen.

You can also start profiling from the console using `console.profile()` and `console.profileEnd()` shown earlier. One asset of using the console instead of the Record button is that you can record several profiles at a time.

Whatever the method you choose, do not forget to deactivate breakpoints you may have set in the Scripts section so that there is no interference with the profiling. Also note that, unlike the other tools in the Web Inspector, the profiling tool is global for all browser windows and tabs, so it might be useful to close all windows except the one you need to study.

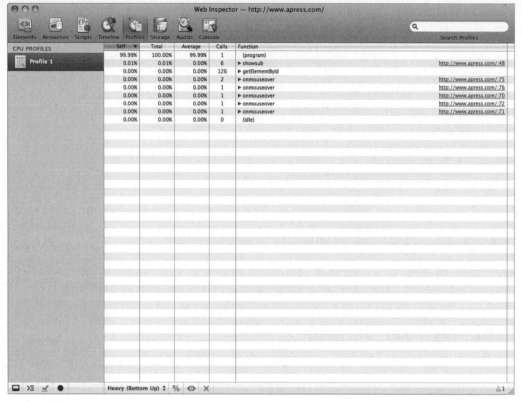

Figure 3–28. *The profiler*

For each new profile, a profile icon will show up in the left sidebar. If a profile starts recording within another profile, the upper-level profile will become collapsible with a disclosure triangle.

Understanding the Profiles

We will use the same example as for the script debugger here to illustrate how the profiler works. Open the Web Inspector, click the Record icon, and reload your page. Once the counter has reached 2, click the same icon to stop the recording, and check your newly acquired data (Figure 3–29).

Self ▼	Total	Average	Calls	Function	
91.43%	92.10%	30.48%	3	▶ myTimer	inspector.html:8
7.90%	100.00%	7.90%	1	(program)	
0.39%	0.39%	0.00%	200000	▶ toString	
0.29%	0.29%	0.00%	200000	▶ Object	
0.00%	0.00%	0.00%	2	▶ incrementCounter	inspector.html:26
0.00%	0.00%	0.00%	2	▶ getElementById	
0.00%	0.00%	0.00%	0	(idle)	

Figure 3–29. *Gathered data is shown in the result table of the profiler*

The profile data is presented as five columns in the right part of the Web Inspector window. It details all the function calls and execution times, by default as a list with the most consuming function on top. The default view shows values as a percentage of total time. You can change these view options using the pop-up menu from the bottom of the window. This way, you can see your functions in tree view, stressing the call stack rather than the resource consumption.

All functions on the right side can be unfolded to reveal the call stack. The base for the call stack is always "(program)." This collapsible area also shows the number of times that the function has been called. This is why myTimer() appears twice in the same group.

Likewise, you can change values for the whole view from percentage to absolute values in milliseconds using the % button next to the pop-up menu. If you are concentrating on a specific column (Table 3–3), you may want to change the data view for that one only. This can be done by double-clicking the columns.

Table 3–3. *Data Columns Description*

Column	Description
Self	Total execution time for the function itself.
Total	Global execution time for the function, including calls to external functions.
Average	Mean execution duration across calls.
Calls	How many times the function was called.
Functions	List of called functions with their related call stack.

Moreover, to perfectly fit your needs, you can change the sort order of a column's data by clicking the column heading.

In the functions list, if one of the function isn't part of the WebKit script engine as shown in Figure 3–29 with getElementById(), a link will be available on the far right that will take you to the relevant file and the relevant line highlighted on the Resources tab.

To make reading such amounts of data easier, you can focus a particular function using the eye icon in the status bar. This of course will be more comfortable if the execution chain is complex. It is also possible to remove functions from the view by clicking the cross icon in the same place. Using one of these options will automatically make a Reload button appear, still on the status bar, so you can seamlessly recover the initial state of the view.

Filtering with the Search Field

From the Profiles section, as from any other section, you can perform a search against your data from the text field at the upper right of the Web Inspector window. This search field will understand character strings when looking for function names or resource URLs. Nonetheless, it should take numerical values and operators, such as <, >, <=, >=, and =. This will allow you, for instance, to find all functions that take more than a certain amount of time to complete. Values would be highlighted in the table, as shown on Figure 3–30.

Self ▼	Total	Average	Calls	Function	
17.73s	17.86s	5.91s	3	▼ myTimer	inspector.html:8
17.65s	17.86s	17.65s	1	(program)	
74.678ms	205.769ms	37.339ms	2	▶ myTimer	inspector.html:8
1.53s	19.39s	1.53s	1	(program)	
75.493ms	75.493ms	0.000ms	200000	▶ toString	
55.565ms	55.565ms	0.000ms	200000	▶ Object	
0.018ms	0.018ms	0.009ms	2	▶ incrementCounter	inspector.html:26
0.015ms	0.015ms	0.007ms	2	▶ getElementById	
0.001ms	0.001ms	0.001ms	0	(idle)	

Figure 3–30. *Searching for >4s will highlight all the relevant table entries*

You can use the same numerical units as in the tabular data, namely, percentage, milliseconds, or seconds. Once your query has returned results, you can navigate different elements by pressing the Return key.

Client-Side Data Storage

One exciting new feature in WebKit is the ability to store data on the user side not only with cookies but also with databases directly set in the browser. We will be getting into further detail for this feature in Chapter 15; for now, we will see how the Storage section (the Database section in older versions) allows you to inspect several client-side storage types (see Figure 3–31).

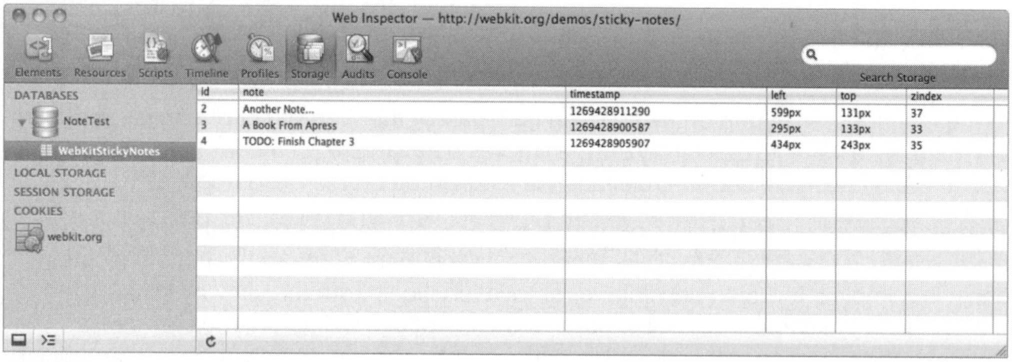

Figure 3–31. *The Storage Inspector*

The Storage Inspector layout should seem familiar at this stage with the usual sidebar and main view. In the sidebar on the left are panes listing storage types, and under each you will see the various storage groups or cookies in use, if any.

Database Storage

The first group is for databases. Each database is collapsible using the arrow preceding the database icon. To reveal the tables of a storage block, just click it. The selected table will be presented on the right side of the window as data grids showing all columns and rows.

As with the Scripts section, if you want to go further with your inspection, you can invoke an interactive shell by clicking the storage block. The shell here is dedicated to SQL commands, allowing you to query data with the help of autocompletion. Note that in the current version, running commands here is the only way to interact with the tables, which cannot be edited directly as you may have done with other storage features. However, the results of your queries will appear immediately on the screen, so the process is rather quick and simple.

Cookies

Cookies are a long-known client-side storage method. Selecting the Cookies pane from the left can hugely simplify your management of cookies. All cookies available to the current page will be presented as a table, with for each its name, value, domain (whether it is a cookie from your page or from third-party sites, as for ads), path, expiry date, size, HTTP, and HTTPS-only flags. You can delete any cookie; however, all cookie deletion is definitive, so use this with care—you may not want to lose your preferences for all your favorite sites by messing this up.

Other Storage Features

Cookie are limited in size to 4KB. Along with database storage, WebKit brings you solutions to store beyond these limitations with local storage and session storage. Each of these has a dedicated pane in the left sidebar. Like cookies, they work as key-value pairs of information. To illustrate this, you can type the following into the console:

```
localStorage.myKey = "Some value";
sessionStorage.anotherKey = "Some other value";
```

This lines will respectively create new storages sections in the local and session storage areas. As will be possible with cookies, you can delete an entry by clicking the cross icon under the table, but unlike cookies and database storage, you can modify value directly from the table and add new entries by double-clicking an empty spot.

Auditing Your Page

The Audits section can help you optimize your site by suggesting guidelines and best practices related to the loading of your pages. These guidelines are mainly based on recommendations from the W3C WebApps Working Group (WWAWG) for better web-based applications. At the time of writing, you cannot extend the audit abilities, but this is a project for future versions, which should allow you to target issue categories specifically, such as security or specific devices.

Again, a list of audits is available from the left sidebar, and the right side of the window holds data and options to run a new audit (Figure 3–32). You will be able to choose between Network Utilization, Page Performance, and All. You can also choose between an audit on page load and an audit of the current state of the page. When you're ready, simply click the Run button at the bottom of the window, and shortly the results of your audit should appear in the inspector.

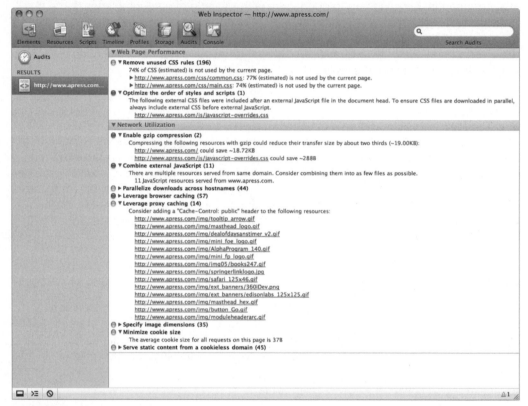

Figure 3–32. *The result of the audit*

Results are categorized depending on how critical they are—red for important issues and green for lesser improvements to be considered. Among recommendations, you may find a list of unused CSS selectors, tips for browser caching, or tips for cookie handling. For instance, you may be advised to put static content on a separate server to prevent useless cookie movement with each new request (images, style sheets, and so on); obviously, this uselessly adds to the traffic weight, because there are few chances that a cookie would be processed on the server by static content such as an image.

If we haven't reminded you enough, you're targeting devices whose connection quality is unreliable and with overall lower performances than desktop computers or laptops.

Every kilobyte spared is time saved and is a step away from seeing your user leave the page, perhaps never to come back.

Still Unsure?

Although we think the WebKit Web Inspector is a great tool for front-end debugging, it is natural that you may prefer some other browser or tool in your developing process. If you're already a front-end developer, you may be used to Firebug on Firefox or Dragonfly on Opera. Even Internet Explorer comes with developer tools with the latest versions. Whatever your situation, be aware that most browsers nowadays have debugging and development tools either built in or available as extensions. The Web Inspector actually wasn't built from scratch: the Console API, for instance, was first used in the hugely successful Firebug. This ultimately is a matter of habits and personal choice.

If you like Firebug or you want more functionality to debug directly on your targeted device, we recommend you follow the updates of Firebug Lite. This tool is a lightweight version of Firebug available to all browsers as a bookmarklet. For now, it isn't very functional on the iPhone, but as it evolves, it may be a serious option for web app developers.

Summary

You now should have a firm grasp of the tools available to you to speed up your developing process. You may also feel reassured that so many helpful tools are available right in your everyday browser to make your developer's life easier. You are not alone, and because the tools we have introduced are built with web languages, the evolutions coming from the community should prove of great help too: who better than web developers can tell what they need? We will be giving more detail about some of these tools when necessary in the following chapters. We bet you sense that things are getting more concrete. In the next chapter, we will be dissecting the generic web app elements, before getting to the core of Mobile Safari development.

## Part II

Web App Design with HTML5 and CSS3

## Chapter 4

The Anatomy of a Web Application

It has been some time now that mobile phones can browse the Internet. Back when Internet access on mobiles devices started, it was nothing like what we know now. Networks had drastically limited speeds and were extremely expensive, screen sizes were small, and devices usually only did black and white. You could read only a few short lines at a time, with a thumbnail-size image if you were lucky. Back then, a web page couldn't go beyond a bunch of kilobytes, partly because of device memories, and users had the chore of navigating mostly with the 0–9 phone keys. Obviously, even if this was some kind of technical revolution, browsing the Internet on their phones wasn't very attractive to end users.

Devices evolved, screens grew wider, and touch phones made an appearance. Phone engines boasted overall better performances, but connections remained expensive, and site layouts weren't ultimately worth it. Although the technologies had largely gotten better since WAP—a kind of lightweight HTML based on XML, the first standard—sites mostly weren't optimized, making page layout and, more annoyingly, navigation a definite issue. Also, because browsing wasn't a phone manufacturer's priority, merely accessing online services generally implied digging into numerous menus and submenus.

That is to say that for a long time, the mobile Internet was around but certainly wasn't an attractive field for developers.

The iPhone Revolution

When Apple released the iPhone, users discovered a new mobile experience, with a full range of possibilities for developers to build on. Accessing the Internet suddenly became seamless, and browsing through pages was a nice, flowing process. Relying on a revolutionary graphical user interface (GUI), the iPhone builds a close relationship between device and the end user based on touch.

Before the release of the iPhone, users—no matter which device they were using—had to have some kind of accessory to interact with content and access functionality, be it a keyboard, mouse, or stylus. After the release of the iPhone, people seemed to reject using these portable devices, and designers progressively abandoned small buttons to emulate the closeness provided by Apple's Multi-Touch system.

Not only is this new connection beyond revolutionary, but Apple also opened the phone user experience to the real Web. By releasing a full range of web-dependent applications and, most importantly, by implementing a real, adapted browser called Mobile Safari, Apple offered a proper sense of immediateness close to that of desktop browsing.

Apple also hugely favored the use of network services on mobile phones with a strong marketing move: on the iPhone's initial release, the company managed to make carriers commercialize the device with mostly trouble-free Internet access, which allowed in most cases a fully satisfying and relatively inexpensive usage of the possibilities of the device.

Belief in Web Apps

Long before the release of the iPhone SDK, Apple counted upon web applications to extend the possibilities of its smartphone. Perhaps the main proof of this was that most web applications were distributed through a dedicated section on Apple's web site (www.apple.com/webapps/), as shown in Figure 4–1. This page is still one of Mobile Safari's default bookmarks.

Figure 4–1. The Apple's web apps dedicated web site

Whereas Apple probably already planned to offer native iPhone applications, it is possible that the wider development of these compared to that of web applications was initiated by developers themselves, who urged Apple to provide a full range of tools to build these specifically. It is nothing unusual nowadays that the eclectic masses, from technology enthusiasts to international firms, have come to develop native iPhone applications (150,000+ to date). Web applications have been temporarily relegated to the background, while native development kits have met great success. However, Apple has sustained projects such as Dashcode. Although primarily designed for desktop widget creation, Dashcode soon became an interesting tool to build web apps too, with new functionality dedicated to Mobile Safari, such as iPhone-inspired web application templates.

Lately, questions have arisen about the possibility of the PastryKit and AdLib frameworks being released to the public respectively for iPhone and iPad development. These two strong frameworks are dedicated to iOS-integrated web applications and bring solutions to perennial issues such as the unavailability of fixed-position elements with CSS. They also bring desirable features meant to enhance the user experience, such as a fixed header that allows users to browse without panning and allows them to navigate as within native applications.

For now, the PastryKit framework seems to be used only on the iPhone user guide (http://help.apple.com/iphone/guide/), shown in Figure 4–2, and probably in your iPhone bookmarks; however, the enthusiasm and curiosity around it is a sign not only that Apple is still working on the future of web applications but also that developers look to produce higher-quality services in this field.

Figure 4–2. *The iPhone user guide on...iPhone*

Other such frameworks have indeed been released by open source believers, showing the urge to find helpers in the iPhone web application development process. Among others, you can check out iUI (formerly iPhoneNav, by Joe Hewitt, the man behind Firebug), which appeared shortly after the first iPhone release; WebApp.Net, which is a lightweight, optimized framework; or jQTouch, which is based on the jQuery library.

Web applications on the iPhone are getting more and more attractive. Mobile Safari's performances are ever-growing, and support for cutting-edge web standards is constantly evolving. Lately, iOS's browser has even gained access to core tools such as geolocation abilities. Because more and more companies are providing web services that can be included in web applications and because the release of the iPad has been greeted with much enthusiasm, the future of the web application field appears even more promising.

But What is a Web App Exactly?

Developing for the iPhone, you have three possibilities: make native applications, build regular web pages, or build web apps (which is somewhere in between the first two). A web application supposedly resembles a native iOS application but is accessible in the same way as a web page and basically uses the same technologies (for instance, HTML and JavaScript).

Apple's guidelines for building web applications stress several points in this regard, which all come down to very close device targeting. According to Apple, the web app should bring a specific answer to a specific need of the user. It should emulate the rest of the iOS interface, thus using special iOS user experience features where appropriate.

The idea is to minimize the feel of a browser experience to favor a closer relationship with the user, in other words, to make the user actually use the page instead of browsing it. For this, Apple recommends strong adherence to web standards and the use of Ajax to avoid reloading pages.

This all makes the difference clearer but certainly not definite. If you are wondering whether the projects you had in mind actually are web applications, and not "just" web pages, be aware that this is all about user orientation: if what you build is dedicated to serving the end user and you think it is a web app, it most likely is. In real life, you could also consider that your page is a web app if your users return to it repeatedly with the same goal. Thus, products such as the iPhone-optimized Gmail or Google Maps can be considered web applications (Figure 4–3).

Figure 4–3. *Two iPhone-optimized Google's web applications*

Planet of the Apps: Who Rules

Many have pounced upon the iPhone application market through the popular App Store. You may be wondering why you should build web applications while native applications are supported by Apple and have already made many people rich in little time. This point needs clarification: the number of applications on the App Store is tremendous; therefore, building up visibility there is a complicated task. Strong marketing is more and more important in order to break through, and few ever meet any success. Moreover, getting to be distributed on the App Store requires approval by Apple, which can take time and extra energy even after you thought you were done with your application. Now, of course, there is more to the debate than just these considerations.

Cross-Platform Master

Building web applications can be better than building native iPhone applications in several ways, and the first convenience that comes to mind is cross-platform compatibility—actually, double cross-platform compatibility.

Indeed, you do not depend on a specific operating system or on specific tools to build web apps. You can basically use anything, from the simplest plain-text editor to complex WYSIWYG editors and IDEs, whereas native applications tend to be inefficient to build without Xcode on Mac OS X.

Then your web application itself should be platform-independent to some extent. Both Google's Android browser and Palm's webOS are based on WebKit and thus will render your pages similarly to Mobile Safari. The WebKit engine is getting more and more popular, not only for desktop browsers (Epiphany has recently made the jump from Gecko to WebKit) but also on a growing number of mobile devices, such as RIM's BlackBerry. No matter how popular the iOS, applications targeting it depend on its underlying platform and APIs and are likely to never work out of the box on any other device.

Hardware Access Is No Forbidden Weapon Anymore

You may have heard that native applications are much more narrowly intertwined with the iOS itself and have access to more hardware power, more resources from the platform, and more possibilities when no connection is available (or desired). This isn't all true anymore.

First, it is unlikely that your application will need more power to run than what is provided through Mobile Safari—and native applications don't use all the power they are given either. As for storage, since version 2.0, you have the option to use JavaScript databases directly on the device, hence making your application data available execution after execution.

Moreover, users can now access web applications in offline mode, which means that all static content will be available even if no connection is. Considering that static elements of your page no longer need to be reloaded each time the page is viewed and considering the new storage abilities of HTML5, you can make a lot of content accessible for users even without a connection.

Finally, although native applications do have more tools available to them from the OS, change is coming for this too: in version 3.0, the iOS gives the browser access to geolocation information. This may be another sign that Apple is betting on the future of web apps.

Free Your Content

The second point where web application development can be more attractive than that of native applications lies in the freedom you, the developer, have for your content. Being distributed in the App Store requires that Apple validates your application, which does imply some limitations in what you can show and what your application is about. The process may be long too, and once you manage to get through this stage, you still have to get the users to choose your application from among the myriads of other applications.

Building web applications, you can release a new application every day, without any concern for Apple, and about most anything you want. You will still have to appeal to users, but, hey! you're making something for them, so, nothing is more natural.

Release Model

On the user side, however easy the process, native applications require an installation and may need updates. The former obviously is not true for web apps, and the latter just happens automatically. For native applications, even updates are dependent on Apple's validation, which necessarily means a delay, even a short one. Finally, web apps are discoverable and available from any device, as long as the user has a browser, which can seem better than being bound to the nonetheless incredible App Store.

Web Apps: Not the Little Brother Anymore

Unlike what is often heard, web applications are no easier to build than native ones. It's just like comparing apples and oranges: they're both fruit, but they're plain different. Freedom doesn't make page creation easier. Unlike native application developers, web application developers will be confronted with a white page each time they undertake a new application. Although displaying elements in a browser can be easier than arranging them for an Objective-C application, the CocoaTouch framework is very efficient in handling this kind of task. Also, we've explained how emulating the iPhone GUI is important, which might make web app development tricky regarding layout and appearance. Building for the iPhone is a whole new range of constraints for the web developer.

Developers should always keep in mind that a web app focuses on specific features that are presented to the user few at a time. Use and access to information must always be as clear as possible. Nonetheless, don't get worried. Frameworks exist that can help you through the process. And what's more, we will too.

Web Apps on Mobile Safari

You're going to make web apps for Mobile Safari running on iOS. Although this entails much fewer platform limitations than making native applications, you must be fully aware of the characteristics of the devices you are targeting. Especially, you should know how you web app will be seen. Up to now, the targeted devices, the iPhone and iPod touch, had exactly the same screen size, visual behavior, and GUI recurrences. With the release of the iPad, you'll have to take into account both a different screen size and slightly different GUI components.

Master the Browser

If there's one element you should get to know inside out, it's Mobile Safari. As Apple likes to put it, it is not a browser miniature: unlike many mobile products on the market, it is a fully-grown web interpreter, with full support for HTML, CSS, and JavaScript— including Ajax technologies. This means that, more or less, any site will display correctly on Mobile Safari if it is built upon the web standards. Not only is it a proper browser, but it can also boast advanced support for cutting-edge features of HTML5 and CSS3 specifications (although these are still at working draft stage). A minor limitation to this may be that none of the three devices we are talking about uses a mouse. All emulate mouse events through touch events, thus allowing more natural interaction than solely with a mouse. In most cases, this difference will not harm usability.

We can only recommend again and again that you keep closely up-to-date with the all the evolutions initiated by the World Wide Web Consortium (W3C; www.w3.org) and the Web Hypertext Application Technology Working Group (WHATWG; www.whatwg.org). This is where you'll find most of tomorrow's web technologies.

Browser Metrics

The default behavior of Mobile Safari is to scale page contents to fit into the screen. This, of course, makes the browsing experience different from that on a desktop browser or from the experience on Opera Mini, which reorders and resizes pages so that they are readable on small screens. Users, with the help of specific gestures, have to adapt the view to what they want like to read. This is done by pinch-opening (zooming in), pinch-closing (zooming out), and double-tapping (focusing a particular page element). Moreover, the "page" metaphor doesn't exist for Mobile Safari as it does for desktop browsers. This means that users will not scroll a page up, down, left, or right, with visual assistance on the side and bottom of the screen. They will pan the view up, down, or sideways by finger-flicking it to uncover whatever content they want to see in the viewport.

The visible area of your page will not only be limited by the size of the screen; you will also have to cope with the address bar and the navigation bar, respectively at the north and south of the screen. However, the address bar will move up as the user pans and be made accessible by tapping the status bar to save screen real estate. The iPad topography here is slightly different: as the screen is wider, the address area and navigation options are grouped in a single bar at the top of the screen. This bar will not disappear as the user pans.

Table 4–1 lists the dimensions you will be working with. Keep them in mind. You should take them into account every time you design a web application for Apple devices.

Table 4–1. *Browser Metrics in Safari and Full-Screen Mode*

Device	Portrait Mode	Landscape Mode
iPhone, iPod touch	320x460 minus 44px for navigation bar minus 60px for address bar minus 50px for console	480x300 minus 32px for navigation bar minus 60px for address bar minus 50px for console
iPad	768x1004 minus 58px for navigation bar minus 50px for console	1024x748 minus 58px for navigation bar minus 50px for console

These metrics are not absolute limits, because all three devices allow web apps to be run full-screen. In that case, only the status bar will be visible, and your application will run freely on the rest of the screen.

Think "Web App"

The problem with this browsing model is that it conflicts with the core principles of the web app experience. The aim of a web application is to seamlessly supply a service. For the end user, having to zoom to access a menu or specific content can easily be deceptive, and visitor loyalty from your point of view would suffer. You must acquire full control over the space dedicated to your application. For that, you have to know it perfectly and focus completely on the core functionalities you are providing. The default browser navigation should disappear, leaving the user to an efficient inner navigation handled by the web application. We will soon explain how to bring your user to add your application to the home screen and how to let him launch it in full-screen mode. This will make your web app look more a like a native app.

Ajax is great help in achieving an application experience, yet it does raise new problems when used exclusively over complete page refresh. Be careful not to spoil your application with poor navigation or an imperfect application experience. For instance, it is important that the user is able to easily return to some specific part of your web application directly from an URL. Not to give away too much of the following chapters, but we will be introducing at least two ways to create web applications that can be navigated with unique URLs without ever refreshing the page. One relies on a widely used JavaScript method (`window.location.hash`), and the other one uses a cutting-edge CSS3 tool (the `:target` pseudo-oselector). One great advantage of these methods is that if the user bookmarks a page and comes back to it later, you can display the right content relative to the URL, not just the default loaded content.

Configuring the Viewport

The viewport concept on iOS doesn't represent the dimensions of the client part of the browser—even less the size of the screen. It is a logical area where a web page can be displayed. It can be larger or smaller than the device screen. When landing on a page, the overall contents will be resized to fit best in the viewport while keeping the same aspect ratio. The default width of the viewport is set to 980 pixels, which is adapted to a great majority of web sites nowadays. However, you know that the approach for a web application is different. You don't want your page to be scaled: users should get direct access to the content they are coming for, with an absolute minimum actions. Making them start with a zoom gesture is bad. You have to build your page to prevent this.

The viewport options can be defined with the viewport meta tag, inside the <head> tag of your web pages. The code shown here will fit your needs in most cases, and we recommend you use it for the majority of your pages. What it does is set the initial zoom to 1.0 and then prevent the user from zooming:

```
<meta name="viewport" content="initial-scale=1.0; maximum-scale=1.0; ↵
```

```
user-scalable=no">
```

Hence, your application won't be scaled on load, and no matter whether it's on an iPhone or an iPad, it will be displayed at the optimal size you have decided. Now, you may be wondering how your page will display correctly if the default viewport is 980px wide and your web app isn't zoomed. The trick is that the `viewport` meta tag has other options, which we haven't used here because they are deduced from those we have written. Here, the `width` option, which you could set to whatever you want, is assumed to be equal to the device screen width as the initial scale is set to `1.0`. Therefore, the previous meta rule is the same as this:

```
<meta name="viewport" content="width=device-width; initial-scale=1.0; ↵
    maximum-scale=1.0; user-scalable=no">
```

It is recommended you use the `device-width` and `device-height` constants rather than hard-coded values in the meta tag whenever possible. This is the best guaranty that your page will occupy on the device screen, even when changing from portrait to landscape orientation and reversely. It also is a good idea to make your pages fluid, that is, to make them occupy all the space they can on the screen to make sure your application will appear full-screen whatever the user's configuration.

All parameters are optional, meaning Mobile Safari will guess values for the ones you do not specify. The rules for the `content` attribute can be declared in any order, as long as you separate them with a colon followed by a space. Table 4–2 lists all the properties and values available for the viewport meta tag. All have been around since the first version of iOS.

Table 4–2. *Viewport Properties*

Property	Description
width	The width of the viewport in pixels. The default value is 980, and the range is from 200 to 10,000. This property can also take the `device-width` and `device-height` constants.
height	The height of the viewport in pixels. The default is calculated based on the value of the `width` property and the aspect ratio of the device. The range is from 223 to 10,000 pixels. This property can also take the `device-width` and `device-height` constants.
initial-scale	The initial scale of the viewport as a multiplier. The default is calculated to fit the web page in the visible area. The range is determined by the `minimum-scale` and `maximum-scale` properties. Setting a value of 1.0 here automatically changes the width default value to `device-width`.
minimum-scale	Specifies the minimum scale value of the viewport. The default is 0.25. The range is from 0 to 10.0.
maximum-scale	Specifies the maximum scale value of the viewport. The default is 1.6. The range is from 0 to 10.0.
user-scalable	Determines whether the user can zoom in and out. The default is "yes". Set to "yes" (or 1) to allow scaling and "no" (or 0) to disallow scaling.

Seriously Appy: Using Stand-Alone Mode

Now that you have a web application that will just fit in the user's device screen, you'd like your application to be truly used like an application. The good news is that not only do iOS users have the option to put a web page in their bookmarks, but they can also put shortcuts to web pages on their home screen as web clips. This makes the web application as quickly accessible as any native app, notably making it accessible with Spotlight. The user just has to select the "Add to home screen" option and choose a name for the shortcut. After that, tapping the new icon on the springboard will bring up your web application in Mobile Safari straightaway.

Showcasing a Proper Icon

The default icon that will be generated for the user's home screen is a screenshot of your application, resized to fit the size of other icons on the page. Although a little gloss is added to make this more icon-like, the truth is it isn't very attractive or very recognizable (see Figure 4–4). You want your end user to find your web app easily and recognize it at first glance, even in the middle of various other shortcuts.

Figure 4–4. *The default icon built with web page screenshot...not very sexy*

To achieve this, you have to make your own icon for your web application. It's best to make it a reminder of your application, be it by using the same colors, similar shapes, and so on. It will be used for any page that is turned into a web clip, just like a favicon in traditional web browsers, so you want something sexy. The easiest way to make iOS use your icon is to save it as *apple-touch-icon.png* format at the root of your site.

Having your icon displayed in the springboard is good, but making it shine is better. The typical shine and drop shadows from the iPhone GUI will be automatically superimposed on your icon, so if you create an icon that is square and is large enough to display in a good quality, it will look just like a native icon to the user (see Figure 4–5).

Icons on iPhone are 57 pixels wide, while the default iPad icon size is 72 pixels. Building icons to common sizes such as 128 or 256 pixels seems a rather good practice. Simply be careful not to add light effects yourself, which could interfere with the default effects added by the OS.

Figure 4–5. *Apress icon before and after styles are applied by the springboard*

Nevertheless, there are cases where the gloss just doesn't fit in and cases where you want to make something slightly different. If you make an application listing places to see Eastern European naïve painters, you may want to have an icon that is rather flat-looking. Shiny curves would just look out of place. To prevent the OS from applying the full range of effects, simply rename your icon to *apple-touch-icon-precomposed.png*. You will still have rounded corners and a drop shadow, but the icon itself will remain unchanged (see Figure 4–6).

Figure 4–6. *Icon using the "precomposed" option*

Having one icon for your web application when it has a small range of different services is enough. However, if you build a tabbed application, with different categories, sections, or services, setting contrasted icons for various parts of the application can bring extra value to the user. You can achieve this on a per-page basis using a `<link>` tag in the head of your page, with the special `rel` attribute values `apple-touch-icon` and `apple-touch-icon-precomposed`. The full code to use an icon for just one page would be something like this:

```
<link rel="apple-touch-icon" href="/path/to/custom-icon.png">
<link rel="apple-touch-icon-precompsed" href="/path/to/custom-icon.png">
```

These values yield the same results as their icon-name counterparts, and the same rules apply.

Running Your Application Full-Screen

You've made another important step in your application-not-browser experience. However, if this icon launches Mobile Safari with your web app inside it, the browser presence cannot be hidden. This is where another meta option comes in. Since version 1.1.3 of iOS, you can tell your page to open full-screen by default. Only the status bar remains visible; the rest of the screen will be dedicated to your page. The so-called stand-alone mode doesn't run your web page in Mobile Safari; it uses the same rendering engine as Mobile Safari, the user will have access to functionalities from Mobile Safari, but the view itself will be your application.

Here is how you do it:

```
<meta name="apple-mobile-web-app-capable" content="yes">
```

Do not forget: your application will not be running in Mobile Safari or in a "lite" version of it. It is a different mode, which should be thoroughly tested to be sure nothing goes wrong regarding display and behavior. Also, be sure to make a clear and efficient navigation system available to the end user, because none of the navigation options from the browser will be at hand. Landing on an application page where one can't actually do anything or where one quickly gets stuck is obviously deceptive for any user.

When needed, you can check whether this mode is currently enabled with JavaScript with the `window.navigator.standalone` boolean. It is a read-only property, so you won't be able to change it dynamically; however, we will show how to play with options and actions specific to this mode later in this chapter.

An Awesome Startup

Special `<link>` tags also allow you to trigger an image to display as a splash screen when your application first loads. The default behavior when a page is opened is to show the page as it was on last visit, until it is loaded sufficiently to be displayed. This not only is rather impersonal, but it can also leave users with the impression that the application freezes on startup and drive them away.

On the iPhone, the OS lets you change this behavior by specifying a startup image, as in the code that follows. Be aware, however, that this is not possible on the iPad; that will systematically show a screenshot of your page.

```
<link rel="apple-touch-startup-image" href="/path/to/startup-image.png">
```

Your image should be 460 pixels high and 320 pixels wide (portrait orientation). Do note that this height takes the status bar height into account. If your image occupies the whole span of the device screen, 20 pixels will be hidden behind the platform interface.

Tweaking the Status Bar

You have noticed that the only iOS interface element always visible to the user is the status bar. Although it integrates easily with many different designs, you may want some control over its appearance. This is Apple: you won't be able to really change the look of the status bar. However, you can choose between variations so that it better fits your needs.

To change the look of the status bar, use another meta tag in the head of your page.

```
<meta name="apple-mobile-web-app-status-bar-style" content="default">
```

The `content` attribute has three options available. Other than `default`, you have a choice between `black` and `black-translucent`. Remember that this option will work only in full-screen mode. You cannot use it if the application changes to full-screen after it has loaded. Again, this isn't possible on the iPad, neither in stand-alone mode nor for native applications.

Staying in Stand-Alone Mode

The main problem with stand-alone mode is that, natively, whenever users tap a link to move on to another page, they will launch Mobile Safari in normal mode, and that's most of your hard work reduced to nothing. The workaround here is to handle all links with JavaScript and prevent the default behavior.

If your application is primarily Ajax driven and you have only a couple of links on your page, this is no big deal. You can bind an event to your link directly from the HTML code, like this:

```
<a href="http://www.apress.com/" ↵
    onclick="window.location.href=this.href; return false">Apress Web Site</a>
```

What happens here is straightforward enough. `this.href` gathers the linked address from the `href` attribute; `window.location` tells the browser to refresh this page using the given address; and finally, `return false` prevents the default anchor behavior from taking place, which would have been to open a new page. You can even take this further by moving part of the work to an external function, which could look something like this:

```
function openLink(anchor) {
    window.location.href = anchor.href;
    return false;
}
```

Your function would be called from each anchor tag as follows:

```
<a href="http://www.apress.com/" onclick="return openLink(this)">
    Apress Web Site</a>
```

Nonetheless, if your application uses links more extensively, as in classic web navigation, we recommend you used a more advanced link-handling system. That could work something like this:

```
/* Create a document-wide click listener */
```

```
document.addEventListener("click", clickHandler, false);

function clickHandler(e) {
    var element = e.target;

    /* handle clicks only on anchor elements */
    if (element.localName.toUpperCase() != 'A') {
        return;
    }

    /* ignore elements with a target value specified since "target"
       cannot be handled in full-screen mode
       those links shall open regularly in Mobile Safari */
    if (!!element.getAttribute('target')) {
        return;
    }
    var url = element.href;

    /* ignore links other than HTTP(S) and to different origin */
    var match = url.match(/^https?:\/\/(.+?)\/.*$/);
    if (!match || match[1] != window.location.host) {
        return;
    }

    /* finally open the link in full-screen view and prevent default behavior */
    window.location.href = url;
    e.preventDefault();
}
```

As you can tell from the comments in this code, this specific script doesn't handle complex (or less complex...) situations. More importantly, it doesn't handle links that have child tags. For instance, if you had an HTML block as common as this:

```
<a href="/pictures/question-mark.png" title="See this picture full screen">
    <img src="/pictures/question-mark.png" alt="A question mark">
</a>
```

then the script wouldn't work, because it would be the image, and not the link, that would receive the event. However, this solution is easily extended, and its main asset is to be unobtrusive, that is, to separate HTML markup and JavaScript code. And, of course, it will safely keep you in stand-alone mode as long as you are linking to other parts of a page or other pages that are part of the web application. For external links, it seems reasonable to always let the OS launch the proper browser, because you cannot be sure that distant sites will be appropriate for stand-alone mode, nor should you want them to be too closely associated to you own web site.

Build Your First Web App Base Project

With all these basics clear enough in mind, it's time we got into web app building. To make things coherent, we're going to show how to build a base project from scratch. This will make examples easier to follow throughout the chapters, and, as you extend this template, it can greatly benefit your workflow. Respectful of the guidelines we put forward earlier in this chapter, and to make things easier, we will be sticking to the iOS default colors and metrics. This will also be the time to announce a few tips to use CSS where images would have been used not so long ago (these tips will be properly explained later, in the relevant chapter).

Your Document Template in Komodo Edit

To create a new project in Komodo Edit, select **File ➤ New ➤ New Project**. Call the new project *Web App Template*, or whatever pleases you, and choose in which directory you want to save your files. If the project's sidebar is activated, you will see your new project there with the name you gave it and the Komodo Edit project extension *.kpf*. If the sidebar is not open, you can activate it from the **View** menu, specifically, **View ➤ Tabs & Sidebars ➤ Projects**.

> **NOTE:** This project definition is basedon Komodo Edit 5.*x*. Menu Layouts and options may differ in newer versions of the editor.

Now, let's add your first HTML file. You can do this either by right-clicking the project name in the sidebar and choosing **Add ➤ New file** or by selecting the menu item **Project ➤ Web App Template.kpf ➤ Add ➤ New file**. A new window will pop up. From its right column, choose the appropriate file type, HTML for now. Choose *index.html* as the file name in the text field underneath the columns; you will notice that the correct folder to save it in is already selected, so just click Open. Your new file will be displayed in the editing area.

This file is not blank. Because you've chosen an HTML file type, Komodo Edit has already done some work for you, and your basic structure is already there. However, to fit our needs exactly, we are going to change or add some elements. This is what your file should look like for the next step:

```
<!DOCTYPE html>
<html>
<head>
    <title>Web Application Template</title>
    <meta name="apple-mobile-web-app-capable" content="yes">
    <meta name="apple-mobile-web-app-status-bar-style" content="default">
    <meta name="viewport" content="initial-scale=1.0; ↩
        maximum-scale=1.0; user-scalable=no">

    <link rel="stylesheet" href="styles/main.css">
    <script src="scripts/main.js"></script>
</head>

<body>
    <div class="view">
        <div class="header-wrapper">
            <h1>Web App Header</h1>
        </div>

        <div class="group-wrapper">
            <h2>iPhone</h2>
            <p>Hello World!</p>
```

```
        </div>
    </div>
</body>
</html>
```

You can see the special tags we have been talking about in this chapter. Of course, if you want all of them to act as expected, you should create an *images* folder in your root folder and populate it with a *startup.png* file, as explained earlier. You should note that we have changed the DOCTYPE from what it was in Komodo Edit's default HTML file. This is the HTML5 doctype, which we are going to use throughout this book in order to showcase the new features of HTML5 while still producing a valid document. The uppercase letters are an old front-end developer's habit; since HTML5, the doctype declaration is case-insensitive.

If you open this file in your browser now (or choose to see it directly in Komodo Edit, using **View ➤ Preview in browser** from the menu), you probably won't be impressed. No styles are applied, and there hardly is any content. However, you will notice that our template skeleton has several classes and IDs. These are going to help you target elements and style them to look like a proper application.

Create a new folder, still at the root of your site, called *styles*. Now, create a CSS file as you did a few minutes ago for the HTML file, and call it *main.css*. This file is already called in the head of your document, so whatever you change in it should be applied immediately, so let's add some style.

Following the recommendations we went through earlier, the first style rule you will add to your style sheet will state that the document should take the entire screen height. To mimic the iOS UI, you will also set the generic font to Helvetica.

Further chapters will get deeper into CSS possibilities, so we will not explain everything here. Simply, you could be unfamiliar with the -webkit- prefix. It is a proprietary prefix (which means it isn't interpreted by browsers other than WebKit-based browsers) used for properties and values that are either specific to the browser or considered unstable regarding the CSS3 specifications or their implementation.

```
html { height: 100%; }
body {
    height: 100%;
    margin: 0;
    font-family: helvetica, sans-serif;
    -webkit-text-size-adjust: none;
}
```

To always make text as readable as possible, Mobile Safari automatically changes the size of text each time the viewport orientation changes. This isn't always desirable, because it can break your layout or end up looking odd if you design your pages in a particular manner. To prevent this behavior and keep control over the appearance of your pages, we set the -webkit-text-size-adjust to none, which disables automatic text resizing.

Next, using the `-webkit-gradient()` background extension, we create a general background without even using images. This background is built so that all you have to do to change the color of the element without losing the iOS look is change the `background-color` property. As for the `.view` rule, it applies to the main container of the document views.

```css
body {
    -webkit-background-size: 100% 21px;
    background-color: #c5ccd3;
    background-image:
        -webkit-gradient(linear, left top, right top,
            color-stop(.75, transparent),
            color-stop(.75, rgba(255,255,255,.1)) );
    -webkit-background-size: 7px;
}

.view {
    min-height: 100%;
    overflow: auto;
}
```

Then, add the header style using the same rule applied to the body background.

```css
.header-wrapper {
    height: 44px;
    font-weight: bold;
    text-shadow: rgba(0,0,0,0.7) 0 -1px 0;
    border-top: solid 1px rgba(255,255,255,0.6);
    border-bottom: solid 1px rgba(0,0,0,0.6);
    color: #fff;
    background-color: #8195af;
    background-image:
        -webkit-gradient(linear, left top, left bottom,
            from(rgba(255,255,255,.4)),
            to(rgba(255,255,255,.05)) ),
        -webkit-gradient(linear, left top, left bottom,
            from(transparent),
            to(rgba(0,0,64,.1)) );
    background-repeat: no-repeat;
    background-position: top left, bottom left;
    -webkit-background-size: 100% 21px, 100% 22px;
    -webkit-box-sizing: border-box;
}
.header-wrapper h1 {
    text-align: center;
    font-size: 20px;
    line-height: 44px;
    margin: 0;
}
```

And finally, this is what will allow to display our content with style:

```css
.group-wrapper {
    margin: 9px;
}

.group-wrapper h2 {
    color: #4c566c;
```

```
    font-size: 17px;
    line-height: 0.8;
    font-weight: bold;
    text-shadow: #fff 0 1px 0;
    margin: 20px 10px 12px;
}

.group-wrapper p {
    background-color: #fff;
    -webkit-border-radius: 10px;
    font-size: 17px;
    line-height: 20px;
    margin: 9px 0 20px;
    border: solid 1px #a9abae;
    padding: 11px 9px 12px;
}
```

The last exciting feature presented here is the `border-radius` property, which will let you bring rounded borders to any kind of element. Now, reload your page in a browser (Figure 4–7). Does that ring a bell?

Figure 4–7. Et voila, *your first web app!*

Hiding Mobile Safari's Address Bar

As long as you view your site in full-screen mode, this is all very well. However, you can't be absolutely sure that your end user will use it that way. A desirable trick would be to hide the address bar—and the error console, if necessary—when the site is seen in

Mobile Safari. Take a look at the situation. These page elements disappear as the user pans the viewport. The page will take up at least 100 percent of the view height, which means that it won't necessarily be high enough to cover the whole screen if part of its elements move out of focus. Therefore, our goal will be to readjust the page's height if needed so it occupies 100 percent of the viewport, even if part of it is hidden.

Let's get to the code. Create a new directory in your project named *scripts*. From Komodo Edit, create a JavaScript file called *main.js*, and copy the following code to it:

```
if (!window.navigator.standalone) {
    document.addEventListener("DOMContentLoaded", adjustHeight, false);
}

function adjustHeight() {
    var html = document.documentElement;
    var size = window.innerHeight;

    html.style.height = (size + size) + "px";
    window.setTimeout(function() {
        if (window.pageYOffset == 0) {
            window.scrollTo(0, 0);
        }
        html.style.height = window.innerHeight + "px";
    }, 0);
}
```

What this snippet does is check for stand-alone mode; if the user is not viewing your page full-screen, the `adjustHeight()` function will be associated with the DOM finishing loading. The function makes the page twice the height of the screen, which will be enough in most cases, because user interface elements will rarely take as much space. The `window.setTimeout()` gives the page enough time to be modified before the magic occurs. The magic takes two steps: we move the page up so the top of the page is at the top of the screen with the `scrollTop()` method; then, we readjust the page height to make it just fit the screen height again.

You may find it strange to readjust the page position only if the vertical page offset equals 0. Actually, as long as a single pixel hasn't moved out of the screen, the `pageYOffset` will have a value of 0. Even if the user pans half the height of the address bar, the `pageYOffset` value will stay at 0. Thus, we can maintain the page position call after call. The result is that when the user loads the page, it will show almost full-screen, giving maximum focus to the application.

Handling Screen Orientation Changes

However, because the height of the page has been modified dynamically, if the user rotates the screen when not in full-screen mode, the page would become too high for the screen. We must add an event listener for this case also. Note that the `pageYOffset` test is especially useful here, because the position won't be reinitialized with each rotation. Here is the line that handles rotation:

```
window.addEventListener("orientationchange", adjustHeight, false);
```

This code will let us know when the user turns his device. The event listener must be set on the DOMWindow object attached to the current window, not on the document. You will be able at any time to check the value of the orientation using the `window.orientation` property, as done in the following example, for instance to modify styles appropriately:

```
switch (window.orientation) {
    /* Normal orientation, home button on the bottom */
    case 0:
        document.body.className = "portrait";
        break;

    /* Rotated 90 degrees to the left */
    case 90:
        document.body.className = "landscape";
        break;

    /* Upside down */
    case 180:
        document.body.className = "portrait";
        break;

    /* Rotated 90 degrees to the right */
    case -90:
        document.body.className = "portrait";
        break;
}
```

This way, we avoid using a timer, which would have been hard on the battery, to regularly check the dimensions of the window for changes—the notification is automatic. Note that on the iPad you can also target one orientation or the other using CSS or the link tag with the `media` attribute.

```
<link rel="stylesheet" media="all and (orientation:portrait)" href="portrait.css">
<link rel="stylesheet" media="all and (orientation:landscape)" href="landscape.css">

<!-- Or in a style tag or stylesheet -->

<style>
    @media all and (orientation:portrait)  { /* Your style here */ }
    @media all and (orientation:landscape) { /* Your style here */ }
</style>
```

This is possible only on the iPad. For other devices, a good practice is to add a `class` or `id` on the body tag with JavaScript to apply different styles when the orientation changes.

Final Touch

The previous piece of JavaScript handles the viewport if the user is opening your application in Mobile Safari. If he is not, we have seen that you should handle links with JavaScript; we are going to add the relevant script to our *main.js* to prevent the default behavior in this case. For that, add an event listener as follows, and append the `clickHandler()` function to your *scripts* file:

```
if (!window.navigator.standalone) {
    document.addEventListener("DOMContentLoaded", adjustHeight, true);
    window.addEventListener("orientationchange", adjustHeight, true);
} else {
    /* Target only standalone mode */
    document.addEventListener("click", clickHandler, true);
}
```

Ready to Go

The files and file structure you have built here are just what you will need to start most web app projects. If you've installed Komodo Edit, you can now save this project as a template to easily reuse it in your regular working process. To do this, choose your project name from the **Project** menu, and click **Create template from project**. The default location for templates is the *Template* folder in the user folder that was created when Komodo Edit was installed. You will be able to create new projects from this template from the **Project** menu by choosing **New project from template**.

If you haven't chosen to install Komodo Edit, we recommend you find some other way to easily reuse this code and structure. From this chapter, you have learned how important the requirements our template stub answers are to the satisfaction of the user—and the success of your web app. Using templates as helpers will help you quickly get past the somewhat annoying first stages of the project. It also is a first step to make your web application meet its primary goal: to be a proper application.

## Chapter 5

User Experience and Interface Guidelines

The heart of the previous chapter is not the information about screen dimensions, technical possibilities, or even understanding of how iOS behaves on the iPhone, iPod touch, and iPad. Of course, you have to master these aspects to build quality web applications for these devices, but the techniques for doing so are simply tools to succeed in the process. The advice in this book all comes down to the user. The touch-interaction system of Apple's portable devices establishes a specific relationship between the device and the user that is definitely user-centric. This means that you, the developer, need to seriously consider the design of your applications.

Applied to computer development, cognitive ergonomics is the practical science that aims to make an application's functionality easy to understand and access for the user. The Apple engineers have considered some of the ergonomics of the iOS already. For instance, the Multi-Touch interaction model allows users to easily perform common tasks for most sites, such as zooming, focusing, or opening a contextual menu.

An important aspect of ergonomics in Apple products in general, and even more critically on Apple portable devices, is aesthetic appeal. The iOS has a strong visual identity that has been made even more recognizable by the success of native applications tightly integrated into the iPhone's GUI. Therefore, the quality of an application from a user point of view is often judged by how its visual quality compares to the iOS GUI.

Of course, relying solely on design won't make your web application successful. Although a pretty face can allure users into an application, if they don't find the expected quality when actually using it, they will quickly move on. This is especially true in the wildly competitive field like application development.

In this chapter, we will go through a number of rules and best practices that will help you build better web applications, that is, applications where the user experience, which is different on mobile devices than on desktop computers, is at its best.

From the Web on the Desktop to the Mobile Web

It is a common but dangerous mistake to consider that the Web is the same regardless of the platform it is accessed on. Although web applications are built using web technologies, they are completely different from classic web pages. Obviously, device capabilities are different. If you view a web application such as Gmail on Desktop Safari or Mobile Safari, you will see a notably different interface.

Still, using Gmail on your iPhone is possible because Mobile Safari is meant to adapt to the limited screen real estate. However, the experience for the user is not as good as when using an iMac or even a MacBook. The scaling makes the content harder to read and interact with, as demonstrated in Figure 5–1. As a result, Google tries to offer adapted versions—with lighter interfaces, generally less features, and optimized loading times—of its web applications for mobile devices.

Figure 5–1. *Although the rendering is the same between Desktop Safari and Mobile Safari, the scaling does affect user experience*

A different screen size doesn't only mean a different view: changing devices implies a completely different experience, with different behaviors and expectations. Developing web applications, you should tightly relate interface and interaction schemes to functionality, independently from the device. Likewise, web technologies such as CSS or JavaScript should always be considered as tools that can be used to define interfaces and interaction possibilities, inherent to specific functionality—but should by no means dictate what the interface and functionality should be.

Forget the Desktop

Typically, the desktop metaphor is one to forget, together with the habit of intensive multitasking. Get used to the fact that iOS devices—not to say all mobile devices—do not work that way. Using a desktop computer, the end user can perform various tasks at a time, handling multiple windows that he can, if he wants, display side by side at any time. For all these tasks, he enjoys plenty screen estate and, most importantly, will interact with the desktop using feature-rich devices, that is, a mouse and keyboard.

Computers embrace the desktop metaphor, and they can boast productivity tools and a practical or playful approach to many activities. With iOS, though you can have several background tasks such as playing music, downloading applications, or fetching e-mail, running several native applications side by side isn't possible. iOS aims to let the end user efficiently accomplish one task at a time. The small screen means the user successively focuses on one area—and hence one series of actions—at a time.

Change Navigation Habits

When developing for the mobile Web, it is important not to lose your end user halfway through the web application experience. The traditional web experience lets the user access all parts of the site from any other part of the site. This is usually done using both a navigation bar and numerous internal links. As a user of the Web, you've probably already been confronted with a site that you just couldn't figure out. If all went right, you found what you were looking for fast enough; if not, like most users, you probably have moved to the next site.

This situation is even more critical on the mobile Web. The user expects to find a clear, straightforward path from one point to another. The important notion is that of *flow*. Although it may seem obvious not to interrupt the user in whatever process is set in motion, displaying a modal dialog box can easily interrupt the user. For such cases, you should always offer the user an easy way to close the dialog box that makes the subsequent events obvious.

Developers may be tempted to make an application more personal for the end user by requiring input, be it through text fields or radio buttons. On the iPhone, this will slow down the user's experience and postpone them from achieving their goal.

The consequence may be even more annoying on an iPad. Apple suggests that iPad applications should work in a nonlinear way, meaning users should see the content of their tasks in a master view and be able to access options and interaction tools from the navigation part of the screen. That is to say, users should be able to perform most tasks no matter what they are doing in the application. Even if it seems relevant to you, be careful when asking the user to choose between things, because this both breaks the user's flow in the master view and may result in cutting off options in the navigation area, which can be frustrating. For instance, in a mail application, you wouldn't want to lose the "compose" option because the user is reading mail. As a rule of thumb, you should be careful making assumptions about the context in which the user is and what the user is likely to want to do.

Also keep in mind that manufacturers have already thought through the usability of their devices. Therefore, you shouldn't re-create functionality that already exists and that the user is used to using.

Show Ads Thoughtfully

Sites often offer free content and rely on advertisements for pecuniary income. If this is your plan, you should seriously think about how you're going to do it. On traditional web pages, various studies have proven that users are widely "trained" to not even notice advertisements. Although you may think this is less a problem on the iPhone, because advertisements necessarily take up more of the screen estate and the display is usually less cluttered, you shouldn't overload your page. There is a clear risk that forcing the user to pan past irrelevant content or to zoom away from it may quickly drive the user away from your web application.

For web applications and native applications, ad standards have already been long established; you would generally display a small banner at the top or at the bottom of the page. Native applications, however, take this further and automatically hide advertisements after a short delay in most cases, leaving the entire space to the actual content. This has the advantage of driving the attention of the user to the ad while not being intrusive. It would be a positive move to bring such a behavior to web applications, especially because, using CSS transitions, you hardly have to use any JavaScript. The following is a simple example that you can easily test using the template created earlier in the book. To begin, add the following to the <head> of your page:

```
.ads {
    z-index: -1;
    position: relative;
    -webkit-transition: margin-top 0.35s ease-out;
    border-bottom: 0;
    margin: 0 auto 34px;
    width: 320px;
}

.ads img { display: block; }

.ads .tab:before {
    color: red;
    content: 'AD ';
}

.ads .tab {
    position: absolute;
    background-image:-webkit-gradient(
        linear, left top, left bottom,
        from(black), to(#666));
    color: white;
    font: bold 11px/24px verdana;
    height: 24px;
    bottom: -24px;
    left: 0;
    width: 100%;
```

```
        padding: 0 5px;
        -webkit-box-sizing: border-box;
}
```

First, you define styles so that the advertisement stacks beneath the header by modifying the z-index and position values for the advertisement. Then, you create the styles applied to the advertisement area and to the block that should remain visible once the advertisement has appeared. The code relative to the transition is in bold type and indicates that a smooth 35ms transition should occur when the margin-top property is changed.

Next, you rely on a script to trigger the animation:

```
function hideAds() {
    setTimeout(hide, 5000);
}

function hide() {
    var ads = document.querySelector(".ads");
    ads.style.marginTop = (-ads.offsetHeight) + "px";
}

function reveal() {
    var ads = document.querySelector(".ads");
    ads.style.marginTop = "";
    hideAds();
}
```

> **NOTE:** The querySelector() method returns the first occurrence that matches the CSS selector passed as parameter. It is part of the W3C Selectors API, fully supported by Mobile Safari.

This way, whenever you want to hide your advertisement, you will simply have to call the hide() function, which will determine a new margin-top value based on the height of the banner and launch the animation.

The reveal() function will allow you to show the advertisement again by restoring the initial value of margin-top and triggering the animation again. Here is the relevant HTML markup:

```
<body onload="hideAds()">
...
    <div class="header-wrapper">
        <h1>Web App Header</h1>
    </div>

    <div class="ads">
        <img src="some-ad.gif" alt="Advertisement" width="320" height="50">
        <div class="tab" onclick="reveal()">
            Apress sales. 20% off on all books.</div>
    </div>
...
```

Figure 5–2 shows the result. The user will be able to click the tab to see the advertisement again, and the hiding process will happen again after five seconds. Chapter 9 covers more about CSS transitions.

Figure 5–2. *The advertisement is automatically hidden after a few seconds*

Also, you should avoid pop-over elements. As explained earlier, you should limit anything that negatively affects the flow of the user experience. Therefore, you should consider using pop-over elements only at specific moments, such as the first page load. In all cases, there should be an obvious and easy way for the user to close the advertisement—using the default X from the iPhone UI is a reasonable choice (Figure 5–3). Overall, you should thoroughly consider how your advertisements affect your application.

Figure 5–3. *You should always supply the user with an easy way to hide advertisements*

On the iPad, similar processes can be used, only with different formats. Although with its large screen the iPad comes closer to what the desktop Web is, a special connection is established between the user and the device, as explained in the previous chapter. Therefore, you should consider new, adapted ways to introduce advertising into your pages. The possibilities available to you, including sound, video, and rich interaction, should encourage you to make the user a central character in promotional content.

Whatever ideas you come up with, keep in mind the usage characteristics that have been and will be presented in this book—as well as elements gathered from your own iPhone user experience.

Let Users Decide by Themselves

Finding the appropriate attitude as a developer between guiding users through a seamless experience, letting them choose what they want from the web application, and not intervening throughout the process can be really tricky. However, there are times where clearly enough you should leave the decision to the user. Although the frustration of the user isn't directly a question of user interface or design, it will have a negative effect on the perceived quality of your application. For instance, filtering users based on the device they use and blocking them with "iPhone Only" messages is something you should avoid. First, it is a better and overall more efficient practice to target functionalities rather than user agents. Then, if your web application works on the iPhone, it probably will work similarly on an iPad but also on an Android, a webOS device, and so on.

Likewise, you shouldn't impose an iPhone-specific site on iPhone users. Users may have reasons to prefer using the regular, desktop site. You've seen that Mobile Safari renders sites in a similar way than Desktop Safari and provides tools to view pages in the best conditions. Give the user a choice (Figure 5–4), remember that choice (be it with cookies or other storage means), and always gives users a chance to change their minds.

Figure 5–4. *The mobile version of Google Translate offers users the option to use the regular web version*

Simplicity and Ease of Use

What is true for traditional desktop development and web development is even more critical when it comes to the mobile Web. Because portable devices are meant to be used in mobile situations, chances are users may be focusing simultaneously on something else at the same time. This is why you have to make it obvious to users how to achieve their goal with your application. Although repeated panning can be annoying, you shouldn't concentrate most of your content at the top of the page; instead, if you have a lot of content, you should categorize it and make your categories clear. The user should be able to immediately identify the primary function of your web application, together with how the application globally works, even while focusing on other things at the same time.

Avoid Clutter

The overall iOS user interface is simple and polished, with subtle gradients, a limited set of colors, and clean lines. This is a standard by which users will judge your web applications, and Apple's choice is by no means random. Clutter begins with loud colors, too many colors, and colors that make your content difficult to scan. The same applies to elements of your web application. Scattered content can be difficult to take in and will distract the user from what is important. Figure 5–5 shows an example of a cluttered application.

Figure 5–5. *eBay is not optimized for the iPhone and leaves an impression of clutter, while still remaining efficient because there is only one search field*

This doesn't mean you should make extensive use of whitespace. Using too much whitespace on the iPhone will force the user to pan a lot, with limited visibility on the content as a whole. Misusing whitespace on a larger screen like that of the iPad is likely to dilute the content and leave the impression of a scattered experience.

In the case where your web application intrinsically contains many different content elements, the key to a satisfying user experience is probably an efficient menu. Again, you cannot keep the habits you may have built developing for the desktop Web. Your menu has to get to the point quickly, limiting user actions to a minimum while still making the different available options clear. Short, expressive text should be preferred over long and descriptive or drop-down menus. If you're confident that your targeted public will know technical words or abbreviations that could make their options clear in fewer characters, use them. Everything regarding navigation should be fast to scan and use, so these guidelines similarly apply to buttons, links, and the odd pop-up window. Simply, do not forget that all these elements are secondary and should not draw attention away from the main service you are providing. Appropriately balancing all of this will greatly help catch user attention and ultimately increase user loyalty.

User Interface

In a mobile context with limited screen sizes, the notion of a user interface should be considered with a curious mind. We are talking about someone who frequently uses your web application while on the move, though on a screen smaller than what one is used to and using solely finger gestures to interact with your application and the device as a whole.

Developing desktop applications, you could confidently line up buttons at the far edge of a full-screen window to make them easily clicked. Developing for the Web, you could rely on mouse-over tooltips to guide your users in the right direction. These techniques aren't relevant when developing on iOS. Nothing specifically prevents users from missing the far edges of the screen, and there is no actual mouse hovering by which the user could rapidly "explore" the page. For the user interface to remain what it was on the desktop—a set of graphical elements acting as a whole to make functionality easily accessible—you have to reconsider what key rules you should apply.

Adapt to Touch

The first parameter you should take into account is the pointing device—the user's finger. Apple suggests that the fingers of most users need an area roughly 44 pixels wide to quickly tap something without missing. If you want to use smaller buttons or links, be sure to make enough surrounding space available so that several active areas aren't clicked simultaneously.

Another crucial point is that actions should be clearly indicated. There is no point in having perfectly sized tapping areas if nobody ever actually thinks of tapping them. Make your elements look tappable. The best way to guarantee that a user will recognize a button is to follow the prevalent Apple user interface. If you move away from it, you should be careful that people won't misunderstand your elements. On the iPhone, general advice to create tappable elements would be to make them "look real." Apple buttons stand out on the screen because of their gradients and drop shadows (see Figure 5–6). They look like buttons you could actually touch—which is precisely what you need to suggest.

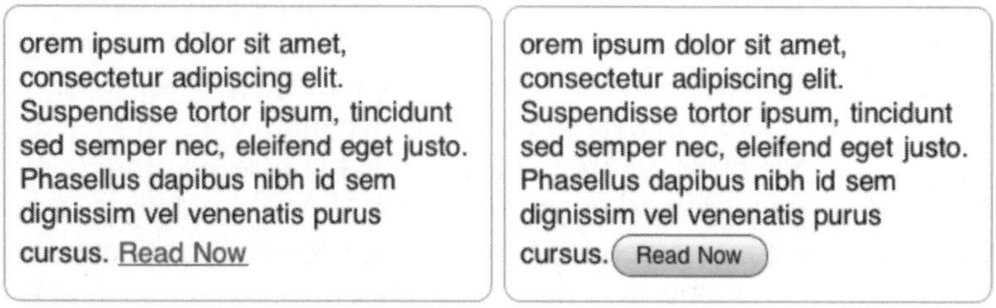

orem ipsum dolor sit amet, consectetur adipiscing elit. Suspendisse tortor ipsum, tincidunt sed semper nec, eleifend eget justo. Phasellus dapibus nibh id sem dignissim vel venenatis purus cursus. Read Now

orem ipsum dolor sit amet, consectetur adipiscing elit. Suspendisse tortor ipsum, tincidunt sed semper nec, eleifend eget justo. Phasellus dapibus nibh id sem dignissim vel venenatis purus cursus. Read Now

Figure 5–6. *Users will be more likely click the button than the plain link*

This will be even more important when developing for the iPad: it is probable that real-world-like application interfaces will be taken a serious step further as the number of applications and sites specifically designed for the iPad's larger screen increases.

Finally, don't forget that unlike when using a mouse the user has no means to activate hover states. If it relies on tooltips or complex hover effects, your application is likely to simply drive disappointed users away.

Adapt to Size

The fact is, there are chances you may not be developing for mobile devices with much larger dimensions in mind. Although screen resolutions may enhance the experience for the user, screen sizes, if devices are to remain mobile, are unlikely to get any larger. The iPad is a quite different experience. Although it has a larger screen, it shouldn't be considered as a new kind of laptop, and although it definitely shouldn't be considered as a larger iPod touch, the following applies to iPad development too: always be extremely careful that all your text content is readable. Small fonts on a wide screen annoy many people—on an mobile device screen, it can completely put your user off.

Of course, one solution is to offer the ability to increase or decrease font size (Figure 5–7). However, ultimately, the best technique is to test your fonts on a device, being honest as to the accurateness of your own eyesight. Create icons with the same limitations in mind. When you make an area efficiently tappable by its size, remember the purpose of an icon is to express an action, a shortcut, or a link faster and more universally than text. This is extra true on mobile devices.

Figure 5–7. *The Twitterific application offers a button in the navigation bar to change text size*

Avoid Unnecessary Interaction

We've stressed that the experience for the user should be as fluid as possible. Whereas filling in forms on the traditional Web can discourage users from going further, on the mobile Web, it can quickly become a chore. In all cases, you should prefer radio buttons, check boxes, or drop-down options to text fields, because typing on an iPhone can be difficult depending on circumstances. The same guideline should be followed concerning the iPad; Apple recommends making iPad applications entirely usable with one hand only, while using two hands should bring extra comfort and speed to access functionality.

Make Use of New Input Types Capabilities

Nowadays, forms are part of a web user's everyday life. People are used to filling in forms and think about it less and less. Therefore, they may be less patient and have higher standards regarding aesthetics and usability. This is especially true on mobile devices, where browsing conditions tend to make users impatient and where input processes can be difficult.

HTML5 introduces a number of new input types to address these issues, which are backward compatible. Table 5–1 lists the types supported by Mobile Safari.

Table 5–1. *New Input Types Supported in Mobile Safari*

Type	Description
tel	A phone number (usually a set of numeric characters)
search	A search field
url	An absolute URL
email	One or several valid e-mail addresses
number	A numerical value

The core idea is that the browser should be able to supply an interface for the user and submit the format to the developer when handling forms. Mobile Safari brings a contextual keyboard for user submission with these input types. For example, tapping a tel type input will trigger a numerical keyboard, as shown on Figure 5–8.

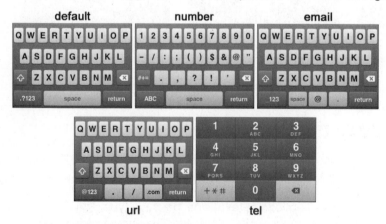

Figure 5–8. *All the supported keyboards*

Such features can obviously make the user experience better by requiring fewer actions for a seamless interaction. The iPhone, up to version 2.0, provided similar functionality to some extent, by automatically firing a numeric keyboard for `input` elements named `zip` or `phone`. However, this feature was dropped in iOS 2.0 and was not available until version 3.1 began to support these new types.

Ponder Upon User-Supplied Information

Although user input can be made easier, always ask yourself whether you really need the information you plan to ask for, or in other words, if it will be a primary concern for the end user. If your application returns a list of books depending on various criteria, it seems secondary to ask whether hardback products, a specific editor, or any year of publication are preferred. In such a case, the best would be to break queries into stages, as done by Amazon (Figure 5–9). First, search by title, author, or topic—ideally, this requires only one text field, leaving the server-side script to determine which is relevant. Then, offer to filter results, for instance by date, editor, or cover type. Finally, you can let your user classify the last results, let's say by price or availability in book stores.

Figure 5–9. *Amazon doesn't load the search area with filters. Instead, it delays filtering to the result page*

Another way to speed up such an application is to keep track of user input. Here, it is likely that your loyal user will mostly be looking for books from the same publishers. You can store the user's choices using traditional cookies or HTML5's latest client-side storage tricks that we will be using in Chapter 15. This way, whenever the user comes back to your web application, the user will be grateful for not having to type *Mephistofeles's Antique Bookshelf Treasures* again.

The key principle behind user input is that for whatever information you ask for, you should give as much extra functionality in return. Of course, gathering information about your user can greatly improve the quality of the service you are providing. The point is to make the "greatly" as great as possible relative to the "gather."

Avoid Multiplying Steps

In the previous example, the user goes through three steps—filter, search, and sort—of which only the first is required. As we have stated earlier, the functionality the user came to find should be available as soon as possible, through a straightforward process. Cutting the book search application into three separate pages only to lighten up each stage—as is often seen with traditional Web, for example in account creation forms—wouldn't be appropriate here. The benefits of such a decision—less panning, less clutter—would be hindered by the fact that the user is forced to wait, perhaps without even knowing how long the process will take or which step is next. Also, for the developer, it is a risky bet to consider that the network will be efficient three time in a row.

The Spirit: Be Focused

The iPhone is not a computer, nor is the iPad. Don't expect users to handle them as such, and don't develop your web applications with computer applications in mind. An iOS application should focus on bringing a specific and satisfying solution to a particular demand or problem and should focus almost only on providing what is expected in the most straightforward manner. The viewport holding your web app should therefore be a place holding selected elements that behave as a whole and a place that is uncluttered, discrete, and clear, as with the Clock application (Figure 5–10).

Although this may originate in hardware limitations—slow rendering under heavy activity, limited screen estate—it has become an expectation of the user, whose loyalty will reward you for providing the appropriate answer to the user's primary question. This becomes true for the iPad also, at least by inheritance, so, always focus on bringing one appropriate service rather than several approximate ones.

Figure 5–10. *The Clock application focuses on what is expected: time services*

Make Things Responsive

Users on mobile devices expect things to happen quickly. Any action should entail a reaction immediately. We've explained in the previous chapter that the default start-up screen for full-screen mode web applications was a view of the last web application screen state, which could leave the impression that the application or the device had become unresponsive. This at least can be frustrating for the user. Even a rather short wait can repel some, and in all cases will harm user loyalty.

Make Your Web App Responsive

This remains true all the way through the web application experience. You should avoid multiplying actions that are heavy on the processor, too much JavaScript , and actions that are too long to complete like heavy server-side activity to show results. This should all be thoroughly considered in the optimizing stage of your development, but also right from the start, in brainstorming and feature designing stage.

To minimize wait times right from your web application loading, always limit the use of images to a minimum, be careful with file sizes, and avoid pages that are too long and will require a lot of panning to use. Regarding images, as we will see in later chapters, you can replace many by using CSS gradients, canvases, or web fonts. You should be aware that as long as the document hasn't fully loaded, the rest of your page is likely to be unavailable to user interaction—without the user actually understanding why, because the part of the page still to load will be out of view. Finally, although separating markup, styles, and functionality (that is, HTML, CSS, and JavaScript) and resorting to external files is a good practice, you should send as few HTTP requests as possible, because again you cannot predict connection type or quality and because server response times may be longer on mobile devices.

Of course, apparent latency steps in the experience you provide are likely to be inevitable. If at some stage you have to initiate an action that is going to take a fair amount of time, always remember to give the user feedback on the web application activity (Figure 5–11). While every action should lead to a quick answer, if this is not doable, users will be more patient and tolerant if you keep them up-to-date with what is happening. This by the way is true for most kinds of user interaction.

Figure 5–11. *The Mail application uses a spinner during the connection and then a progress bar for the potentially longer loading of messages*

For waiting stages, unless you're absolutely sure the awaiting is going to be short, regardless of connection quality, a progress bar is better than a spinner, because it tells the user about the evolution of current processes. Likewise, if several actions are taking place, it would be beneficial to tell users about what is happening, step after step. Visual elements changing on the screen tell users that something is really going on, that is, that the web application hasn't just frozen on a spinner view—and if you do things nicely, it can even be entertaining to some extent.

Make Your Web App Reactive

In a similar way, you should guide your user through actions, even if they are not going to take time to complete. iOS comes with built in feedback for tapped buttons using the `-webkit-tap-highlight-color` CSS property. You can take this as an example of what can be done to strengthen the connection between the user and his device—and your application—because the screen reacts to finger actions like a proper button. On the traditional Web, this is often achieved with hover states: a menu item changes color when hovered over, a tooltip appears, elements are zoomed in upon, or their opacity is toggled.

You know that this isn't an option on mobile devices because with no mouse, there is no actual hover action. Instead, you should give extra attention to whatever should happen when the user taps. Another inspiring example from native iOS functionalities is the toggle on-off button. Instead of a regular check box, or even a button that looks pressed in when a feature is activated, Apple designers use a "switch" metaphor. This gives the user a superior sense of concreteness of the GUI elements, while the change in the state becomes a discreet animation, acknowledging that the action has been taken into account. Nonetheless, always be careful when mimicking the native iOS UI, because users will expect your elements to behave exactly like those they imitate. Hence, a different behavior or result would be deceiving and negatively impact the perceived quality of your applications.

As an iOS developer, it can be interesting in many cases to go further than the `-webkit-tap-highlight-color` effect in this kind of process by creating your own effects (keep in mind however that things should remain simple and easily understandable), by managing your own custom effects, or, for instance, by mimicking entry or menu selection list native effects.

iOS Interface Design Good Practices

Beyond the usability guidelines introduced earlier, there are a number of user interface design guidelines that you should consider when developing your web application. These originate in the specificities of the devices or in the native iOS GUI. Following them can help you serve an experience as good as the user expects and is an important step to a successful application.

Adaptability

A tricky specificity of the iOS is that it allows users to choose at any time between portrait and landscape orientation for the viewport. This is unusual compared to traditional web developers, who can easily rely on minimum screen sizes and ultimately on scrolling. Moreover, there is little chance that a user would change the size of the browser window repeatedly in one visit of a page, which means there won't be a direct comparison of different displays. The situation is made even more complicated with the release of the iPad, which has a screen five times as large as that of the iPhone and iPod touch. To provide a satisfactory experience to users, it is critical that your web applications perfectly adapt to these circumstances.

Because, following the advice found in this book, you have prevented zooming on your web application, you have to make sure it will adapt to the width of the viewport (set to device-width). If you are a front-end web developer, you know what a fluid layout is. The basic idea is that you page occupies 100 percent of the screen, whatever the size of the screen, without breaking into a bunch of disorderly elements. This means you should prohibit fixed sizes for all layout elements and, as a general rule, avoid them altogether. There will be plenty examples in this book on how to achieve this. You have already seen in the project template you built that the title and paragraph take all the width of the screen, regardless of the orientation.

Another method available to you is to apply CSS rules depending on the viewport orientation. This is to be used with caution, because you can easily double file sizes if you end up applying completely different rules to each configuration. The best method is to keep in mind that your page will have two possible layouts and test both at each development stage. If you have built your markup and styles this way, you probably will not have to use specific styles.

List vs. Icon Approach

Looking to present data in a clear and straightforward manner, you will be using lists quite a lot. Apple recommends using lists for web pages and applications that target devices running iOS, and indeed lists have many advantages. They allow you to be more concise by cutting the number of complete sentences, and they make large amounts of information stand out as clear groups of data. In addition, they are similar in form to the default menus of the iOS and desktop application menus, so they will be familiar to the user.

Be careful, however, not to make lists too long. Although the points presented earlier all intersect with good practices we have already written about, lists—even web pages—if they become too long, they will force users to pan, possibly missing what they were looking for or getting lost in the information. Another serious issue with long lists is that they generally make the browser slower, which again will frustrate the user. To avoid lists becoming too lengthy, as explained previously, you should ask yourself what information is most important and how you can categorize it.

Because lists exist in the iOS GUI, there are existing styles you can mimic to achieve an appealing interface for your web applications. Three types of list are available, namely, edge-to-edge lists, lists with rounded borders, and icon grid lists (see Figure 5–12).

Figure 5–12. *Three different list types in three different applications (Yahoo Finance, Settings, and LinkedIn)*

If you follow all the examples in this book and create templates from the files and snippets we suggest, you will soon have a solid base that you can pick from to build web applications.

The first list type is especially adapted to long lists. It is compact, simple, and readable. If you've started building your project template and template files, you can create a new HTML file and add the following code into the `.view` container:

```
<div class="list-wrapper">
    <h2>A</h2>
    <ul>
        <li>Apple</li>
        <li>Application</li>
    </ul>
</div>
```

Next is the CSS to make your basic list look iPhone-like. Append it to the *styles.css* style sheet you have already started in the web application template:

```
.list-wrapper h2 {
    line-height: 1;
    font-size: 18px;
    padding: 1px 12px;
    font-weight: bold;
    text-shadow: rgba(0,0,0,0.5) 0 1px 0;
    background: left 1px -webkit-gradient(linear,
            left top, left bottom,
            from(rgba(0,0,0,0.18)), color-stop(0.65, transparent))
        rgba(178,187,194,0.89);
    -webkit-box-sizing: border-box;
```

```css
    height: 22px;
    border-bottom: solid 1px rgba(0,0,0,0.18);
    overflow: hidden;
    white-space: nowrap;
    margin: 0;
    color: #fff;
}

.list-wrapper ul {
    padding: 0;
    background: #fff;
    font-size: 20px;
    line-height: 23px;
    margin: 0;
}

.list-wrapper ul li {
    border-bottom: 1px solid #dfdfdf;
    padding: 10px;
}
```

The second list type is very similar to the edge-to-edge list type, but it has rounded borders on the first and last list items. Therefore, it is better used on not-too-long lists, so the top and bottom edges of the list are seen at once. The HTML is very similar to the previous markup, though the styles will transfer the padding directly to the links, so effects applied to the focused elements take the border radius into account. To see what happens, simply put the following code inside a .group-wrapper:

```html
<h2>Group List</h2>
<ul>
    <li><a href="item1.html">Item 1</a></li>
    <li><a href="item2.html">Item 2</a></li>
    <li><a href="item3.html">Item 3</a></li>
</ul>
```

And the relevant styles go into the same style sheet:

```css
.group-wrapper ul {
    background-color: #fff;
    -webkit-border-radius: 10px;
    font-size: 17px;
    line-height: 20px;
    margin: 9px 0 10px;
}

.group-wrapper ul li {
    padding: 11px 9px 12px;
}

.group-wrapper ul {
    font-weight: bold;
    margin-bottom: 20px;
    list-style: none;
    padding: 0;
    border: solid 1px #a9abae;
}
```

```
.group-wrapper ul li:not(:last-child) {
    border-bottom: inherit;
}

.group-wrapper ul li a {
    padding: inherit;
    color: inherit;
    text-decoration: inherit;
    margin: -11px -9px -12px;
    display: block;
}

.group-wrapper ul li:first-child a {
    -webkit-border-top-right-radius: 10px;
    -webkit-border-top-left-radius: 10px;
}

.group-wrapper ul li:last-child a {
    -webkit-border-bottom-right-radius: 10px;
    -webkit-border-bottom-left-radius: 10px;
}
```

Your third list alternative, the icon grid display, is appropriate when many options have to be presented in a minimal area. It allows for an intuitive display that can be used to present options to the user. You can also use this display to replace labels in contextual menus, as when a user long-presses to use copy-and-paste functionality. Just remember to always make tappable areas large enough to be usable.

Considering UI Alternatives

Along with considerations about usability design, you thoroughly rethink actual graphical design for your web applications. You have several options here, which are all legitimate. Since there are quite a few orientations regarding interface design for mobile devices, it is your choice to which extent you will follow these guidelines.

Mimicking the iOS UI

Mimicking the native GUI from the device you are targeting is a rather safe bet when developing your web applications. Using a look and feel that users already know will speed up their navigation experience and favor positive impressions regarding your application. You should aim to serve a fluid experience, so making your application mimic the overall Apple interface and using well-designed elements provided by Apple seems like an obvious idea.

The main drawback to mimicking the iOS is that your application may feel out of place if viewed on another device. A webOS or Android user will see your web application just as it could be seen on an iPhone—but the surroundings, the built-in functionalities, and even the device itself will not be an iPhone.

Finally, you would be right to consider that mimicking the iOS UI, even if Apple recommends it, isn't very personal, which could ultimately make your application less memorable than one with similar functionality but a more recognizable identity.

Without actually mimicking the native interface, there are times where you should rely on it. iOS has specific built-in behaviors regarding form `<select>` elements and pop-up modal windows. Moving away from Apple's implementation, these typically would be difficult to render in a usable way, especially because it should be clear for users what is going to happen when they perform actions on such elements.

There are also times when you will have no choice but to rely on the iPhone UI. If you want to use special URL schemes such as `mailto:` or `tel:`, you will be leaving the control to the OS again. The same is true when resorting to audio or video players, because Mobile Safari doesn't integrate these functionalities directly on the iPhone and iPod touch.

Building the iPad Experience

The iPad is new to the developing market. Although it shares its GUI with the iPhone and iPod touch, because it too works with iOS, you should think your design principles over again for this device. The iPad will most probably bring users a brand new experience as a device—it is up to you to build a new, relevant application experience.

The screen of the iPad is more or less netbook size, and it has a greater resolution than that of the iPhone and iPod touch. However, you shouldn't develop your application with a laptop in mind or simply considering the iPad to be a larger iPhone. The functionality the iPad brings is clearly different from that of computers and smartphones.

Not a Laptop, Not an iPhone

The initial orientation of the iPad is the portrait orientation, and there is no scrollbar. The importance of a clear experience remains as critical as with the iPhone. Just because you have more screen estate available for your application definitely doesn't mean that you should try to use all of it. Keep focusing user attention on one purpose of your web app, and keep ways of interacting with it easy to understand. In general, apply the same guidelines as for iPhone development.

Again, the iPad isn't a large iPhone. If following iPhone UI guidelines, you should adapt wherever is possible or necessary. You can keep a preference for lists, though you might consider making the amount of content for each item more complete. Also, you might consider where you had two views on an iPhone application, you can combine elements in the iPad to make one view if it seems relevant, as Figure 5–13 shows.

Figure 5–13. *A creative and realistic way to implement split view*

An interesting way to design content layout for the iPad is called *split view*. The idea is that, because the iPad has a larger screen, developers can separate the main focus from auxiliary content and more advanced functionality in a master-detail style.

In portrait orientation, the detail view would appear full-screen, and the master would float over it; users toggle from a visible state to hidden by tapping an button. In landscape orientation, you would transform the floating box of your application into a sidebar. This has serious advantages, but do not forget to always let users choose by themselves. If you are thinking that you should suggest to use landscape view or even force it, you're probably producing poor design or making an application that is not really an iPad application.

On the iPad, touch is maintained as the ideal way to interact with the OS, applications, and content. This is important because it strongly influences how users use and perceive your pages and applications. Because the screen size allows you to more easily mimic real-life elements, with higher detail, you can rely on a new level of realism to make your application easier to understand and use. Take a look at iBooks (Figure 5–14), which goes far with the library metaphor. The application is very intuitive, because the user is invited to take a book to read it.

Figure 5–14. *iBooks stand as in a real library on the iPad, inviting users to take a book*

As you have more space available to you, interaction in space is no longer limited to vertical movement, and it becomes less of a chore too, be it only because users will have more visibility on what they are doing. The applications presented first on the iPad are to read books, keep a calendar up-to-date, and even do text processing. These are all desktop activities (we're talking about a proper, wooden desktop here), ported to a cleaner, mobile life. This is strong suggestion that you should allow for similar physical sensation of what the user is doing.

Creating the Interface for the iPad

If you are going to extensively use split view (Figure 5–15) in your application design, you should once more seriously consider building a reusable template to speed up your developing process. There are several points where building a split view can be a little tricky.

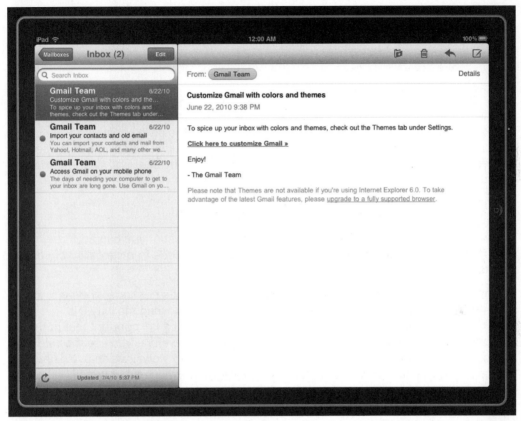

Figure 5–15. *A classic split view with the Mail application*

First, you will have to target the iPad specifically—obviously split view would break on a 320x480 pixels screen. This is achieved using the CSS @media rule, as follows:

```
@media only screen and (min-device-width:640px) { ... }
```

This means we are targeting only screen devices with a minimal width of 640px. This means you could put this in your main style sheet:

```
@media only screen and (min-device-width:640px) {
    body {
        background: #e1e4e9;
    }

    .header-wrapper {
        color: #727880;
```

```
            text-shadow: rgba(255,255,255,0.7) 0 1px 0;
            border-top-color: #fff;
            border-bottom-color: #3e4149;
            background: -webkit-gradient(linear,
                left top, left bottom,
                from(#f4f5f7), to(#a8adb8));
            -webkit-background-size: 100%;
        }

        .group-wrapper p,
        .group-wrapper ul {
            -webkit-box-shadow: 0 1px 0 #fff;
            border-color: #b2b5b9;
        }
    }
```

For the moment, you only change the color of the header to fit with the color scheme of the iPad. However, it is unnecessary to overload your iPhone style sheet uselessly, because you can also load a different, specific file when your web application is used on an iPad or desktop browser. This is done by specifying the device width in the `media` attribute of the `<link>` tag:

```
<link rel="stylesheet" href="styles/big.css" ↵
    media="only screen and (min-device-width:640px)">
```

This way, nothing will be loaded if your user is on an iPhone, but you can add appropriate styles for the larger devices. Add the previous code to a file called *big.css* in your template *styles* directory.

Now that you have your iPad-specific style sheet waiting, let's get some code in it to achieve the split view mentioned earlier. You will apply it following the way it is implemented on native iPad installed applications. Note that it is important that both columns in landscape orientation have the same height. Therefore, you use the `table` and `table-cell` display property value for main and auxiliary views, which avoids having to resort to JavaScript or visual illusions using background images that would be heavier on the rendering engine, longer to load, and less elegant and maintainable altogether.

```
.split-view {
    display: table;
    width: 100%;
    height: 100%;
}

.split-view .view {
    display: table-cell !important;
}

.split-view .view:first-child {
    border-right: solid 1px black;
    width: 320px;
}
```

And your markup would be as simple as this:

```
<div class="split-view">
    <div class="view">
```

```
        ...
    </div>
    <div class="view">
        ...
    </div>
</div>
```

Now, simply do not forget to hide the auxiliary content from iPhone users, by putting the following in your main style sheet:

```
.split-view .view:first-child {
    display: none;
}
```

This will not be applied on the iPad, because you have specified `!important` on the `display:table-cell` rule earlier. The `!important` statement overrides all other rules in the style sheet or inline.

Be Creative and Innovative

You now have knowledge and tools to efficiently start building iPhone and iPad applications. An easy way to start moving away from the defaults is to keep the overall layout unchanged—you understand how the presented layout choices have positive effects on the usability of your web app—but tweak the color scheme applied. The default colors of iOS are distinguished but can be a little cold for some purposes. The relevance also depends on the public you may be targeting. The gray and blue choice may, for instance, feel boring to a teenage target.

An easy yet entertaining way to play with color schemes is to go the site `http://kuler.adobe.com/`. There, you can choose between numerous user-submitted themes or create your own. The idea for you is to easily generate color associations that fit into the initial spirit of Apple's design. You can also go there to get a sense of what's popular or find inspiration.

Of course, the best way to find original ways to design your web applications is to actually use the devices you target as much as possible. Knowing them well, not only as a developer but also as a user, will immensely help you understand what "works" and what doesn't.

Mimicking the UI of the OS you target is a good start to make your application more accessible. Even lazy users should easily adapt to an environment they are familiar with. Therefore, the interface to your application should be well designed and intuitive, building upon what already exists.

Still, you should often be able to find good inspiration in your everyday life. Do you like to sort papers to get yourself organized? Do you need a soothing landscape painting to work in good conditions? Find ways to port this to your applications. Chances are you are not alone in your case, and this kind of innovation can make the difference between good and great. To offer a different experience, build upon the simple, clear iOS interface, creating beautiful, new environments.

Summary

Developing for mobile devices isn't easy. You'll have to move away from a number of principles and habits that ruled on the traditional Web to produce successful web applications. All iOS-based devices provide excellent support for standards, a clean interface, and nifty features for your applications—and thus users—to benefit from. Nonetheless, this comes with its share of constraints. You should be extremely careful not to disappoint your users and always bring them the best experience possible, taking into account the standards they have become used to seeing.

Think about your design process from the ground up but without forgetting what you may have learned from previous development. You have plenty tools available to you, so make the most of them by creating a relevant and unique experience. In the next chapters, we will be getting into more thorough detail of what is possible to achieve with the WebKit and iOS technologies.

## Chapter 6

Interesting CSS Features for Your Web Application User Interface

HTML5 takes document semantics even further than previous versions of the language. However, if you've been a front-end developer for some time, you must be conscious that an appealing design often implies hard dilemmas and superfluous markup. In this chapter, we'll go through a number of CSS features that are going to make your web application developing process much faster, richer, and cleaner. Some make long-awaited enhancements hassle free and easy to maintain, and others are more complex but are going to open a whole new range of layout and design opportunities for your web application on Mobile Safari.

Note that many of the features explained in this chapter are either pretty new and considered unstable or WebKit specific and therefore are prefixed with the WebKit's proprietary -webkit-. This can be needed for property values and is required for most of the properties we are going to explain. As a good practice, you should always declare the WebKit-specific rule followed by the proper, non-prefixed rule to achieve maximum forward compatibility.

Keep all this in mind, and dive into the new wonders that Mobile Safari is making available to you.

Improving the User Experience with CSS

Before we introduce a number of CSS treats brought by the CSS3 specification and some others often sacrificed to browser compatibility, let's go through a few Mobile Safari–specific CSS features. Although the CSS goodness to be presented in this chapter will help you increase and refine your control over the layout and design of your pages, you are targeting a specific OS and browser, both of which have strong user interfaces and have created habits and expectations for their users. The Mobile Safari possibilities we are going to start with will let you build applications that integrate even better into the user's device to improve their user experience.

User Feedback

On a device with such close interaction between the user and the interface, it is important that actions on the user side trigger visual feedback in your web applications, as we explained in Chapter 5.

The initial interaction state implemented in Mobile Safari is based on the -webkit-tap-highlight-color property, which defines a color for the overlay box that will highlight tappable areas of the viewport on user action. It can be seen, for instance, on any tapped link. The following rule would darken (Figure 6–1) such areas whenever the user touches a tappable element:

```
a { -webkit-tap-highlight-color: rgba(0, 0, 0, 0.5); }
```

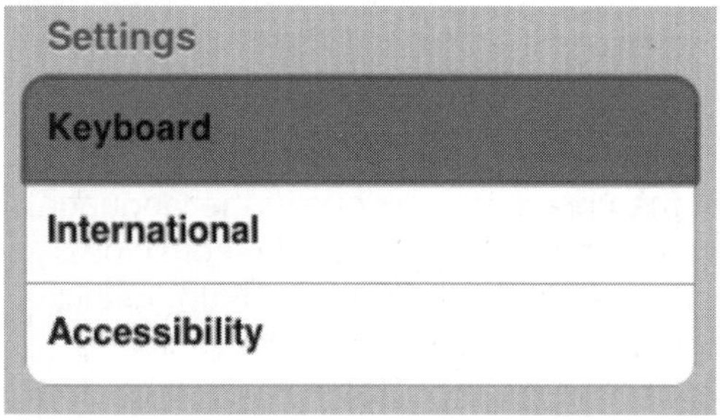

Figure 6–1. *A touched element with custom highlight color*

You may have been thinking that there was no other "clicked" state in Mobile Safari. This isn't entirely true. However, it takes a little trick to access this property with the CSS :active and :hover pseudo-classes.

Many recommend using the mouseover and mouseout Multi-Touch equivalents touchstart and touchend by adding and removing a specific class with an event handler. This indeed works, but it is somewhat clumsy and heavy to use, especially considering there is a much simpler way to achieve this.

You can activate these equivalents by adding an event handler on the window, and without even adding functionality to this handler, it just works and triggers the desired behavior. Therefore, the following code added to the *main.js* file in our web application template will allow us to add the subsequent rule to our *main.css* file, as shown in Figure 6–2:

```
/* main.js */
document.addEventListener("touchstart", new Function(), false);

/* main.css */
.group-wrapper ul li a {
    ...
```

```
    -webkit-tap-highlight-color: transparent;
}

.group-wrapper ul li a:active {
    color: #fff;
    background: #015de6
        -webkit-gradient(linear,
            left top, left bottom,
            from(rgba(255, 255, 255, .25)), to(transparent));
}

.group-wrapper ul li a:active * {
    color: #fff;
}
```

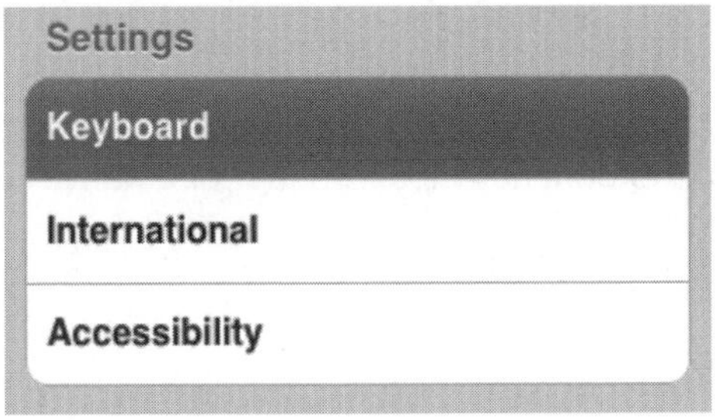

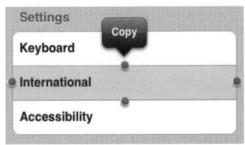

Figure 6–2. *Just like a native iPhone menu*

Again, we have made these styles in a way that makes them easily adaptable. Here, a simple change of the background color will allow you to change the aspect of the button, without altering the gradient.

Disabling Copy/Paste Functionalities

Users can easily initiate a long press action on elements of your page, which would trigger the copy/paste feature with an ugly box that could spoil the user experience to some extent, as shown in Figure 6–3.

Figure 6–3. *A long press may trigger the copy/paste feature*

This behavior can be disabled when it is not desired or when you want to add some custom functionality to this action. You do this using only CSS, with the -webkit-user-select property. This takes either the value auto, to allow selecting; text, to let users select only text; or none, to disable it altogether.

Nonetheless, be careful not to let usability dwindle, for instance by removing the ability to select text fields. The following code takes care of this for you, using common selectors:

```
*:not(input):not(textarea):not(select),
    input[type=image],
    input[type=file],
    input[type=submit],
    input[type=button],
    input[type=reset] {

    -webkit-user-select: none;
}
```

This will prevent selection for all elements apart from text inputs (taking into account all the new input types), making your web application experience closer to that of a native Mobile Safari application.

Control Over Callout

The touch and hold action on a link will trigger the menu shown in Figure 6–4. If your web application has been made to resemble a native application, this behavior is probably not needed, desired by you, or expected by the user.

Figure 6–4. *Touching and holding on elements such as links or images may trigger an option callout*

Luckily, it can be disabled, again with simple CSS, by setting the -webkit-touch-callout property to none. As with the previous property, do consider cases where the functionality may be expected by the user, to not entail frustration on that side.

```
body {
    ...
    -webkit-touch-callout: none;
}
```

Adding this rule for the body of your documents will be enough to globally disable the behavior for all elements.

Selectors

Before getting into the magic of CSS3 layout and styling features, we think it is important to spend some time going through one of the most exciting aspects of writing CSS for modern browsers: selectors. Indeed, if you used to target elements using IDs, classes, and descendants only, you have been missing most of the fun. WebKit browsers implement all of the CSS1 and 2 selectors, along with most of those introduced by CSS3.

> **NOTE:** All the selectors discussed here can be used in the search field of WebKit's Web Inspector found under the Develop menu, which again can prove very useful in your development process.

This gives you almost full control over which element you want to target, without having to identify too many tags with extra identifiers. CSS selectors allow you to precisely move across the document structure choosing only elements with given characteristics.

Overview of Available CSS Selectors

With CSS3, the number of available selectors has become quite impressive, but we will only get into the details of those that appear more complex to handle. You can find the complete list with a description for each selector on the specification page, at www.w3.org/TR/css3-selectors/#selectors.

You will see that most of the selectors presented there are either known already or pretty self-explanatory. You will probably notice some interesting newcomers that allow for negative selection or selection on only part of an attribute. In Chapter 9, we will also be using the very versatile :target, which can save you a fair amount of JavaScript. Other selectors, however useful, may be a little less obvious. Here are a few notes and explanations for those.

First, pseudo-elements are now differentiated from pseudo-classes by the use of a double colon mark (::) instead of a single one. This may seem trivial, but CSS2 didn't make this difference. It has a meaning in the nature of selectors: pseudo-elements are not part of the document tree. Typically they belong to the document text content and couldn't normally be accessed with the document language, while pseudo-classes are meant to further identify elements based on their position in the DOM.

Second, you should be careful with spaces, because an "empty selector" can target any element.

```
/* 2 equivalent definitions... (with space) */
p ::first-letter { ... }
p *::first-letter { ... }

/* ...but different from */
p::first-letter { ... }
```

Next, be aware that you can chain selectors. You could, for instance, want to add a visual mark to the end of all your articles. Assuming that the very last child of the <div> is a paragraph element, this could be done as follows:

```
div p:last-child::after {
    content: "The End";
    font-weight: bold;
}
```

This can be quite complex, because there is virtually no limit to how precise you get, as you can imagine from what follows:

```
a.class1.class2:not(#id1):first-child:hover {
    color: red;
}
```

Here, we target any anchor that has the classes .class1 and .class2, but not the ID id1, and that is the first child of its parent in order to apply a specific color to its hover state.

Position in Suite Selectors: Structural Pseudoclasses

You may be accustomed to using the :first-child and :last-child selectors. If so, you probably know that they can be frustrating, for two reasons.

The first limitation is that, obviously, they allow you to target only the first and last children, respectively. Yet, it can often be desirable to apply different styles to the penultimate child of an element, every other element, or the first child of such or such type.

The second reason is that both of these selectors have an ambiguous behavior where p:first-child doesn't target the first <p> element, but the first element of the parent, if it is of type <p>. Thus, in the following code, no paragraph would be styled differently:

```
<style>
    div p:first-child {
        font-weight: bolder;
    }
</style>

<div>
    <h1>Some Title</h1>
    <p>First paragraph, but not first element: will not be bold text.</p>
    <p>Second paragraph.</p>
</div>
```

All of these limitations are addressed in CSS3. However, the syntax for these new selectors deserves some explanation. The selectors we are going to look at here are those that imply counting elements within the tree, :nth-child(), :nth-last-child(), :nth-of-type(), :nth-last-of-type().

These all share a peculiar syntax where the count of the element you want to target can be represented either by a single number, to target the nth child only, or by an expression matching the xn+y pattern. Both xn and y can be omitted if they equal 0, but one of them must be different from 0. Also, y can have a negative value. Here is an application:

```
<style>
    /* Here there will be no repetition, equal to nth-child(3) */
    ul li:nth-child(0n+3) {
        font-weight: bolder;
    }

    ul li:nth-child(2n) {
        /* Every other row will be affected */
        color: red;
    }
</style>

<ul>
    <li>Item</li>
    <li>Red Item</li>
    <li>Bolder Item</li>
    <li>Red Item</li>
    <li>Item</li>
    <li>Red Item</li>
</ul>
```

xn always represents the variable increment part of the expression, and the number after the + is the position where the increment should begin. When the variable is set to 0n, you target only one element, as in our first example.

Hence, the expression ul li:nth-child(1n+3) would have to target all <li> elements starting at the third child of its parent. Using nth-child(4n+1) would target every fourth element starting the count at the first child (1, 5, 9, 13...).

For nth-last-child(), the syntax is the same, except n is a decrement factor. :nth-last-child(2n+0) targets every even element counting from the end. Also note that for both forward and backward counting, the +y can be a -y, as in (3n-1).

Understanding this syntax gives you plenty of possibilities to style repetitive layout patterns or target specific elements without resorting to additional markup. Also note that all these selectors can take the odd and even keywords as a parameter. Thus, the two following rules are identical:

```
section div:nth-child(2n+0)::after { content: "even"; }
section div:nth-child(even)::after { content: "even"; }
```

As are these two:

```
section div:nth-child(2n+1)::after { content: "odd"; }
section div:nth-child(odd)::after  { content: "odd"; }
```

On the other side, the former examples may or may not be identical to the following, because the starting point is different:

```
section div:nth-last-child(2n+0)::after { content: "odd or even"; }
section div:nth-last-child(even)::after { content: "odd or even"; }
```

Finally, note that the expressions taken by these selectors as parameters should be free of whitespace. The following is invalid and will be ignored:

```
ul li:nth-child(0n + 3) { font-weight: bolder; }
```

As we said, these global child selectors search through all children of a container, regardless of their type. It can often be preferable to target only one kind of children, as in our first example. Here it is again, modified to work as expected:

```
<style>
    div p:first-of-type {
        font-weight: bolder;
    }
</style>

<div>
    <h1>Some Title</h1>
    <p>First paragraph now bolder!</p>
    <p>Second paragraph.</p>
</div>
```

Hence, you can have complete control over the selection of your elements.

Advanced Handling of Backgrounds

Although many inspiring designs have been achieved with the possibilities offered by previous versions of CSS, these usually made the task of setting a background a difficult one.

From a designer's point of view, background definition possibilities with CSS2 could be called a rough cut. Nonetheless, backgrounds are used extensively today as designs grow more complex and richer and incorporate more page elements.

Moreover, backgrounds apply on structures that are more intricate and complex than before. Therefore, developers need to more precisely display backgrounds.

CSS3 offers a new set of background properties to make formerly tricky and cumbersome tasks easier and more efficient. Better positioning and multiple layer backgrounds are available. We are going to explain those that are currently supported by Mobile Safari.

NOTE: Many CSS3 features temporarily require a -webkit- prefix. This allows you to implement new specifications earlier but also implies that these rules will be replaced and disappear. Therefore, in your style sheets, you should always declare the -webkit- prefixed rule followed by what should be the proper, unprefixed rule, to avoid surprises when future versions don't support the "draft" implementation. Also, because the definitive implementation will possibly be better (either faster, cleaner...), you will want that to be applied rather than the draft as soon as it is ready. Therefore, it should be declared second.

Origin of the Background

When defining a background, it is typically applied to a box, with some padding, a border, and a margin. The background color would run from the outer edges of the borders to meet at the center of the box, while a background image would be positioned relative to the inner edge of the border.

This can be fine-tuned with the CSS3 background-origin property, which in a way extends background-position by allowing you to specify the origin for positioning. This will be made most clear with a couple of examples:

```
<style>
    div {
        float: left;
        border: dashed 10px #000;
        background-color: #ccc;
        padding: 20px;
        width: 240px;
        height: 240px;
        margin: 20px;
        background-position: bottom right;
        background-repeat: no-repeat;
        background-image: url(images/flower.jpg);
    }

    div:nth-of-type(1) {
        -webkit-background-origin: border-box;
    }

    div:nth-of-type(2) {
        -webkit-background-origin: padding-box; /* default */
    }

    div:nth-of-type(3) {
        -webkit-background-origin: content-box;
    }
</style>

<!-- Our 3 boxes -->
<div></div>
<div></div>
<div></div>
```

For this example, we have created three boxes with the same dimensions, the same background color, and the same background image. The only difference is the value of the background-origin property. You can check their behavior in Figure 6–5.

The values determine whether the background image should be placed relative to the whole box, including borders; to the box with its padding; or only to the actual content area. The default value for this property is padding-box, the illustration in the middle.

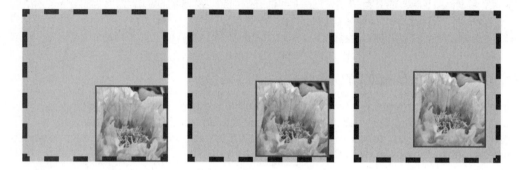

Figure 6–5. *Three possible origins for the background, namely the border, the padding (default), and the content of the box*

Of course, you may think this was achievable with CSS 2.1 properties—you could determine the position of a background, taking into account the width of the borders and of the padding. This obviously had serious limitations.

For instance, you couldn't make the image move into the border area, even by setting a negative value to make it move from the padding area back into the border. Also, defining fixed values for styles such as a background-position typically leads to less reusable code and a multiplication of similar rules, because values would have to be updated for each individual block size. Using the background-origin property not only gives you more possibilities, but it also allows for more global styles, thus letting you write less, more efficient code.

Global Background Clipping

The benefits for design explained in the previous section apply also for the next property, background-clip. While the "origin" of the background affected only background images, the background-clip property allows you to state rules for all background elements, that is, images and colors, by defining the background painting area.

We can almost use the previous example by simply replacing origin with clip in the styles—because the values for this property are the same as for background-origin.

```
<style>

    div {
        ...
```

```
        background-position: bottom right;
        background-repeat: no-repeat;
        background-image: url(images/flower.jpg);
        -webkit-background-origin: border-box;
    }

    div:nth-of-type(1) {
        -webkit-background-clip: border-box; /* default */
    }

    div:nth-of-type(2) {
        -webkit-background-clip: padding-box;
    }

    div:nth-of-type(3) {
        -webkit-background-clip: content-box;
    }

</style>
```

This would result in the behavior shown in Figure 6–6.

Figure 6–6. *The three possible states for background clipping: from the outer edge of the border (default), then excluding the border, then the padding (starting within the content area)*

The default behavior is to extend the background color into the borders of the box. The other values prove to behave as for the background origin, only including background colors too.

Be careful, however, when using the content-box value for the background-clip property: WebKit has implemented it as defined in an early version of the CSS3 specification. However, because this value has been removed from the specification, you should prefer, where possible, to combine background-clip with one of its other two values to achieve the desired effect, in case the value is removed from the browser. It is probable that for the background-clip property, the padding-box value is the most interesting, because it allows rich styling of borders with images—as we will soon see—or translucency.

Text-Based Background Clipping

WebKit also offers the possibility to clip the background in relation with the text from the container using the value text, as shown in Figure 6–7.

```
<style>
    div {
    background-image:
        -webkit-gradient(linear,
            left top,
            left bottom,
            from(yellow), to(red));
    -webkit-background-clip: text;
    color: transparent;
    }

</style>

<div>Background Clip</div>
```

Background Clip

Figure 6–7. *Image-less text rendered as a gradient*

As you can see in the code, the text color needs to be set to transparent so that the container background shows through. The problem with this is that versions of the browser that do not support this background value will show practically no text. Luckily, you can work around this using a WebKit-specific property supported only by versions that also support the background property value in question, -webkit-text-fill-color. You would use it like this:

```
-webkit-text-fill-color: transparent;
color: red;
```

This way, the text will be red for browsers that don't support these recent properties but will still be rendered as a gradient on latest versions of Mobile Safari.

Sizing the Background

Another shortcoming in CSS2 backgrounds that you have probably cursed is that background images, unlike proper HTML images, couldn't be resized. CSS3 brings an easy-to-use solution to this annoying problem with the background-size property (prefixed with -webkit-).

We are soon going to see how you can use this new feature to bring the attractiveness of the Photos native application to your web applications. One aspect of the Photos application that makes it visually attractive is that all the pictures are presented in a regular grid of thumbnails with the same format and alignment—small squares of the same size, as shown in Figure 6–8. This results in a consistent layout, without harming the quality of the pictures because they are all scaled or cropped to fit in the format.

Figure 6–8. *The Photos application presents a homogeneous gallery, where pictures all have the same display size*

Developing a native application, you could use the `UIImageView` object from the Cocoa Touch framework to make images fit into whatever container size using aspect fit, scale to fill, or aspect fill parameters, as shown in Figure 6–9. We are going to use the new CSS features made available to us to achieve a very similar design. The Mobile Safari resize algorithm is good, so you can obtain excellent results.

Figure 6–9. *The aspect fit, scale to fill, and aspect fill modes can now be achieved simply by applying a style to the container*

The `background-size` property takes two values: a horizontal value and a vertical value, and of course you can specify only one value that will apply for both. You can give values using the usual CSS units of your liking; however, for our example, percentages are the best choice, because they make the code easily reusable.

The most obvious value to use is scale to fill, so you needn't know the horizontal/vertical ratio of your pictures. The image will be resized to fill the available space and be stretched or squashed appropriately:

```
/* Scale to fill */
-webkit-background-size: 100%;
```

The other values for the background-size property require that you know the orientation of your images. To obtain an aspect fill effect, you should set the narrowest part of your picture to 100% and the other to auto. This means your image will be cropped vertically for a portrait and cropped horizontally for a landscape.

```
/* Aspect fill for landscape images... */
-webkit-background-size: auto 100%

/* ... and portrait images */
-webkit-background-size: 100% auto;
```

Reversing these values would result in an aspect fit resize, meaning the whole image will appear in the dedicated area, leaving blank space either vertically or horizontally. Specifying both values explicitly would force the resized image dimensions.

> **WARNING:** Be careful that your images are not more than twice as high as your container. There is a bug in Mobile Safari's handling of such a situation, which shows a cropped image. The only way to avoid this problem is to use smaller images.

The CSS3 specification has values to easily achieve the desired effect. However, these values—contain and cover—are not supported as of iOS version 3.2.

Developing a Photos-Like Gallery

In this section, we will show a live example of the possibilities offered by these new CSS properties and values by using them to reproduce the appearance of the Photos gallery shown earlier. One of the characteristics that makes this gallery so efficient and appealing is that, whatever the initial format of the pictures displayed, they all fit nicely into the square area allotted to them.

As usual, we are going to build upon our Komodo Edit project and the directory structure we have already worked with. First, you will need to add a new physical folder to your project, named *images*, where you will store all the pictures for your gallery.

In Komodo Edit, go to **Project ➤ Add ➤ New Live Folder**, and click the appropriate icon to create a new directory called *images*. Then select it.

Next, because we are going to use PHP to read the *images* folder contents and dynamically add references to the images inside it to some JavaScript code, you will have to rename your *index.html* file to *index.php*. This is what it should look like:

```php
<?php require_once("index_code.php"); ?>
<!DOCTYPE html>
<html>
<head>
    <title>Gallery Demo</title>
...
    <link rel="stylesheet" href="styles/main.css">
    <link rel="stylesheet" href="styles/gallery.css">
...
    <script src="scripts/main.js"></script>
    <script>
        var images = <?php writeImages('images'); ?>;
    </script>
    <script src="scripts/gallery.js"></script>
</head>

<body onload="showImages()">
...
    <h1>Gallery</h1>
...
    <div id="gallery"></div>

</body>
</html>
```

Then, create a *index_code.php* file at the same level as *index.php*. It will hold the functions necessary for the galley to work. In other words, it allows you to gather the list of images from the *images* folder. Here it is:

```php
<?php

# Parse the given folder and return an array of the collected files

function getImages($path) {
    $handle = opendir($path);
    $files = array();

    if ($handle) {
        while (($name = readdir($handle)) !== false) {
            if (is_file("$path/$name")) {
                $files[] = "$path/$name";
            }
        }
    }

    closedir($handle);
    return $files;
}

# Transform our PHP array into a JavaScript array

function writeImages($path) {
    $all = implode('", "', getImages($path));
    echo !$all ? '[]' : '["'. $all . '"]';
}
?>
```

Now, create a *gallery.css* file in your *styles* folder, and link to it in the head of your document. The following are the styles you will be using:

```
.header-wrapper {
    background-color: #444;
}

.view {
    background-color: #fff;
}

div#gallery {
    padding: 2px;
    float: left;
}

#gallery > div {
    border: solid 1px rgba(0,0,0,0.1);
    width: 75px;
    height: 75px;
    margin: 2px;
    float: left;
    -webkit-box-sizing: border-box;
    -webkit-background-size: 100%;
    background-position: center top;
    background-repeat: no-repeat;
    -webkit-background-origin: border-box;
}

#gallery > div.portrait {
    -webkit-background-size: 100% auto;
}

#gallery > div.landscape {
    -webkit-background-size: auto 100%;
}
```

These styles ensure that each image extends into the borders of its container so that all images have exactly the correct size. In addition, the translucent border makes sure that the overall look is consistent, even with pale-colored pictures.

You will have noticed that, because the contain and cover values aren't supported, we have to apply different rules, whether the picture is in portrait or landscape orientation. We will use the following JavaScript code, to be put in a new *scripts/gallery.js* file, to determine for each image which class should be added:

```
function showImages() {
    var container = document.getElementById("gallery");
    container.innerHTML = "";

    for (var i = 0; i < images.length; i++) {
        loadImage(container, images[i]);
    }
}

function loadImage(container, src) {
    var img = new Image();
```

```
    img.src = src;

    var div = document.createElement("div");
    container.appendChild(div);

    img.onload = function() {
        div.className = (this.width < this.height) ? "portrait" : "landscape";
        div.style.backgroundImage = "url(" + this.src + ")";
    }
}
```

The showImages() function first empties the gallery container so that there is no display problem when loading new content. Then, it uses the global images array to fetch the pictures to be displayed and for each new item calls the loadImage() function. This function creates a new <div> container for each new item with the right class and image background. The Image object is used only to determine the current orientation once each image has been loaded.

Now, if you open the URL to this page in Mobile Safari, you should see a consistent gallery similar to that of the native Photos application, as shown in Figure 6–10.

Figure 6–10. *A homogeneous picture gallery*

To be more search engine friendly, you can also add the images directly to the markup on the server side and apply an onload attribute directly to each image. However, you would then need to replace all the images' src with a blank pixel image in order to finally display only the background.

Multilayer Backgrounds

As you can see, the effects you can achieve with CSS3 backgrounds are much richer than those of CSS2. Yet this is not all the new specifications have in store for you. Working with background images, you can now handle multiple backgrounds applied to only one element. By using a comma-separated list of values for the URL of your background, all images will be taken into account, stacking up with the first declared one on top. The main limitation to this is that you can specify only one background color that will be on only the lowermost layer.

However, WebKit extends this functionality by allowing it not only for the background-image property but for all background properties apart from the color. This means, for instance, the end of the sliding-doors technique or more possibilities for fluid layouts, because gradient backgrounds drawn with -webkit-gradient() will be resizable. Rather than using a background repeat, you could also achieve effects like the one shown in Figure 6–11 using the following code:

```
.multiple {
    width: 400px;
    height: 300px;

    background-repeat: no-repeat;
    background-image: url(flower.jpg);

    background-position:
        90px 90px,
        70px 70px,
        50px 50px;

    -webkit-background-size:
        60% auto,
        50% auto,
        40% auto,
        30% auto,
        20% auto;
}
```

Figure 6–11. *Images stack up, from the first at the bottom to the last on top*

In this example, we leave the background-image property unchanged for all background layers, but we progressively change its position and size to mimic a zoom-in effect.

It is important here to understand how the interpreter handles values when there are more layers than values for some property. The rule applied is to repeat the list of available values in a loop until they meet the right count.

However, be careful: although the specifications indicate that the number of layers should be determined solely by the number of `background-image` properties, WebKit duplicates this property if other background properties have a higher count. Because, following the specifications, superfluous values should be ignored, we advise that you should not rely on this for your designs, because it is likely that either WebKit's implementation or the specification will evolve.

This property will, for instance, let you set a different background for elements that are selected. We shall use it in our next chapter on the canvas and SVG to add an arrow to list items, and this is used in our web application template header combining gradients and the new color definition possibilities that we are going to explain next.

Colors

Color is essential to design, and its use has become more and more complex as its rendering has improved on devices. However, building interfaces with complex color associations often required that we resorted to images (for instance to handle transparency) or to third-party tools (typically to build a color scheme). The CSS3 specification brings a new set of options that will help you build image-less interfaces that are more complex yet more lightweight, while making your workflow more efficient.

The Alpha Channel

Colors using CSS2 would most often be defined using the RGB notations, namely, `#rrggbb`, `#rgb`, and the `rgb()` function. This is extended in CSS3 to allow for an alpha channel, using the `rgba()` function. The value for the alpha channel is a floating number within a range from 0 to 1. This is especially useful when dealing with transparent box backgrounds, because the traditional use of the `opacity` property has the inconvenience of being inherited. For instance, to set a translucent background on a box while still having fully readable text inside it, you would have needed to resort to background images or complex positioning. This is no longer necessary, because you can simply set transparency for the `background-color` property.

The following code illustrates how this will change your life:

```
<style>
    body { background-color: yellow; }
    .main { position: relative; }

    .opacity-layer {
        position: absolute;
        background-color: blue;
        opacity: 0.25;
        left: 0;
        right: 0;
```

```
        top: 0;
        bottom: 0;
    }

    .content-layer {
        position: relative;
        color: red;
    }
</style>

<div class="main">
    <div class="opacity-layer"></div>
    <div class="content-layer">
        <h1>Some Title</h1>
        <p>A nice paragraph.</p>
    </div>
</div>
```

Here is equivalent code using the new color functions:

```
<style>
    body { background-color: yellow; }

    .content-layer {
        background-color: rgba(0,0,255,0.25);
        color: red;
    }
</style>

<div class="content-layer">
        <h1>Some Title</h1>
        <p>A nice paragraph.</p>
</div>
```

Of course, the other advantage of the alpha channel is that, because it is simply a color definition, you can apply it to anything that takes a color as value, including text or borders. You will also find it can be used to create sophisticated CSS background gradients.

New Color Definitions

The alpha channel can also be used with a new CSS3 color definition function: hsl(). Although RGB is commonly used and many front-end developers are quite fluent with it, it is often considered unintuitive. Indeed, in "everyday life", people are used to subtractive synthesis of colors (as when mixing paint colors), while RGB is based on additive synthesis (as in "blending all colors together produced pure white," which is the case for light). It is common that RGB users actually get used to it by subconsciously translating it to a change in hue, saturation, and light.

The hue (the *h* in the hsl() and hsla() functions) is an angle, measured in degrees (without specifying the unit) with a value from 0 to 360. It is usually represented by a circle, where each degree represents a shift in color, from red (0) to red (360). Saturation and lightness are specified as percentages.

```
hsl(<hue>, <saturation>, <lightness>)
hsla(<hue>, <saturation>, <lightness>, <alpha>)
```

Here is a set of equivalent CSS rules:

```
.red { color: red; }
.red { color: #f00; }
.red { color: rgb(255, 0, 0); }
.red { color: hsl(0, 100%, 50%); }
.red { color: hsl(360, 100%, 50%); }
.red { color: hsla(0, 100%, 50%, 1.0); }
```

Because the progression around the hue "circle" is easy to grasp, you can quite easily move around it, as represented in Figure 6–12, a laid-out version of the circle, with stop points to situate basic colors.

red	yellow	lime	aqua	blue	fuchsia	red
#F00	#FF0	#0F0	#0FF	#00F	#F0F	#F00

| 0 | 60 | 120 | 180 | 240 | 200 | 360 |

Figure 6–12. *Conversion table between basic colors*

HSL makes it easier to move around color values in a natural way. If you want orange, you just pick a value between red and yellow (0 and 60 degrees). Want a lighter orange? Just add some lightness. Need an orange that is less vivid? Remove some saturation.

With the `rgb()` representation, you would have had to determine an amount of each color, while with the #rrggbb representation, you would have had to cope with the extra difficulty of converting to hexadecimal values for each color.

Using Gradients

The previous properties allowed for the fine-tuning of background properties. However, WebKit features new properties that allow you to use code instead of images for a most interesting purpose: gradients. This can make a great difference in the way you handle design elements, because it has quite a few advantages.

First, CSS gradients will be more lightweight for the end user, because no images will have to be loaded, and of course, there will be no extra HTTP request—which, as we have indicated before, can be quite slow on mobile devices.

Second, CSS gradients, once you have mastered them, are faster and more straightforward to modify on your site, because you will need only one tool—which often means only one person, too—and you don't have to worry about dimensions.

Basic Syntax

As of this writing, there is no specification about the actual syntax for CSS gradients; each browser vendor has implemented this feature in its own way. Here is the most elementary syntax to create a gradient for WebKit browsers:

```
-webkit-gradient(
    linear,
    left top,
    right bottom,

    from(black),
    to(yellow)
)
```

For instance, you can apply this to the background of an element using the following:

```
<style>

    button {
        background-image:
            -webkit-gradient(
                linear,
                left top,
                right bottom,

                from(white),
                to(lightgrey)
            );
        border: 1px solid gray;
    }

</style>

<button>Click Me</button>
```

This example draws a linear gradient that spans from the upper-left corner of the box to the lower-right corner and will create a transition from white to lightgrey, as shown in Figure 6–13. In our examples, we are going to use named colors for clarity, but you can use any color naming convention supported by CSS3, including transparent values.

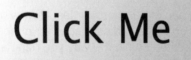

Figure 6–13. *A simple button with a linear gradient*

You can determine positions using named positions, pixels (with implicit unit), or percentages: the left top and right bottom values in our example are equivalent to 0 0 and 100% 100%, for instance.

A gradient value can be applied to properties that support an image, namely, background-image, border-image, list-style-image, and even content. However, it is not possible for now to set this value for a color property—meaning you won't be able to directly apply gradients to text.

Changing the Size of the Gradient

With backgrounds, the default behavior of gradients is to extend to the dimensions of the box to which they are attached. Because the -webkit-gradient() function is considered as an image, you can tweak this behavior using the properties explained earlier, noticeably with background-size, which will change the drawing area for the gradient.

Setting the background size to 5px, for instance, will limit the span of the gradient to a square 5 pixels on a side. The default value of the background-repeat is repeat, so if you haven't set a value, the gradient will repeat as a pattern to cover the box area, as shown in Figure 6–14.

```
.gradient-box {
    ...
    -webkit-background-size: 5px;
}
```

Figure 6–14. *Because the drawing area has been redefined, the gradient has become a repeating pattern*

Of course, your gradient could be cut off, if the drawing area is not large enough to hold the whole gradient. This would typically occur using fixed dimensions (as you will have to do to use radial gradients).

Complete Gradient Syntax

Although gradients offer a good range of new possibilities for the styling of HTML elements, there is more to the implementation of gradients by WebKit. Here is the complete syntax as described in the WebKit documentation:

```
-webkit-gradient(<type>, <point> [, <radius>]?, <point> [, <radius>]? [, <stop>]*)
```

As with regular expressions, the question mark indicates that the item can occur none or one time, and the asterisk shows that it can be used one or several times, or not at all. Of course, specifying a gradient with no color seems like a strange idea.

You can create two kinds of gradients with CSS: linear gradients, as you have already seen, and radial gradients. To define a radial gradient, you have to specify a radius together with the elements we have already introduced. Note that the value for the radius is expressed in pixels only, though the unit should not be specified. You cannot use relative units to fit your gradient whatever the size of your box, and therefore you can achieve only regular circles, not more complex ellipses. You can see the effect of the radial type gradient (shown in Figure 6–15) by replacing your gradient code in the first example by the following:

```
-webkit-gradient(
    radial,          /* gradient <type> */
    100 100, 25,     /* <point> and <radius> (for radial gradients only) */
    100 100, 100,

    from(black),     /* 2 <stop> values */
    to(yellow)
);
```

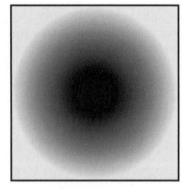

Figure 6–15. *A simple radial gradient*

This syntax can seem a little tricky or confusing. It is important to understand exactly what each value represents. The first pair of values, after the gradient type, is the position where the gradient should originate. It is followed by the radius of the area that should be entirely filled by the first color stop.

The second pair again indicates the destination circle of the gradient, the last number being the radius by which the color blend should occur. The rest of the available space out of this last circle will be filled with the last color stop, plain.

The last values determine the colors that will be used to draw the gradient. As shown previously and as we'll explain in the next section, you can set as many colors as you like for these values.

Advanced Color Handling

The from() and to() functions are both shorthand expressions for the color-stop() function, which has the following signature:

color-stop(*<stop value>*, *<color>*)

The first parameter can be defined either as a percentage or with a float ranging from 0 to 1. The second takes any valid CSS color definition. This function thus allows you to determine the entire color palette for your gradient, along with the steps where they should start, stop, and blend. from(*<color>*) and to(*<color>*) hence are the same as color-stop(0, *<color>*) and color-stop(1, *<color>*).

This opens new ways to use your gradients, because you can use the `color-stop()` function as many times as you want for a single gradient. Here is the preceding example, with an extra color:

```
-webkit-gradient(
    radial,
    100 100, 25,
    100 100, 100,

    from(black),
    to(yellow),
    color-stop(50%, red)
);
```

If you use Photoshop, this logic should seem familiar, and you will recognize the Gradient Editor, as shown in Figure 6–16.

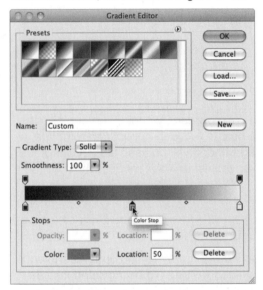

Figure 6–16. *Photoshop Gradient Editor with color stops and midpoint circles between stops*

However, with CSS, the only way to give more importance to one color over another as you would with the color midpoint in Photoshop or to build irregular gradients is to add more stops with the same color.

Order is not important when you specify these color stops, unless several occur in the same place, for instance when building a sharp transition, as in the following example (Figure 6–17):

```
-webkit-gradient(
    radial,
    50% 50%, 0,
    50% 50%, 100,

    from(red),
    color-stop(50%, red),
```

```
        color-stop(50%, yellow),
        color-stop(99%, yellow),
        color-stop(99%, transparent),
        to(transparent)
);
```

Figure 6–17. *Two concentric circles drawn using several* `color-stop()`

Using this technique, you can draw circles with crisp borders, without worrying about the ending color of the gradient filling the entire box. In our web application template, we have used this technique to add a hashed background. It will be used also in Chapter 9 to create an attractive tab bar, in association with the flexible box model, which will be explained later in this chapter.

Boxes and Borders

Traditionally, "boxes" in CSS haven't been supplied with many styling options. Beyond a handful of unevenly supported border styles, you had to resort to background images, with all the duplicate styles and the approximations that the process entails, to bring some extra shine to your elements.

A simple web search yields hundreds of pages promising the ultimate beveled or rounded border solution; this has resulted either in superfluous markup, heavy JavaScript, or extra images. CSS3 is almost making these practices obsolete, with several very interesting features supported by recent browsers, including Mobile Safari.

Box Sizing

Before we get into the styling of boxes, let's take a look at a new feature regarding box sizing. The `box-sizing` property resulted from the observation of the non-compliant Internet Explorer that didn't calculate box sizes as described in the CSS2 specification. Although HTML renderers should process the box size as the sum of its width, padding, borders, and margins, Internet Explorer considered the padding part of the content width, instead of adding it.

```
.box {
    -webkit-box-sizing: border-box;
}
```

The default value for the box-sizing property is content-box, which is the behavior expected in CSS2. However, setting the value to border-box will cause the padding and borders to be counted inside the content area instead of around it. Figure 6–18 shows the difference.

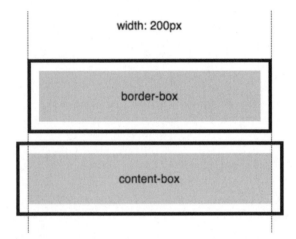

Figure 6–18. *The transparent padding and black borders show the difference between both box models*

This may seem unusual to you if you've been using the CSS2 box model for some time. Nonetheless, using this property value means you won't have to worry about giving a 100% width to a box or adding a border to your containers.

Typically, you would design a site with a global container, a 680 pixels wide left column for the main content, and a 300 pixels side column. Changing the padding for your boxes or adding a border to your side column would have proven a daunting task. Here, you wouldn't have to worry about this, because your boxes would preserve their outer width.

Rounded Box Corners

Adding rounded corners to elements on your pages has been very popular for some time now; however, again, this could be difficult to implement in a flexible way. Furthermore, the iPhone user interface extensively uses rounded corners. To achieve a design consistent with this, it is likely you will want to emulate iOS boxes too.

CSS3 brings the ultimate solution with the border-radius property. With a simple CSS declaration, you should be able to achieve most of your designer dreams regarding corners, as shown in Figure 6–19.

Note that WebKit (and, necessarily, Mobile Safari) doesn't exactly comply with the specification. This is a limitation only in that the specification allows you to generate differentiated borders in a single declaration. With the syntax for WebKit, you will have to declare each corner separately if you want different effects.

The syntax for Mobile Safari is arguably more intuitive, though. You refer to the targeted border in the property name and set the radius as the value. Thus, your rule would be presented as follows:

```
/* Same value for the four corners */
-webkit-border-radius: 16px;

/* The same as separated declarations */
-webkit-border-top-left-radius: 16px;
-webkit-border-top-right-radius: 16px;
-webkit-border-bottom-left-radius: 16px;
-webkit-border-bottom-right-radius: 16px;
```

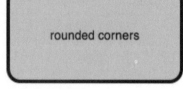

Figure 6–19. *A simple box with rounded corners*

Of course, you are not limited to regular shapes. Although giving the same value to every corner will return a regular box with rounded corners and end in a perfect circle, you can create a more elliptic shape by specifying parallel values for the width and height, as in Figure 6–20:

```
/* Again, same value for the four corners */
-webkit-border-radius: 24px 48px;

/* And again, the same as separated declarations */
-webkit-border-top-left-radius: 24px 48px;
-webkit-border-top-right-radius: 24px 48px;
-webkit-border-bottom-left-radius: 24px 48px;
-webkit-border-bottom-right-radius: 24px 48px;
```

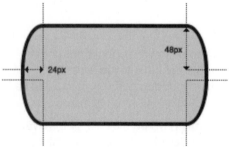

Figure 6–20. *A box with distorted corners*

The property is applicable to all elements, just as with the border property, but it doesn't depend on the actual use of a border. Likewise, you can use any measure unit, be it fixed values such as pixels or relative values such as ems or percentages.

Using percentages, the value of the radius will be evaluated relative to the overall width and height of the box (that is, the dimensions considered as when using the border-box value for box-sizing). Also note that you won't have to worry about your backgrounds overflowing their containers, because they will be clipped appropriately.

Borders Drawn with Images

However awesome the border-radius CSS3 feature may be, there is more to borders than actual border lines with the new specification. Indeed, you can also integrate more elaborate border styles with the border-image property. This will take care of adapting an image to the size of your borders, either by scaling it or by repeating it.

In the following examples, we will use the image in Figure 6–21, which is 300 pixels wide and high, as a pattern for a border divided into nine different areas. These will be declared in the same order as for margins, padding, or borders, with two modes, stretch and repeat. The main limitation to this method is that you cannot specify a different mode for opposite borders.

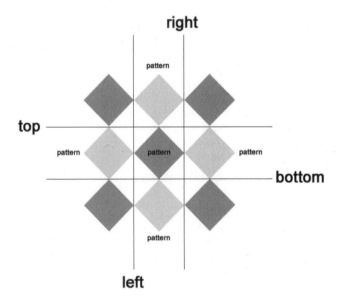

Figure 6–21. *A pattern to be used as a border image*

Figure 6–22 shows the result of the following code, changing only the mode:

```
.border {
    -webkit-border-image: url(diamonds.png) 100 100 100 100 stretch stretch;
    width: 400px;
    height: 350px;
    border-width: 100px;
}
```

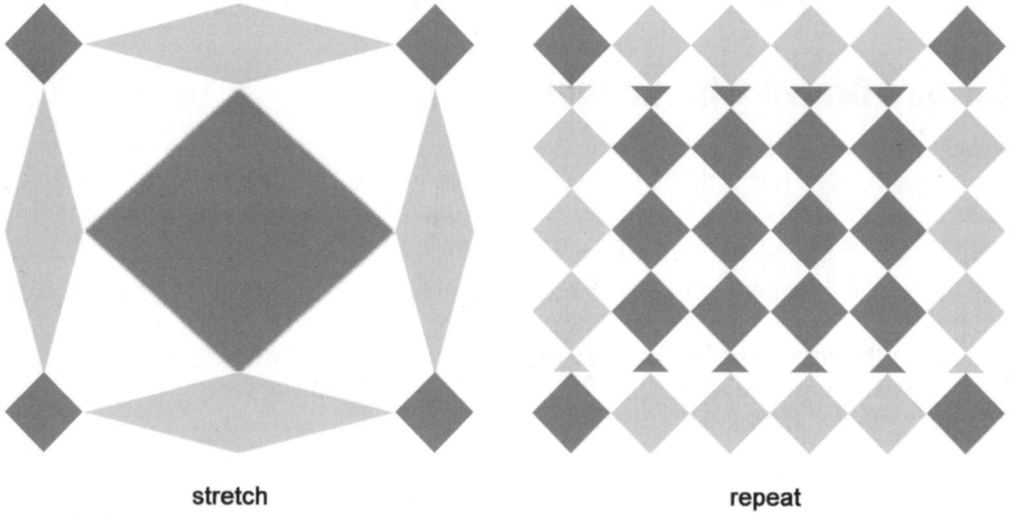

stretch   **repeat**

Figure 6–22. *The resulting box with stretch and repeat mode*

There is a third mode, round, that would repeat the pattern and scale it so that it is not truncated. However, this mode is not yet supported by Mobile Safari. As a consolation, because a border with an image primarily is a border, you can specify the border width directly in your border-image declaration, as shown here:

```
.border {
    -webkit-border-image: url(diamonds.png) 100 / 100px stretch stretch;
    width: 400px;
    height: 350px;
}
```

This is shorthand for the property. Because all sides have the same dimensions, we group the slice areas together. This value doesn't take a unit; pixels are implicit for the parts of the image. A slash separates the slice area from the size of the border to avoid any confusion.

Because the areas in our image are 100 pixels wide doesn't mean we need to have borders that wide: by defining a thinner border, the area of the image shall be scaled to fit into the border width. Thus, in the following example, our image will be made, respectively, 50px, 25px, 100px, and 25px wide for the top, right, bottom, and left borders (Figure 6–23).

```
.border {
```

```
    -webkit-border-image: url(diamonds.png) 100 / 50px 25px 100px stretch;
    width: 400px;
    height: 350px;
}
```

Figure 6–23. *Each border has its own thickness*

This rule can be very useful when creating attractive buttons to replace the default operate system ones.

Shadows

More control over borders is an interesting feature in building web pages because identifying blocks helps readability and can be a way to make content stand out. CSS3 offers another long-awaited feature in this respect, namely, outer shadows for blocks with the box-shadow property. WebKit browsers also implement the CSS2 text-shadow property. Because this property is part of an official recommendation and is considered stable, you needn't use the -webkit- prefix.

Both of these features not only allow for drop shadows but also make it possible to draw glowing effects, which is useful creating button effects. Beyond the visual attractiveness, one advantage of this solution is that shadows don't extend the dimensions of your blocks or text, meaning your layout will not be affected. Also, you have the possibility to apply multiple shadows to the same element, using only one declaration.

Box Shadows

The syntax for box shadows is quite simple. The box-shadow property takes four parameters: the color, horizontal offset, vertical offset, and blur radius. Setting the blur to 0 would result in a neatly cut shadow; the greater the value, the fuzzier and more transparent the shadow.

The most usual use of such a property would probably be the outlining of page sections or provide user feedback while pressing a button. Nonetheless, in the following example, we are going to use it to create an iOS-looking icon, using only one image, that of the icon itself.

```
<style>
    .icon {
        display: inline-block;
        text-shadow: rgba(0,0,0,0.5) 2px 2px 2px;
        color: #000;
        font: bold 11px helvetica;
        text-align: center;
        margin: 8px;
    }

    .icon div {
        -webkit-border-radius: 8px;
        width: 57px;
        height: 57px;
        margin: 0 auto 4px;
        -webkit-box-shadow: 0 4px 4px rgba(0,0,0,0.5);
        -webkit-box-sizing: border-box;
        background-image:
            -webkit-gradient(radial,
                50% -40, 37,
                50% 0, 100,
                from(rgba(255,255,255, 0.75)),
                color-stop(30%, rgba(255,255,255, 0)),
                color-stop(30%, rgba(0,0,0, 0.25)),
                to(rgba(0,0,0, 0))
            ),
            url(flower.png);
        -webkit-background-size: auto auto, 100% 100%;
    }
</style>

<div class="icon">
    <div></div>
    Flowers
</div>
```

The first thing you'll notice in Figure 6–24 is that the shadow follows the borders. Therefore, if you apply a radius to corners, the shadows will be rounded too.

Figure 6–24. *An icon in the iOS Dashboard style*

> **NOTE:** The zoom property is not valid CSS. First implemented by Internet Explorer, it has been implemented by other browsers without ever making its way to any specification.

What is interesting using this code is also that it is fully resizeable. For instance, setting the zoom property to 0.57 would change your 57 pixel icon to the regular 32 pixel iPhone menu icon; just changing one value will result in a modified icon size while preserving the overall measurements and quality.

Text Shadows

The previous example uses another kind of shadow, applied to text. The syntax for the text-shadow property is very similar to that of box-shadow; the only difference is that you should declare the color value first, instead of last. The two following classes, respectively, apply a drop shadow and a glow effect to the piece of text they are applied to (Figure 6–25):

```
.shadow {
    text-shadow: #000 2px 2px 5px;
}

.glow {
    text-shadow: #000 0 0 2px;
    color: #fff;
}
```

Figure 6–25. *Shadow and glow effect*

As we have seen in our web application template, drop shadows can be used for more than shadows. Previously, we have used drop shadows to create embossed effects.

Using JavaScript, you could even extend and reduce dynamically the blur of the text shadow dynamically to create a vibrant glowing animation.

Text Effect with Shadows and Outline

With the `text-shadow` property, you have learned to create a realistic glow effect that's quite similar to an outline. To explore the richness of possibilities offered by Mobile Safari in this field, let's draw a more advanced heading using properties that will let you finely control the rendering of the text stroke:

```
<style>
    div {
        color: lightgrey;
        -webkit-text-stroke: 2px gray;
        font-size: 100px;
        text-shadow:
            gray 1px 1px 0,
            gray 2px 2px 0,
            gray 3px 3px 0,
            gray 4px 4px 0,
            gray 5px 5px 0,
            gray 6px 6px 0
    }
</style>

<div>Text Stroke</div>
```

The `text-stoke` property is a shorthand to the `text-stroke-width` and `text-stroke-color` properties. This makes defining an outline extremely simple, as illustrated in Figure 6–26. In this example, we also add a drop shadow to enhance our title visually.

Figure 6–26. *The outline is simply defined using a CSS property*

This again is an illustration of how new CSS features can save you the use of images and make your developing and maintenance processes faster and easier. In this particular case, this would be especially true when dealing with different languages. You will see in the next chapter that this kind of optimization is made even more acute with the use of downloadable fonts.

Adding a Button to Your Header

This is a lot to take in at once. Why not have a break and add something to your web application template? Adding the following code to your *main.css* style sheet will let you use a stylish button in the header of your web applications:

```
.view {
...
    position: relative;
```

```
}

.header-wrapper .header-button {
    /* Button size and position (anchored right) */
    position: absolute;
    top: 7px;
    right: 6px;
    width: auto;
    height: 29px;
    min-width: 44px;      /* Minimum size for a tappable element */

    margin: 0;
    padding: 0 10px;

    /* Box style for a rounded button */
    -webkit-border-radius: 5px;
    border: solid 1px rgba(0,0,0,.25);
    border-top-color: rgba(0,0,0,.6);

    -webkit-box-sizing: border-box;
    -webkit-box-shadow: 0 1px 0 rgba(255,255,255,.3);

    /* Text style */
    font-family: inherit;
    font-size: 12px;
    font-weight: bold;
    text-shadow: rgba(0,0,0,.4) 0 -1px 0;
    text-decoration: none;
    text-align: center;
    line-height: 29px;
    color: #fff;

    /* Shiny effect for the background */
    background-color: rgba(0,0,0,.3);
    background-image:
        -webkit-gradient(linear, left top, left bottom,
            color-stop(0, rgba(255,255,255,0.25)),
            color-stop(0.1, rgba(255,255,255,.4)),
            color-stop(1, rgba(255,255,255,.1)) ),
        -webkit-gradient(linear, left top, left bottom,
            from(transparent),
            to(rgba(0,0,64,.05)) );
    background-repeat: no-repeat;
    background-position: top left, bottom left;
    -webkit-background-size: 100% 14px, 100%;
}
.header-wrapper .header-button:disabled {
    color: rgba(255,255,255,0.65)
}

.header-wrapper .header-button:active:not(:disabled) {
    background-color: rgba(0,0,64,.5);
}
```

The button described would be drawn on the right side of your header. To move it to the left of the screen, simply add the following class to your styles:

```
.header-wrapper .header-button.left {
```

```
        left: 6px; right: auto;
}
```

This code is easy to use and reuse, be it to create form buttons or simple links. The following code results in the area shown in Figure 6–27:

```
<div class="header-wrapper">
    <h1>Web App</h1>

    <a href="edit.php" class="header-button">Edit</a>
    <button class="header-button left">Back</button>
</div>
```

Figure 6–27. *Two buttons in the header*

The header-button class uses the method called *adaptive styles*, meaning the color of the button automatically adapts to the background color of its parent. This method was used already for the header itself. Because it uses only translucent black and white for backgrounds and borders, it will only darken or brighten the color that shows through, without blending—just like native iOS buttons.

If you, however, wanted to create a colored button, like the blue action buttons on the iPhone, you would simply change the value for background-color, as follows:

```
.header-wrapper .header-button.action {
    background-color: #0f6cd7;
}
```

As you can see, this code is easily reusable and adaptable. It's exactly what you need for lightweight web applications.

Columns Layout

In Chapter 4, we used a table type display to create the split view we needed for the iPad. The main container had its display property set to table and its inner boxes with a display set to table-cell extended to have exactly the same height. This also allowed you to center content vertically. It can seem attractive to use this method to emulate a column layout like in a newspaper or a magazine.

However, this would result in semantically superfluous markup. What's more, it would prove hard to maintain, and even to achieve, because you would have to evaluate a length for each piece of content and enclose each one appropriately.

CSS Column Properties

Better than layout tricks, CSS3 automatically handles column flow. This feature is implemented in iOS since version 2.0. You don't have to think about the length of your content, nor do you even have to physically represent your columns by enclosing pieces of content inside HTML tags. Mobile Safari will determine where to cut the text, either to achieve a number of columns or to achieve a column size. This allows for global styles, which will end in a consistent layout within many container sizes. The following code will result in a different layout whether you view the page on an iPhone or an iPad, as shown in Figures 6–28 and 6–29:

```
.newspaper {
    -webkit-column-width: 200px;
    -webkit-column-gap: 20px;
    -webkit-column-rule: 1px dotted black;
    padding: 20px;
}
```

Figure 6–28. *One column on iPhone...*

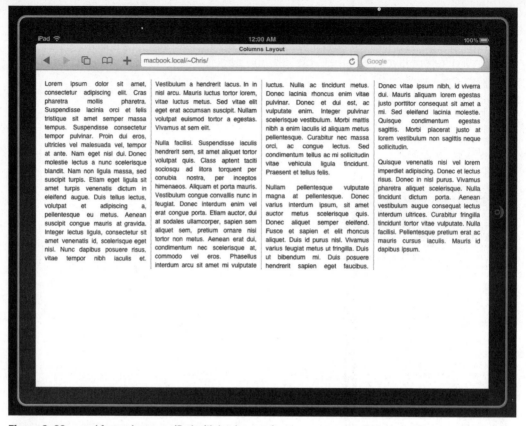

Figure 6–29. *...and four columns on iPad with landscape view*

In our example, we define a minimum width of 200 pixels for our columns. The rendering engine will try to stay as close as possible to this value, while still adapting to the available space. This is why the column on the iPhone is 280 pixels wide.

These properties are pretty self-explanatory. Note how the `column-gap` property solves a common issue met with horizontal layouts, namely, the whitespace between different blocks. Here, you don't have to worry about a incongruous margin sticking out on one side of your layout. What happens is that Mobile Safari evaluates the amount of content that is to be shared between columns and the width of the container.

Also note that the `column-rule` property is shorthand that can take the same styling values as the `border` property and allows you to define, for instance, a color or width as independent rules.

As long as the container has enough free space left, a new column will be created. When the renderer has determined the ideal number of columns, the content will be distributed as evenly as possible.

If you have a close enough idea of how long your content will be, you can enclose your content inside a fixed-height box. Simply be aware that, if your text grows longer than expected, new columns will continue being generated to the left, beyond the container.

A fourth column layout property is available to you, column-count. This acts inversely to column-width, because it allows you to specify a number of columns where your content should be distributed. Mobile Safari will try to render the expected number of columns (be aware that it may judge one letter wide columns acceptable) but will let them grow them vertically if there is not enough space available horizontally.

Of course, it is possible to associate both properties, for instance to render two 300 pixel wide columns inside a 1,000 pixel wide container. When using both properties together, remember that column-width will prevail.

Porting Press Content to the Web

These already interesting features of CSS3 have a new light shed on them by the release of the iPad, for which an obvious use could be online newspapers and magazines. In the following example, we are going to try to reproduce a magazine layout using CSS3 properties. First, we create a file named *magazine.html* with the following code:

```
<!DOCTYPE html>
<html>
    <head>
        <title>Columns Layout</title>
        <meta name="viewport" content="width=device-width; ↵
            initial-scale=1; maximum-scale=1; user-scalable=0">
        <link rel="stylesheet" href="page.css">
    </head>
    <body>
        <div class="mag">
            <hgroup>
                <h1>Flowers</h1>
                <h2>Lorem ipsum dolor sit amet, consectetur adipiscing elit. Cras
                    pharetra mollis pharetra. Suspendisse lacinia orci et felis
                    tristique sit amet semper massa tempus. Suspendisse consectetur
                    tempor pulvinar.</h2>
            </hgroup>

            <p>Lorem ipsum dolor sit amet, consectetur adipiscing elit. Cras pharetra
                mollis pharetra. Suspendisse lacinia orci et felis tristique sit amet
                semper massa tempus. Suspendisse consectetur tempor pulvinar. Proin dui
                eros, ultricies vel malesuada vel, tempor at ante. Nam eget nisl dui.
                Donec molestie lectus a nunc scelerisque blandit. Nam non ligula massa,
                sed suscipit turpis. Etiam eget ligula sit amet turpis venenatis dictum
                in eleifend augue. Duis tellus lectus, volutpat et adipiscing a,
                pellentesque eu metus. Aenean suscipit congue mauris at gravida. Integer
                lectus ligula, consectetur sit amet venenatis id, scelerisque eget nisl.
                Nunc dapibus posuere risus, vitae tempor nibh iaculis et.</p>
        </div>
    </body>
</html>
```

Next, add the appropriate styles in a file called *page.css*:

```
* { margin: 0; }
html { height: 100%; }
body {
    height: 100%;
```

```css
    color: white;
}

.mag {
    background: black url(flower.jpg) center center no-repeat;
    -webkit-background-size: auto 150%;
    width: 100%;
    min-height: 100%;
    padding: 20px;
    -webkit-box-sizing: border-box;
    position: relative;
    font-weight: bold;
    text-shadow: 1px 1px 3px black;
}

h1 {
    margin: 0;
    font-size: 50px;
}

p {
    margin: 0;
    position: absolute;
    max-width: 420px;
    -webkit-column-gap: 20px;
    -webkit-column-width: 200px;
    -webkit-column-rule: 1px dotted white;
    font-size: 16px;
    text-shadow: 1px 0 0 black;
    bottom: 20px;
    right: 20px;
}

p:first-letter {
    font-size: 36px;
    margin-right: 4px;
    margin-bottom: -6px;
    float: left;
}

p:after {
    content: '';
    display: inline-block;
    width: 10px;
    height: 10px;
    background-color: white;
    margin-left: 10px;
    -webkit-box-shadow: black 1px 1px 1px;
}
```

As shown in Figure 6–30, however simple the markup, we achieve an interesting result. We make sure the background will take all the visible space by setting its size to 150 percent of the container space—though you could use the method explained earlier to have a more adapted result whatever the image format. Then, with a simple title, subtitle, and paragraph association, we build a simple magazine-style layout that will appear consistently whatever the device orientation.

Figure 6–30. *A nice page*

WARNING: Safari has a bug preventing it from correctly evaluating text size when a vertical shadow is applied to the content. The algorithm actually truncates the letters instead of making columns higher or shifting text to the next column.

As usual, you can build specific rules to serve a slightly different page whether it is viewed on an iPad or on a smaller screen. This could be done like this:

```
@media only screen and (max-device-width:760px) {
    h1 { font-size: 30px; }
    h2 { font-size: 20px; margin-bottom: 20px; }
    p  { position: relative; bottom: auto; right: auto; }
}
```

This way, your text will simply look scaled on an iPhone or iPod touch with you still having control, and the overall layout will not break because of a lack of space.

The Flexible Box Model

As explained earlier, in a previous chapter, we have used the interesting `table` and `table-cell` display properties to gain more control over the placement and sizing of our elements. This is a simple and efficient method, but CSS3 brings even more control over the box model. What we are going to explain here is among the most interesting features brought by the latest specification—and yet it seems ill-known, because it has been implemented ever since the first version of Mobile Safari!

A Clean and Flexible Way to Handle Column Layouts

This "box model" method is simple, efficient, and extensive. It allows for full control over subsequent boxes. Let's begin with a simple example. This is the relevant code:

```
<style>
    .group {
        display: -webkit-box;
        min-height: 100px;
        padding: 5px;
        background-color: lightgrey;
    }

    .group .box {
        text-align: center;
        border: 10px groove green;
        padding: 10px 30px;
        margin: 1px;
        background-color: white;
    }
</style>

<div class="group">
    <div class="box">Box 1</div>
    <div class="box">Box 2</div>
    <div class="box">Box 3</div>
</div>
```

The first thing you should notice in this code is that no superfluous markup is needed. Now, taking a look at Figure 6–31, you will see the interest for layout purposes.

Figure 6–31. *A new way to achieve column layout*

The height of our three boxes adjusts to the outer box, and as explained next, if you specify a box-flex value, our boxes will occupy 100 percent of the width of their parent, solving two problems that have been around since front-end developers have moved from table to CSS layout. The box value makes the container behave as a block element. You can also trigger an inline block—keeping your elements in the document flow— behavior by using the value inline-box.

Ordering Boxes

This of course is very useful, yet there is much more to this new box model. In our example, you probably weren't surprised that our inner boxes appeared in the document flow in the same order as that of their appearance in the code. This is the default behavior for boxes, which is equivalent to using the box-direction property with the value normal. Setting the value of this property to reverse would result in our boxes being presented from last to first, as in Figure 6–32.

```
.group {
    display: -webkit-box;
    min-height: 100px;
    ...
    -webkit-box-direction: reverse;
}
```

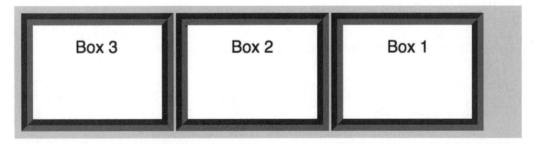

Figure 6–32. *Seamlessly reversing the layout*

You can even go further in box ordering by using the box-ordinal-group property. This property takes an integer as a value, with 1 being the default. This allows you either to reorder boxes, for instance putting box 3 in the first position and box 1 in the second, or to group them. You can also combine this with CSS3 selectors, for instance with a rule such as this:

```
.group .box:nth-child(2) {
    -webkit-box-ordinal-group: 2;
}
```

In this example, because all boxes left unchanged have a box-ordinal-group value of 1, the second box will end up in third position, because all the other boxes have a prevalent position, as shown in Figure 6–33.

Figure 6–33. *Box 2 has been moved to the last position because of its ordinal group value*

This property can be used with `box-direction`. If this is set to `reverse`, the meaning of the ordinal groups will also be changed, together with the boxes in each group.

Flexibility

The default behavior for boxes here is to line up horizontally. This too can be changed using the `box-orient` property. Setting the value to `vertical`, the boxes will stack up vertically, and there's more: setting their `box-flex` value to `1.0`, our boxes will adapt vertically, meaning that each box in our example would be one-third high (Figure 6–34).

```
.group {
    display: -webkit-box;
    min-height: 200px;
    ...
    -webkit-box-orient: vertical;
}

.group .box {
    ...
    -webkit-box-flex: 1.0;
}
```

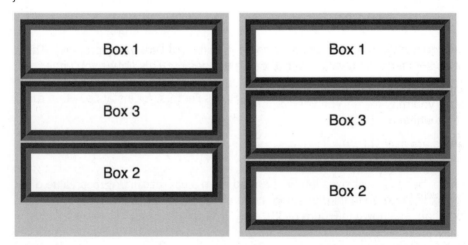

Figure 6–34. *Layout with default box-flex value, which is (0.0), and box-flex set to 1.0*

The box-flex property determines the degree of flexibility of each box. By default, vertically stacked boxes take 100 percent of the available width and only the necessary vertical space. By giving boxes a flex value, they will try to fill the entire available vertical space.

Thus, if all boxes have a flex value that is identical, they will expand to fill their container, all by the same degree. If one or several boxes have a higher flex value, they will expand more. For instance, with the following code, the second box will be made wider or higher, depending on whether your boxes line up or stack up.

```
.group .box:nth-child(2) {
    -webkit-box-flex: 2.0;
}
```

Be careful that this does not mean your second box will be twice as wide or high as the others, as shown in Figure 6–35. It means only that it is more flexible, so it will be larger to some extent. However, giving a box flexibility allows you to use boxes with a fixed width or height and still have an area entirely occupied.

Figure 6–35. *The flexibility is relative; the second box is not twice as big as the others*

Of course, because these properties have to do with the page flow, you cannot use them with elements that are absolutely positioned or are floated. The behavior not only wouldn't be what is expected, but it could also unpredictably break your layout, whereas the general fallback for these properties is the regular box model.

Packing and Alignment

Flexibility as you can see and imagine is full of potential. However, there are times when a more definitive layout is more desirable. In such cases, it is likely you will want to have some control over how elements behave when they do not exactly fit together.

If there is space still available in a box container when all children have reached their definitive size, you may want to decide where the child elements should be displayed relative to that whitespace.

Two properties are available to you in this quest: box-pack and box-align. Modifying the styles of the .group class in our previous example illustrates this:

```
.group {
    display: -webkit-box;
    min-height: 100px;
    ...
    -webit-box-pack: justify;
    -webkit-box-align: end;
}
```

The results are shown in Figure 6–36.

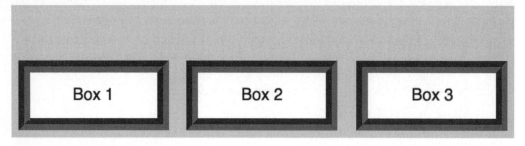

Figure 6–36. *Boxes take the available horizontal space because of the justify value and align at the bottom of their parent because of the end value*

Indeed, the box-pack and box-align properties tell the boxes where to settle within the container. box-pack tells the children how to align on the axis of their orientation; box-align shows how to align perpendicular to the axis of their orientation. Both can take the values start, end, and center. The box-pack property can also take justify as a value, while box-align can take baseline and stretch. The latter is the default value, which is why boxes take all the available space if nothing is specified.

Used together, all these properties allow you to fine-tune the layout of your elements. Of course, you can use these values and properties on any kind of element, meaning this control can be used not only for overall layout but also for small areas of your code, such as an evenly laid out tabbed menu. Although this set of properties is only a draft, it is quite reliable, because it has been implemented since Desktop Safari version 3.0 and from the first version of Mobile Safari. We have listed only the properties that seem the most interesting to us, but there is more to this part of the specification, so feel free to dig further!

Targeting WebKit Specifically

Although we are targeting Mobile Safari, as we have stated earlier, many devices nowadays have good support for standards, and your web applications are likely to work satisfactory on portable devices using other browsers. If you plan to support such browsers to some extent, you could want to serve some rules only to Safari. This can be done using a WebKit-specific targeting feature, related to the pixel ratio of the device. Here is how to do it:

```
@media screen and (-webkit-min-device-pixel-ratio:0) {
    /* Your specific CSS here */
}
```

Or, using the link element:

```
<link rel="stylesheet" href="some.css" ←
      media="screen and (-webkit-min-device-pixel-ratio:0)">
```

This appears to be supported also by Opera 9.5+. At the time of this writing, you can work around this using the following for Opera:

```
@media all and (-webkit-min-device-pixel-ratio: 10000),
    not all and (-webkit-min-device-pixel-ratio: 0) {
        /* Your code here, only for Opera */
}
```

However, hacks are by nature precarious, and there is no warranty that the previous will not be obsolete by near-future versions of the major browsers on the market.

Summary

You just got a glimpse of the possibilities the latest version of CSS and its implementation by Mobile Safari. Designed with modern functionality and aesthetic features in mind, it solves many problems met by front-end developers in the near past. You are now limited only by your own imagination, and launching a quick search on the Internet for *CSS3 tutorials and showcases* will finish persuading you if this chapter hasn't. With all this, you can mimic the iOS UI using hardly any images or JavaScript. Indeed, CSS is a serious way to limit file sizes and bandwidth usage (by requesting fewer images) and overall can lead to better code. These principles have guided the development of our web application template in Chapter 4.

As a general recommendation, we suggest limiting the number of classes you need in your markup. Remember that classes and IDs have a purpose; strive not to create a new ID every time you build a new block, and avoid multiplying duplicate style declarations. Classes are meant to visually group elements that share common characteristics. Therefore, you should use classes to define characteristics that are to be used many times in your code. On the contrary, IDs should be used for very specific modules, and when applying them, choose the outermost block you can. As you have seen, CSS selectors can hugely help limit the need for identifiers in your code.

In following chapters, we will get into further detail about other, exciting CSS3 features implemented in Safari such as downloadable fonts with SVG, animation, and hardware transformations, so start practicing with them and building crisp and elegant web applications.

## Chapter 7

Bitmap and Vector Graphics and Downloadable Fonts with Canvas and SVG

The one element of Mobile Safari that has drawn the most attention is that it has no support for Adobe Flash. The Web has become a place where multimedia and animation hold an important role, and while being unable to create Flash-based web sites and casual gaming might not be a problem for most people, the main problem is that Flash is used in some manner on most sites nowadays, be it for graphic animation in headers, advertisements, or videos. Not supporting Flash can be a real issue for the iPhone and iPad user experience when viewing classic web sites.

Although canvases and SVG are often presented as alternatives to Flash on iOS devices, they can be used for more than creating interface elements and definite modules only at great expense. The lack of authoring tools makes their development for intensive use unproductive. However, there are many interesting applications to these new technologies, especially with the WebKit-specific extensions that we will introduce in this chapter.

By using these two features, which are newly supported on Mobile Safari, together with some scripting, you will be able to achieve many graphics and effects that formerly would have required heavy images or server-side processing.

Working with the Canvas Area

The new <canvas> tag, introduced in HTML5, doesn't do anything by itself, but it lets you work with the browser in a entirely new way; it lets you define an area in which you will be able to draw directly using a powerful JavaScript API. This is how you should insert it into your code:

```
<canvas id="area" width="200" height="200">
    Fallback information.
</canvas>
```

The id attribute you place on the <canvas> tag is very important, because it is the identifier by which you will be able to interact with the defined drawing area. Any content between the opening and closing <canvas> tags will appear only if the end user has disabled scripts on the device.

If, however, the user has for some reason disabled scripts in Mobile Safari, the <canvas> tag will be useless, because nothing could be drawn to the area defined by it. In this case, the text you insert should indicate that scripts are required to access the unavailable content, and you should give information on how to do this.

The scope of the canvas area should be defined with the width and height attributes, a 200 pixel wide square in our example. If you determine the size of the canvas with styles, the rendering engine will scale the canvas drawing area to fit in the default boundaries, instead of rendering the script output as expected. If you do not specify these dimensions, the default size of the area is 300 pixels horizontally and 150 pixels vertically.

Note, however, that using styles to set the size of the canvas area can be useful to maintain your layout in case scripting is disabled, because the width and height attributes will be ignored in that case. You should also set the display property of the canvas to inline-block if it is not floated, to keep the default inline behavior of the area.

```
#area {
    display: inline-block;
    width: 200px;
    height: 200px;
    font-weight: bold;
    color: red;
}
```

Regarding dimensions, also keep in mind that whenever you resize the canvas area by the means of a script, the entire drawing area is cleared and reset.

The drawing area bound by the canvas is transparent. You could therefore use it as you would a PNG image with an alpha channel. This opens its usage to plenty of possibilities; for instance, it allows you to replace GIF images, which, unlike PNG images, allow for animation but only support fully transparent and fully opaque pixels (see Figure 7–1).

Figure 7–1. *Using PNG or the* `<canvas>` *tag, edges are clean no matter what background the image is superimposed on, whereas quality is poor with GIF*

The latter of course is a problem as soon as you want to draw curved or diagonal lines to a transparent image background, because the line shown would be rough and irregular. Typically, you couldn't use a GIF image for a logo implying a circular shape if you wanted it to be adaptable to several backgrounds.

Despite these preliminary assets of the `<canvas>` tag, be careful not to use it where some other tag would be semantically more appropriate, primarily because of accessibility issues. An image with an `alt` attribute makes it clear what kind of content is present and should describe the content to a sufficient extent.

The first of the following examples is an appropriate use for the `<canvas>` tag because the spinner has no particular meaning and can be easily ignored, while the second should be avoided.

```
<!-- This is recommended -->
<canvas width="45" height="45" id="spinner">Page loading</canvas>
<i>Please wait...</i>
```

```
<!-- This is not -->
<canvas width="450" height="200" id="comic-strip-cell">A comic strip</canvas>
<i>Have fun!</i>
```

The `<img>` tag would fit perfectly with the type of data presented in the second example. Using a canvas here could result in poorer accessibility for disabled users and surely would be poorly taken into account by search engines. Note that we will explain further in this chapter how to use a canvas as a proper image.

Now, we bet you are impatient to see the exciting JavaScript API in action. Let's go.

The Drawing Context

To access the canvas and work with it, the first thing to do is get a context. This can be done using the `getContext()` method from the API. The following will allow you to work with a two-dimensional bitmap context:

```
var canvas = document.getElementById("area");
var context = canvas.getContext("2d");
```

Once you have obtained a reference to the context in this way, you can start drawing to the canvas area. Every call of `getContext("2d")` will return the same instance. Keep in mind that none of what you will create inside the canvas area will be accessible through any DOM interface. You will simply be drawing pixels on the drawing surface. For instance, to animate a line, you have to draw the line all over again; you cannot move it or change its properties as you would a DOM element.

> **NOTE:** Be aware that, for now, only two-dimensional contexts can be used. A very promising 3D version is being studied, primarily by the Khronos Group. It is based on OpenGL ES 2.0 and will be called WebGL. One asset of its evolution is that it is bound directly to the hardware (GPU accelerated), making much more complex and fluid animations possible. We hope this technology will be available soon on the iPhone.

WebKit introduces another, versatile way to define canvases, by allowing you to use a canvas directly from a style declaration, thus letting you use canvases as backgrounds or as a value for any other property that can take an image. This, for instance, will let you easily create a spinner, without actually using images. This of course not only will save you some bandwidth and loading time but will also allow for real alpha transparency and color adaptability, as explained earlier.

```
/* Using a canvas as a value in a CSS declaration is extremely simple */
.css-canvas {
    background-image: -webkit-canvas(area);
}
```

In the previous example, we indicate that a new canvas should be created with the area identifier. This canvas does not exist at this stage, but from there, you can initialize it and get a context for it with the getCSSCanvasContext() method from the document object, as follows:

```
var context = document.getCSSCanvasContext("2d", "area", 37, 37);
```

As with getContext(), the first parameter is the desired context type, and the second, as you will guess, is the identifier for your canvas. The two following parameters are the dimensions you expect your canvas to have. Each call to this canvas with the same parameters will return the same instance, while changing the dimensions in a call to this method would result in the canvas being cleared, as in the regular canvas-handling process.

One interesting characteristic of this use of canvases is that the defined canvas can be used simultaneously on as many elements as you like. In our example, if you create an animation in it, the animation will be drawn for any element that uses the class .css-canvas.

Now, let's take our animated spinner example further and see the code that can make it live. In the pieces of code that follow, we are going to use quite a few properties of HTML canvases, but don't worry: all will be explained in due time.

First, we are going to define the object that will enable you to initialize and animate our canvas easily to be added to our web application template. Again, if you are not used to object-oriented JavaScript programming, worry not. This will all be explained in Chapter 10. For now, you can just as well see this code as a series of reusable functions.

```javascript
/* Object constructor */
var BigSpinner = new Function();

BigSpinner.prototype.init = function(id, color, shadow) {
    /* Initialize the canvas and save the context */
    this.context = document.getCSSCanvasContext("2d", id, 37, 37);

    /* Line style for the spinner */
    this.context.lineWidth = 3;
    this.context.lineCap = "round";
    this.context.strokeStyle = color;

    /* Define a shadow for the spinner */
    if (shadow) {
        this.context.shadowOffsetX = 1;
        this.context.shadowOffsetY = 1;
        this.context.shadowBlur = 1;
        this.context.shadowColor = shadow;
    }

    /* Animation variables */
    this.step = 0;
    this.timer = null;
}

BigSpinner.prototype.draw = function() {
    /* Clear the canvas at every frame */
    this.context.clearRect(0, 0, 37, 37);

    /* Prepare canvas state and draw spinner lines */
    this.context.save();
    this.context.translate(18, 18);
    this.context.rotate(this.step * Math.PI / 180);

    for (var i = 0; i < 12; i++) {
        this.context.rotate(30 * Math.PI / 180);
        this.drawLine(i);
    }
    this.context.restore();

    /* Increment the animation */
    this.step += 30;
    if (this.step == 360) {
        this.step = 0;
    }
}

BigSpinner.prototype.drawLine = function(i) {
    /* Draw one line with varying transparency depending on the iteration */
    this.context.beginPath();
    this.context.globalAlpha = i / 12;
    this.context.moveTo(0, 8 + 1);
    this.context.lineTo(0, 16 - 1);
    this.context.stroke();
}

BigSpinner.prototype.stop = function() {
```

```
        if (this.timer) {
            this.context.clearRect(0, 0, 37, 37);
            window.clearInterval(this.timer);
            this.timer = null;
        }
    }

BigSpinner.prototype.animate = function() {
    /* Already running? exit... */
    if (this.timer) {
        return;
    }

    /* The execution context (this) will be the window object with setInterval()
       Save the correct context in "that" variable and run the timer */
    var that = this;
    this.timer = window.setInterval(function() {
        that.draw();
    }, 100);
}
```

From there, it becomes very straightforward to create a new custom spinner. Simply create a new instance of the BigSpinner object and initialize it with the init() method, passing the ID of the canvas, a color, and, optionally, a shadow color as parameters, and launch the animation with the animate() method, as shown here:

```
var spinner = new BigSpinner();
spinner.init("area", "red", "rgba(0,0,0,0.5)");
spinner.animate();
```

The code that follows is intended to imitate the start-up screen of Mac OS X, as shown in Figure 7–2.

```
<!DOCTYPE html>
<html>
    <head>
        <title>Startup Screen</title>
        <meta name="viewport" content="initial-scale=1.0;
            maximum-scale=1.0; user-scalable=no">

        <style>
            html { height: 100% }
            body {
                height: 100%;
                background-color: lightgrey;
                color: gray;
                margin: 0;
            }

            .bigSpinner {
                background-image: -webkit-canvas(spinner);
            }

            .useSpinner {
                background-position: center 70%;
                background-repeat: no-repeat;
                width: 100%;
```

```
                min-height: 100%;
                padding-top: 20%;
                -webkit-box-sizing: border-box;
                text-align: center;
                font-size: 100px;
            }
        </style>

        <script>
            /* The BigSpinner class definition goes here
               ... */

            var spinner = new BigSpinner();
            spinner.init("spinner", "gray");
            spinner.animate();
        </script>
    </head>
<body>

<div class="bigSpinner useSpinner">
    &#63743;<!-- Apple logo -->
</div>

</body>
</html>
```

Figure 7–2. *The Mac OS X start-up screen, drawn with the Canvas API*

As you can see, this solution is both simple and easily customizable. Because it is likely
that you want to use the same spinner several times, it is profitable to make a simple
definition in one CSS class (.bigSpinner) and develop it in another (.useSpinner).
Because only one element is loaded, such a practice represents a notable gain in
download times and memory usage.

Indeed, the same spinner as an animated GIF image would require more than 3KB, whereas this code, which is less than 3KB, allows you to create as many spinners as desired, customize them, and seamlessly execute them. Moreover, HTTP compression is widely used on servers nowadays. Because GIF images are already compressed, the file size for the GIF spinner wouldn't change, while the code for the canvas spinner is likely to be compressed to less than 1KB.

Of course, it would be preferable to launch the animation only at the time it is needed in order not to uselessly consume battery power. For this, you can use the stop() method, together with animate(), to control the activity of the spinner.

You can also take a more conventional approach to using canvases in your styles. The toDataURL() method of the canvas object is meant for that, because it allows you to transform the data from the canvas into an URL. This way, you can use binary, base64-encoded data right in an HTML page, for instance. The background of an element thus could be modified from a canvas like this:

```
var data = canvas.toDataURL();

/* Use the canvas as a background of the first <div> of the document */
var object = document.getElementsByTagName("div");
object[0].style.backgroundImage = data;

/* Use canvas data in a <img> tag */
var image = document.images[0];
image.src = data;
```

The default format is PNG, which is the only format required for implementation by the specifications. However, other formats, like JPEG, can be used to pass the MIME type (image/jpeg) as a parameter to the toDataURL() method. For now, we are going to get into the details of the Canvas API.

Drawing Simple Shapes

With the Canvas API, the simplest shapes to draw are rectangles. To draw more complex shapes such as circles, you have to handle complex path functions (which we will soon explain). On the contrary, to draw a rectangle, you have three options, all of which are pretty straightforward. All three take the same parameters: the origin as a couple of reference points (x,y) and the dimensions for the box (width,height). Figure 7–3 shows how this works.

```
/* Paints a rectangle using the current fill style */
context.fillRect(10, 10, 180, 80);

/* Draws the box outlining the given rectangle
   using the current stroke style */
context.strokeRect(10, 110, 180, 80);

/* Clears the area to transparent */
context.clearRect(50, 50, 100, 100);
```

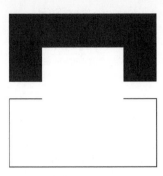

Figure 7-3. *Simple shapes drawn with the Canvas API*

Notice that when executing this code, the lines of the rectangle drawn with the `strokeRect()` method are a little fuzzy and bolder than expected—the default border width being 1 pixel. To solve this problem, you would usually just have to add 0.5 to origin points, as follows:

```
context.strokeRect(10.5, 110.5, 180, 80);
```

This is because, although the lines are not drawn along a pixel grid, the drawing process does depend on the undividable pixel unit. Because it is impossible to draw a half pixel, the renderer uses anti-aliasing to lessen the density of the line and give the impression that the line is along the axis, with the expected width. By moving the line by half a pixel, you make it possible to draw the line on a full pixel, no longer two halves, and the line looks crisp. Figure 7-4 stresses this behavior, where each line is an axis and each square is a physical pixel.

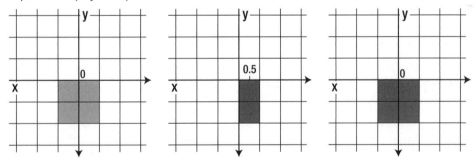

Figure 7-4. *Different pixel rendering depending on the position and the width of the lines*

All three represent the drawing of a 2 pixel high line. The first example illustrates the issue described earlier, with a 1 pixel width at the coordinates (0,0). The pixels are anti-aliased and extend to both sides of the vertical axis. By positioning the same line on the points (0.5,0), the extension happens on the new axis, and the line fits on the physical pixel. No visual effect is needed. The illustration to the right in Figure 7-4 shows a line with the same characteristics as the first, but 2 pixels wide. In this case, each pixel can be displayed on one side of the axis.

Colors, Gradients, and Patterns

The default drawing and fill color in a canvas is black, though of course you can modify this at any stage. This is done as follows:

```
context.fillStyle = "red";
context.fillRect(10, 10, 180, 80);

context.strokeStyle = "rgba(0, 255, 0, 0.5)";
context.strokeRect(10, 110, 180, 80);
```

In these processes, you can use any CSS colors that we have seen in the previous chapter, including colors with an alpha channel, as shown in both previous examples. Syntaxes are also available to you to use gradients and even patterns.

Using Gradients

The syntax for gradients in the Canvas API is quite similar to that found in CSS, with -webkit-gradient(). You should choose between a linear or radial gradient to use the appropriate method to instantiate a new CanvasGradient object.

```
/* createLinearGradient(x0, y0, x1, y1) */
var linear = context.createLinearGradient(0, 0, 100, 100);

/* createRadialGradient(x0, y0, r0, x1, y1, r1) */
var radial = context.createRadialGradient(100, 100, 90, 100, 100, 10);
```

The first example will draw a linear gradient stretching from point (0,0) to point (100,100)—thus along a diagonal. Beyond these points, the colors will continue to fill the entire canvas area. The coordinates refer to points in the space of the canvas; therefore, the display will change depending on the position of the shapes that use this gradient.

The second example should draw a radial gradient, with parameters that specify the center of the initial circle (100,100), its radius 10, and the position of the second circle (100,10), with a radius of 90 pixels.

Once you have defined an area and stop points for your gradient, you can add color to it with the addColorStop() method. As previously, the definition looks a lot like that found with CSS.

```
linear.addColorStop(0.0, "yellow");
linear.addColorStop(1.0, "green");
```

The first parameter is the offset from where the color should start, ranging from 0.0 to 1.0; the second of course is the color. Now that you gradient is ready, you can use it with the methods shown earlier both for the stroke and for the fill (Figure 7–5).

```
context.fillStyle = linear;
context.strokeStyle = linear;
```

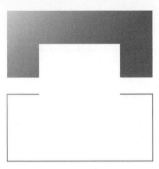

Figure 7–5. *You can use a gradient both for fill and for stroke*

This already allows for quite a few possibilities. Nonetheless, the Canvas API also allows for the use of an image object, a video, or even a canvas (including the current canvas) as patterns inside your drawing area.

Defining Patterns

New patterns are created with the createPattern() method from an image, video, or even canvas object, which takes two parameters, the source object and a repeat mode, as shown in the CSS background-repeat property.

```
var image = document.getElementById("someImage");
var pattern = context.createPattern(image, "repeat-x");
```

Once you have created a new pattern, it can be used, just like plain colors and gradients, with the fillStyle and strokeStyle properties. However, remember that, once you have created your pattern object, it will not be changed, even if, for instance, the source image used to create it was altered or the source canvas was cleared and drawn differently. Therefore, you cannot automatically animate a pattern, even using a video or multilayer GIF image.

More Complex Shapes with Paths

All the previous methods and properties of course can have many appreciable uses. However, for now, you are still limited to straight lines and rectangles. Of course, there is more to the API. Using paths, similar to those used in Illustrator or in Photoshop with the water pen tool, you can achieve very complex illustrations.

In the canvas area, paths should be defined using one or more subpaths, which are themselves composed of several points on a straight or curved line. A subpath can be indicated as closed, meaning its last point is connected to its first by a straight line. Table 7–1 lists the different methods used to define paths.

Table 7–1. *Methods Used to Define Paths*

Method	Description
context.beginPath()	Resets the list of subpaths.
context.moveTo(x, y)	Creates a new subpath with the given point.
context.lineTo(x, y)	Adds the given point to the subpath connected to the previous one by a straight line.
context.rect(x, y, w, h)	Adds a new closed subpath representing the given rectangle.
conext.arc(x, y, radius, startAngle, endAngle, anticlockwise)	Adds points to the subpath representing the given arc, connected to the previous one by a straight line. Angles are in radians.
context.arcTo(cpx1, cpy1, cpx2, cpy2, radius)	Adds two control points defining, using last point of the previous subpath, two intersecting segment tangents to the circle defined by arguments. Resulting subpath is an arc starting at intersection point with the first tangent and ending at intersection point with the second tangent. The first point is connected to the previous subpath by a straight line.
context.quadraticCurveTo(cpx, cpy, x, y)	Adds the given point to the subpath, connected to the previous one by a quadratic Bézier curve with the given control point.
context.bezierCurveTo(cp1x, cp1y, cp2x, cp2y, x, y)	Adds the given point to the subpath, connected to the previous one by a cubic Bézier curve with the given control points.
context.fill()	Fills the subpaths with the current fill style.
context.stroke()	Strokes the subpaths with the current stroke style.
context.closePath()	Closes the current subpath explicitly and starts a new one with the same point as the previous point.

Paths should be initialized with the beginPath() method of the context object, which empties the subpath's list. The closePath() method closes the current subpath (not the path itself), drawing a line from its last point to its first point, as shown in Figure 7–6.

The fill() and stroke() methods make closing the subpath implicit but don't close the active path, like the closePath() method would. There can be only one current path at a time, which is why you should always specify to the engine when a path begins and where to close a subpath. This is critical if several subpaths are to be defined with similar styles but shouldn't be connected.

```
context.beginPath();

/* Draw a first triangle */
context.moveTo(20, 90);
context.lineTo(70,40);
context.lineTo(120,90);

/* Then move and draw another triangle */
context.moveTo(80, 110);
context.lineTo(130,160);
context.lineTo(180,110);
context.closePath();

/* Fill subpaths and stroke */
context.fill();
context.stroke();
```

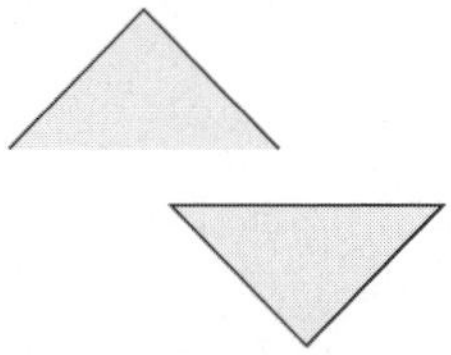

Figure 7–6. *The first triangle is implicitly closed, while the second is closed with the* closePath() *method*

In this example, we begin by creating a first subpath to draw a triangle with only two sides, and then we move within the path using moveTo() to start another subpath in another area. Therefore, the closePath() method will close only the second subpath.

Drawing Arcs

There once again are quite a few possibilities using the previous methods; however, these examples still stick to straight lines. To unleash the full range of possibilities offered by the Canvas API, you will have to handle the most complex path methods, namely, those used to draw curves. Starting with the arcTo() method, you will notice that the two points it takes as parameters don't even actually belong to the subpath that it allows you to draw. They are control points, that is, points that will be used to calculate the position of the arc from its starting point to its ending point.

Figure 7–7 shows an arc drawn with the following code:

```
context.beginPath();
context.moveTo(120,18);
context.arcTo(140, 20, 110, 100, 100);
context.lineTo(200, 100);
context.stroke();
```

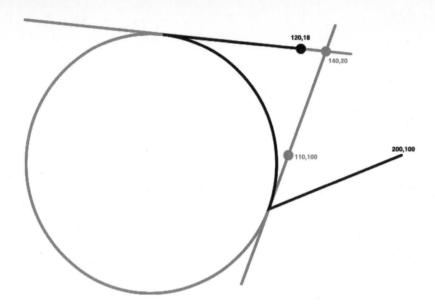

Figure 7–7. *An arc is defined by its control points (the gray dots) relative to the last point from the previous subpath (black dot)*

As you can see, neither of the lighter dots—the control points—are part of the subpath. Instead, they are used only to define tangents, whose intersection points are used to situate the points of the actual subpath, as the arc spans from one to the other. As explained in Table 7–1, the first point is attached to the previous subpath by a straight line.

Drawing Curves

There are two other curve types: quadratic and cubic b-splines. They're drawn using the quadraticCurveTo() and bezierCurveTo() methods, using one and two control points, as shown on Figure 7–8. These are widely used in the graphic industry, be it for 3D creation or in the car design industry, where they were developed.

```
/* A quadratic curve */
context.beginPath();
context.moveTo(20, 100);
context.quadraticCurveTo(100, 20, 180, 100);
context.stroke();

/* A cubic curve */
context.beginPath();
context.moveTo(20, 100);
context.bezierCurveTo(70, 20, 140, 180, 180, 100);
context.stroke();
```

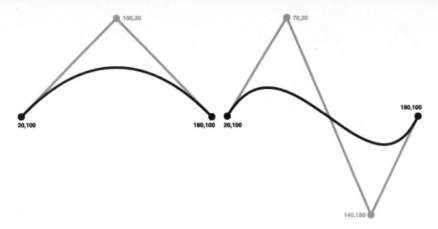

Figure 7–8. *Two Bézier curves—one quadratic, one cubic*

Once again, the lighter points indicate control points. You will notice that the actual curve is much lower than the corresponding control point. Basically, to draw a Bézier curve is to draw a definite line from the center of one definite line to the center of the next definite line connected to it. This gives you the initial position of the curve. The newly created lines will be used in the same manner as explained earlier. Of course, this is very schematic, but it is the basics of the process, and along with some training, it should allow you to obtain the results you expect.

Line Styles

All the previous methods are configurable, so you can style all lines in quite a few manners, beyond the colors and gradients introduced earlier. The configuration is available with the context object.

Thus, `lineWidth` allows you to tweak the thickness of your lines, `lineCap` will let you choose an ending style for each line, and `lineJoin` will let you indicate how lines should meet. These are illustrated respectively in Figures 7–9 and 7–10.

```
context.lineCap = "butt";   // Default, also 'round', 'square'
context.lineJoin = "miter"; // Default, also 'round', 'bevel'
```

Figure 7–9. *Different line endings*

Figure 7–10. *Different line blending options*

The default size for the miter is 10.0. This can be modified with the miterLimit property. If the rendering engine doesn't find enough space to draw the miter, it will extend it to the defined limit and then cut it as with the bevel parameter.

Enhancing Your Menus with Style

Now that you know how to create paths with different styles, you can add a new feature to your web application templates: the missing chevron in your list menu. Add the following styles and scripts to the main.css and main.js files, with the result shown in Figure 7–11.

```css
/* main.css */

.group-wrapper ul li a {
...
    background: -webkit-canvas(chevron-normal) right center no-repeat;
}

.group-wrapper ul li a:active {
...
    background:
        -webkit-gradient(linear,
            left top, left bottom,
            from(rgba(255, 255, 255, .25)), to(transparent) ),

        -webkit-canvas(chevron-active) right center no-repeat #015de6;
...
}
```

```javascript
/* main.js */

initChevron("chevron-normal", "hsl(0, 0%, 50%)");
initChevron("chevron-active", "hsl(0, 0%, 100%)");

function initChevron(id, style) {
    var context = document.getCSSCanvasContext("2d", id, 22, 13);

    context.save();

    context.clearRect(0, 0, 20, 13);
```

```
        context.strokeStyle = style;
        context.lineWidth = 3;

        context.beginPath();
        context.moveTo(4, 1);
        context.lineTo(10, 6.5);
        context.lineTo(4, 12);
        context.stroke();

        context.restore();
}
```

Figure 7–11. *Your template menus have moved yet another step toward native application styles*

In the previous chapters, you created styles to differentiate the `:active` and `:hover` states. Here you simply extend the relevant classes, taking advantage of multiple background support.

Once again, this code is easily reusable and customizable, and you can, for instance, use different drawing styles for the normal and active states.

Applying Transformations

The Canvas API offers several methods to achieve transformations, letting you adopt a fluid workflow. You will be able to modify the scale, apply a rotation, or move the grid for your canvas together with the points from your elements. These transformations will apply only to the shapes that are to be drawn—shapes that have already been stroked will not be altered.

```
/* Moves the grid by 100 pixels in both directions */
context.translate(100, 100);

/* Rotates the grid by 60 degrees */
context.rotate(60 * Math.PI / 180);

/* Scales the grid, double in width, half in height */
context.scale(2, 0.5);
```

All transformations are calculated from the origin of the grid, initially the top left (0,0). The translate() method allows you to change this value. The rotate() method, which takes a value in radians, will be calculated from the new point defined by the previous call to translate(), clockwise. The advantage of these methods is that the scaling will not simply multiply pixels. As with a vector graphics editor, proper scaling will take place.

These basic transform methods actually are affine transformations, calculated with matrices, with each new transformation bringing a new transformation to the previous matrix. You can define your own matrices with the following form.

NOTE: If you are not familiar with matrices, don't worry, because this is only for very advanced usage of the canvas transformations. You'll see in Chapter 9 how to easily calculate resulting matrices with the CSSMatrix object.

$$T = \begin{bmatrix} a & c & e \\ b & d & f \\ 0 & 0 & 1 \end{bmatrix}$$

This is done with one of the following methods:

```
context.transform(a, b, c, d, e, f);
context.setTransform(a, b, c, d, e, f);
```

The first method multiplies the matrix defined by the current matrix parameters. The second method clears the transformation matrix, before acting like the transform() method, applying the new matrix.

```
/* These methods... */
context.translate(100, 100);
context.rotate(45 * Math.PI / 180);

/* ... are analogous to the following */
var cos = Math.cos(45 * Math.PI / 180);
var sin = Math.sin(45 * Math.PI / 180);
context.transform(cos, sin, -sin, cos, 100, 100);
```

To completely reset the whole transformation matrix, you can use this very useful piece of code:

```
context.setTransform(1, 0, 0, 1, 0, 0);
```

This way, you will not have to work back through all your previous transformation operations. This of course will make your code simpler and will make it more lightweight.

Simplifying Drawing State Modifications

The method illustrated in the previous section lets you easily reset all transformations. However, the HTML5 specification allows for fine-tuning on the successive transformations that you operate, by providing means to save and restore different states of the canvas.

Each context can keep in memory a stack of the different drawing states. Thus, any previously defined line end, color, or transformation property can be pushed to this stack with the save() method and popped later with the restore() method, following the last-in-first-out principle. The following code illustrates this behavior:

```
/* this is the current state */
context.strokeStyle = "red";

/* Push the current state to the stack
   and draw a green rectangle */
context.save();
context.strokeStyle = "green";
context.strokeRect(10, 10, 180, 180);

/* Restore and draw a red rectangle */
context.restore();
context.strokeRect(20, 20, 160, 160);
```

You can call the save() method as many times as you like without calling restore(), which can be useful, for instance, if you are building several functions that draw distinct graphic elements, because you wouldn't have to worry about the state of the drawing context. Nonetheless, each call of the save() method requires that you at some stage call the restore() method to return to the initial state.

This again is both a code weight saver and a good optimization operation, because these methods are natively executed by the script engine, without being interpreted.

Using Text

Although the rendering of text is part of the Canvas specification, it is not properly implemented as of version 3.2 of iOS. However, all the methods and properties of the Text API can be accessed without raising any exception. You will simply see no result in the canvas area. Nevertheless, because this part of the specification is already implemented in Desktop Safari, we believe these features will be added soon to future versions of Mobile Safari.

The font and its characteristics should be defined similarly to what is found in CSS with the font shorthand. The default is sans-serif, 10px, with a weight of 400 (aka normal). However, you cannot change the line-height, which is set at a common value and will be ignored if defined.

```
context.font = "italic 18px Georgia";
```

As with CSS, you can define font sizes with relative values such as ems. In such a case, the actual font size will be calculated based on the computed `font-size` property value applicable to the canvas at the moment it is created—not on any previous `font` declaration with the `context` object. On the other side, if the canvas is dynamically generated with JavaScript and wasn't in the source code of the document, relative values will be based on the default values for the context `font` property.

```
<style>
    div { font-size: 13px; }
</style>

<div>
    <canvas id="area" width="200" height="200"></canvas>
</div>

<script>
    var canvas = document.getElementById("area");
    var context = canvas.getContext("2d");

    context.font = "italic 1.4em Georgia";
    context.fillStyle = "red";
    context.fillText("Some Text", 10, 100);
</script>
```

In this example, because the size of the font is relative, it will be computed relative to the CSS definition found in the style declaration. Because the `<canvas>` tag inherits from its `<div>` parent, the font size would be 18px (13*1.4).

Later in our description of canvases, we will also see how the font face can be changed to some other font than those installed on the device with the `@font-face` rule and downloadable fonts.

Drawing the Text

To draw pieces of text, you have two methods available to you: either draw the text fill as in classic HTML or draw only the outlines of the text. The following illustrate both methods:

```
/* Classic rendering */
context.fillText("Some Text", 0, 20);

/* Outlined text */
context.strokeText("Some Text", 0, 20);
```

Both methods should take a third, optional parameter, `maxWidth`, that limits the content width to the definite value. If the text would have spanned beyond this width, it is compressed to stay inside the defined area. However, this third parameter is not yet supported in Safari. Therefore, you will have to use a scaling method together with the `measureText()` method, which returns the size of the passed text. The following example shows how to use this to obtain such results, and Figure 7–12 shows the result:

```
context.font = "bold 15px 'Marker Felt'";
```

```
/* The string to be drawn */
var str = "The quick brown fox jumps over the lazy dog.";

/* Measurement */
var maxWidth = 200;
var metrics = context.measureText(str);

/* Draw with and without constrains */
context.fillText(str, 0, 20);
if (maxWidth < metrics.width) {
    context.scale(maxWidth / metrics.width, 1);
}
context.fillText(str, 0, 40);
```

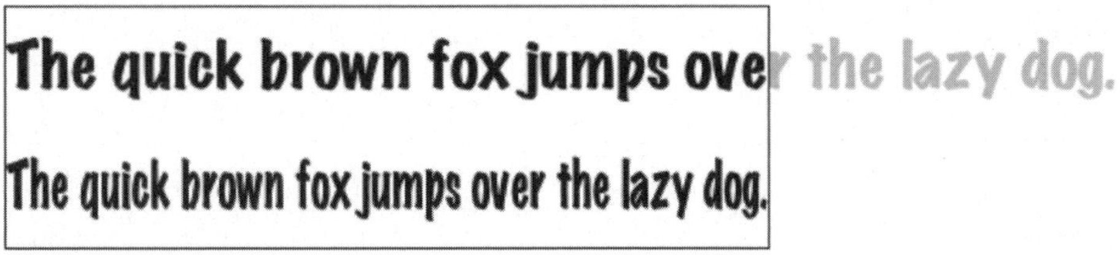

The quick brown fox jumps over the lazy dog.

The quick brown fox jumps over the lazy dog.

Figure 7–12. *The first definition lets the text span beyond the edges of the canvas; with the second method, the full text is rendered visibly*

The only FontMetrics property available for now is width, which is read-only. It represents the rendered width of the string passed as a parameter to the measureText() method. Unfortunately, there is no way to determine the line-height or the actual height that the rendered text will take, which means you won't be able to determine whether your text will vertically fit into the area you expect. This can be especially problematic, for instance, when attempting to draw an object, such as a button, or when centering your text vertically inside the container.

Text Baseline

Nonetheless, knowing the size of your font can let you get a pretty close evaluation of the vertical space your content will take. Hence, you will want to determine how the text will be displayed within the space occupied. This can be tuned with the textBaseline property. Although the default baseline for text content is the baseline of the square em measure, you can, for instance, force your text to align in the middle of this area by setting textBaseline to middle.

> **NOTE:** A square em (pronounced "M," not "e.m.") is a fixed height (it varies, however, depending on the font size) within which any character in the font set can be drawn—including accents on uppercase letters, ascending and descending letters, and so on.

Other available values for the textBaseline property are alphabetic (default), top, and bottom. These values are illustrated in Figure 7–13. There are other values; however, they are currently not supported.

top of the em square

middle of the em square

alphabetic baseline

bottom of th em square

Figure 7–13. *Different values for the* `textBaseline` *property*

This of course will make the results of your code more predictable. The following example would center your text inside its container (see Figure 7–14).

```
context.font = "15px Zapfino";
context.textBaseline = "middle";
context.strokeRect(50.5, 0.5, 100, 80);
context.fillText("Zapfino", 50, 40);
```

Figure 7–14. *Vertically centered text*

In our example, we know that the Zapfino font is quite large, so we draw a frame slightly higher than the 15 pixels given for the font size. Our text is then drawn from the left side of the frame and centered vertically. To center it horizontally too, we could, of course, use `measureText()` to calculate its position depending on the text size. However, there is a far simpler method.

Text Alignment

Horizontal alignment works in roughly the same manner as vertical alignment, though there is no em square consideration—just a `start`, a `center`, and an end for the text, which will be values for the `textAlign` property. The text in our previous example thus can be easily centered both ways by adding this declaration to our text (Figure 7–15):

```
...
context.textAlign = "center";
context.fillText("Zapfino", 100, 40);
```

Figure 7–15. *The text is perfectly centered in the frame*

The preceding value depends on the text direction as defined in the HTML document with the `dir` attribute. The default value for `dir` is `ltr` (left to right), meaning that the default value, `start`, will make the text begin at the given position and expand from left to right; using `end`, the reverse will happen. If you gave the `dir` attribute the value `rtl`— such as when writing in Hebrew or Arabic—these behaviors would be reversed.

If you do not want your canvas to depend on the text direction, you can use the direction-insensitive `left` and `right` values. Of course, the value `center` will not be a problem, because the text would evenly expand to both sides of the initial point.

Shadows

As with CSS and HTML, you can apply shadows to everything drawn inside the canvas. Shadows are defined using four properties of the context object. To see the effect of a shadow definition, simply add the following lines to the code of our previous example (results in Figure 7–16):

```
...
context.shadowColor = "gray";
context.shadowOffsetX = 2;
context.shadowOffsetY = 2;
context.shadowBlur = 4;

context.textAlign = "center";
context.fillText("Zapfino", 100, 40);
```

Figure 7–16. *The equivalent of a text shadow within your canvases*

With these few lines of code, all the rendered shapes will gain a drop shadow. Be careful that `shadowColor` can take only a color as a value, unlike `strokeStyle` and `fillStyle` that can take a gradient or a pattern. Canvases are not yet ready for rainbow shadows. Also remember that offsets are not affected by transformations. Hence, the shadow will always go the same sense, even after a rotation, and will always have the same size, even after a scaling operation.

> **NOTE:** A resilient bug in WebKit's implementation affects all browser versions. If the shadowBlur property has its value set to 0 (the default), the value for shadowOffsetY will systematically be treated as negative. The easiest way to avoid this problem is to give the shadowBlur property a forbidden value, namely, NaN, Infinite, or a negative value. Moreover, the shadow will not work at all if the shape style is based on a gradient or pattern.

The shadowBlur property gives you control over the fuzziness of shadow. Its value should be either positive or null, and it applies a two-dimensional Gaussian blur to the shadow. Any other value should be ignored but will be automatically set to 0 by WebKit.

Clipping and Compositing

By default, all shapes are drawn one on top of the other in the area allotted to the canvas. However, you can constrain the drawing to a specific area of the canvas.

Clipping to the Drawing Area

To bind the rendering of an element to a specific area, you should use the clip() method. What this method does is define the current path as a drawing area beyond which no point or line will be drawn. The following example illustrates this behavior, and the results are shown in Figure 7–17:

```
/* The path */
context.beginPath();
context.moveTo(30, 70);
context.lineTo(70, 70);
context.lineTo(100, 30);
context.lineTo(130, 70);
context.lineTo(170, 70);
context.lineTo(100, 160);

/* Clip and implicitly close the path (for clipping only) */
context.clip();

/* Create a gradient and draw a filled box */
var linear = context.createLinearGradient(50, 70, 100, 200);
linear.addColorStop(0.0, "red");
linear.addColorStop(0.6, "yellow");

context.fillStyle = linear;
context.fillRect(0, 0, 200, 200);

/* Prepare a shadow */
context.shadowOffsetX = 3;
context.shadowOffsetY = 5;
```

```
context.shadowColor = "rgba(0,0,0,0.3)";

/* You can stroke your path too since it is drawn across the line (3 in, 3 out) */
context.lineWidth = 6;
context.closePath();
context.stroke();
```

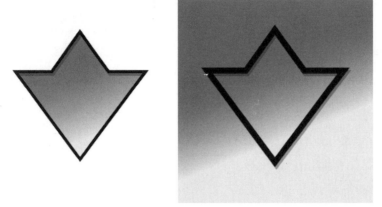

Figure 7–17. *The same shape drawn with and without clipping*

This code defines a shape to which the subsequent drawing will be bound. As you can see Figure 7–17, multiple operations can be applied to one path—clip() and stroke() in our example. We have added a shadow to the path stroke, which is drawn only inside the clipping area. If you comment the context.clip() line, you will see the same drawing unclipped, with a broader line style and a shadow spanning beyond the figure area. Thus, clipping can let you create slightly inset shadows.

Calls to the clip() method are cumulative, which means each new clipping area you define will itself be clipped to any previously defined clipping area. Consequently, you couldn't, for instance, restore the initial clip state by calling the clip() method with the dimensions of the canvas itself. You will have to resort to the save() and restore() methods as explained earlier.

Another limitation to the clip() method is that it can apply only with paths. Although paths are the major part of canvas drawing, you won't be able to define a clipping area using text, for instance. If you want to clip using text content, you can define a pattern containing the desired material and use it as fillStyle or strokeStyle, as in previous examples.

Compositing and Global Transparency

Canvases are initially transparent, which means you can create effects combining a background on an HTML element behind your background and the elements in your canvas.

To go further, you can also benefit from advanced compositing features of the Canvas API, using the globalCompositeOperation property. Compositing is an operation by which you can combine several images to create one final illustration. The following code is used to draw Figure 7–18:

```
/* Draw the source over the destination (default) */
compositing("source-over", 0, 0);

/* Apply a eXclusive OR between the source and the destination */
compositing("xor", 160, 0);

/* Fill blank pixels with the source shape */
compositing("destination-over", 320, 0);

function compositing(mode, x, y) {
    context.save();
    context.translate(x, y);

    context.fillStyle = "yellow";
    context.fillRect(0, 0, 100, 100);

    context.globalCompositeOperation = mode;
    context.fillStyle = "blue";
    context.fillRect(50, 50, 100, 100);

    context.restore();
}
```

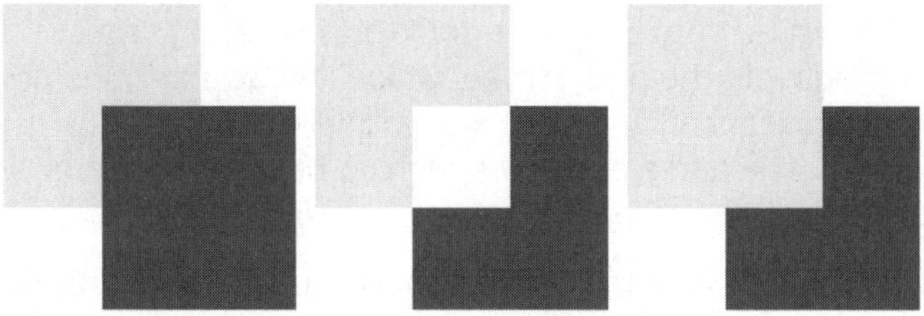

Figure 7–18. *An illustration of compositing abilities*

Table 7–2 lists all the values supported by Mobile Safari for the globalCompositeOperation property. Be careful: all values are case sensitive. The blending occurs between the element to be drawn and the current canvas contents, taking into account either the transparent pixels (with an alpha value less than 1.0 but more than 0.0) or the non-transparent ones.

Another feature regarding compositing is brought by the globalAlpha property, which we have already used in our spinner example. We used it to play with the opacity of the spinner lines. As made clear by its name, the globalAlpha property allows you to define an opacity value (from 0.0 to 1.0) for all rendered elements. This makes it possible to apply an alpha channel, even to elements that do not support one by themselves, such as images. Note that shadows that are not affected by transformations take the alpha value defined by the globalAlpha property.

Table 7–2. *Supported Values for the* globalCompositeOperation *Property*

Value	Description
source-over	The source is drawn over the destination. This is the default behavior.
source-atop	The source is drawn atop the destination. The destination behaves like a mask.
destination-over	The source is drawn under the destination. It is the inverse of source-over.
destination-out	Deletes intersecting pixels from the destination.
lighter	Displays the sum of the source and destination image, with color values approaching 1 as limit.
darker	Same as lighter but with color values approaching 0 as limit.
xor	Applies an eXclusive OR operation between the two images, removing fully opaque intersecting pixels.

Working with Canvas Pixels

Drawing shapes within your canvas can yield excellent results. However, to take things much further, it is possible to include image contents directly with the Canvas API. The following methods will let you use complete images as part of your canvas, as shown in Figure 7–19:

```
context.drawImage(image, dx, dy);
context.drawImage(image, dx, dy, dw, dh);
context.drawImage(image, sx, sy, sw, sh, dx, dy, dw, dh);
```

The called image can be an <img> element, a video, or a canvas (either an external canvas or the current canvas). In the cases of videos, the browser will consider only the frame at the current playback position for insertion. These methods are subject to the same constraints as other features such as compositing or clipping.

> **NOTE:** In the current version of Mobile Safari, trying to access a video frame always raises a SECURITY_ERR exception. This should occur only if the drawImage() method was used to copy an image from an origin other than that of the executed code. This bug is not present in Desktop Safari.

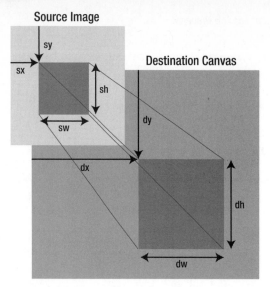

Figure 7-19. *The* `drawImage()` *method with different arguments*

The following code will draw an image with rounded corners:

```
<canvas id="area" width="400" height="300"></canvas>

<script>

    /* Create a new Image object and attach an onload handler to it */
    var image = new Image();
    image.onload = drawImage;
    image.src = "panda.jpg";

    function drawImage() {
        /* Get the canvas context */
        var canvas = document.getElementById("area");
        var context = canvas.getContext("2d");

        /* Read image dimensions */
        var w = canvas.width;
        var h = canvas.height

        /* Prepare a rounded rectangle and use it as clipping area */
        context.save();
        roundedRect(context, 20, 20, w - 40, h - 40, 64);
        context.clip();

        /* Finally, draw the image */
        context.drawImage(this, 20, 20, w - 40, h - 40);
        context.restore();
    }

    function roundedRect(ctx, x, y, w, h, radius) {
        var x1 = x + radius,
        var x2 = x + w - radius;
        var y1 = y + radius;
        var y2 = y + h - radius;
```

```
        ctx.beginPath();
        ctx.arc(x1, y1, radius,  Math.PI * 1.0, Math.PI * 1.5);
        ctx.arc(x2, y1, radius,  Math.PI * 1.5, Math.PI * 2.0);
        ctx.arc(x2, y2, radius,  Math.PI * 2.0, Math.PI * 0.5);
        ctx.arc(x1, y2, radius,  Math.PI * 0.5, Math.PI * 1.0);
        ctx.closePath();
    }

</script>
```

This example should be pretty clear. We define a path that draws a box with rounded corners that we use as a clipping area. Of course, we push the context state to the stack so that the clipping will be reset. Then, the image is rendered inside this area with the drawImage() method. Figure 7–20 shows the resulting canvas.

Figure 7–20. *An image with rounded corners*

The image must be loaded with the call to drawImage(), or nothing will appear. This is why we call our function after the image onload event. The first parameter to the drawImage() method is set to this, because the execution context is the object that sent the event—the image defined earlier.

Though using images in such a manner offers interesting possibilities, the API allows us to go even further by directly accessing the pixels of the canvas. Thus, you will be able to apply special effects. In our next example, we will simply turn the image used from color to black-and-white and invert its colors.

```
<img src="flower.jpg" onload="snap()" width="400" height="300">
<canvas id="area" width="400" height="300"></canvas>

<script>

    function snap() {
        var canvas = document.getElementsByTagName("canvas")[0];
        var context = canvas.getContext("2d");
```

```
/* Draw the image into the canvas */
var w = canvas.width;
var h = canvas.height;
context.drawImage(document.images[0], 0, 0, w, h);

/* Get the input buffer and create an output buffer */
var inp = context.getImageData(0, 0, w, h);
var out = context.createImageData(inp.width, inp.height);

/* Iterate through the image pixels */
for (var y = 0; y < inp.height; y++) {
    var line = y * inp.width * 4;

    for (var x = 0; x < inp.width; x++) {

        /* Get a pixel and calculate its brightness */
        var pixel = x * 4 + line;
        var light = 255 - (inp.data[pixel + 0] * 0.30        // Red
                     +  inp.data[pixel + 1] * 0.59        // Green
                     +  inp.data[pixel + 2] * 0.11);      // Blue

        var out_r = light;
        var out_g = light;
        var out_b = light;
        var out_a = inp.data[pixel + 3];     // Alpha

        /* Write the new pixel into the buffer */
        out.data[pixel + 0] = out_r;
        out.data[pixel + 1] = out_g;
        out.data[pixel + 2] = out_b;
        out.data[pixel + 3] = out_a;
    }
}

/* Flush the buffer to the canvas area */
context.clearRect(0, 0, w, h);
context.putImageData(out, 0, 0);
}

</script>
```

The brightness of a color is made of roughly 30 percent red, 59 percent green, and 11 percent blue components. To reverse the colors of an image, you have to invert these three values and give the new ones to each color. In our example, we read the component of each pixel color found in the data array of the ImageData object returned by the getImageData() method—and obtain the result shown in Figure 7–21.

Figure 7–21. *The original picture and the picture transformed with the Canvas API*

To hold the transformed pixels, we use a buffer created with the createImageData() method that can take either the dimensions of the buffer or an existing ImageData object from which the dimension data will be obtained. In both cases, the buffer will be empty. The data property is a one-dimensional array that holds the color components for each pixel under the RGBA notation, which is why we multiply by four to move from one pixel to the next.

Once the buffer holds all our transformed pixels, we write the data to the canvas with the putImageData() method to the canvas, with an ImageData object as a parameter and the coordinates where the image should be drawn. Optionally, you can specify with this method a "dirty" rectangle, that is, the area to update, so that only the defined rectangle is rendered to the canvas.

Using Vector Graphics

The great advantage of vector graphics over bitmap images is that they are independent of the resolution to which they are rendered and can be scaled without loss of quality. This is useful to draw the same background at full screen size, whatever the size of the device—for instance, on an iPhone and an iPad.

SVG is a presentational markup language based on XML. Like the Canvas API, it is lightweight, easily compressible (because it is text), and is thus fast to load on portable devices that, like Mobile Safari on iPhone, support HTTP compression even for complex documents. Note, however, that you will obtain poorer performance with SVG than with a canvas.

Taking advantage of the fact that it is based on XML (and, unlike the canvas, which works with an unalterable drawing process), SVG is provided with specific DOM interfaces, similar to that of HTML, that make it both dynamic and potentially interactive. Moreover, dynamism isn't accessible only through scripts. It has good native support of animations through the Synchronized Multimedia Integration Language (SMIL) integration, a specification based on XML that aims to ease the creation of interactive audiovisual presentations.

Inserting SVG into Your Documents

HTML5 lets you use the `<svg>` tag directly in your markup, without even having to specify a namespace. Unfortunately, this is not yet supported by Mobile Safari. To embed an SVG document into your pages, you will have to resort either to the `<img>` tag, specifying the file locations in the `src` attribute; to the `<iframe>` tag (this method is not recommended, because it proves inflexible in Mobile Safari); or to the `<object>` tag, with the SVG location as a value for the `data` attribute, as shown in the following example (Figure 7–22):

```
<img src="tiger.svg" alt="A tiger">
<object data="tiger.svg" width="400" height="400" type="image/svg+xml"></object>
```

Figure 7–22. *The famous vector tiger drawn with SVG*

Mobile Safari ignores any width and height value given to an `<iframe>`, because it automatically sizes the frame to contain the linked document. This of course is problematic with SVG documents, which inherently have no defined size.

Understanding the Coordinates System

This is not the place to get into too much detail, but it is essential to understand how the browser renders an SVG document. Hence, we are going to explain the necessary basics to understand how an SVG document will be scaled inside an HTML page in Mobile Safari.

The dimensions of an SVG canvas are initially infinite, but they are generally fixed by the width and height attributes on the `<svg>` tag. The size will be considered in pixels if no measure unit is given. For the rendering, coordinates are converted to pixels based on a

96dpi resolution. This means a 4-centimeter line—as long as the viewport for the HTML document is correctly set for scaling and the scale is set at 1.0—will be rendered as 151 pixels – 4 / 2.53 * 96 (where 2.53 is a rounded value for 1 inch).

As an example, let's take a simple SVG document where a rectangle and a circle are drawn with the <rect> and <circle> tags (Figure 7–23). Note that the XML declaration and doctype are not mandatory.

```
<?xml version="1.0" ?>
<!DOCTYPE svg PUBLIC "-//W3C//DTD SVG 1.1//EN"
        "http://www.w3.org/Graphics/SVG/1.1/DTD/svg11.dtd">
<svg xmlns="http://www.w3.org/2000/svg">

    <rect x="0" y="0" width="100%" height="100%" fill="lightgrey"
        stroke="black" stroke-width="4" />

    <circle cx="110" cy="110" r="100" fill="yellow"
        stroke="red" stroke-width="2" />

</svg>
```

To add this to our HTML document, we are going to use the <object> tag. The <img> tag is not the best solution to insert SVG elements, and it is unlikely that you will ever really have to choose that option. Therefore, we will systematically use the <object> tag and bring more information when notable behavior differences arise. For now, let's make our object 320 square pixels.

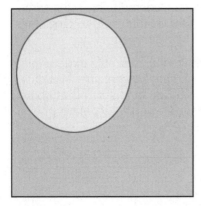

Figure 7–23. *A simple SVG document inside an HTML document*

Because we haven't specified any dimension for the SVG canvas, those indicated on the <object> tag will be used to set the rendered size, which will be the same as the SVG viewport, that is, the area in which the document will be drawn. In Figure 7–23, the rectangle thus completely outlines the viewport, and, as expected, the circle has a 100 pixels radius (the r attribute) and spans 200 pixels.

Now, let's explicitly set the document viewport size by adding width and height attributes to the <svg> tag:

```
...
<svg xmlns="http://www.w3.org/2000/svg"
```

```
    width="400" height="400">
...
</svg>
```

Because the viewport, as defined, is larger than the `object` area, the rectangle spans beyond the area (Figure 7–24), and the content is clipped. Here, the behavior would be different using an `<img>` tag. Indeed, using img, the SVG document is considered as a bitmap element, so it will be scaled to fit into the area defined by its own attributes, without consideration of the initial ratio.

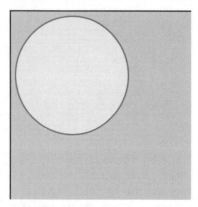

Figure 7–24. *With a viewport explicitly larger, the document is clipped*

If a value isn't defined inside the SVG document, it will be considered to have the same dimensions as the host HTML document. This seems to us a limitation of the `<img>` tag, although in some specific cases it can come in handy.

This limitation is especially sensible because, in cases where it is desirable to determine an area of the document that would stretch to fit into some specific container—as to apply a focus on such an area—it can be done with the `viewBox` attribute. This attribute allows you to set coordinates of the rectangle to bind to the viewport. By default, the scaling will occur while preserving the initial ratio (Figure 7–25).

```
...
<svg xmlns="http://www.w3.org/2000/svg"
    width="320" height="320" viewBox="0 0 150 800">
...
</svg>
```

Figure 7–25. *The same document using the* viewBox *attribute*

To clarify things, we adjust the dimensions of the viewport again to make them fit with those of the <object> element. As you can see in Figure 7–25, the viewBox attribute has an effect on relative coordinates such as those defined for the rectangle but doesn't clip drawn lines, and the circle spans beyond the area. Moreover, because the area defined is higher than the viewport (800px), the image is scaled.

This default behavior can be modified with the preserveAspectRatio, for instance by setting it to none. This way, the scaling will occur regardless of the defined area and will span on either side to fill the viewport, as shown in Figure 7–26.

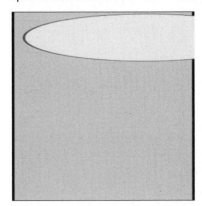

Figure 7–26. *The aspect ratio can be changed with an attribute*

Those are the main features available to you using SVG in HTML documents. All work with the <object> tag. Using an <img> tag, not only will the behavior regarding dimensions be different, but animations will not be rendered, and you will not be able to use scripts or interactions defined in the document. Moreover, you will lose access to the SVG DOM through JavaScript from the hosting document.

Drawing Shapes

As stated earlier, SVG is a presentational language that provides plenty of tags to draw most of the shapes commonly used in vector graphics—lines, rectangles, polygons, and paths—and to define colors, stroke styles, fills, gradients, and transitions. All the options available for the canvas area are available in SVG also, though instead of being handled with scripts, they are described with XML. The following code gives examples for a fair range of the available shapes, with the results in Figure 7–27:

```
<svg xmlns="http://www.w3.org/2000/svg">
    <g fill="yellow" stroke="red" stroke-width="4" transform="translate(5,5)">
        <circle cx="45" cy="45" r="45" />
        <rect x="100" y="0" width="90" height="90" rx="10" ry="10" />
        <ellipse cx="245" cy="45" rx="45" ry="30" />
    </g>

    <g fill="yellow" stroke="red" stroke-width="4" transform="translate(5,105)">
        <polyline
            points="0,0
                    0,90 20,90    20,80 30,80
                    30,90 40,90   40,80 50,80
                    50,90 60,90   60,80 70,80
                    70,90 90,90   90,45" />

        <polygon transform="translate(100, 0)"
            points="0,0
                    0,90 20,90    20,80 30,80
                    30,90 40,90   40,80 50,80
                    50,90 60,90   60,80 70,80
                    70,90 90,90   90,45" />

        <line x1="200" y1="0" x2="290" y2="90" />
    </g>
</svg>
```

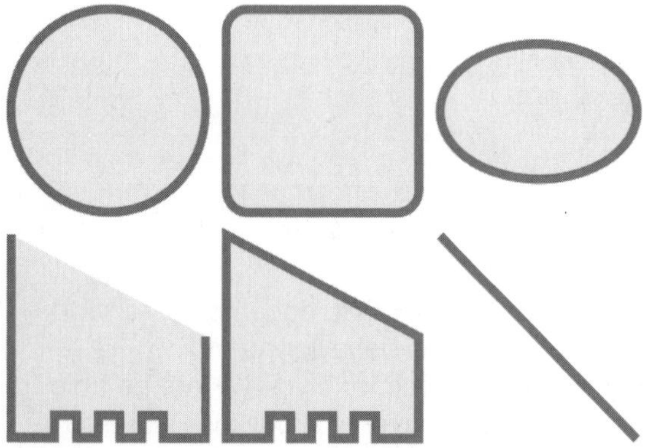

Figure 7–27. *Some basic shapes available with SVG*

This piece of code already gives you a look of the kind of possibilities SVG has. As you can see, you don't need to use paths to draw rounded corners on a rectangle, setting the optional attributes rx and ry on the rect element. You will also notice that the only difference between the `<polyline>` and `<polygon>` elements is that the former doesn't automatically close the shape.

To make this more obvious, our two shapes use the same points, apart from the initial coordinates (so that the second doesn't cover the first). Finally, the `transform` attribute doesn't only allow translation: you can also rotate, scale, or skew (horizontally or vertically, with `skewX` and `skewY`) or use a custom matrix, as with Canvas. Note that although skewing isn't available natively with the Canvas API, it is easily achievable using a matrix. As previously stated, all transformations are actually affine transformations.

We are not going to get into the details of actually writing SVG, because the most effective way to create SVG documents probably is to use a dedicated tool such as Adobe Illustrator or Inkscape. Paths, for instance, are often complex and will be easier to grasp, draw, and modify with a mouse and visual feedback. For the same reasons that we put forward regarding Komodo Edit, we suggest using Inkscape, a solid, feature-rich, free, open source SVG graphical editor.

> **NOTE:** Inkscape is the reference open source tool for vector graphics creation. It is available on all operating systems and can be downloaded for free and with no restriction from the official web site, `www.inkscape.org`.

Interoperability

Once your document is created, you can add it to your HTML document. Because it is often desirable to do more with images, especially SVG images, rather than just leave them in the middle of the screen, we are going to take the possibilities of SVG further. To demonstrate interoperability, let's start by creating the same chevron as we did in an earlier example in a canvas and use it as a CSS background. Because it is a rather simple drawing, we can create it directly in Komodo Edit, without resorting to a specific authoring tool. Here is the code from the *chevron.svg* document:

```
<svg xmlns="http://www.w3.org/2000/svg" width="23" height="13">
    <polyline
        fill="none" stroke="gray" stroke-width="3"
        points="4,1 10,6.5 4,12"
    />
</svg>
```

This will yield exactly the same result as the previous canvas JavaScript but by simply using XML. You can replace your CSS rules for the chevron with the following:

```
/* main.css */
.group-wrapper ul li a {
    ...
    background: url(images/chevron.svg) right center no-repeat;
}
```

Note that the no-repeat rule is crucial. Not only can you not apply repetition to a SVG image, chances are that not applying the no-repeat rule to such an image would just result in nothing being rendered to the screen. Moreover, it would no longer be possible to use the CSS3 background-size property.

> **NOTE:** As you may know, it is possible to enable the accessibility features from the iPhone and iPad settings. Doing this, you would notice that the zoom for partially sighted people doesn't take advantage of the scaling advantages of SVG documents. Indeed, this option applies a zoom to the screen pixels: it doesn't scale the SVG graphics or fonts.

With this new definition, your chevron will be perfectly rendered whatever the resolution of the screen and the scale that may be applied. For instance, you can set the viewport to a scale factor of 2.4 to make your web application take the same width on the iPhone and the iPad (unlikely you would want to do that) with the following code:

```
<meta name="viewport" content="initial-scale=2.4; maximum-scale=2.4; user-scalable=no">
```

With this configuration, you should see a clear difference in the quality of your graphics, as shown in Figure 7–28.

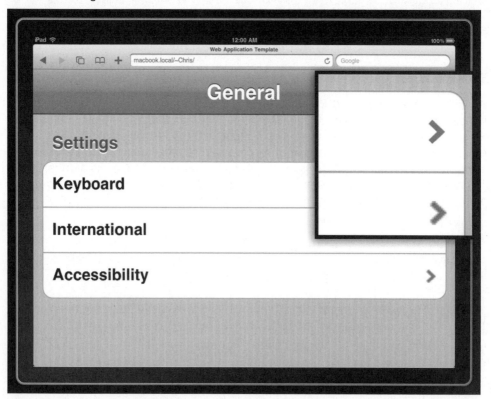

Figure 7–28. *When zooming, the difference between bitmap (canvas) and vector (SVG) is noticeable*

Nevertheless, for now, you can't do everything with SVG that you can do with a canvas. Indeed, in our earlier example, we could easily modify the color of our chevron using the `initChevron()` function. This cannot be done the same way with SVG used as an image.

To be able to change the color, we are going to add the SVG code directly to the JavaScript code—which is no problem because the code is really short—and load it using the data URL scheme, which is an IETF standard (RFC 2397) that allows for instance inline inclusion in HTML, CSS, or JavaScript files. This will also help save some HTTP requests.

The scheme can take either base64-encoded data (especially useful to hold binary data such as images) or encoded URLs, which we are going to use right now.

Let's start by putting our SVG document into a JavaScript variable, taking care to delete line feeds:

```
/* Initial document in plain text so that it is easy to modify */
var chevron = '<svg xmlns="http://www.w3.org/2000/svg" width="23" height="13"> ↵
    <polyline fill="none" stroke="ADD_COLOR" stroke-width="3" ↵
    points="4,1 10,6.5 4,12" /></svg>';

/* URL encode the string */
chevron = encodeURIComponent(chevron);
```

Doing this, note that we have replaced the stroke color by `ADD_COLOR` in order to easily replace the string later. Then, the data URL will take this form:

```
chevron = "data:image/svg+xml;charset=utf-8," + chevron;
```

The URL begins with the relevant scheme, `data:` in this case. You then declare the MIME type for SVG documents and the character set separated by semicolons. The actual data starts after the comma. Now, let's see how this is handled in the main.css style sheet:

```
/* main.css */
.group-wrapper ul li a {
    ...
    background: url(#chevron,gray) right center no-repeat;
}
.group-wrapper ul li a:active {
    ...
    background:
        -webkit-gradient(linear,
            left top, left bottom,
            from(rgba(255, 255, 255, .25)), to(transparent) ),

        url(#chevron,white) right center no-repeat #015de6;
    ...
}
```

We have added an identifier in order to allow communication with the SVG, and for more flexibility, the color is added to the styles directly, which is logical really! Of course, this style declaration is perfectly valid CSS, because the #chevron is a hash that should call part of the current document. Next, we need a script that will dynamically modify the CSS definition using the data URL:

```
/* main.js */
var list = { "chevron": chevron };
applySVGBackground();

function applySVGBackground() {
    /* Get all CSS attached to the document */
    var css = document.styleSheets;

    /* Parse them all looking for a background url() */
    for (var i = 0; i < css.length; i++) {
        var rules = css[i].rules;

        for(var j = 0; j < rules.length; j++) {
            var rule = rules[j].style.getPropertyCSSValue("background-image");

            /* Return an single objet, an empty collection.
               Be sure to always have a list of objects */
            if (!rule) {
                continue;
            } else if (!rule.length) {
                rule = [rule];
            }

            for (var k = 0; k < rule.length; k++) {
                /* Only handle certain objects */
                if (!rule[k].getStringValue) {
                    continue;
                }

                var r = rule[k],
                    text = r.getStringValue(r.CSS_URI) || "";

                /* If we have a hash, try to apply the SVG style */
                var start = text.indexOf("#");
                if (start != -1) {
                    var defs = text.substr(start + 1).split(",");
                    r.setStringValue(r.CSS_URI, getSVG(defs[0], defs[1]));
                }
            }
        }
    }
}

function getSVG(id, color) {
    if (list[id] != undefined) {
        color = color.replace("[", "%28").replace("]", "%29");
        return list[id].replace("ADD_COLOR", color);
    }
}
```

First, we save our chevron to the `list` object, which will allow communication between the hash read in the CSS file and the data URL to use. The `applySVGBackground()` function gathers a collection of objects using the `document.styleSheets` property that holds the styles from the HTML document, regardless if they are declared as links to external style sheets or style declarations inline. This collection is parsed to look for rules relevant to our purpose. The parsed rules are in computed style, which is why we can access the `background-image` property where the `background` shorthand is used in the actual style sheet. We must be careful here to handle multiple background definitions, not to lose styles in the process.

Next, once we have obtained a two-element long array (identifier and color), we pass the array to the `getSVG()` function. This function returns the data URL relative to the identifier, inserting the passed color at the expected place. From there, everything is automatic.

All CSS2.1 color definitions can be used, as well as the named colors introduced by SVG. On the other side, for colors written as an `rgb()` declaration, you should replace the parentheses with square brackets, so you don't generate an erroneous CSS rule that would not be accessible and thus not alterable by our script. The `getSVG()` function will take care of changing the square brackets back to the usual form.

```
/* Invalid definition */
url(#chevron,rgb(0,0,0))

/* Correct definitions */
url(#chevron,rgb[0,0,0])
url(#chevron,black)
url(#chevron,#000)
```

The strong point of this script is that it is very generic and can be used without any changes. To use it with other SVG documents, the only thing to do (other than declaring styles in the CSS) is add it to the list object with the identifier and the encoded data.

```
var list = { "chevron": chevron , "identifier": svgDataUrl };
```

Now, you may wonder what happens working with more complex documents, if you wanted to affect the DOM directly. As we have said earlier, this is not possible when using the `<img>` tag to insert SVG document—and it is not possible when the SVG is used as a `background-image` either. However, if your SVG is brought to the document using the `<object>` tag, you can communicate with the SVG document, as long as its DOM has been entirely loaded and has the same origin as the HTML and scripts (that is, it is on the same domain). In this case, we could use the `onload` event of the HTML document; instead, we are going to experience the communication possibilities between SVG and HTML.

Communication

As we have said, SVG has support for scripting, so we can add JavaScript directly into the SVG document. This is how we modify our previous file:

```
<?xml version="1.0" ?>
<!DOCTYPE svg PUBLIC "-//W3C//DTD SVG 1.1//EN"
        "http://www.w3.org/Graphics/SVG/1.1/DTD/svg11.dtd">
<svg xmlns="http://www.w3.org/2000/svg" onload="notify()">

    <rect x="0" y="0" width="100%" height="100%" fill="lightgrey"
        stroke="black" stroke-width="4" />

    <circle cx="110" cy="110" r="100" fill="yellow"
        stroke="red" stroke-width="2" />
```

```
<script type="text/ecmascript"><![CDATA[
    function notify() {
        parent.svgLoaded(this);
    }
]]></script>
</svg>
```

The onload event is added directly to the SVG document. The called function notifies the HTML document that the SVG is ready. From there, the SVG document can access the HTML elements using the parent object. By default, the scripting language for SVG is ECMAScript, a specification from which JavaScript inherits. Therefore, the code should be pretty clear. Inside the HTML document, we add the following code and JavaScript:

```
<script>
    function svgLoaded(svg) {
        var circles = svg.document.getElementsByTagName("circle");
        circles[0].setAttribute("r", 200);

        var ellipse = ↵
            svg.document.createElementNS("http://www.w3.org/2000/svg",  "ellipse");

        ellipse.setAttribute("cx", "50%");
        ellipse.setAttribute("cy", "50%");
        ellipse.setAttribute("rx", "150");
        ellipse.setAttribute("ry", "50");

        circles[0].parentNode.appendChild(ellipse);
    }
</script>

<object data="notify.svg" width="320" height="320"
        type="image/svg+xml"  id="mySVG"></object>
```

The svgLoaded() function receives a reference to the SVG document, modifies the radius of the circle, and creates an ellipse to be inserted into the document. It is necessary here to use the namespace version of the createElement() method. Otherwise, the object will be created with the wrong element type and will be impossible to add to the SVG document.

> **NOTE:** In this example, the SVG establishes a communication with the HTML document. The JavaScript in the HTML is not explicitly asking for access to the SVG document (as we will do later in this section). Therefore, it can be useful to identify the document in question. To do this, you can use the location property of the SVG document object, which holds the various parts of the document URL. To get an ID, it is possible, for instance, to add a hash to the URL in the data parameter of the <object> tag that holds your SVG and collect this using the hash property of the Location object.

In Figure 7–29, this method is used on the document object of the SVG document, but we also could have used it on the document object of the HTML DOM.

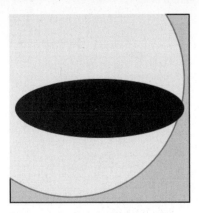

Figure 7–29. *The modified document*

You can also acquire full control over your HTML document from the host file. The following is the code that we would have used to create HTML tags in the HTML document from a script in the SVG.

```
/* Create a new <div> element in the host document */
var div = document.createElementNS("http://www.w3.org/1999/xhtml", "div");
div.style.width = "100px";
div.style.height = "100px";
div.style.backgroundColor = "green";

parent.document.body.appendChild(div);
```

Here, it is the SVG that should indicate when it is available so that it can be referenced by its host. If we had used the onload event of the HTML document, we could have used the getSVGDocument() method to get a reference to the SVG. This could, for instance, look like the following:

```
var svg = document.getElementById("mySVG").getSVGDocument();
```

From there, the rest of the code is still valid and should yield the same results. It is merely another method to access the SVG code from the HTML document. These techniques will even allow you to animate your pages with scripting, both from the XML and from the HTML.

Animation with and Without Scripting

Though you can animate SVG elements with a scripting language, this is not the only way to do it. Indeed, SVG integrates the Synchronized Multimedia Integration Language (SMIL), which is widely used today to produce multimedia content, and more specifically the SMIL Animation Specification, which was collaboratively established by the SMIL and SVG Working Groups. SVG inherits much of its functionality and animation possibilities from these technologies.

Once again, we are going to take our spinner example first created in a canvas and adapt it to pure SVG. The first step is to draw the spinner using XML.

```
<svg xmlns="http://www.w3.org/2000/svg"
```

```
        xmlns:xlink="http://www.w3.org/1999/xlink"
        viewBox="0 0 37 37">

<defs>
    <line x1="0" y1="9" x2="0" y2="15" id="line" />
</defs>

<g transform="translate(18,18)" stroke="rgb(0,0,0)" opacity="0.5"
        stroke-width="3" stroke-linecap="round">

<use xlink:href="#line" transform="rotate(-30)" opacity="0.85">
  <use xlink:href="#line" transform="rotate(-30)" opacity="0.85">
    <use xlink:href="#line" transform="rotate(-30)" opacity="0.85">
      <use xlink:href="#line" transform="rotate(-30)" opacity="0.85">
        <use xlink:href="#line" transform="rotate(-30)" opacity="0.85">
          <use xlink:href="#line" transform="rotate(-30)" opacity="0.85">
            <use xlink:href="#line" transform="rotate(-30)" opacity="0.85">
              <use xlink:href="#line" transform="rotate(-30)" opacity="0.85">
                <use xlink:href="#line" transform="rotate(-30)" opacity="0.85">
                  <use xlink:href="#line" transform="rotate(-30)" opacity="0.85">
                    <use xlink:href="#line" transform="rotate(-30)" opacity="0.85">
                      <use xlink:href="#line" transform="rotate(-30)" opacity="0.85" />
                    </use>
                  </use>
                </use>
              </use>
            </use>
          </use>
        </use>
      </use>
    </use>
  </use>
</use>

<animateTransform attributeName="transform" attributeType="XML"
        type="rotate" values="0;30;60;90;120;150;180;210;240;270;300;330"
        calcMode="discrete" repeatCount="indefinite" additive="sum" dur="1.2s" />

</g>

</svg>
```

The logic behind this code is still very close to what has been done with the Canvas API, and you will see that the result is the same as that of the canvas. Even the line ends and the stroke styles are calculated in the same manner, pixel for pixel.

First, we add the namespace that allows us to reference objects from some tags. The `<defs>` tag is meant to define reusable elements and, in our example, is very useful to create the primary line with a rounded end that we will repeat inside the `<g>` tag.

On the `<g>` tag, we add several attributes that let us define the basic styles for its children. SVG can also take CSS rules, so this could have been done with the code that follows. However, be careful when doing this, because it will no longer be possible to modify element attributes with the `setAttribute()` method.

```
<!-- Styles defined with the style attribute -->
<g transform="translate(18,18)"
```

```
      style="stroke:rgb(0,0,0);opacity:0.5;stroke-width:3;stroke-linecap:round">
</g>

<!-- Styles defined using the <style> tag -->
<defs>
    <style type="text/css"><![CDATA[
        g {
            stroke: rgb(0,0,0);
            opacity: 0.5;
            stroke-width: 3;
            stroke-linecap: round;
        }
    ]]></style>
</defs>
```

Next, we add a number of <use> tags so that each inherits from its parent, and then, altogether, they draw our 12-branched spinner. Hence, the definition is the same for each branch, but because each one inherits from its parent and rotation and opacity are relative to the parent, we end up with a circular shape with a progressive fade-out effect.

The <use> tag lets you reference an object defined with its id through the xlink:herf attribute. From there, as with any other shape, you can attach style or transformation attributes to it.

The last tag in use is the <animateTransform> tag. Its purpose is, quite obviously, to bring animation to the transformations applied to objects—rotate() in our example. To avoid interpolation between the different steps of the animation and instead obtain a fluid movement of the shape as a whole, we use the values attribute that lets you define a series of values to be applied to the property you want to be animated. The calcMode attribute set to discrete is what avoids interpolation. This way, the shape itself seems not to move, and what appears to take place is a color rotation. To have a full turn that takes 100ms, we have fixed the dur attribute to 1.2s—because there are still 12 steps.

The additive attribute set to sum makes the animation cumulative so that no transformation is lost. If it had been set to replace, we would have lost the translation, and the shape would have changed its origin from the first iteration.

Of course, the spinner drawing could have been made shorter and thus perhaps easier to maintain—but we wanted the code to be clear to understand. You can, for instance, replace all the <use> tags with the following script after the <g> tag:

```
...
<script type="text/ecmascript"><![CDATA[

    var g = document.getElementsByTagName("g");
    var use, prev = g[0];

    for (var i = 0; i < 12; i++) {
        use = document.createElementNS("http://www.w3.org/2000/svg", "use");
        use.setAttributeNS("http://www.w3.org/1999/xlink", "href", "#line");
        use.setAttribute("transform", "rotate(-30)");
        use.setAttribute("opacity", "0.85");

        prev.appendChild(use);
```

```
            prev = use;
        }

]]></script>
...
```

To create objects appropriately, we once again use `createElementNS()`, and then we use `setAttributeNS()` to set the `href` attribute that isn't part of the SVG namespace. The loop will create the 12 `<use>` tags for you, which in turn will draw the 12 branches, entwining them as with the previous XML code.

The new spinner is now ready to be added to any of your HTML documents, with the same quality at any size, as shown on Figure 7–30. Indeed, because we have used `viewBox` in our example, the SVG drawing will adapt to fill its container. All you have to do is set the `width` and `height` attributes to fit your needs.

Figure 7–30. *A pretty big spinner*

Coping with Temporary Bugs

The only bad news is that a recent bug in Safari prevents SVG graphics from appearing as translucent when inserted using a holder tag. This means that a white background will always appear behind fully or partially transparent areas. This can be remedied at least in cases where you can define a plain background for your graphics by adding an option to our previous script, as we had done for the chevron color. Again, we can grab this option from the hash. The `<object>` definition looks like this:

```
<object data="spinner.svg#green,red,0.5"
        width="320" height="320" type="image/svg+xml"></object>
```

Then, simply add the following to the end of the previous script in the SVG document:

```
var hash = window.location.hash;

if (hash != "") {
    var defs = hash = hash.substr(1).split(",");

    /* Create the background color */
    if ((defs[0] || "transparent") != "transparent") {
```

```
    var rect = document.createElementNS("http://www.w3.org/2000/svg", "rect");
    rect.setAttribute("width", "100%");
    rect.setAttribute("height", "100%");
    rect.setAttribute("fill", defs[0]);

    g[0].parentNode.insertBefore(rect, g[0]);
}

/* Additionally change the spinner color and opacity if defined */
if (defs[1]) {
    g[0].setAttribute("stroke", defs[1]);
}
if (defs[2]) {
    g[0].setAttribute("opacity", defs[2]);
}
}
```

The SVG code will be able to identify this information in the URL, still using the location.hash property, and use them to alter the background color (green), the spinner color (red), and the opacity of the branches (0.5).

One interest of this method compared to using a script in the host HTML document to apply modifications is that you won't have to worry about waiting for the SVG document to load before calling the function. Because there is no dependence between the documents, handling functionalities is easier.

Preinstalled and Downloadable Fonts

Using fonts other than the default serif, sans-serif, and monospace is often a crucial step on the way to more attractive web pages. iOS comes with a number of already installed fonts that you can safely rely on. The following is the list, and Figure 7–31 shows what each font looks like on-screen:

- American Typewriter
- Arial
- Arial Rounded MT Bold
- Courier New
- Georgia
- Helvetica
- Marker Felt
- Times New Roman
- Trebuchet MS
- Verdana
- Zapfino

The quick brown fox jumps over the lazy dog.
The quick brown fox jumps over the lazy dog.
The quick brown fox jumps over the lazy dog.
The quick brown fox jumps over the lazy dog.
The quick brown fox jumps over the lazy dog.
The quick brown fox jumps over the lazy dog.
The quick brown fox jumps over the lazy dog.
The quick brown fox jumps over the lazy dog.
The quick brown fox jumps over the lazy dog.
The quick brown fox jumps over the lazy dog.
The quick brown fox jumps over the lazy dog.

Figure 7–31. *Fonts natively available on iOS*

Other fonts are installed, but they are used only to render different alphabets, such as Hebrew, Japanese, or Arabic. You cannot simply use these by their names in your style sheets, because they are extended character sets meant to be system fonts for foreign alphabets. However, some do offer interesting versions of the Roman character set. For instance, you could try "Heidi J" or ".Helvetica LT MM" (don't forget the leading point).

NOTE: If you want to discover all the font available on your device, you can download the free Typefaces application (formerly Cédille) by Tomoaki Nakano from the App Store.

Nevertheless, you can also use fonts that are not actually installed on the system, if the installed fonts don't necessarily fit your specific needs. You probably have resorted to images and more or less complicated CSS tricks in such cases. Creating a header on every page with this kind of technique can prove unproductive and annoying, especially with multilingual sites—which can lead to leave your initial design aside.

Mobile Safari, starting with version 3.1, supports the CSS3 `@font-face` property, which will let you specify a downloadable font from the growing list of appropriately licensed fonts. This of course is much more flexible, because this will make the font available almost like any other font that would be installed on the OS.

> **WARNING:** The most important limitation to this property is the question of licensing. That a font is installed on your own system or is downloadable for free doesn't necessarily mean it can be used in all cases and for all purposes. For any font you choose to use, you should check whether it is all right to use in your specific case. Always check the license or contact the author prior to using a font.

Mobile Safari has support for SVG fonts only. SVG allows you to define several fonts using the `<font>` tag, and you can add them directly to the document. However, because character definitions often use many complex paths and need a long kerning definition, it is more productive to use a font creation application.

FontForge is a powerful, open source font editor and converter that works on all platforms and won't cost you a thing. It can handle TrueType (TTF), OpenType (OTF), and of course SVG. You can download it from the SourceForge web site at `http://fontforge.sourceforge.net/`.

Generally, you will not be creating your own fonts; you will simply want to convert existing ones. Be it a font that is installed on your system but is known not to be common on some other system or a font that you have downloaded, the software will ask you to choose a font when you launch it. Quite evidently, it is unlikely that you would want to convert a font such as Arial, Verdana, or Times for `@font-face` inclusion. Table 7–3 gives you the default folders for font files on different operating systems.

Table 7–3. *Availability of Fonts on the Main Operating Systems*

Mac OS X	Windows	Linux
~/Library/Fonts/ /Library/Fonts/ /System/Library/Fonts/	%windir%\fonts\ (%windir% is usually C:\Windows)	~/.fonts/ /usr/share/fonts/

Choose the font you want to work with, and click OK. If the font holds some license information, FontForge will ask you whether you have the necessary rights to edit the font (see Figure 7–32).

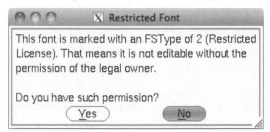

Figure 7–32. *FontForge may ask for permission to load the font*

Once you have loaded the font into the software, a new window will appear containing all the available glyphs (Figure 7–33). From the menu in this window, choose **File ➤**

Generate Fonts..., give a name to your font, select SVG format, and save. You are almost done.

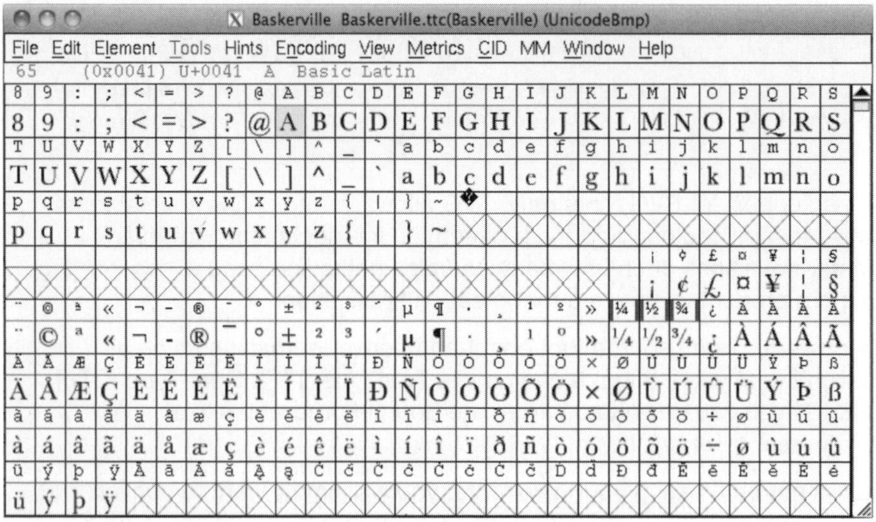

Figure 7–33. *The font window with the font glyphs and the export dialog box*

We write *almost* because, as explained earlier, the namespace definition is required for Mobile Safari to correctly interpret the font—however, FontForge doesn't add this. Therefore, you will need to edit the font source, for instance by using Komodo Edit. What you need to modify is the <svg> tag, as follows:

```
<svg xmlns="http://www.w3.org/2000/svg">
```

Once this is done, simply save the document. Now your font is ready for the Web! All you have to do is add the following rule into the relevant style sheet. Whereas Desktop Safari will ask for permission before downloading the font, the mobile version of the browser will just do it without complaining.

```
@font-face {
    font-family: "My Font Face";
    src: local("Baskerville"), url("pathto/mybaskerville.svg#fontID") format("svg");
}
```

There are several important steps here. First, you need to name your font for further use with the font-family property. For this, avoid using real font family names so it doesn't conflict with other fonts. In our example, we have exported the font "Baskerville" and named it "My Font Face".

Because nothing proves the font will not be installed in future versions of iOS, you will not want it to be downloaded systematically—in case it could be useless. Therefore, the first source we indicate for the browser to look for the font is the proper font name, to be searched directly in the OS fonts. This is done with the local() function. The url() function, as with background-image, is used to indicate a remote URL, in this case, the path to the downloadable font. Specifying the format is necessary for the rule to work, as is the reference to the <font> tag identifier in the hash of the URL (fontID in our example). Note that the latter is required even if there is only one font tag in the document. Because SVG is primarily a format meant to describe vector documents, it is absolutely possible to define several fonts in one document. This of course can be useful if you need to define several SVG fonts, because it would limit the number of HTTP requests.

Your newly defined font can now be used in your documents as any other (Figure 7–34).

```html
<!DOCTYPE html>
<html>
    <head>
        <title>Definition</title>
        <meta name="viewport" content="initial-scale=1.0;
            maximum-scale=1.0; user-scalable=no">

        <style>
            body {
                background: #fce9cb -webkit-gradient(linear,
                    left top, left 50%,
                    from(rgba(95,66,21,0.5)), to(transparent)) repeat-x;
                color: #5f4215;
                font-family: "Marker Felt";
                font-size: 16px;
                margin:15px;
            }
            h1 {
                font: 100 normal 35px/50px "Anagram";
                text-shadow: #fce9cb -1px -1px 3px;
                border-bottom: 1px dotted currentColor;
                text-align: center;
            }

            p:nth-of-type(3) {
                font-family: "Zapfino";
                text-align: right;
            }

            @font-face {
                font-family: "Anagram";
                src: url("anagram.svg#Anagram") format("svg");
            }
        </style>
    </head>

<body>

    <h1>Anagram</h1>

    <p>Lorem ipsum dolor sit amet, consectetur adipiscing elit. In tristique sodales
        dui, in porttitor orci sodales quis. Vivamus et lobortis nisl. Nullam et varius
        ante. Sed ante erat, laoreet vitae tristique sed, placerat ut lacus. Sed at
        dictum odio. Nam iaculis dictum quam, et fermentum tellus ultricies vel.</p>

    <p>Pellentesque habitant morbi tristique senectus et netus et malesuada fames ac
        turpis egestas. Donec fringilla odio vel arcu ullamcorper pretium. Mauris arcu
        ipsum, semper eu auctor accumsan, dignissim et diam.</p>
```

```
    <p>by Lorem Ipsum</p>

</body>
</html>
```

Figure 7–34. *A nice presentation using the Anagram font by Nick Curtis and built-in fonts*

If you have exported the font as we have explained, you may have noticed that the file size is rather large. This is because the SVG font contains all the glyphs that the original font had—which may not be necessary for your purposes. One typical case is that some font definitions copy the uppercase glyphs into the lowercase ones. For such cases, you can easily benefit from the scripting possibilities of FontForge.

Once you have selected a font, you should notice that selecting a glyph will make some information appear at the top of the window, noticeably the Unicode code for the glyph (Figure 7–35)—this is just what we need to select only some glyphs to add to our exported SVG font.

Figure 7–35. *The scripting window*

We are going to use a script to export only the characters that we need. The scripting functionalities are accessible from the menu **File ➤ Execute Script**.... In the new window that appears, select FF from the bottom—to activate FontForge mode—and type the following code:

```
Select(0u0041);
```

This command selects only the uppercase letter *A*. To select several glyphs at a time, you need only specify the first and last glyphs of your series. The following code would select all uppercase letters from *A* to *Z*:

```
Select(0u0041, 0u005a);
```

What the `Select()` function does is allow selecting character groups with pairs of references, the first of character of the list, and then the last of the list. All characters in the interval will be selected. If you want to select only one glyph, specify only one reference; if you want to select a single glyph inside a list of intervals, you should simply specify the same start and end points for the glyph. Here is the code that will allow you to export our SVG font as we need it:

```
Select(0u0030, 0u0039, 0u0041, 0u005A, 0u0061, 0u007a, 0u00ab, 0u00ab, 0u00bb);
SelectInvert();
Cut();
Generate("exported.svg");
SelectNone();
Revert();
```

This code exports the 0–9, a–z, and A–Z sets, together with left and right angle quotes. Then, we invert our selections to use the `Cut()` function and delete our unused glyphs from the font. Naturally, be careful to enter a correct path for the `Generate()` function. To finalize our script, we cancel our selection and revert to the initial font to avoid accidents. Your font file should now be notably lighter.

Note that if you want to use only uppercase letters, you should be careful that all your text is written in capital letters or, better yet, let a style rule take care of this for you:

```
.upper {
    text-transform: uppercase;
}
```

Nonetheless, remember that fonts imported with @font-face have some limitations in WebKit browsers. The main one is that, even if you have imported the uppercase glyphs, you won't be able to give the font-variant the small-caps value. Although the specification explicitly notes that user agents should use scaled uppercase letters for small capitals if these are not defined, WebKit simply ignores @font-face-defined typefaces if a font-variant rule is set and reverts to the default inherited font.

```
.small-caps {
    font-size: 0.71em;           /* Reduce text */
    text-transform: uppercase;
}

.small-caps::first-letter {
    font-size: 1.41em;           /* Reset to 100% of the inherited font-size */
}
```

Although this solution covers only the first letter, it can be enough for quite a few uses. Another limitation that you should keep in mind is that, unlike fonts that are already installed on the system of the user, web fonts have to be downloaded (on the first visit, they may be cached). This can be long, because SVG fonts are inherently heavier than TTF or OTF and take more time to be rendered, especially if your font is complex and depends on a lot of code. Beware that Mobile Safari might freeze, and always limit this practice to reasonable file sizes.

Summary

The examples used in this chapter gave you only a glimpse of what can be done with canvas and vector graphics. However useful the spinner we have created can be—used in association with Ajax, for instance, to give feedback to the user—we have used small amounts of code and simple, repetitive shapes. If you have some experience with some vector graphics creation software, you will soon see what possibilities SVG support can offer you. The use of canvas also has huge potential, for those who prefer scripting to graphic design. Also, look into our following chapters about video and animations, which help you bring your graphics to life.

We are going to use these technologies in following chapters, for instance in Chapter 14 to build a compass, and in Chapter 12, where our spinner will be used to give the user feedback during Ajax requests. Work your way into the richness of these new features, but always ask yourself which solution is best between the two and whether either is better than another alternative, for instance, a CSS-based solution. As for bitmap images, Flash, and most things on the Web, use them when they will create a better user experience.

## Chapter 8

Embedding Audio and Video Content in Your Web Application

As we have stated before, Mobile Safari doesn't support Flash content. iOS, however, is an extraordinary multimedia platform that inherits the quality of the iPod for audio and video content. That the YouTube application is shipped by default on the OS is symptomatic of the importance given to multimedia both by Apple and by third-party web sites. The number of companies that optimize their sites for the iPhone and the iPad is ever growing, such as Vimeo (as shown on Figure 8–1), where the popular Adobe Flash content is replaced by H.264 videos, the format pushed by Apple. Even YouTube is providing a new mobile version of its web site, surpassing the iPhone built-in native application using the new HTML5 features.

Many signs indicate that web actors are taking alternate web-specific formats more and more seriously—even Adobe has implemented H.264 in its Flash Player. This movement also follows from the excellent support of the latest web standards by mobile browsers such as Mobile Safari, which allows for efficient support of multimedia content. Indeed, as you are going to see, Apple no longer advises you to use the <embed> tag under Safari and recommends you use the new HTML5 <audio> and <video> tags, which come with solid APIs that will let you control many aspects of the playing and collect real-time information on the state of the content using a full range of events.

Figure 8–1. *The iPad-optimized web application by Vimeo*

> **NOTE:** To illustrate this chapter, we are going to use the great animation film *Big Buck Bunny* (Creative Common license, © Blender Foundation) that you can download in many formats— including iPhone—from www.bigbuckbunny.org.

Before HTML5, because there was no standard to embed media content into a web page, browsers usually resorted to external plug-ins, possibly requiring installation by the user, which wouldn't be possible under Mobile Safari. This is no longer necessary— it's up to you to get started.

Embedding Video Content

Video probably is the most popular media on the Web nowadays. Even if you don't produce your own content, you can easily add media to your site. Using YouTube, for instance, this is easily done with code similar to the following:

```
<a href="http://www.youtube.com/v/VIDEO_IDENTIFIER">
    <img src="poster.jpg" alt="Breaking News Video Poster">
</a>
```

VIDEO_IDENTIFIER is the value for the v parameter found in all YouTube video URLs. However, embedding such video content in this way will launch the YouTube application, and at the end of the sequence, the user will be left inside this application.

Of course, building your web app, your aim will be to keep the user inside the application as long as possible and make the experience as close as possible to that of a native application. With HTML5, playing media directly from inside the browser is as easy as using the new <video> tag. This is a simple though rich way to embed video content, similar in some aspects to the formerly used <embed> tag, with which it shares several attributes.

```
<video src="myvideo.m4v" poster="preview.png"
    id="myvideo" width="320" height="240"></video>
```

As with the <canvas> tag, the default size for <video> tag is 300 pixels wide and 150 pixels high, and you should specify any other dimensions using the width and height attributes. If the ratio of the movie is different from that of the defined area, black stripes will be displayed along the unoccupied space, and the video will be resized, keeping its initial ratio. Unfortunately, there is no way to change the color of the stripes, such as by applying a background color, as you might expect.

By default, the <video> tag is an inline element, and it should be closed as in our example; if not, the code that follows it will be considered to be fallback content. As you'll see soon, the <video> tag can contain not only fallback information but also other tags, such as an <object> or <embed> tag, or other elements that let you refine the media type definition and bring additional functionality to enhance simple playing.

Getting Information About the Video

If for some reason you do not specifically know the initial ratio of the movie you are embedding, you can access this information using the properties of the HTMLVideoElement object and, for instance, adjust the size of your container appropriately. This could prove useful if you use a default format for your movie but offer several formats based on the connection speed of the user's device.

> **NOTE:** Using the width and height properties in the adjustVideo() function, the returned values are those of their attribute counterparts. However, if these values are not set or are set using a percentage, the returned values will not be exploitable. Therefore, we prefer the DOM offsetWidth and offsetHeight properties.

```
var video = document.getElementById("myvideo");
video.addEventListener("loadedmetadata", adjustVideo, false);

function adjustVideo(event) {
    var video = event.target;

    /* Intrinstic size (read only) */
```

```
        var vw = video.videoWidth;
        var vh = video.videoHeight;

        /* Element size */
        var ew = video.offsetWidth;     // Could be video.width
        var eh = video.offsetHeight;    // Could be video.height

        /* adjust container size if needed */
        var vratio = vw / vh;
        var eratio = ew / eh;

        if (vratio != eratio){
            video.height = ew / vratio;
        }
}
```

If the browser hasn't downloaded a minimum of information to identify the video, the data specific to the movie won't be available. The `preload` attribute—which indicates that the video metadata should be preloaded with the HTML page—is currently not supported by Mobile Safari, primarily to limit HTTP traffic. This kind of information will be accessible only once the `loadedmetadata` event is raised. The API attached to the new HTML5 media tags offer many other specific events, such as `timeupdate`, that will let us handle custom subtitles. We'll cover them later in the chapter.

The Video Placeholder

On Mobile Safari, no data regarding the video is downloaded until the video is launched—at least nothing that can be of any use to you. As you wait for this data, if the `poster` attribute is set, the defined image will be used as a placeholder, with the same image ratio as the movie itself. Of course, the image you choose should be as representative as possible of the video. If no image is defined or the source URL is wrong, on both the iPhone and the iPod touch a blue gradient will be used as a placeholder, as shown in Figure 8–2.

Figure 8–2. *The default video placeholder on the iPhone*

This is true for versions of the OS prior to 3.2, but with the latest versions (including 3.2 that ships with the recent iPad), if no `poster` attribute is specified, the whole video area will appear black, with no other indication. This is probably because one of the great steps taken by the iPad is that you can play movies directly in the browser, without launching the QuickTime Player full-screen as would happen with earlier versions. Hence, you can create media content that integrates into your page, and the neutral black can make this operation more versatile.

Playing the Video

On the iPhone and iPod touch, to play a video, the user has to tap the placeholder, which will launch the external player (Figure 8–3). Naturally, as we leave the browser context, you may assume that all events attached to the tag will be lost. This actually isn't true. The use of an external player doesn't prevent events related to the videos or actions upon videos to be executed, such as resizing the container, as shown earlier.

Figure 8–3. *The QuickTime media player on the iPhone*

On the iPad, using the `<video>` tag will not yield the same results. The movie won't launch automatically, and nothing will happen if you tap the placeholder. To allow the video to be played, you will have to either add the `controls` attribute, which indicates that the player should display standard controls visible to the user, or use the `play()` method on the video object to launch the video dynamically. The first way, the player will have a play button, as on previous versions. When controls are enabled, they cover part of the movie (as shown in Figure 8–4), but they disappear automatically after a few seconds, making the experience seamless for the end user, as with most modern media application nowadays.

```
<video src="myvideo.mp4" poster="preview.png"
    id="myvideo" width="320" height="240" controls></video>

<!-- Handle video playing using javascript -->
<button onclick="document.getElementById('myvideo').play()">Watch Video</button>
```

Figure 8–4. *With controls enabled, a play icon appears on the video. Pressing the button launches the movie and shows other controls*

Note that the video element itself doesn't support the onclick event so that it doesn't interfere with these controls, even if it is enclosed in some other container. This is why you use a separate button, which should be outside the video placeholder.

Whatever solution you choose, the video can be launched only after an action by the end user. The autoplay attribute is supported only in a very specific case, which we'll explain later in this chapter. The same limitations apply to the play() method, which means you couldn't use a window.setTimeout() method to launch your video after a delay. This most likely is because when using cellular networks, it is still common to be charged per data unit, and being charged a fortune because a web application designer has made you download a heavy file without your consent is bad user experience.

Embedding Audio Content

The <embed> tag used to be recommended not only for video but also for audio content. With HTML5, this has changed, because a new elegant solution is now offered to developers, as shown here:

```
<audio src="myaudo.mp3" id="myaudio"></audio>
```

The associated DOM interface is HTMLAudioElement, and you can easily create an audio object dynamically with JavaScript, with the usual createElement() DOM method but also using a new HTML5 constructor that takes a source URL as a parameter. The benefit of this method is that, because only sound is involved, the element can be initialized and played immediately without being added to the document tree.

```
var audio1 = document.createElement("audio");    // DOM way
var audio2 = new Audio("myaudio.mp3");           // HTML5 way
```

Because there is no image or sequence to display, the width and height attributes are not supported. The block will default to a block that's 200 pixels by 16 pixels. On the iPhone and iPod touch, the same placeholder as for the <video> tag will be shown with these dimensions, which allows the audio content to be launched by tapping and allows it to be resized using styles. This placeholder is the only way to launch sound on the device without resorting to JavaScript.

On the iPad, the configuration is slightly different. The default display for the <audio> tag is a plain blank area, which will be replaced by proper controls (Figure 8–5) when the controls attribute is set, as shown with the <video> tag. With controls enabled, sound control is rendered with the default dimensions or with the dimensions defined by any style rules. Be aware, however, that the controls can be made wider but cannot be forced to be taller. If you specify a height value larger than 16 pixels, the controls will simply be aligned vertically inside the defined area.

Figure 8–5. *The iPad audio controls*

In either case, the audio player isn't specially attractive. Finding an alternative solution would allow you to both enhance the user experience and unify the cross-device experience—without resorting to the DOMWindow navigator.platform or navigator.userAgent property. You can easily attach an event to an image, such as an album cover, and launch the play() method for your <audio> tag this way.

Keep Things Reasonable

As you have seen, it has become extremely easy to embed audio content into your pages. Be careful, however, not to overdo it. If you want to display a list of videos on a page, for instance, as is done on YouTube or Vimeo (see Figure 8–6), we don't recommend using a <video> tag for each element. Because on the iPhone and iPod touch tapping the player launches QuickTime, you could be tempted to do this to make accessing your content easier. Nonetheless, you should be aware that multiplying media tags on the same page can considerably slow down navigation and make the browser less snappy.

Instead, you could display a list of images, each one sending the user to a dedicated play page. This will enhance user experience, especially for iPad users who will play the video directly in the browser and expect a viewing experience superior to that provided by a small-sized video in a thumbnail list.

Figure 8–6. *A video list in the YouTube web application*

Take Control Over Your Content

As stated earlier, once the user has launched the video or audio content, you can gather information about this content. The API bound to the new HTML5 media tags ships with a whole range of new DOM events that will let you know exactly what is going on while media content is played.

To illustrate some of the possibilities offered by the API, we are going to create a page that will display real-time information about the state of a playing movie. Mainly, we will use the `TimeRanges` object—used in the `HTMLMediaElement` interface from which the video and audio objects inherit—and its attached properties for the audio and video objects.

This interface is very simple, containing only a `length` property that holds information about the number of available ranges, and two methods, `start()` and `end()`, that give data in seconds about the range with the index passed as a parameter. If an error occurs with this parameter, that is, if it is out of range, an `INDEX_SIZE_ERR` exception will be thrown.

Understanding and Using Ranges

The HTMLMediaElement interface has several properties, including buffered, which gives information about the state of downloaded data available to play the media content, and played, which indicates the already played ranges. Note that in Mobile Safari, it is most often considered that the played property has only one range.

The seekable property, which also uses the TimeRanges object, indicates which ranges are seekable by the browser. We are not going to use it here, because it generally returns a range equal to the range from the startTime property (for the video object) to the duration property. Cases where this is not true include media on web servers that do not support *HTTP range* that allows for partial download—which is used, for instance, to let users resume an interrupted download. Also, on older versions of the iOS, the range will be set to the available buffer and will raise an INDEX_SIZE_ERR if you try to set the currentTime property out of this range.

> **NOTE:** Although media is played directly in the browser on the iPad, information is updated also on the other iOS devices. Nonetheless, with versions prior to 3.2, the played property holds no range, which shouldn't be a problem because it is generally preferable to use the startTime and currentTime properties to get the play position.

For our example, let's start with the HTML markup of our application:

```
<!DOCTYPE html>
<html>
    <head>
        <title>Media Demo</title>
        <meta name="viewport" content="initial-scale=1.0;
            maximum-scale=1.0; user-scalable=no">

        <link rel="stylesheet" href="styles/video.css">
        <script src="scripts/video.js"></script>
    </head>

    <body onload="setup()">
        <div class="info">
            <h1>Big Buck Bunny</h1>
            <p>A fantastic movie under Creative Commons License
                freely available for download to everyone.</p>
        </div>
        <div class="video">
            <div class="media">
                <time>Waiting...</time>
                <video src="media/BigBuckBunny_640x360.m4v"
                    width="100%" height="360" controls></video>
            </div>

            <div id="buffered"><meter></meter><mark></mark></div>
            <div id="played"></div>
        </div>
```

```
    </body>
</html>
```

Note that the <div> identified as `buffered` has two children. The first will be a progress bar attached to the buffer completion, while the second will hold an arrow indicating the current play position. The played ranges will be added to the <div> identified as `played`.

Next, we create a specific style sheet for our video pages that we unsurprisingly name *video.css*:

```css
body {
    background-color: #444;
    color: white;
    font-family: helvetica;
    text-shadow: black 2px 2px 2px;
}

.video { margin-right: 200px; }
.media { position: relative; }

.media time {
    position: absolute;
    top: 0;
    left: 0;
    right: 0;
    background-color: rgba(0, 0, 0, 0.5);
    padding: 5px;
    color: white;
    font: bold 10px verdana;
}

.media video {
    display: block;
    background: black;
    -webkit-box-shadow: 0 4px 20px black;
}

.info {
    float: right;
    width: 190px;
    font-size: 13px;
}

.info h1 { font-size: 18px; }

#buffered, #played {
    position: relative;
    background-color: black;
    -webkit-box-shadow: 0 4px 20px black;
    margin: 1px;
}

#buffered {
    background-color: #444;
}

/* Progress bars */
```

```css
meter, mark {
    display: block;
    height: 10px;
}

#buffered meter {
    background-color: gray;
    -webkit-box-sizing: border-box;
    border:1px solid black;
    border-width:0 1px;
}

/* Arrow indicator */
#buffered mark {
    position: absolute;
    border: 5px solid transparent;
    border-bottom-color: white;
    margin: -10px 0 0 -5px;
    height: 0;
}
```

Finally, this would all be pointless without the appropriate scripts to display the expected information. We create a file called *video.js* to which we add the adjustVideo() function shown earlier. Then, the first function we create is the one called with the document onload event; it initializes the watchers.

```javascript
function setup() {
    var video = document.getElementsByTagName("video")[0];

    window.setInterval(checkBuffered, 500, video);
    video.addEventListener("timeupdate", checkPlayed, false);
    video.addEventListener("loadedmetadata", adjustVideo, false);
}
```

The checkBuffered() function checks the buffer state of the video every 500 milliseconds and displays this data as a gray progress bar under the video. Using Desktop Safari, much more memory would be available, but on portable devices, the browser is allotted less memory, which means the buffer will constantly change without ever holding all the length of the movie. Also note that we use a timer because the progress event, corresponding to the update state of the buffer, is currently not supported.

```javascript
function checkBuffered(video) {
    if (video.buffered.length && video.duration) {
        var pos = calcPosition(video.buffered.start(0), ↵
            video.buffered.end(0), video.duration);

        var bar = document.getElementById("buffered");
        updateBar(bar.firstChild, pos);
    }
}
```

Next, the checkPlayed() function displays the played range, again as a progress bar under the video. In Mobile Safari, because there is never more than one already played range that spans from the beginning of the video to the current play state, only one bar will be displayed, whereas on Desktop Safari each range will be rendered independently.

Thus, a new range will be added, for instance, when you jump to another frame of the movie using the time cursor. When two ranges overlap, they are merged to make just one range and reduce the number of ranges. This is why we clear the played container with each updatetime event, making the progress bar update.

```
function checkPlayed(event) {
    var video = event.target;

    /* Update the time cursor position */
    var progress = document.getElementById("buffered");
    progress.lastChild.style.left = (video.currentTime / video.duration * 100) + "%";

    /* Update the textual video time progression */
    updateTime(video);

    /* Clear and add played ranges if any */
    var container = document.getElementById("played");
    container.innerHTML = "";

    for (var i = 0; i < video.played.length; i++) {
        var pos = calcPosition(video.played.start(i), ↵
            video.played.end(i), video.duration);

        addRange(container, pos);
    }
}

function addRange(dest, pos) {
    var bar = document.createElement("meter");
    bar.style.backgroundColor = ↵
        "hsl(" + (pos.from * 360 / 100 | 0) + ", 100%, 50%)";

    updateBar(bar, pos);
    dest.appendChild(bar);
}
```

The following functions calculate the progress and control the display of the progress bar. The first function determines the percentages required for the second to correctly position the bars in their container and visually represent the played range passed as a parameter to calcPosition().

```
function calcPosition(start, end, max) {
    return {
        from: (start / max * 100),
        to:   (end   / max * 100)
    }
}

function updateBar(bar, pos) {
    bar.style.width = (pos.to - pos.from) + "%";
    bar.style.marginLeft = pos.from + "%";
}
```

Finally, we need to handle duration. The updateTime() function evaluates the elapsed and remaining time and converts them from seconds to a more readable time format using the formatTime() function.

```
function updateTime(video) {
    if (video.duration) {
        var elapsed = video.currentTime - video.startTime;
        var state = video.paused ? "Paused" : "Playing";

        document.getElementsByTagName("time")[0].textContent = state + ": " +
            formatTime(elapsed) + " / " +
            formatTime(video.duration) + " (-" +
            formatTime(video.duration - elapsed) + ")";
    }
}

function formatTime(time) {
    /* Do we have hours? */
    var cut = time < 3600 ? 4 : 1;
    var str = "";

    for (var i = 2; i >= 0; i--) {
        var step = Math.pow(60, i);
        var part = (time / step) | 0;              // Quick way to do a Math.floor()

        time -= part * step;
        str  += ":" + ("0" + part).substr(-2);     // Add a leading 0
    }

    return str.substr(cut);
}
```

Now, open the created page in Mobile Safari—or your development browser to see multiple ranges—and launch the video. You should get a result similar to Figure 8–7.

Figure 8–7. *The time is displayed in the upper part; the buffer and playback progression are shown as bars at the bottom*

As in Mobile Safari, the video download will begin only on an action by the user. Absolutely no data will be available, including the length of the movie, until this has occurred. Once the download has begun, the information will be gathered and displayed, and the progression will be accurately represented.

A Number of Supported Events

Only a handful of available events have been covered in our previous example, and there are many more that you can use. Table 8–1 shows the complete list of supported events with their meaning on iOS. The Event object passed as a parameter to the handlers has no specific property related to the event type itself like the current playback time with the timeupdate event. The necessary data is available directly through the object receiving the event, as you have seen in the example (event.target).

Table 8–1. *List of Events Supported by Mobile Safari*

Event Name	Description
abort	The fetching has been interrupted before the browser has completed downloading the media.
emptied	An already initialized media has been reinitialized to its initial state.
play	Playback has been initiated, for instance after the user has pressed a play button.
pause	Playback has been paused, for instance after the user has pressed the pause button.
loadedmetadata	Dimensions and duration data about the media are available.
loadeddata	Data required for media playback have just been made available.
waiting	Playback has stopped because the next frame is not available.
playing	Playback has started.
canplay	Data is available for playback, without certainty that it will be playable without buffering.
canplaythrough	Data is available to play the media, and the browser estimates that it will be playable without buffering.
seeking	The browser has to find a new playback position. This event will be triggered only if the searching takes longer than is reasonable.
seeked	The browser finished seeking a new position.
timeupdate	The current playback position has changed.
ended	The playback has stopped because the media has come to an end.
ratechange	The playback rate has been modified.
durationchange	The length of the media has changed, for instance if the source of the media has been modified.
volumechange	The volume has changed. Modifying the volume using the controls on the player doesn't trigger this event.

Some behaviors for these events can be surprising. The ratechange and volumechange events are supported but are of limited use on Mobile Safari. Indeed, the associated properties on the media objects currently have no effect. Modifying the values for the properties playbackRate, defaultPlaybackRate, and volume—which should change the playback speed and volume—will trigger the event but won't affect the playback.

To implement a fast-forward function, you have to use the currentTime property, but you will not benefit from the same playback fluidity as using the properties directly affecting the playback rate.

Using the currentTime property will automatically trigger a seeked event. Technically, using currentTime changes the seeking property to true to indicate that a search is being performed. The seeked event will be sent when the property is set back to false. If the process takes more time than expected, and in this case only, a seeking event will be triggered.

The same event is also triggered when the media content comes to an end and the loop attribute on the <audio> or <video> tag is set. In such a case, the ended event is never triggered, because the playback isn't expected to stop. Therefore, you will have to manually check whether the playback is complete using the currentTime and duration properties along with the seeked event. This would be useful if you wanted the media to be looped only so many times.

Adding Subtitles and Chapters to Your Media

The HTML5 specification plans for external resources to be linkable to media content that would make media more accessible, notably for disabled users. At the time of writing, this feature is still a work in progress and hasn't been implemented in any browser. Eventually, you should be able to specify one or several resources using the <track> tag, as in the following example:

```
<video src="myvideo.mp4" poster="preview.png"
    id="myvideo" width="320" height="240">

    <track kind="subtitles"
        src="mysubtitles-us.srt" srclang="en-US" label="English Subtitles">

    <track kind="subtitles"
        src="mysubtitles-fr.srt" srclang="fr-FR" label="Sous-Titres en Français">
</video>
```

Specific attributes allow you to determine the resource types—subtitles in our example—as well as the language in use, in the BCP 47 format, similar to that returned for the browser with the navigator.language property of the window object. The label attribute contains the title for the track, which can be used in a menu to select resources. Therefore, it shouldn't be left empty, should be representative, and ideally should be different for an attribute value with the same kind value.

Creating Your Own Custom Subtitles

Because subtitles can be a desirable feature prompt to enhance user experience and make your web applications more attractive, we are going to build some code to replace the unsupported <track> tag. Of course, subtitles will be of interest only if you are targeting devices that support playing media directly inside the browser—you cannot add functionality to an external player. On the contrary, navigating through chapters will be possible on all devices, because events can be passed to the player.

From our previous examples, you learned how to gather the current playback position. Hence, you only have to find a way to insert the relevant elements into your page at the right time. For this, we are going to use a simple, widely used format for our subtitles: SRT. .srt files were initially created for the SubRip application, which is used to extract subtitles in real time from a video stream. This format is close to the WHATWG format in progress, WebSRT, and is simpler than the current W3C Timed Text Markup Language (TTML), which is why we are going to use it.

Displaying Subtitles

SRT files are text files with series of multiline blocks representing the following information:

- A period number
- The range in which the subtitle should appear
- The text of the subtitle (which can span several lines and include new lines, but no blank lines)
- A blank line indicating a new subtitle is coming

For our example, we will use an SRT file with five subtitles and allow HTML markup so we can easily transform our content:

```
1
00:00:16,000 --> 00:00:18,000
Tweet tweet! I'm a bird!

2
00:00:19,500 --> 00:00:20,000
Tweeet... <span>Ouch!</span>

3
00:00:20,000 --> 00:00:21,000
Tweeet... Ouch!

4
00:00:47,000 --> 00:00:50,000
Oh, it's already morning.
What a beautiful day!

5
00:01:03,000 --> 00:01:05,000
Humm, that smells nice... what is it?
```

Obviously, these subtitles are of limited interest, but they are enough to convey speech to our animated characters. Still using the *Big Buck Bunny* movie, we are going to explore the possibilities offered by this solution.

First, let's define a style sheet that will allow us to make text evolve, such as between subtitles 2 and 3. We want the text ("Tweeet...") not to flicker when the "Ouch!" part appears after a few seconds. In the style sheet from the previous example, add the following:

```
#textual span {
    visibility: hidden;
}
```

Of course, you'll also need generic styles to position and style the subtitles. You will place them at the bottom of the video and apply a `text-shadow` so that the text remains readable no matter what the rendered video image is.

```
#textual {
    position: absolute;
    left: 0;
    right: 0;
    bottom: 16px;
    text-align: center;
    color: white;
    font-weight: bold;
    text-shadow:
        black 0 0 3px,
        black 1px 1px 2px;
}
```

Next, let's modify the HTML code to add the container for the subtitles (with the ID textual):

```
...
<div class="media">
    <div id="time">Waiting...</div>
    <video src="media/BigBuckBunny_640x360.m4v"
        width="100%" height="360" controls>

        <track kind="subtitles"
            src="srt/subtitles-us.srt" srclang="en-US" label="English Subtitles">

        <track kind="subtitles"
            src="srt/subtitles-fr.srt" srclang="fr-FR" label="Sous-Titres en Français">

    </video>
    <div id="textual">(Press Play)</div>
</div>
...
```

Now, you'll put this altogether, using JavaScript:

```
var TimedInfo = function(media, container) {
    this.owner = media;
    this.element = container;

    /* Active track */
```

```
        this.current = 0;

        /* Self initialization */
        this.parse();
        var that = this;
        this.owner.addEventListener("timeupdate", function() {
            that.shouldDisplay();
        }, false);
    }

    TimedInfo.prototype.parse = function() {
        var tracks = this.owner.getElementsByTagName("track");

        /* Push all available tracks information */
        this.data = [];
        for (var i = 0; i < tracks.length; i++) {
            this.data.push({
                src:   tracks[i].getAttribute("src"),
                label: tracks[i].getAttribute("label") || "Untitled",
                readyState: 0
            });
        }
    }

    TimedInfo.prototype.loadResource = function(index) {
        var that = this;
        var req = new XMLHttpRequest();
        req.open("get", this.data[index].src);
        req.onreadystatechange = function() { that.handleAsyncState(this, index) };
        req.send();
    }

    TimedInfo.prototype.handleAsyncState = function(req, index) {
        if (req.readyState == 4) {
            if (req.status != 200) {
                this.data[index].readyState = 3;
            } else {
                this.data[index].srt = this.extract(req.responseText);
                this.data[index].readyState = 2;
                this.shouldDisplay();
            }
        }
    }

    TimedInfo.prototype.extract = function(text) {
        var i, j, res = [];
        var parts = text.split("\n\n");

        /* Iterate through each block */
        while ((i = parts.shift())) {

            /* Split the block lines ... */
            i = i.split("\n");
            j = i[1].split(" --> ");

            /* ... and take the time information (start and end) */
            for (var n = 0; n < 2; n++) {
```

```
                j[n] = j[n].split(":");

                for (var t = 0, m = 0; m < 3; m++) {
                    t = t * 60 + 1 * j[n][m].replace(",", ".");
                }

                j[n] = t;
            }

            /* Push information */
            res.push({ time: j, text: i.slice(2).join("<br>") });
        }

        return res;
    }

    TimedInfo.prototype.shouldDisplay = function() {
        if (!this.checkReadyState(this.current)) {
            return;
        }

        /* Data have been loaded */
        var st = this.data[this.current].srt;
        var ct = this.owner.currentTime - this.owner.startTime;

        /* Look for a suitable subtitle */
        this.element.innerHTML = "";
        for (var i = 0; i < st.length; i++) {
            if (ct >= st[i].time[0] && ct < st[i].time[1]) {
                this.element.innerHTML = st[i].text;
                break;
            }
        }
    }

    TimedInfo.prototype.checkReadyState = function(index) {
        if (index == -1) {
            return false;
        }

        /* Check whether the data is available */
        switch (this.data[index].readyState) {
            case 0:
                this.loadResource(index);
                this.data[index].readyState = 1;
            case 1:
            case 3:
                return false;
        }

        return true;
    }
```

This is quite a chunk of code. You create an object, TimedInfo, partly inspired by the
TimedTrack object from the HTML5 specifications. This object will read the <track> tags
related to the media passed to the constructor and then display the subtitles using a

handler on the timeupdate event. This way, the subtitles will appear appropriately both in play mode and in seek mode.

You can initiate an instance of the object simply by passing the media object and the container for the subtitles. The constructor will keep these parameters, get the required data on the tracks using the parse() method, and then register for timeupdate notifications and display subtitles appropriately using the shouldDisplay() method.

```
var ti = new TimedInfo(mediaObject, containerObject);
```

The parse() method will read the attributes from the tracks and collect them in the data array. Because at this moment no data is available, we add a readyState property set to 0, indicating that the resource has not been downloaded.

When a timeupdate event is triggered, the shouldDisplay() method checks whether the active resource is available. If this isn't the case, it asks for the SRT file to be downloaded using the loadResource() method and changes the readyState property to 1, showing that a download request has been initiated. As long as the resource is unavailable, the shouldDisplay() method simply waits. Once the data is loaded, the method looks for the subtitle relevant to the current playback time and displays it if any.

The XMLHttpRequest object, which we will detail in a coming chapter, is used by loadResource() to launch the resource download in asynchronous mode. Once the request has completed, the handleAsyncState() function extracts the data returned by the server via the responseText property and passes them to extract(), which will split the SRT file and return an array with organized data.

Once this object is added to the *video.js* file, you simply have to modify the setup() function created earlier and add the following lines:

```
var timed; // Globally stored for future use

function setup() {
...
    timed = new TimedInfo(video, document.getElementById("textual"));
}
```

Launching your page in Mobile Safari will show you the movie, with subtitles corresponding to the played picture, as shown in Figure 8–8.

Paused: 00:17 / 09:56 (-09:38)

Tweet tweet! I'm a bird!

Figure 8–8. *Real-life subtitles*

Language Auto-selection

You have used only a few attributes of the <track> tag, and you are using only the first <track> tag in the HTML code, although you have gathered all those that were defined. With the following code, you'll use the srclang attribute to automatically select a language for the subtitles depending on the browser language. The information will be saved to the array.

```
TimedInfo.prototype.parse = function() {
...
    for (var i = 0; i < tracks.length; i++) {
        var l1 = tracks[i].getAttribute("srclang");
        var l2 = window.navigator.language;
        if (l1.toLowerCase() == l2.toLowerCase()) {
            this.current = i;
        }

        this.data.push({
            language: l1,
...
        });
    }
}
```

To test this code, you simply have to add the language relative to your browser in the second position in the <video> tag and create the associated SRT files. Here is the French version of the subtitles:

```
1
00:00:16,000 --> 00:00:18,000
Cui cui ! Je suis un oiseau !

2
```

```
00:00:19,500 --> 00:00:20,000
Cuuiii... <span>Aïe !</span>

3
00:00:20,000 --> 00:00:21,000
Tweeet... Ouch!

4
00:00:47,000 --> 00:00:50,000
Oh, et bien c'est déjà le jour.
Quelle belle journée !

5
00:01:03,000 --> 00:01:05,000
Humm, ça sent bon... Qu'est-ce que c'est ?
```

Don't forget to check the language for your browser to appropriately set the srclang attribute for your tests. You can easily check this by typing window.navigator.language in the console.

Let the End User Choose

Automatic selection is good, but, as usual, letting users choose for themselves is better. This is why you'll now add methods to get the list of tracks available for a given kind and activate the track you want.

The specifications allow for several values for this attribute, as presented in Table 8–2. These values can give you ideas of what you can create while waiting for proper support for this feature. Of course, some keywords will be hard to implement, because they are tightly related to the system and the ability to communicate with it, such as the descriptions value.

Table 8–2. *The kind Keywords As Defined by the HTML5 Specification*

Keyword	Description
subtitles	A translation for the media used when the sound is present but not understood
captions	Transcription of the soundtrack in case the sound is muted and for disabled viewers
descriptions	Transcription of the images displayed, for use with vocal synthesizers for blind people
chapters	Chaptering meant to make parts of the media more easily accessible
metadata	Tracks defined by the developer to be used with scripts

In the parse() method, you do not gather information for the kind attribute. You do that with the following code to filter the track types:

```
TimedInfo.prototype.parse = function() {
...
    this.data.push({
        kind: tracks[i].getAttribute("kind"),
        src: tracks[i].getAttribute("src"),
        label: tracks[i].getAttribute("label") || "Untitled",
        language: l1,
        readyState: 0
    });
...
}
```

Next, let's add two simple methods that get the list of available tracks for a defined kind and activate the relevant resource. The activate() method will add a class to the container for the textual data based on the kind to eventually add different styles depending on its value.

```
TimedInfo.prototype.getFilteredIndex = function(kind) {
    var list = [];

    for (var i = 0; i < this.data.length; i++) {
        if (this.data[i].kind == kind) {
            list.push(i);
        }
    }

    return list;
}

TimedInfo.prototype.activate = function(index) {
    if (index >= 0 && index < this.data.length) {
        this.current = index;
        this.element.className = this.data[this.current].kind;
    }
}
```

From here, you can build a select box from the data returned by getFilteredIndex():

```
function buildList() {
    var list = timed.getFilteredIndex("subtitles");
    var select = document.createElement("select");

    for (var i = 0; i < list.length; i++) {
        var index = list[i];
        var option = document.createElement("option");

        option.textContent = timed.data[index].label;
        option.value = index;
        option.selected = (timed.current == option.value);

        select.appendChild(option);
    }

    select.onchange = selectionChanged;
    return select;
}

function selectionChanged(event) {
```

```
        timed.activate(event.target.value);
}
```

The `buildList()` function creates a `<select>` element populated with the labels from the tracks, directly reading the `data` property from the `TimedInfo` object. Because now the language is selected automatically when the `parse()` method is initialized, you just have to activate the associated `option` not to display the wrong information to the user. A handler is added to the `<select>` tag to immediately change the language when the section is modified.

You can now modify the HTML code to add the list container to receive the `<select>` tag:

```
<div class="info">
...
    <form id="list"></form>
</div>
```

Here are the rules to style the select box and position it above the video on the right:

```
#list {
    height: 20px;
    border: 1px solid gray;
    -webkit-border-radius:4px;
    -webkit-box-shadow:2px 2px 4px black;
    background-image:-webkit-gradient(
        linear, left bottom, left top,
        from(transparent), to(rgba(255,255,255,0.2))
    );
}

#list select {
    border: 0;
    background: none;
    color: white;
    font-size: 13px;
    line-height: 18px;
    text-shadow: black 1px 1px 1px;
}

/* Create a small arrow on the left */
#list::before {
    content: '';
    display: inline-block;
    width: 10px;
    height: 10px;
    margin-right: -10px;
    border: 5px solid transparent;
    border-left-color: gray;
    -webkit-box-sizing: border-box;
}
```

On Mobile Safari, the `<select>` element can be fully styled. You can, for instance, remove the border and arrow, as we do here.

The final touch is to call the function `buildList()` and add the returned object to the markup. Once more, you alter the `setup()` function, adding a line at the end:

```
function setup() {
...
    document.getElementById("list").appendChild(buildList());
}
```

Now, test all of this in your browser; it should look something like Figure 8–9.

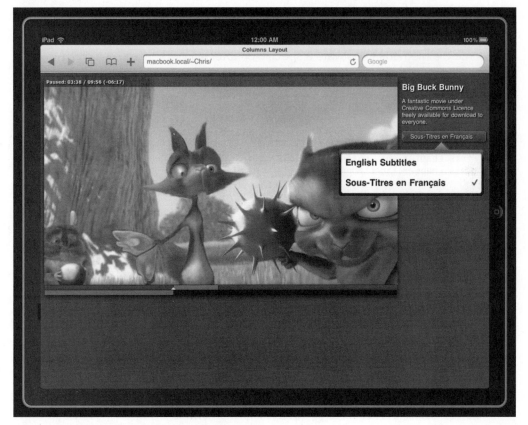

Figure 8–9. *The user can easily select a language now*

As you can see, the default `<select>` on the iPad doesn't need any further styling.

Easier Media Browsing with Chapters

With the previous examples, you are already adding appreciable functionality to the default media implementation. To make the experience closer still to that of a proper media player application, we are now going to offer the user the possibility to move from one part of the media to another specifically or to load several sounds in the same media tag and trigger one or another for some action by the user. We are going to continue expanding the previous example.

First, add an object to the JavaScript code that will handle tracks with the chapter type:

```
TimedInfo = function(media, container) {
...
    /* Active track */
    this.current = 0;
    this.chapter = { index: -1 };
...
}
```

Then come the methods to activate a specific chapter (number) based on a given resource (index):

```
TimedInfo.prototype.play = function(index, number, shouldStop) {
    /* Don't request twice the same chapter while loading SRT file */
    if (index != this.chapter.index || number != this.chapter.number) {
        this.chapter.index = index;
        this.chapter.number = number;
        this.chapter.shouldStop = shouldStop;
        this.chapter.timeChanged = false;

        this.handleChapter();
    }
}

TimedInfo.prototype.handleChapter = function() {
    if (!this.checkReadyState(this.chapter.index)) {
        return;
    }

    var nb = this.chapter.number - 1;
    var st = this.data[this.chapter.index].srt;

    /* We have data, we can set the current position */
    if (!this.chapter.timeChanged) {
        if (this.owner.paused) {
            this.owner.play();
        }
        if (this.owner.readyState == this.owner.HAVE_NOTHING) {
            return;
        }
        this.owner.currentTime = this.owner.startTime + st[nb].time[0];
        this.chapter.timeChanged = true;
    }

    /* If we have to stop at the end of the chapter */
    if (this.chapter.shouldStop) {
        var ct = this.owner.currentTime - this.owner.startTime;
        var et = st[nb].time[1];

        if (ct >= et) {
            this.chapter = { index: -1 };
            this.owner.pause();
        }
    }
}
```

The handleChapter() method is the trickiest because you must consider many parameters. As shown previously, you must download the SRT file asynchronously, but you must also handle the state of the media data to avoid getting an INVALID_STATE_ERR exception when fixing the currentTime property.

> **NOTE:** The decompression algorithm integrated into the device doesn't allow for precise positioning. You may have to move your timing a few seconds forward to get the exact place. The position written in currentTime isn't guaranteed, though there is no problem reading this property.

First, you check whether the video is being played, reading the paused property, and launch the playback if necessary. Then, you check the state of the readyState property, which must at least have a value of 1 (HAVE_METADATA), the minimal value indicating that data is available for playback (see Table 8–3). If the value is lower, the previously noted error will be raised. From there, we can set the reading position depending on the data of the chosen chapter.

Setting a value for currentTime that doesn't fit into the ranges seekable by the browser will throw an INDEX_SIZE_ERR exception on the iPhone and iPod touch. However, on the iPad, the browser will begin downloading a new range to make reading at the indicated position possible.

Table 8–3. *Possible Values for the* readyState *Property*

Constant	Description
media.HAVE_NOTHING (0)	No information about the media is available.
media.HAVE_METADATA (1)	The available data is enough to determine the duration of the media. For videos, dimensions are also known. The available data is not sufficient to play the media.
media.HAVE_CURRENT_DATA (2)	The available data is sufficient to play the current position of the media but not to move forward in it.
media.HAVE_FUTURE_DATA (3)	Enough data has been gathered to play the media without immediately interrupting.
media.HAVE_ENOUGH_DATA (4)	There is enough data to correctly play the media.

The shouldStop property determines whether the playback should stop after the chapter is completed. If it is set to true, we test the value for currentTime to tell whether the playback has reached the end of the video and use the pause() method if it has. To handle this option, handleChapter() has to be called too during the timeupdate event. To achieve this, you have to group both methods in the same handler.

```
TimedInfo.prototype.handleTracks = function() {
    this.handleChapter();
    this.shouldDisplay();
}
```

Of course, you must modify the listener with this new handler:

```
TimedInfo = function(media, container) {
...
    /* Self initialization */
    this.parse();
    var that = this;
    this.owner.addEventListener("timeupdate", function() {
        that.handleTracks();
    }, false);
}

TimedInfo.prototype.handleAsyncState = function(req, index) {
...
        } else {
            this.data[index].srt = this.extract(req.responseText);
            this.data[index].readyState = 2;
            this.handleTracks();
        }
...
}
```

Finally, you must prevent the activation of a chapter as a subtitle:

```
TimedInfo.prototype.parse = function() {
...
    if (tracks[i].getAttribute("kind") != "chapters" &&
        l1.toLowerCase() == l2.toLowerCase()) {
        this.current = i;
    }
...
}
```

This way, if you modify the HTML code to add a reference to a chaptering resource, it won't be selected by mistake.

```
<video src="BigBuckBunny_640x360.m4v" width="100%" height="360" controls>

    <track kind="subtitles"
        src="subtitles-us.srt" srclang="en-US" label="English Subtitles">

    <track kind="subtitles"
        src="subtitles-fr.srt" srclang="fr-FR" label="Sous-Titres en Français">

    <track kind="chapters"
        src="srt/chapters-us.srt" srclang="en-US" label="English Chapters">
</video>
```

By now, you can display a list of chapters using something similar to the buildList() function used to display subtitle options and launch the chapter using the play() method of the TimedInfo object. With our previous code, you could, for instance, have the following SRT file:

```
1
00:00:00,000 --> 00:00:24,000
In the begining...

2
00:00:24,900 --> 00:00:50,300
The rabbit wakes up.
```

You would then activate the second chapter using code similar to this:

```
<button onclick="timed.play(2, 2, false)">The rabbit wakes up.</button>
```

However, on Mobile Safari, jumping directly to a specific chapter will be possible only if the playback is initiated by an action by the user, as explained earlier. Because media resources are downloaded asynchronously, the actual play() call is deferred from the action by the user and therefore will not be applied. Still, as soon as the user launches the media, this code will work.

Workarounds...Let's Go

Automatic playing of a media resource is not supposed to be possible on Mobile Safari, because an action by the user should be required to start playback. This can be annoying, because you may want to automatically play, for instance, a sound file, considering that it could be no larger than an average image file. Your sound file thus would be rather quickly downloaded, as quickly as other files that wouldn't suffer any restriction. You can work around this limitation on iOS 3.2 (and newer) using the load() method. This method forces the media to be downloaded, which will make it automatically playable, using code such as the following. Note that you may have to wait a short time for some buffer before to call play().

```
var audio = document.getElementsByTagName("audio")[0];
audio.load();
audio.play();
```

Hence, to launch a chapter immediately after the SRT has been loaded, you would simply have to add a call to the load() method in the setup() function.

```
function setup() {
    var video = document.getElementsByTagName("video")[0];
    video.load();
...
}
```

In reality, the browser always downloads minimal information to check the integrity of the media, which is how you can get a ruled-out play button (Figure 8–10) on your player when the format related to the src attribute is not supported by Mobile Safari. The browser also sets the networkState property to 1 (NEWTWORK_IDLE), indicating that a resource is active although the network isn't in use at that precise moment. This, however, doesn't trigger any event, not even loadedmetadata, until the user taps the play button, initiating the actual download of playable data.

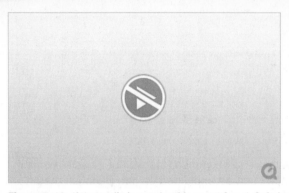

Figure 8–10. *If the media is not playable or not found, Safari will display a ruled-out play button*

When the load() method is called, the browser will first check the networkState and, if it is not set to 0 (NETWORK_EMPTY, indicating that the element hasn't been initialized), will reset it and successively send two events—abort and then emptied—and restart the initialization from the beginning. Finally, once the resource has been validated, it will resume the download of the metadata and of the data necessary for playback.

Using this method, you will be able to launch your audio and video media without the previously presented restrictions. Nonetheless, be aware that Mobile Safari can play media only one at a time, because some media can be played only using the hardware directly, meaning several sources cannot be simultaneously decoded. This means you cannot, for instance, overlay several sound effects.

Media Content for the iPhone and iPad

On a computer, Safari can handle many different audio and video formats using a number of codecs from third-party sources, but iOS supports only a few. Nevertheless, most of the supported formats are based on very rich standards, with widespread implementation. They are also quite easy to use, once you can tell the specificities for each.

Understanding Video Formats

Video decoding is a very resource-hungry operation, which is why the iPhone uses a specific chip that decodes video bitstreams directly from the hardware. This is much more lightweight than using the main processor and thus saves precious battery lifetime.

WARNING: The use of the H.264 codec is subject to royalties, be it for the distribution or the use of video content. As a video content producer, you should be sure that you have the appropriate license for your needs, which will not ship with the video compression software that you may be using to produce H.264-readable media. All Apple and Adobe software comes with a license to benefit from the codec for personal and noncommercial use. However, the Internet Broadcast AVC Video license specifies that the distribution of content for free won't be subject to royalties until 2015. If you are specifically interested in this subject, you may get thorough information from the MPEG LA site at `www.mpegla.com`.

Table 8–4 presents the currently supported characteristics that will allow you to appropriately configure you video creation software.

Table 8–4. *Supported Video Formats*

Video/Audio	Max Bit Rate	Max Format	Frame/Channel	Video Profile	Container
H.264 AAC-LC	1.5 Mbps 160 Kbps	640x480 48 KHz	30 fps stereo audio	Low-Complexity of the Baseline Profile	.m4v, .mp4, .mov
H.264 AAC-LC	2.5 Mbps 160 Kbps	640x480 48 KHz	30 fps stereo audio	Baseline Profile Level 3.0	.m4v, .mp4, .mov
MPEG-4 AAC-LC	2.5 Mbps 160 Mbps	640x480 48 KHz	30 fps stereo audio	Simple Profile	.m4v, .mp4, .mov
H.264 AAC-LC	14 Mbps 160 Kbps	1280x720 48 KHz	30 fps stereo audio	(iPad only) Main Profile Level 3.1 in 720p	.m4v, .mp4, .mov
M-JPEG PCM	35 Mbps	1280x720 μ-law coding	30 fps stereo audio	(iPad only) Motion JPEG	.avi

H.264 is often referred to as MPEG-4/AVC or MPEG-4 Part 10. This is not the same as MPEG-4 (Part 2) in the table, which depends on a different industry standard and uses a different compression method. However, the supported formats globally are MPEG-4 standards, which are widely used nowadays and also used in the 3GP format, a low-quality video format often used for multimedia mobile services, because it is easily readable on mobile networks and is widely supported by mobile phones. The M-JPEG is widespread on numeric cameras with video capabilities.

The associated profiles and levels determine the specificities supported with the format, such as compression modes, bitrates and framerates, maximum resolution, and so on. iOS's support for levels is incomplete, which is why the highest possible value is indicated in the table.

Of course, you don't have to understand every detail about these codecs to use them. Be aware, however, that the *Low-Complexity Baseline Profile* isn't part of the MPEG-4/AVC standard but is a simplified variant of the *Baseline Profile* with only one reference frame. The compression of videos is based upon the differences between one or more frames in the video and save this difference only, thus making the amount of data to hold lesser. With a reference frame, the picture to be displayed is solely calculated from one frame, which also simplifies the decoding process but entails lesser compression efficiency and lower quality.

The soundtrack for video media uses Advanced Audio Coding – Low Complexity (AAC-LC), the most commonly used nowadays. AAC is a lossy compression format that follows MP3 but produces a better-quality sound with similar bitrate and more flexibility. However, as with MPEG-4, support isn't full and is limited to a sample rate of 48KHz in stereo, as with MP3, where AAC itself can reach 96kHz with 48 channels—for a much better quality. AAC, unlike MPEG-4, isn't subject to any license for distribution, and media using it can be freely distributed, whatever the distribution mode.

Dealing with Supported Audio Formats

Naturally, Apple devices have support for other formats that you can use with the `<audio>` tag. Table 8–5 presents a non-exhaustive list.

Table 8–5. *Supported Audio Formats*

Format	Description
AAC (MPEG-4 Advanced Audio Coding) and HE-AAC (High Efficiency)	HE-AAC is an extension to the AAC format optimized for low bitrate, ideal for application that, for instance, use streaming.
ALAC (Apple Lossless)	A format created by Apple. Unlike MP3 and AAC, the compression is lossless, you will not see lesser quality. The compressed video should be around half of the size of the original.
IMA4 (IMA/ADPCM)	Interactive Multimedia Association (IMA) is a compression algorithm designed to be used in entertainment multimedia applications. It is particularly fast to encode and decode.
Linear PCM (uncompressed, linear pulse-code modulation)	As WAV (Windows) and AIFF (Mac), it is a uncompressed format played in software. Requires little processing because it needn't be decoded but can represent large file sizes.
MP3 (MPEG-1 audio layer 3)	The widespread format everyone knows. The compression ratio is better than that of AAC, but the quality isn't as good. The VBR mode (Variable Bit Rate) is also supported.

There are chances you will choose to serve your user a format that offers good quality; still, you should take into account the target audience that you aim for. A WAV file will be larger than an AAC file, will require more bandwidth, will require longer download times, and potentially will be more costly for the user.

If you know that your audience is likely to be affected by such drawbacks, you can consider formats such as Internet Low Bitrate Codec (iLBC); μ-law and a-law, which are low-quality formats used in telecommunications (generally for voice encoding); or Adaptive Multi-Rate (AMR), used to bring sound to Multimedia Messaging Services (MMS).

Encoding for the Web

When planning to encode any kind of media, especially video content, you should begin with high-quality material, because compression is generally lossy. Likewise, if you want to test or produce several formats, always use the original source for each new production, because successive compressions could result in disastrous quality.

This is important, because, when working on the Web, it is a good practice to offer several formats from which QuickTime can choose depending on the circumstances—especially network conditions—under which the user is trying to view your content. The latter behavior is made possible by the use of a reference movie.

A *reference movie* is a binary file that references links to different resources relative to network considerations. It is automatically generated by the QuickTime Player when you export a video for the Web, as we'll explain.

If you cannot or do not want to use professional software such as Apple's Final Cut or Adobe's Premiere, you can, as a Snow Leopard user, count on QuickTime X, which allows you, with no extra fee, to export video media for the iPhone. For Windows users and Mac OS X users with a version prior to 10.6, you will need to buy QuickTime Pro (7 or newer). This remains far below the prices of the professional software cited previously.

Using QuickTime Player

The process using QuickTime Player is very simple. Launch the software and load a video from the menu using **File ➤ Open File....** A new playback window appears with the first frame from the movie. Still from the **File** menu, simply choose **Save For Web....** An option window will appear, as shown in Figure 8–11.

Figure 8–11. *The export window in QuickTime*

To finalize your export, give a new name to your video, choose a directory to save it to (here, *Desktop*), and select the formats you need to export to. As a general rule, you can leave all checked formats. For instance, the first will be used with a Wi-Fi connection on iPhone, the second for a 3G or EDGE connection, and the third for a Wi-Fi connected iPad or a computer.

Click the Save button, and a progress window will appear (Figure 8–12). Wait for the export to complete; the progress bars will disappear as the export completes.

Figure 8–12. *The Export Progress window*

Once all operations have completed, your chosen directory will contain a new folder with several files; here we're still using the same example movie:

- *Big Buck Bunny – Computer.m4v*

- *Big Buck Bunny – iPhone (Cellular).3gp*

- *Big Buck Bunny – iPhone.m4v*

- *Big Buck Bunny.html*

- *Big Buck Bunny.jpg*

- *Big Buck Bunny.mov*

The first three are the videos themselves, using different formats and the same naming as specified in the export window. The HTML file holds the relevant markup and information to embed your media into a regular web page. The JPEG file should be used in the `poster` attribute of your `<video>` tag, whereas the `.mov` file is to be set as the `src` attribute—this is the reference movie. Also, don't forget to place the video files at the same level as the `.mov` files so that the player can find all the data when parsing the reference movie.

An Encoder Alternative

This is a very simple—and for lucky Snow Leopard users, a cost-effective—method to compress video content; however, you have no control over the dimensions or bitrate of your media. If you target iPad users, it is likely you will want larger formats and better quality. Moreover, developers on other platforms will be frustrated to be forced to pay for such a service, not to mention Linux users who cannot natively install QuickTime. Therefore, once again, we are going to introduce a free, open source, cross-platform alternative that also offers better control over the export options.

The name is HandBrake, and you can download it from `http://handbrake.fr/`. Once the download has completed and you have been through the pretty straightforward installation process, you can launch the program. The file selector should appear and let you choose a media to convert from your file system. If this didn't happen, just click the Source button at the top of the window.

When the chosen movie is loaded, the interface will update (Figure 8–13) with the default output parameters depending on presets appearing in the right sidebar (**Regular** ➤ **Normal**). You have the possibility to change these to fit your needs. Start by choosing the **Apple** ➤ **iPhone & iPod Touch** profile from the sidebar to filter the options available to you and make your configuration easier. This, for instance, will disable the B-frames option on the Advanced tab, which is not supported by the device.

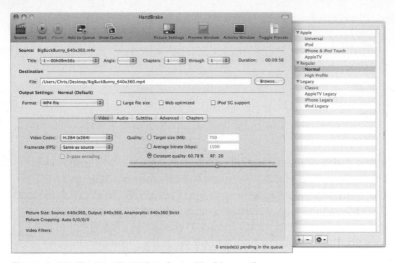

Figure 8–13. *The HandBrake interface with video settings*

On the Video tab (close to the center of the window), you can access configuration options for the video stream encoding. By default, primacy is given to quality. Hence, the bitrate will be evaluated to obtain the best possible quality, which isn't necessarily the best choice when working with web devices in mind. Appropriately, we can set a specific bitrate.

Using QuickTime, the default was 80 Kb/s for the cellular version of our media, 1 Mbit/s for a Wi-Fi connected iPhone, and 5 Mbit/s at best quality. We are going the aim for these values by selecting the "Average bitrate" option under the Quality section.

NOTE: The more important the video dimensions, the higher the bitrate should be to keep an optimal quality. Always preview your content before beginning the encoding process to check whether the result is what you expect. Also keep in mind that the higher the bitrate, the more difficult the video will be to view on a cellular network.

Now, we are going to make a video with the lowest bitrate (80 Kb/s) and scale the video down to get a satisfactory quality. This is done by clicking the Picture Settings button in the toolbar (or the Picture tab, if you are not on a Mac) and choosing "none" from the Anamorphic combo box in the window that appears (Figure 8–14). Change the width to 176, keeping the aspect ratio so that your media isn't deformed, and close the window.

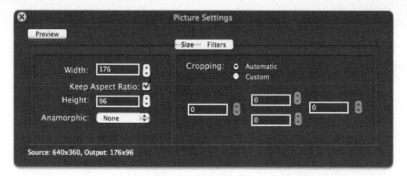

Figure 8–14. *The Picture Settings window*

On the Video tab again, if it isn't already so, set Video Codec to H.264 (x264) instead of FFmpeg (for MPEG-4 Part 2), and set Framerate to Same as Source to keep good fluidity while playing the media.

Then, on the Audio tab, as shown on Figure 8–15, check that the audio codec is set to AAC (CoreAudio) if you are on a Mac user or the poorer but only available AAC (faac) on other platforms. If you need to, you can explicitly reduce audio quality by limiting the sample rate, the bitrate, or both. This could be necessary, for instance, if the source bitrate were over 160 Kb/s, the support limit for the devices you target.

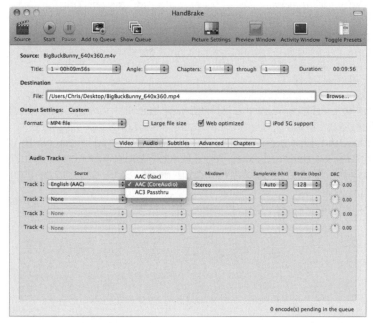

Figure 8–15. *Audio settings*

You can now finalize the configuration to export for the Web. In the upper area of the window, under Output Settings, the format should be set to "MP4 file." You should also select the Web Optimized option to allow progressive download and let the user play the video before all data is available.

To check the quality of your video before you export it, click the Preview Window button in the main window, and in the window that pops up, click Live Preview, as shown on Figure 8–16. If the result is as expected, click Start to launch the conversion.

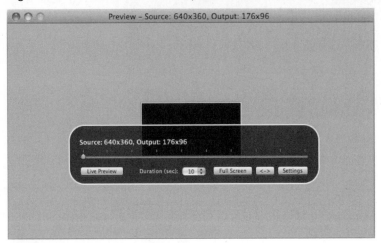

Figure 8–16. *The HandBrake preview window*

This should give you enough all the options to create exactly the media formats you need. HandBrake is a powerful tool that will also let you create batches and group-encode your media. The documentation on the software web site is very rich; you can use it to discover the best way to get the exact result you were seeking.

Summary

As you have seen, embedding media content the HTML5 way is both more specific and much richer than the earlier possibilities offered to developers. Not only does it make your markup more semantic, but it also comes with a full panel of ways to interact with your media, and it offers the user a better, deeper, more customizable experience. Combined with the <canvas> tag and its related API and the use of SVG, you can create applications that really come to life, giving users the impression of immediacy and movement that they are likely to expect on their devices.

## Chapter 9

Handling Transformations, Animations, and Special Effects with CSS

Desktop Safari has long enabled you to make advanced visual effects directly from the style sheets, and logically Mobile Safari inherits these capabilities. Not only is it possible to apply two- and three-dimensional effects to many elements of your pages, but it is now also possible to precisely define advanced animations to make your web applications visually more lively and attractive—all of this without using a single line of JavaScript or relying on external plug-ins. Again, Flash no longer is a necessity when moving away from still pages. These enhancements are available thanks to the new CSS3 specification, and there are some extra treats from WebKit itself, such as CSS masks.

Transform Your Elements

Transformations have been supported since version 2.0 of iOS. Transformations can be applied in a manner similar to what we have seen for canvases or SVG elements, using matrices. All are available using the `transform` CSS property, prefixed with `-webkit-`, though this property has been supported for some time now.

There are four basic transformations, namely, `rotate()`, `translate()`, `scale()`, and `skew()`. Most allow several variations, which we will go through in this chapter. You can also define your own matrices using the `matrix()` function.

The `transform` property takes a list of space-separated transformations as a value. However, keep in mind that transform rules are not cumulative, meaning that every new rule definition of the `transform` property will clear the previous definition.

```
.transformation {
    -webkit-transform: rotate(90deg) scale(2.0) translateX(15px);
}
```

In the previous code, we already are doing quite a lot. First, we rotate our element clockwise by 90 degrees, then we double its dimensions, and finally we move it by 15 pixels to the right of the x-axis. Note that the x-axis is relative to the element position in space, which means that in our example, moving to the "right" means moving downward.

In the previous example, transformations are not applied one after the other. The rendering engine processes the different transformations to apply the resulting matrix. This has the advantage of being very efficient. Efficiency is also enhanced because the transformations are handled on the hardware, which makes an appreciable difference compared to canvases or SVG, which can be slower on the iPhone when several elements are drawn.

> **NOTE:** All style rules affecting the transformed elements are also modified by the transformation. Therefore, drop shadows combined with a rotation will show relative to the element they are attached to, instead of being coherent with surrounding elements. This is different from the behavior of canvases.

Also, note that, like elements with a `position` set to `relative` or `absolute`, elements to which a `transform` has been applied do not affect the flow of the document. Transformations are applied in place.

There are differences, however, regarding the `overflow` value of the parent element. As with relatively positioned elements, transformed elements will not show beyond the boundaries of a parent with an `overflow` set to `hidden`; however, as with absolutely positioned elements, a block that has been transformed will not cause scrollbars if the `overflow` value of the parent is set to `auto`. Finally, transformations cannot be applied upon inline elements.

Checking Transform Support

To try transformations only in browsers that support them, you can rely on a media query to target them using the following code:

```
@media all and (-webkit-transform-2d) { ... }
```

This will allow you to build fallback behaviors directly from your style sheets, without resorting to JavaScript.

Applying Rotations

Rotations are defined clockwise using the `rotate()` function. Because we are working in a two-dimensional area, the function takes only one parameter, an angle in degrees (denoted `deg`), that is applied from the center of the element by default.

> **NOTE:** Keep in mind that block elements take all the available width unless you specify a `width` value. Therefore, the center of your element may well be the center of the screen, and you may wonder, after your rotation, where the content of your block has disappeared to. One solution to this is to change the `display` value of your block to `inline-block`, because it will then adapt to the width of what it contains.

Using this function, you can draw text vertically or diagonally, a technique often used with images, either to conserve screen real estate or to create a more attractive design.

```
<style>

ul {
    background: lightgrey;
    height: 44px;
    font: bold 12px/2.5 sans-serif;
    margin: 0;
    padding: 0;
    list-style: none;
    border: solid 1px black;
}

li {
    -webkit-transform: rotate(-45deg);
    width: 100px;
    background: white;
    display: inline-block;
    margin: 0 -65px 0 10px;
    text-indent: 10px;
    border: black 1px solid;
}

div {
    overflow: hidden;
    padding-bottom: 30px;
}

</style>

<div>
    <ul>
        <li>Home</li>
        <li>Tools</li>
        <li>Contact</li>
    </ul>
</div>
```

The previous code will result in the layout shown in Figure 9–1. Once the rotation is applied, the page flow remains unchanged, and the tabs are too far from one another. This is why we add a negative margin to each list item.

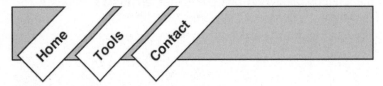

Figure 9–1. *Tabs are tipped by 45 degrees*

Such abilities can make your developing process easier and your web applications more efficient in terms of weight. For instance, you can now obtain the effect seen in the Photos application of the iPad without resorting to various images displaying different orientations.

Translating Element Coordinates

The translate() function allows you to reposition elements relatively to their physical position in the page without affecting the layout. It takes the x and y offset values for the translation as parameters, although the specification also provides the shortened functions translateX() and translateY() to work with only one coordinate.

The previous example could therefore be easily enhanced to bring visual feedback to the user, by moving our tabs on mouse hovering, with the following rule:

```
li:hover {
    -webkit-transform: rotate(-45deg) translateX(-10px);
}
```

This already lets you achieve quite a few visual effects. Nonetheless, translations (and more generally transformations), as we will see, are of much greater interest combined with transitions, which will let you animate elements over time using only CSS.

Scaling Page Contents

The scale() function works in a way similar to translate(), and the shortened functions scaleX() and scaleY() are also available. scale() takes two scaling coefficients as parameters to apply on the x- and y-axes. If you specify only one value, it will be used for both parameters. As with all transformation functions, the origin for the transformation is the middle of the element.

As when using the CSS zoom property, all styles are scaled, which means the rendered quality will remain even with extreme values. One asset of the scale() function over the zoom property is that you have control over both axes; therefore, you can stretch elements one way only, as shown with the text in Figure 9–2. Yet, for images, you will notice that the limitations are the same as when forcing the size of an image using CSS or the width and height attributes on the <img> tag. The bigger the difference from the original image size, the lesser the displayed quality.

Figure 9–2. *Quality isn't affected as the coefficient changes*

Distorting Elements

The specification will let you apply a distortion matrix to your elements using the skew() function. The parameters to this function are angles by which the transformation should be applied (Figure 9–3).

```
<style>

div {
    width: 320px;
    border: 5px solid black;
    padding: 5px;
    font: bold 15px helvetica;
    text-align: center;
    -webkit-transform: skewX(-30deg);
}

</style>

<div>Some text content.</div>
```

Figure 9–3. *A -30 degree skew operation along the x-axis*

As with translate() and scale(), you have two shortened functions, skewX() and skewY(), to build one-way transformations.

Custom Transformations with Matrices

Instead of chaining predefined transformations to achieve a goal, the specification will also let you define a complete transformation matrix using the matrix() function. This can be useful to make your code smaller or to create your own custom transformations. The matrix() function takes six parameters, which are used in the following matrix:

$$T = \begin{bmatrix} a & c & e \\ b & d & f \\ 0 & 0 & 1 \end{bmatrix}$$

All options available to you can be combined to give you full control over the effects you want to create with the transform rule. This lets you define a full set of transformations in a single declaration, reducing file sizes for styles but also the readability of the whole code. This corresponds to what the layout engine computes before applying the transformation. We will see more about using matrices for transformations later in this chapter, with the JavaScript CSSMatrix object.

The Origin of the Transformation

As stated earlier, the default origin for transformations is the center of the transformed element. This can be modified using the transform-origin property (Figure 9–4).

```
<style>

.box {
    width: 100px;
    height: 100px;
    background-color: black;
    float: left;
}

.box + .box {
    background-color: gray;
    -webkit-transform: rotate(-45deg);
    -webkit-transform-origin: 50% 50%;
}

</style>

<div class="box"></div>
```

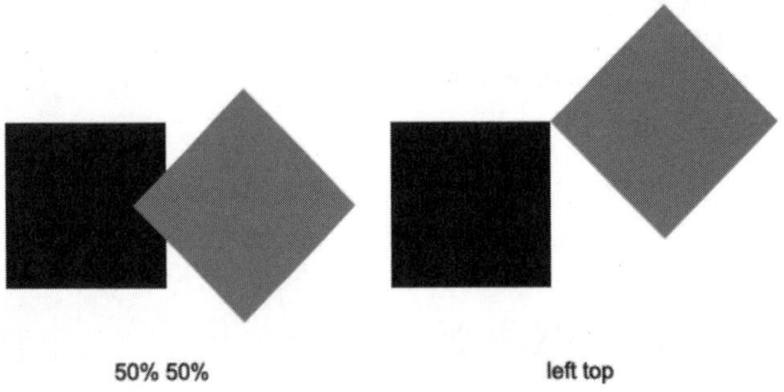

50% 50%   left top

Figure 9–4. *The same rotation based on different* transform-origin *values*

This property can take all the usual position keywords as parameters, as well as any CSS numerical value (px, em...), as used with the background-position rule, for instance.

Working in a Three-Dimensional Environment

Not only does Mobile Safari offer the possibility to handle two-dimensional transformations, but it also implements features from the CSS specification to create three-dimensional effects. This makes it possible to render elements on the x-, y-, and z-axes. The specification also offers new properties that will let you define the perspective level, as well as how to handle the back face of your elements.

Nevertheless, be conscious that unlike applying changes to the x- and y-axes, styles won't be scaled for transformations upon the z-axis, and quality will dwindle as the factor for the transformation changes.

As with 2D transformations, you can target only those browsers with support for the features using the `-webkit-transform-3d` condition in a media query.

New Transform Functions

The specification extends the 2D Transforms module by adding new functions to handle the z-axis. New variants of the two-dimensional functions, ending with `Z()` and `3d()`, are now available. Because rotations can now be executed in full space, the new `rotateX()`, `rotateY()`, `rotateZ()`, and `rotate3d()` are also available to you.

All functions for 3D use a 4x4 homogeneous matrix that will let you work in the three-dimensional space and apply perspective projection. The `matrix3d()` function thus takes 16 values, in column-major order (reading the matrix members from top to bottom and left to right), as represented here:

$$T = \begin{bmatrix} m11 & m21 & m31 & m41 \\ m12 & m22 & m32 & m42 \\ m13 & m22 & m33 & m43 \\ m14 & m24 & m34 & m44 \end{bmatrix}$$

Considering the previous matrix, the following definitions are equivalent:

```
  matrix(a, b, c, d, e, f)
matrix3d(a, b, 0, 0, c, d, 0, 0, 1, 0, e, f, 0, 1)
```

> **NOTE:** Again, you don't have to fully understand the matrix in order to use it. The `CSSMatrix` will be there to help. The most useful information to be extracted from the matrix will be the m41 and m42 members, giving the computed x and y positions of the element.

However, using 3D alternatives will have no notable effect as long as the perspective level is not specified, because no projection will be observable. A rotation on the y-axis, for instance, would compress the element only horizontally, without projecting it.

Setting the Perspective

Perspective can be rendered using either of two processes: the `perspective()` function, which you can use within the `transform` property to modify one element type, or the `perspective` property, which you can use to change the perspective for the transformed children of the element to which the property is attached. Both take a positive or null value, with no explicit unit.

```
/* Element level */
.perspective {
    -webkit-transform: perspective(500) rotateY(45deg);
}

/* Children level */
.perspective {
    -webkit-perspective: 500;
}

.child {
    -webkit-transform: rotateY(45deg);
}
```

The great asset of this method is that all children are rendered within a uniform 3D environment, which will allow you to create animations with rich and realistic depth effects.

To estimate values for the perspective property, you should consider it as the distance between the observer and an element on the z-axis. An element with its z position set to 0 will show in its normal size, whereas an element with a position set to half the distance will be twice as big.

```
/* The element will look twice as big */
.perspective {
    -webkit-transform: perspective(1000) translateZ(500px);
}
```

> **NOTE:** Keep in mind that translations are applied relative to the plane of the element. Therefore, with a 90-degree rotation on the y-axis, the translation will apply on the perceived x-axis instead of the z one.

As the observer gets closer, distances grow smaller, vanishing points get closer to one another, and parallel lines head apart, creating an extreme perspective effect (as shown in Figure 9–5). Hence, the smaller the value, the more stretched the element will be on the z-axis; the bigger the value, the lesser perceivable the perspective effect will be. Generally speaking, the value for a perspective should span between 500 and 1000.

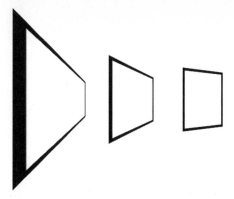

Figure 9–5. *A 100x100-pixel element with a perspective value set successively to 125, 250, and 1000*

The position of the vanishing point defaults to the center of the element. This can be changed with the perspective-origin (prefixed with -webkit-). It can take three values indicating the position of the point in a three-dimensional environment—the x point first, then y, and finally z. This means you can also change the distance, changing only the value for z and keeping the perspective value.

Preserving the 3D Aspect

When an element is rendered in perspective within its parent, it is actually drawn to the screen to give the impression of perspective. However, if a transformation is applied to the parent in the 3D environment, the child elements will be flattened in the plane of their parent regardless of their own position in space. Of course, it would be preferable that each element keep their depth so that everything is coherently rendered within a 3D space using the same perspective. The following code shows how to achieve that:

```
<style>

div { border: 5px solid black; }

.perspective {
    border: 0;
    -webkit-perspective: 150;
}

.parent {
    margin: 0 auto;
    width: 100px;
    height: 100px;
    padding: 10px;
    -webkit-transform: rotateY(60deg);
    -webkit-transform-style: preserve-3d;
}
.child {
    height: 100%;
    -webkit-box-sizing: border-box;
    -webkit-transform: translateZ(-50px) rotateX(45deg);
}
```

```
</style>

<div class="perspective">
    <div class="parent">
        <div class="child"></div>
    </div>
</div>
```

As shown in the Figure 9–6, using the default value for the transform-style property, flat, elements will not be projected "outside" their parents. The result will be similar to applying a rotation to an element in two dimensions, as with an image. The preserve-3d value allows you to maintain the depth of each element, which will let you create very realistic effects, especially with CSS animations, that we will soon be going through.

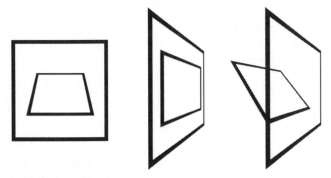

Figure 9–6. *The second illustration uses the flat value for the* transform-style *property; for the third, the value is set to* preserve-3d

Back Face Visibility

In the 3D space, an element has two faces, somewhat like a transparent card. The side that initially shows is the classic HTML display. When rotating the element by 180 degrees around the y-axis, the other side logically is the same view, just reversed, as shown in Figure 9–7.

Figure 9–7. *The initial state of the element, a 180-degree rotation, and the resulting state*

During an animation, when two elements are placed back to back, if both elements are opaque, normally no inconsistency should show, because pixels will overlap without revealing what is behind the element; however, because both elements use the same space, the rendering isn't what would be expected, and in most cases both elements are alternatively swapped in a disorderly manner.

```
<style>

.parent {
    width: 110px;
    margin: 0 auto;
    -webkit-perspective: 1000;
}

.parent div {
    width: 100%;
    height: 150px;
    line-height: 150px;
    text-align: center;
    position: absolute;
    float: left;
    color: white;
    background: black;
    -webkit-border-radius: 8px;
    -webkit-transition: -webkit-transform 1s linear;
}

.face { -webkit-transform: rotateY(0deg); }
.back { -webkit-transform: rotateY(-180deg); }

.parent:hover .face { -webkit-transform: rotateY(180deg); }
.parent:hover .back { -webkit-transform: rotateY(0deg); }

</style>

<div class="parent">
    <div class="face">FACE</div>
    <div class="back">BACK</div>
</div>
```

In our example, we create two elements back to back. The second one is rotated by 180 degrees so that its front is visible after the transition. Now, if you point your mouse or finger on the element, the card will turn around, but the rendering will be deceptive. You could solve this by moving both elements enough along the z-axis so that they no longer occupy the same space, but you would also have to modify the original position of the transformation, making the handling of positions uselessly heavier.

To address this issue, you should use the backface-visibility property, which can be set either to visible (by default) or to hidden.

```
.parent div {
...
    -webkit-backface-visibility: hidden;
}
```

This will force the engine to hide the backside of the element during the rotation. It will simply disappear, leaving a transparent area that will solve the approximate positioning problem. This new property, together with those presented earlier, lets you finely control your elements within the 3D plane.

Combining Styles with JavaScript

Like all CSS properties, transformations can be read and modified using JavaScript. This can be used to build interactivity with the user or to create animations.

Accessing Current Styles

To access and apply transformations via JavaScript, you should use the webkitTransform property of the CSSStyleDeclaration object, attached to any relevant element.

```
var element = document.getElementById("myElement");
element.style.webkitTransform = "translateX(100px)";
```

Quite naturally, as with any CSS declaration, any modification overwrites any previous ones. If you need to apply a transformation in addition to its current state, you will have to first read its computed style using the getComputedStyle() method of the DOMWindow object. This returns a CSSStyleDeclaration object that will let you access the styles in use (through a style sheet or a script), as with the style property.

```
var iter = 0;

var timerID = window.setInterval(function() {
    var current = window.getComputedStyle(element);
    element.style.webkitTransform = current.webkitTransform + " translateY(10px)";

    if(iter++ == 5) {
        window.clearInterval(timerID);
    }
}, 200);
```

In this piece of code, we move our element downward by 10 pixels every 200 milliseconds. The movement is relative to the previous position, because we add our new transformation to the current state, which takes previous transformations into account. Looking at the value returned by current.webkitTransform, you will note that it is always a unique matrix() function (or matrix3d(), if the element has been transformed in a 3D environment) and not a list of successive function calls; as explained earlier, the engine always computes one matrix that synthesizes all matrices that should be applied.

A Native Object to Compute Matrices

The process used in our previous example yields the expected result but isn't very flexible, nor is it optimal because it forces you to handle potentially long strings that can be cumbersome if many parameters are in line. The specification for transformations brings a new object to remedy this: CSSMatrix. It has been supported since version iOS 2.0 and allows you to easily calculate matrices. Here is how it can be used:

```
var timerID = window.setInterval(function() {
    var current = window.getComputedStyle(element);
    var matrix  = new WebKitCSSMatrix(current.webkitTransform);
    element.style.webkitTransform = matrix.translate(0, 10);

    if(iter++ == 5) {
        window.clearInterval(timerID);
    }
}, 200);
```

As in our example, this object takes the previous matrix as a parameter. To the constructor, you can pass a string containing a matrix() or matrix3d() function or another CSSMatrix object. If no parameter is specified, a new empty matrix will be returned. Table 9–1 shows the different methods available to interact with the matrix.

Table 9–1. *Methods Applicable to the CSSMatrix Object*

Method	Description
matrix.setMatrixValue(newMatrix)	Modifies the matrix using the one passed as a parameter.
matrix.multiply(matrix)	Returns a new CSSMatrix object resulting from the multiplication of the current matrix and the one passed as a parameter.
matrix.inverse()	Returns a new CSSMatrix object that is the inverse of the matrix to which the method is applied.
matrix.translate(x, y, z)	Returns a new CSSMatrix object resulting from the multiplication of the matrix by the translation matrix using the values passed as parameters. The z parameter can be omitted; it will default to 0.
matrix.scale(x, y, z)	Returns a new CSSMatrix object resulting from the multiplication of the matrix by the scale matrix, using the values passed as parameters. z can be omitted and will default to 1. Moreover, y can be omitted also, in which case it will take the same value as x.
matrix.rotate(x, y, z)	Returns a new CSSMatrix object resulting from the multiplication of the matrix by the rotate matrix, using the values passed as parameters. Rotations are applied one at a time in the same order as the parameters. Angles are set in degrees. If y and z aren't defined, in order to be compatible with the 2D version of the CSSMatrix object, the call will be considered to be (0, 0, z).

Method	Description
`matrix.rotateAxisAngle(x, y, z, angle)`	This method allows you to define a new axis and operate a rotation around it. Like the previous methods, this returns a new matrix.
`matrix.toString()`	Returns the matrix as a string holding a `matrix()` or `matrix3d()` function, as defined for the `transform` CSS property.

Only the first method modifies the `CSSMatrix` object. The others just return a new `CSSMatrix` holding the resulting matrix. Surprisingly, there is no `skew()` method, so you will have to create your own matrix. The following is an example of how to do this:

```
/* Define a skew(45deg, 30deg) matrix */
var matrix = new WebKitCSSMatrix();
matrix.b = Math.tan(30 * Math.PI / 180);
matrix.c = Math.tan(45 * Math.PI / 180);
```

Each value for the matrix is accessible through the pertaining properties, named, as shown previously, from `a` to `f` (supported since version 3.0 of the OS) for the 2D version and from `m11` to `m44` for the 3D version. This means six values for the two-dimensional matrix and sixteen for the three-dimensional one. Note that, of course, you could use a similar function to calculate matrices within canvases, with the `transform()` and `setTransformation()` methods of the `CanvasRenderingContext2D` object. This can be done as follows:

```
context.translate(50, 50);
context.rotate(Math.PI * 0.5);
```

That is equivalent to the following:

```
var matrix = new WebKitCSSMatrix().translate(50, 50).rotate(45);
context.transform(matrix.a, matrix.b, matrix.c, matrix.d, matrix.e, matrix.f);
```

As you can see, the specification of angles is different in canvases than it is in the `CSSMatrix` object. However, reading properties from the `CSSMatrix` object, values representing angles will be converted to radians. This object will also let you know where an element is situated at some given moment, for instance reading the current matrix during an animation, as with transitions.

Transitions

We have seen how it is possible to move an element within the page using a timer and the `CSSMatrix` object, which was used to read the current state of the matrix applied to an element. Nevertheless, you can define such transitions without resorting to JavaScript, using CSS rules directly.

WARNING: To obtain better rendering, the engine rasterizes the elements so animations can be handled directly by the hardware. This does not mean you can do anything with CSS without worrying about performance. You could easily end up with jumps in your animations, especially on the iPhone and iPod touch, if your style sheets get too complex. You will often find that too much relatively or absolutely positioned elements will make the task for the rendering engine harder, which will result in poorer quality. Always check for useless styles, and try to find the most efficient solution to your goal.

Many CSS properties can be animated: colors and gradients (as long as they keep the same count of color stops), dimensions, font sizes, and others. You should be able to interact in this way with most style rules. Note that, because opacity and transformations are handled on the hardware level, performance will be better for these than for other styles. Most of the transformations explained earlier gain much richness with transitions.

The transition CSS Property

The principle of CSS transitions is to interpolate an initial CSS value to another, which is simply done using the transition property; it should be used as follows:

transition: *<property>* *<duration>* *<timing-function>* *<delay>*

The transition property is a shorthand to a series of properties relative to transitions. These two declarations hence are equivalent:

```
/* Shorthand */
-webkit-transition: opacity 0.5s linear 200ms;

/* Exploded version */
-webkit-transition-property: opacity;
-webkit-transition-duration: 0.5s;
-webkit-transition-timing-function: linear;
-webkit-transition-delay: 200ms;
```

You can also define several transitions in a single declaration (one use of the transition property) by separating your transitions by comma. The transition-property defaults to all, meaning that all properties supporting transitions will be affected.

Initiating a Transition

The transition begins at the very moment the value of the property is modified, yet after any delay set for the transition-delay property. The modification must occur outside the initial definition of the value, which means you can trigger a transition on some action by the user.

```
<style>

.box {
```

```
        width:100px;
        height:100px;
        background-color: black;

        -webkit-transition-property: -webkit-transform;
        -webkit-transition-duration: 2s;
}

.box:hover {
        -webkit-transform: translateX(100px);
}

</style>

<div class="box"></div>
```

> **NOTE:** On iOS 3.*x*, the hardware acceleration is buggy with some translations, resulting in a staggered rendering. To animate only these properties, you should use the `translate3d()` method to obtain fluid transitions.

In our example, the user pointing his finger on the `<div>` makes the black square move by 100 pixels to the right over a two-second time span. When the user leaves the square area, the value of the property is restored, and the animation is reversed, even if its first movement isn't complete.

However, this means that, if the same transition configuration was used, the animation would be asymmetric, because the starting point would not match the previously expected target point. This of course would seem unnatural to users, who will expect the same reversed movement. This issue shows when using nonlinear timing functions.

The specification describes a specific behavior for such cases, which will maintain consistency when reversing transitions. The rendering engine will compute the curve of the timing function and search the stage it should be at the current keyframe. The reverse animation will then be started from that point.

Timing Function Curve

As suggested earlier, the animation curve isn't always linear—and in most cases, it actually isn't linear at all. Mobile Safari supports several keywords to be used with the `transform-timing-function` property, which allows you to define the most common animation curves, as shown in Table 9–2 and in Figure 9–8.

Table 9–2. *Supported* `transform-timing-function` *Keywords and Their Related* `cubic-bezier()` *Definitions*

Keyword	Configuration
ease (default)	cubic-bezier(0.25, 0.1, 0.25, 1.0)
linear	cubic-bezier(0.0, 0.0, 1.0, 1.0)
ease-in	cubic-bezier(0.42, 0, 1.0, 1.0)
ease-out	cubic-bezier(0.0, 0.0, 0.58, 1.0)
ease-in-our	cubic-bezier(0.42, 0.0, 0.58, 1.0)

All are based on cubic Bézier curves that can be defined using the `cubic-bezier()` function. As parameters, this function takes coordinates for the control points P1 and P2 of the curves, spanning from `0.0` to `1.0`. The origin and destination points (P0 and P3) are considered to be positioned at `(0,0)` and `(1,1)`.

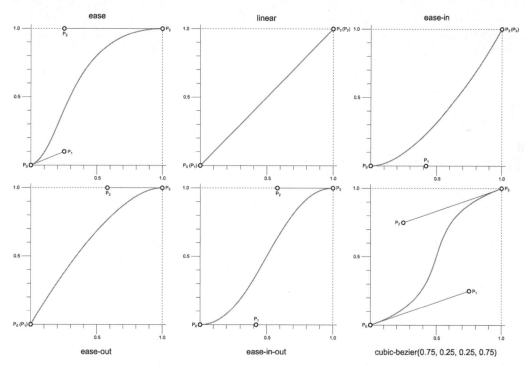

Figure 9–8. *The curves relative to the* `transform-timing-function` *keywords and a custom curve definition*

The idea is to define a progress curve for the animation. For instance, using the last curve from Figure 9–8, the animation will first progress slowly and will temporarily speed up, before taking the same pace as when beginning.

Telling When the Transition Is Completed

In the use of transitions and animations, you will often need to know when they have been completed. Rather than using a timer set to the time span of the transition, you can rely on the `transitionend` event.

```
var box = document.getElementsByClassName("box")[0];

box.addEventListener("webkitTransitionEnd", function(event) {
    alert("The box reached the destination point after " + event.elapsedTime + "s.");
}, false);
```

The event is triggered as soon as the transition is complete, even when the transition is reversed. Of course, this is far more accurate than a timer, because it will always be synchronous with the transition. Moreover, because the handler is executed in the context of the object that triggers the event, you can access this directly using the `event.target` property or the keyword `this`, without previously saving them.

> **WARNING:** In Mobile Safari, the name of the event is case sensitive, meaning you should be careful to use the `webkitTransitionEnd` event, with the appropriate uppercase letters, for the event listener to work.

The event has the `TransitionEvent` type and holds two extra properties, `elapsedTime` and `propertyName`, that will let you know the time taken by the transition (in seconds, regardless of the `transition-delay` property) and the property associated to the transition.

Getting Ready for a Cover Flow–Like Experience

Now that you have an overall idea of how transitions work and how to use them, let's bring all of this together in an example that would have been a CSS dream not so long ago. We are going to create a Cover Flow effect, familiar to anyone who has used iTunes, the Mac OS X Finder, an iPod, or the iPad App Store (Figure 9–9).

Figure 9-9. *A Cover Flow from the French iPad App Store*

Note that this code will not work well on older WebKit versions like Desktop Safari 4 or an earlier version of Mobile Safari because of a bug in the transition implementation.

The Main Document

First let's get our HTML file together. We will need the following code:

```
<html>
    <head>
        <title>Cover Flow Demo</title>
        <meta name="viewport" content="initial-scale=1.0;
            maximum-scale=1.0; user-scalable=no">

        <link rel="stylesheet" href="styles/coverflow.css">
        <script src="scripts/coverflow.js"></script>
    </head>

<body>
    <div id="coverflow">
        <div id="left"></div>
        <div id="right"></div>
    </div>
```

```
</body>

</html>
```

Next come the styles relative to this document:

```
body { background-color: black; }

#coverflow {
    position: relative;
    height: 320px;
    background-color: #333;
    white-space: nowrap;
    overflow: hidden;
    -webkit-border-radius: 32px;
    border: solid 3px white;
    -webkit-perspective: 1000;
}

#left {
    width: 50%;
    height: 100%;
    float: left;
}

#right {
    width: 50%;
    height: 100%;
    float: right;
}
```

We associate an overflow property set to hidden and a white-space rule set to nowrap so that our covers, as they move, do not change position, spanning over several lines or beyond the #coverflow container. For now, the document holds only the main containers, that is, the #coverflow parent defining the perspective and the left and right areas that will hold the actual covers. To add covers, we will use a script to create elements and set colors for them so that they are recognizable during the animations.

Create a new *coverflow.js* file, and add the following to it:

```
function init() {
    var m = 8;          // Covers count
    var s = 360 / m;    // Color step

    /* Add left and right covers */
    var o = document.getElementById("left");
    createCovers(o, m, s);
    o = document.getElementById("right");
    createCovers(o, m, s);

    /* Add current cover */
    o = document.getElementById("coverflow");
    createCovers(o, 1, 0);
    o.lastChild.className ="current";
}

function createCovers(o, max, step) {
```

```
        var color = step;
        for (var n = 0; n < max; n++, color += step) {
            var span = document.createElement("span");
            span.style.backgroundColor = "hsl(" + (color) + ",100%, 50%)";
            o.appendChild(span);
        }
    }
}
```

The number of covers can be modified by changing the value of m in the init() function. This will let you have one eye on performance issues, because each cover will be animated individually.

Now, the following styles will be used to correctly place the covers within their container:

```
#coverflow span {
    width: 160px;
    height: 240px;
    border: solid 5px rgba(0, 0, 0, 0.25);
    margin-top: 40px;
    -webkit-box-sizing: border-box;
    -webkit-border-radius: 16px;
}

#left span {
    float: right;
    margin-left: -130px;     /* 30px between each cover */
    -webkit-transform: translate3d(-30px, 0, -80px) rotateY(+60deg);
}

#right span {
    float: left;
    margin-right: -130px;
    -webkit-transform: translate3d(+30px, 0, -80px) rotateY(-60deg);
}

#coverflow .current {
    position: absolute;
    left: 50%;
    top: 50%;
    margin-left: -80px;
    margin-top: -120px;
}
```

This transforms the covers so that they are displayed with a 60-degree rotation and moves them backward in a three-dimensional plane to make them further back than the focused cover. Because we are working in a 3D environment, we cannot use z-index to handle the element's stack. To make placing the current cover earlier, we place it at the center of the view and position it absolutely.

Next, change the HTML document to execute the init() function when the document is loaded.

```
...
<body onload="init()">
...
```

Your document should now look like Figure 9–10.

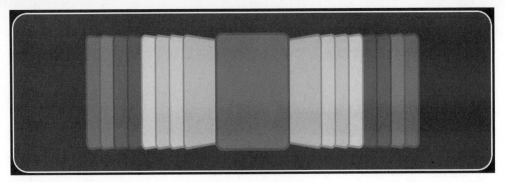

Figure 9–10. *The near to final state of the Cover Flow experience*

For the moment, although the CSS performance is appreciable, there is nothing really useful in our display. However, everything is in place to add the Cover Flow animation to our page.

The Cover Flow Animation

To animate our covers, we will begin by adding buttons to our page to trigger animations:

```
...
    <div id="coverflow">
        <div id="left"></div>
        <div id="right"></div>

        <button onclick="slide(-1)">&laquo;</button>
        <button onclick="slide(+1)">&raquo;</button>
    </div>
...
```

An here are the associated styles:

```
button {
    font-size: 80px;
    color: white;
    text-shadow: black 1px 1px 10px;
    border: 0;
    background: none;
    position: absolute;
    top: 100px;
}

button:first-of-type { left:0; }
button:last-of-type { right:0; }
```

A function slide(), attached to the click event on the button elements, takes a parameter indicating the direction in which the covers should slide. Here is the initial definition, as well as the first functions that will control movement:

```
function slide(dir) {
    document.getElementById("coverflow").className = "slide";
```

```
    /* Move covers */
    moveSides("left",  dir, +1);
    moveSides("right", dir, -1);
    moveCurrent(dir);
}

function moveSides(str, dir, coef) {
    var s = document.getElementById(str).childNodes;
    for (var n = 0; n < s.length; n++) {
        s[n].style.webkitTransform = getMatrix(s[n], dir, coef, 30);
    }
}

function moveCurrent(dir) {
    var s = document.querySelector(".current");
    var styles = window.getComputedStyle(s);

    var matrix = new WebKitCSSMatrix(styles.webkitTransform);
    matrix = matrix.translate(30 * dir, 0, 0);
    s.style.webkitTransform = matrix;
}

function getMatrix(s, dir, coef, move) {
    var styles = window.getComputedStyle(s);
    var matrix = new WebKitCSSMatrix(styles.webkitTransform);

    /* Read values from the matrix */
    var angle = Math.acos(matrix.m11) * 180 / Math.PI * coef;
    var x = matrix.m41 + move * dir;
    var y = matrix.m42;
    var z = matrix.m43;

    /* Return a new matrix */
    return new WebKitCSSMatrix().translate(x, 0, z).rotate(0, angle, 0);
}
```

When the user clicks the button, the slide() function adds a .slide class to the main container. This allows you to define a transition to use, which is defined with CSS only:

```
.slide span {
    -webkit-transition: -webkit-transform .35s linear;
}
```

The moveSlides() function gathers the covers from each side and then uses the transformation of each cover to read the information from their matrices using getMatrix() and the CSSMatrix object. Because the rotation changes the position of the x-axis, we cannot simply apply a new translation to move the covers, or they would go forward or backward instead of to the left and to the right. This is why we re-create the matrix after having calculated the current position of each element. For the focused cover, however, because there is no rotation, we can simply use the translate() function to change its position.

Flipping the Current Cover

If you try this code now, you will notice that all covers move to the left or right. Now to make the focused cover return to the cover stack and switch the focus to next one, we have to intercept the `transitionend` event before resuming the animation.

```
function slide(dir) {
...
    var current = document.querySelector(".current");
    current.addEventListener("webkitTransitionEnd", function(event) {
        this.removeEventListener(event.type, arguments.callee, false);

        document.getElementById("coverflow").className = "flip";
        prepareFlipSide(dir);
        prepareFlipCurrent(dir);
    }, false);
}
```

When the event is received, we immediately delete the listener, because it is defined anew for each `click` event and no longer is of any use. Then we add the following .flip class to the main container again:

```
.flip  span {
    -webkit-transition: -webkit-transform 0.2s ease-in-out;
}
```

Then we call the functions that are responsible for the cover rotations:

```
function prepareFlipSide(dir) {
    var s = document.getElementById(dir > 0 ? "left" : "right").firstElementChild;
    s.style.webkitTransform = "translateX(" + (dir * 80) + "px)";
}

function prepareFlipCurrent(dir) {
    var current = document.querySelector(".current");

    /* Apply a new matrix based on the style of the side covers */
    var base = document.getElementById(dir < 0 ? "left" : "right").firstElementChild;
    current.style.webkitTransform = getMatrix(base, dir, -dir, (80 - 30));
}
```

The side cover to be focused will be repositioned with the `prepareFlipSide()` function; then, the `prepareFlipCurrent()` function gathers the transformation of an element from the stack to apply its matrix to the previously focused element. The last stage is to transfer the nodes of the covers to their new parent so that a new animations can be initiated.

Final Touch to the Animation

To maintain the consistency of the document, we are going to move the covers after the second animation to give them their original styles. This is done with the following code:

```
function prepareFlipCurrent(dir) {
...
    current.addEventListener("webkitTransitionEnd", function() {
```

```
        this.removeEventListener(event.type, arguments.callee, false);

        /* Reset elements to their initial state */
        reset("left");
        reset("right");
        document.getElementById("coverflow").className = "";
        this.style.webkitTransform = "";
        this.className = "";

        /* Append the current cover to its new parent */
        var c, e = document.getElementById(dir < 0 ? "left" : "right");
        e.insertBefore(this, e.firstElementChild);

        /* Append the new current cover to the main container */
        e = document.getElementById(dir > 0 ? "left" : "right");
        c = e.firstElementChild;
        e.parentNode.appendChild(c);
        c.className = "current";
    }, false);
}

function reset(str) {
    var s = document.getElementById(str).childNodes;
    for (var n = 0; n < s.length; n++) {
        s[n].style.webkitTransform = "";
    }
}
```

As previously, we add a listener to be notified of the end of the animation. Then, all elements are reset to their initial states, and the covers are moved.

Double-Check: Preventing Unexpected Behavior

At this stage, if a user clicks the button before an animation is complete, the movement becomes inconsistent because the animations are interrupted, and therefore the matrices are no longer those expected. To address this, we add a variable that will let us check the state of the animation.

```
var animate = false;

function slide(dir) {
    var c1 = (document.getElementById("left").childNodes.length == 1);
    var c2 = (document.getElementById("right").childNodes.length == 1);

    if (animate || (c1 && dir == +1) || (c2 && dir == -1)) {
        return;
    }
    animate = true;
...
}

function prepareFlipCurrent(dir) {
...
    current.addEventListener("webkitTransitionEnd", function() {
...
```

```
        animate = false;
    }, false);
}
```

In addition to the `animate` variable, we add a control in `slide()` on the number of children remaining on either sides of the Cover Flow display. If none of them remain on one pane and the user tries to move elements from that side, nothing will happen.

This is your Cover Flow setup. Of course, the colored squares used in our example aren't very attractive and should be replaced with relevant content. To use this at its best, we suggest you try things with transitions, such as modifying animation curves or adding more covers to estimate the impact on the performance of your page.

Advanced Animations and Key Frames

The transitions explained up to now only allow you to progressively slip from one value to another for some property, and each property needs its own definition. Moreover, they use implicit animation, because the animation is triggered by the change of a property value. Whenever you need finer control over your animation and have to explicitly declare animations from your style sheets, you should resort to Apple's new CSS Animation module. This will let you precisely define a series of events on a timeline, using an at-rule.

Key Frames

A key frame specifies the state of an animation at some definite stage in time. A series of key frames is defined using the @keyframes rule by giving a name to the sequence that will be used by the `animation-name` property and listing CSS rules to be animated.

```
@-webkit-keyframes "mySequence" {
    0% {
        left: 100px;
        top: 0;
        background-color: red;
    }

    25% {
        left: 75px;
        background-color: green;
    }

    75% { background-color: blue; }

    100% {
        left: 200px;
        top: 100px;
    }
}
```

Using this sequence, for instance, on an absolutely positioned element, the element will be set to the position (`100,0`), with a red background. Then, using 25 percent of the defined animation duration, it will slide to the left until it reaches the position (75,0) and simultaneously blend from red to green. Finally, a new color switch will occur over 50 percent of the allotted time, before the element is shifted to the coordinates (200,100) over the 25 percent remaining for the animation.

> **NOTE:** As with transitions, the animations are optimized for some properties, and you are often better off using transformations than regular CSS positioning in order to obtain better performances and thus spare battery life and provide an overall better user experience.

To prepare your animations, you have to determine the initial state (0%), optional transitional states, and a final state (100%). The position of these states must be set using numerical values followed by the % sign, or the rule will not be considered valid. Moreover, the 0% and 100% points are mandatory. Note, however, that they can be replaced with the from and to keywords. The order of the declarations isn't important, but be careful because any single mistake will make the whole sequence invalid and compromise the whole animation.

Starting and Timing the Animation

To trigger an animation, you simply need to use the animation-name property, associating the name of a sequence to it and giving the animation a duration. The timing uses properties similar to those of transitions, and you can use both the animation-duration property to declare the duration and animation-delay to delay the beginning of the animation. The duration will then be split up to determine the duration of each step of the sequence.

```
div {
    -webkit-animation-name: "mySequence";
    -webkit-animation-duration: 10s;
    -webkit-animation-delay: 2s;
    -webkit-animation-iteration-count: 3;
}
```

In the previous example, we indicate that the animation should follow the mySequence sequence and span over ten seconds, after a two-second delay. This delay naturally isn't taken into consideration for the animation duration. The animation will be repeated three times before stopping and hence will last for thirty seconds. The animation-iteration-count property can also be set to infinite, which is quite self-explanatory.

Animation Properties

As with transitions, not all properties can be animated. However, using such a property—box-shadow, for instance—within an @keyframes statement will not raise an error, and the animation will resume, simply ignoring the faulty rule.

When a property is animated, the computed values are affected by the transformations applied all along the animation. Moreover, because all properties pertaining to the animation can take several comma-separated values, it is possible to specify several sequences for one element. In such a case, if the same properties are animated, the last definition will overwrite the previous one.

```
<style>

@-webkit-keyframes "blue-yellow" {
    from { background-color: blue; }
    to   { background-color: yellow; }
}

@-webkit-keyframes "red-green" {
    from { background-color: red; }
    to   { background-color: green; }
}

div {
    width: 100px;
    height: 100px;
    -webkit-animation-name: "red-green", "blue-yellow";
    -webkit-animation-duration: 10s, 2s;
}

</style>

<div></div>
```

In this peculiar example, the animation will begin with a blue to yellow blending, because the same property is animated in both @keyframes, and blue-yellow is called last. However, because the red-green animation lasts longer, the animation will go on as if the red to green animation had occurred and will be resumed with a slightly greenish red block, changing to full green on the tenth second.

Be aware that if the initial state declaration is different from that of the actual element to animate for some property, no transition will occur from one style to the other, and the transition initial state declaration will be applied immediately. This may cause unpleasant effects, for instance a jump of the element before the actual transition. Moreover, unlike what happens with transitions, the state of the element after the animation is complete isn't persistent, and the element will instantly return to its initial state, with the same jump effect.

Always keep these specificities in mind when building animations for your web applications, and don't get stuck because of something that isn't an actual issue but just a subtlety of the implementation.

The Evolution Curve

Animation curves, defined using animation-timing-function, are the same as for transitions and use the cubic-bezier() function. The curve isn't applied globally for the animation as a unit, but one key frame at a time. Thus, you can define a different curve for each step of the animation within the at-rule. The animation-timing-function property is the only property that can be used directly within the at-rule.

```
@-webkit-keyframes "mySequence" {
    0% {
        left: 100px;
        top: 0;
        background-color: red;
    }

    25% {
        left: 75px;
        background-color: green;
        -webkit-animation-timing-function: ease-in;
    }
...
}
```

The timing function must be defined on the destination key frame, or it will either not be applied or not be applied where expected. If you want the function to apply to all steps of the sequence, you can define it directly along with `animation-name`.

Working with Events

Animations come with three new events. The first two, `animationstart` and `animationend`, will let you know when an animation starts or reaches its end; the third, `animationiteration`, is triggered when an animation is run again after its first occurrence because of the `animation-iteration-count` property value.

```
var div = document.getElementsByTagName("div")[0];

div.addEventListener("webkitAnimationStart", function(event) {
    alert('The animation "' + event.animationName + ' has started.');
}, false);
```

As for transitions, the name is case sensitive when used with the `addEventListener()` method, and you should follow the camel case syntax used in the previous example.

All three events use the new `AnimationEvent` object that adds the animation name to the base `Event` object through the `animationName` property. For `animationiteration` and `animationend`, as with transitions, the `elapsedTime` property lets you estimate the time elapsed during the animation.

Of course, this property will always return 0 for `animationstart`, because no delay before the animation is taken into account. The event will actually be triggered only after the delay is determined. Also note that because the `animationiteration` is replaced by `animationend` for the last iteration, you will never get an `animationiteration` if the counter is set to 1.

Special Effects with CSS

The latest versions of WebKit implement new properties that can make the life of web developers much easier, such as reflection or masks. These are not yet part of the CSS3 specifications, so they won't be exportable for some time to other browsers.

Creating Reflections

Although reflection has been a very popular effect for some time now, there is no optimal way to implement it into your pages. Up to now, solutions included creating a specific image for each element you wanted reflected—which isn't very flexible—or stacking 1-pixel high elements underneath your image and applying a positioned background to each one while acting on opacity, which is not very flexible either, because this can only work with images and it takes up a lot of extra markup. Both of these solutions of course are quite heavy on the rendering engine. WebKit comes with the new -webkit-box-reflect property, which should be used as follows:

```
-webkit-box-reflect: <direction> <offset> <mask-box-image>
```

The direction parameter, which determines to which side of the element the reflection should be built, can take either of four values: below, above, left, or right. The offset can be set using any valid CSS size unit, including percentages, and will determine the distance between the original image and its reflection. Finally, the mask can be any image supported for the background-image property, as Figure 9–11 demonstrates. The use of CSS gradients for the mask will of course make the process even simpler and lightweight.

```
<style>
    img {
        -webkit-box-reflect: below 3px
            -webkit-gradient(
                linear,
                left top, left bottom,
                color-stop(0.7, transparent), to(rgba(0, 0, 0, 0.75))
            )
    }
</style>

<img src="panda.jpg" alt="A nice panda">
```

Using a gradient, like any other image format, the most important element is the alpha channel, because pixels visible in the image used as a mask will be visible in the reflection. Therefore, you will most often use PNG, although all formats are supported. Using a format that doesn't support transparency (or an image with no transparent or partially transparent pixel) will be the same as not specifying a mask-box-image parameter: a full mask will be applied, with all pixels visible. Note that the image will be stretched to take all the available space of the reflection box.

Also keep in mind that when defining your reflection mask, even using a gradient, it will be reversed according to the direction: if the reflection is projected on the x-axis, it will be reversed as in a mirror, and it will be shown upside down if the projection is vertical.

Figure 9–11. *A simple reflection using a gradient*

> **NOTE:** On older WebKit versions, reflection doesn't work in association with transformations. Using reflections for your Cover Flow effect, you will see the reflection only for the focused element using iOS version 3.2 or earlier. This has been solved in the latest versions of Safari.

You can of course use SVG, in which case the transparency of the colors will determine the opacity of the pixels, or canvases, using the WebKit-specific -webkit-canvas() function, explained in Chapter 7. This way, you could easily define animations on your masks, for instance, if you wanted to create a wavy water-reflection effect.

Likewise, if the element from which the reflection is built changes—for instance during a hover event—the reflection will take this change into account. Finally, remember that, like shadows, CSS reflections do not change the dimensions of elements nor otherwise affect the layout.

Using Real Masks

The third parameter to the reflection function is a mask, which can let you achieve quite interesting effects once you have mastered their subtleties. Masks in WebKit are also available as such with many advanced options and will let you finely cut out parts of your page elements. The supported items supported for CSS masks are the same as for reflections, that is, images, gradients, SVG, and canvases. Masks are declared much like backgrounds, meaning that all the adjustments used for backgrounds—including those presented in Chapter 6—can be used for masks, and you shouldn't find difficult to master the new possibilities available to you. Figure 9–12 shows the effect of the following rule:

```
<style>
    img {
        -webkit-mask-image: url(mask.png);
        -webkit-mask-repeat: repeat-x;
        -webkit-mask-size: 50%;
    }
</style>

<img src="flower.jpg" alt="A nice flower">
```

Figure 9–12. *The content, mask, and association of the two with CSS*

Not only can you use masks on backgrounds, but they can also be applied on borders using the `-webkit-mask-box-image` property that behaves like the `border-image` property. Note, however, that, unlike border images, border masks do not adapt to the dimensions of the border; this means the corners will be rendered without scaling, and the rest of the mask will be tiled or stretched depending on the parameter you specify, regardless of the border itself.

Create an iOS-Like Tab Bar Using Masks

To convey an idea of the possibilities offered by masks and their options, we will create a tab bar similar to that provided by the UITabBar object of the Cocoa Touch API, which is often used in native applications (Figure 9–13).

Figure 9–13. *The classic tab bar in the bottom of the Phone application*

For this we will rely on canvases, masks, and the flexible box model that we introduced in Chapter 6. Also, we will use the new `:target` pseudo-oclass to activate the current tab, so absolutely no script or images are required.

Getting the Initial Tab Bar Ready

We are going to base our example on the web application template used and extended in previous chapters. Simply add the code associated with our tabs:

```
...
<body>
    <div class="view">
        <div class="header-wrapper">
            <h1>Tab Bar Demo</h1>
        </div>

        <nav class="tabbar-wrapper">
            <ul>
                <li id="tab1"><a href="#tab1"><b><i></i></b>Most Recent</a></li>
                <li id="tab2"><a href="#tab2"><b><i></i></b>Favorites</a></li>
                <li id="tab3"><a href="#tab3"><b><i></i></b>Search</a></li>
                <li id="tab4"><a href="#tab4"><b><i></i></b>Bookmarks</a></li>
                <li id="tab5"><a href="#tab5"><b><i></i></b>History</a></li>
            </ul>
        </nav>
    </div>
</body>
...
```

The :target pseudo-class is going to let us focus the tab relevant to the active hash in the URL. To do this, we add an ID to each list item of the list identical to the hash specified as href to the anchor. The <i> and <b> tags will only be placeholders for the tab icons and their shadows. This will be explained thoroughly later in this chapter.

Next, we add some rules to our *main.css* file to style our tab bar. This shares some resemblance with the header; it is simply higher and uses a slightly different gradient, because the base color is black.

```css
.tabbar-wrapper {
    background-color: black;
    background-image:
        -webkit-gradient(linear, left top, left bottom,
            from(rgba(255, 255, 255, 0.2)),
                to(rgba(255, 255, 255, 0.1)) );
    background-repeat: no-repeat;
    background-position: top left;
    -webkit-background-size: 100% 50%;
    border-top: solid 1px rgba(0,0,0,0.6);
    position: absolute;
    bottom: 0;
    width: 100%;
}
```

Then, here are the rules relative to the list itself:

```css
.tabbar-wrapper ul {
    border-top: solid 1px rgba(255, 255, 255, 0.2);
    height: 48px;
    display: -webkit-box;
    margin: 0;
    padding: 2px;
    text-align: center;
    color: hsla(0,0%,100%, 0.65);
    font-weight: bold;
    font-size: 9px;
    line-height: 1;
    -webkit-box-sizing: border-box;
}

.tabbar-wrapper li {
    width: 100%;
    list-style: none;
    -webkit-box-flex: 1;
    padding: 2px;
    margin-top: -1px;
}

.tabbar-wrapper li a {
    color: inherit;
    text-decoration: none;
    display: block;
}
```

So as not to worry about the size of our tabs, we use the box display mode for our container (<ul>). From there, in order to make the tabs take up all the available width, whatever the number of tabs and their individual width, we set their box-flex property to 1. Thus, even when the user changes the orientation of the device, our tab bar will consistently span across the screen.

A Placeholder for Icons

Before adding icons to our tabs, let's handle the tab selection, as announced, using the :target pseudo-class. This is done as follows:

```
.tabbar-wrapper li:target {
    color: white;
    -webkit-border-radius: 3px;
    background-color: hsla(0, 0%, 100%, 0.2);
    text-shadow: rgba(0, 0, 0, .5) 1px 1px 1px;
}
```

Now, we can add the placeholder for our tab icons. Before applying a mask to draw the icons, we define the containers that will hold the shadow and the blue icon.

```
.tabbar-wrapper li b {
    display: block;
    width: 36px;
    height: 36px;
    margin: -3px auto -1px;
    padding: 2px;
    -webkit-box-sizing: border-box;
}

.tabbar-wrapper li i {
    display:block;
    width:32px;
    height:32px;
    background-image: -webkit-gradient(
        linear, left top, left bottom, from(#bbb), to(#666)
    );
}

.tabbar-wrapper li:target i {
    background-image:
        -webkit-gradient(radial, 72 170, 160, 72 170, 184,
            from(rgba(255,255,255,0)),
            color-stop(0, rgba(255, 255, 255, 0.3)),
            color-stop(0, rgba(255, 255, 255, 0.35)),
            to(white)
        ),
        -webkit-gradient(linear, left top, left bottom, from(#0062db), to(#44d5fe));
    -webkit-background-size: 48px 32px;
    background-position: right top;
}
```

The backgrounds define the gray and blue gradients (Figure 9–14) for the unfocused and focused states of our tabs. They will show through the mask once it is defined. You can already check the behavior of the `:target` pseudo-class by loading the page in your browser.

Figure 9–14. *The gray and blue gradients, before the application of masks*

Icons Management

To create our icons, we are going to use the "sprite" technique, commonly used to limit HTTP requests for background images; it can be used for masks also. As with backgrounds, you will simply have to move the image within the container to show different areas of the mask.

We have defined two containers—one that's 36x36 pixels represented by a `<b>` tag, which will contain the shadow, and the other that's 32x32 pixels represented by an `<i>` tag, which will hold the icon mask. The shadow placeholder is slightly larger than the actual icon placeholder, because in order to be visible, the shadow must span beyond the limits of the icon (in this case, to the bottom right).

For our icons, we need an image whose alpha channel represents the shapes of the pictographs we want to use; we will use canvases to build a template that will represent the successive display stages. Figure 9–15 represents the template we are going to use.

For each shape, we are going to align three areas from this template vertically. The first element represents the icon. The image holding the mask needs to be drawn black on a transparent background, up to 30 pixels wide and high, and offset by 1 pixel from the top and left. For a better result, the icon should be centered in the 30x30 pixels area. Also note that within the black zone, you may draw some transparent pixels. The two additional pixels of the `<i>` container will let us correctly position the icon in the tab bar.

The second element will be used for the shadow on unfocused tabs, which will emboss the icon materialized by a gray gradient, as explained earlier. This area will be drawn directly from the canvas by copying the first area without the 1-pixel vertical offset and setting a lower opacity value. This is why the icon has to be drawn black.

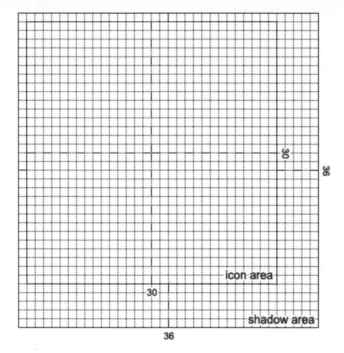

Figure 9–15. *The template used to build an icon*

To draw the last element, the drop shadow, we can copy the first one again and change the opacity value three times (Figure 9–16). Proceeding this way, we needn't worry about the actual shape of the icon we draw to render the shadow.

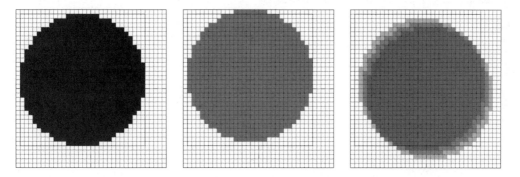

Figure 9–16. *A basic icon as three elements: the icon, the emboss shadow, and the regular shadow*

We can now create our icons and use them in our tabs using masks.

Creating Icons

The canvas definition that holds the different images should be declared within the client code rather than from the main style sheet, because you are likely to need several tab bars in the same web application at some stage. We are going to use the -webkit-canvas() function, as shown in the following code:

```
<style>

.tabbar-wrapper li i {
    -webkit-mask-image: -webkit-canvas(tabbar-icons);
}

.tabbar-wrapper li b {
    background-image: -webkit-canvas(tabbar-icons);
}

</style>
```

As explained earlier, the <i> tag holds the icon, and we will use the previously defined gradients. A mask will let us "cut out" the icon shape from the gradients. The <b> tag will hold a background that will simulate a shadow; we won't need a mask for this, because the shadow will already be defined from the canvas.

Here is how the icons are finally defined:

```
<script>

const AREA_SIZE = 36;

/* Prepare the 3 states of 3 icons */
initTabBarIcons("tabbar-icons", 3, createIcons);

function initTabBarIcons(id, count, src) {
    var ctx = document.getCSSCanvasContext("2d", id, AREA_SIZE * count, AREA_SIZE * 3);

    if (typeof src == 'function') {
        src(ctx);
        createShadows(ctx);

    } else {
        var i = new Image();
        i.onload = function() {
            ctx.drawImage(this, 0, 0);
            createShadows(ctx);
        }
        i.src = src;
    }
}

</script>
```

The initTabBarIcons() function takes three parameters. The two first parameters are rather straightforward—first, the ID of the canvas to hold the icon states, and second, the number of icons in order to correctly fit the canvas width. The last parameter can be either a function or the URL of an image. In the first case, the functions will be called to draw icons to the relevant context (passed as first parameter) using the Canvas API. In the second case, the image will be loaded and then drawn to the canvas using the drawImage() method. The image has to be built according to the scheme explained earlier.

For now, let's draw our icons using the first configuration, with the createIcons() function. We will go through the more common case later.

```
function createIcons(ctx) {
    ctx.save();

    /* Offset of 1x1 pixel */
    ctx.translate(1, 1);
    ctx.fillStyle = "black";

    /* A circle icon */
    ctx.beginPath();
    ctx.arc(15, 15, 15, 0, Math.PI * 2, false);
    ctx.fill();

    /* A square icon */
    ctx.translate(AREA_SIZE, 0);
    ctx.fillRect(0, 0, 30, 30);

    /* A triangle icon */
    ctx.translate(AREA_SIZE, 0);
    ctx.moveTo(15, 0);
    ctx.lineTo(30, 30);
    ctx.lineTo(0, 30);
    ctx.fill();

    ctx.restore();
}
```

Now, our canvas has three basic icons, for which the function createShadows() is going to build shadows, as evoked earlier, by copying the icon and altering its opacity and position. Figure 9–17 shows the final result.

```
function createShadows(ctx) {
    var c = ctx.canvas;
    var w = c.width;
    var h = c.height / 3;

    ctx.save();

    /* Draw the emboss shadow */
    ctx.globalAlpha = 0.25;
    ctx.drawImage(c, 0,0,w,h, 0,h*1-1,w,h);

    /* Draw the drop shadow */
    ctx.globalAlpha = 0.1;
    ctx.drawImage(c, 0,0,w,h, 1,h*2+0,w,h);
    ctx.drawImage(c, 0,0,w,h, 2,h*2+1,w,h);
    ctx.drawImage(c, 0,0,w,h, 3,h*2+2,w,h);

    ctx.restore();
}
```

Figure 9–17. *The final result showing icons and their shadows*

The canvas is now ready, so we need only add styles to position the shadows within their areas. Here is the code to be added to the main style sheet:

```
.tabbar-wrapper li b {
...
    background-position: 2px -34px;
}
.tabbar-wrapper li:target b {
    background-position: 2px -70px;
}
```

Because we have a 2-pixel padding, we adjust the position of the background shadow (<b>) so that it is aligned with the icon (<i>). Then, we select the relevant shadow by moving the canvas upward, depending on the state of the icon.

If you test your page now, you will see that all tabs have the same round icon. To use a different icon for each tab, still using the "sprite" technique, you simply need to move the background by a specific amount of pixels. Because our blocs are 36 pixels wide and the shadow requires a 2-pixel offset, the following code added to our CSS file will take care of that:

```
<style>
...
    .tabbar-wrapper li:nth-child(2) i { -webkit-mask-position-x: -36px; }
    .tabbar-wrapper li:nth-child(3) i { -webkit-mask-position-x: -72px; }
    .tabbar-wrapper li:nth-child(4) i { -webkit-mask-position-x: -36px; }

    .tabbar-wrapper li:nth-child(2) b { background-position-x: -34px; }
    .tabbar-wrapper li:nth-child(3) b { background-position-x: -70px; }
    .tabbar-wrapper li:nth-child(4) b { background-position-x: -34px; }

</style>
```

Because we have only three icons for five tabs, we use two icons twice, as shown in Figure 9–18. Sprites are a very convenient and flexible way to define background images, and as stated earlier, they will generally help making your applications faster to load, because they limit the number of HTTP requests, which is especially appreciable on mobile devices.

Figure 9–18. *Our tabs with icons appropriately positioned*

Custom Icons Using an Image

Our `initTabBarIcons()` function can take an image URL as its third parameter. Of course, this will often be more flexible and familiar to developers than using the Canvas API to draw icons. The image should contain as many black icons as needed, on a transparent background, using the template shown earlier. The following call to the function uses the image presented on Figure 9–19 to create the tab bar shown in Figure 9–20:

```
<script>
    initTabBarIcons("tabbar-icons", 5, "icons.png");
</script>

<style>
...
    .tabbar-wrapper li:nth-child(4) i { -webkit-mask-position-x: -108px; }
    .tabbar-wrapper li:nth-child(5) i { -webkit-mask-position-x: -144px; }
...
    .tabbar-wrapper li:nth-child(4) b { background-position-x: -106px; }
    .tabbar-wrapper li:nth-child(5) b { background-position-x: -142px; }

</style>
```

Figure 9–19. *`icons.png` is used for the tab bar icons*

Figure 9–20. *A tab bar using an external image*

First, the image is copied to the canvas and the building process is launched. Then everything happens exactly like when using a canvas definition, and the icons are positioned. The process is very simple to set up and makes code maintenance easy, because only one image is required to handle both the icons and their shadows.

Summary

Although the new CSS properties introduced in this chapter may seem unfamiliar and somewhat disturbing, you will soon find that they can greatly enhance the user experience for your web applications, both by making them more appealing visually via animations and masks and by allowing better performances relying on hardware optimized transformations.

By limiting the number of images and scripts required to achieve attractive effects, not only should you be able to limit the number of HTTP requests, reduce the overall file size to be loaded for your pages, and make your pages easier to process for the rendering engine, you should end up with code that is easier to maintain, more flexible, and, with some practice, faster to build.

## Part III

Going Futher with JavaScript and Web Standards

## Chapter 10

An Object-Oriented JavaScript Programming Primer

It is more than likely that, as shown in the previous chapters, you will heavily rely on JavaScript to build your web applications. Over time, client-side scripting has become an ever more crucial tool for developers, with the progress of hardware, the evolution of expectations, and, recently, new APIs that bring the most desirable functionality to web content.

However, this language, to be efficiently used, requires that the developer understands some of its specificities, such as weak typing and its object model. We will explain the object-oriented programming part, which should help you bring more modularity to your programs, encapsulate some APIs to make their use more flexible and generic, and make them easier to maintain. This chapter will also help you better understand execution context issues that you are likely to run into when using event handlers or callback functions, as used extensively in the upcoming chapters. You will also find out how to effectively solve the problems of code execution isolation when you need to work with third-party scripts to enhance your web applications or when you provide scripts to other sites yourself.

From the Procedural Model...

The procedural programming model is still widespread nowadays. As in BASIC, this means you use a series of functions to control the state of your program by modifying variables and changing their values. The most common way to do this is as follows:

```
var state = add(5, 6, 7);

function add(a, b, c) {
    return a + b + c;
}
```

Proceeding this way, you multiply the number of independent and possibly redundant functions and variables. Yet, in JavaScript, this is actually already OOP. As soon as you define a function, the scripting engine creates an instance of the Function object. Therefore, the previous code is the same as what follows:

```
var add = new Function("a", "b", "c", "return a + b + c");
```

The Function object takes a series of strings as parameters, the last always being the code to be executed and the others being arguments for use by the defined function. There are several ways to declare these parameters. You can declare them as we did previously, or you can group comma-separated arguments within the same string to form the list of parameters for the function. Hence, the previous example could have been written like this:

```
var add = new Function("a, b", "c", "return a + b + c");
var add = new Function("a, b, c", "return a + b + c");
```

Of course, the function keyword is a very useful shortcut, because declaring a function within a string the way it is done using the Function object would quickly prove difficult to handle.

Using instantiation for our previous example will quite evidently result in code similar to the following example:

```
var add = function(a, b, c) {
    return a + b + c;
}
```

Note that you can also add a name to your function so that it can refer to itself within the function. Specifically, this declaration type is the basis of creating objects.

...to Object-Oriented Programming

When a function is declared, an object is created internally that is attached to the global object of the hosting environment. With JavaScript, in the browser context, this is the DOMWindow object of the browser, accessible using the window property. This means when you declare a function, you extend the window object, and the function will be accessible through this property, as any variable would be.

```
var state = window.add(5, 6, 7);
var result = window.state;
```

Using the faculty of objects to be extended with properties and methods, we are going to create a simple program to illustrate the assets of OOP.

A First Custom Object

Using object-oriented programming, any object inherits from the base object Object, as seen in languages like .NET or Java. This means all properties and methods available to the Object object will be available to the inheriting object. The most common example is the toString() method. So, beginning to create our object, we create an instance of Object with the new keyword. From there we can extend it with the following code:

```
var animal = new Object();

/* Additional properties */
animal.family = "Unnamed";
animal.noise = "Silent";
animal.legs = 4;

/* New method */
animal.makeNoise = function() {
    console.log("The noise of " + this.family + " is " + this.noise + ".");
}
```

Calling the function and reading the properties of our object is easy:

```
animal.makeNoise();
console.log(animal.legs);
```

```
--- result ---
> The noise of Unnamed is Silent.
> 4
```

In our examples, we adopt the naming conventions of the language, that is, *camel case*, with an uppercase first letter for object definitions and a lowercase first letter for its properties.

The keyword this will let you access the current execution context. In our example, this is the instance of the object, which allows us to reach the properties previously defined and use them to build a readable string. The execution context is an important notion that we will explain in more detail shortly.

The effect achieved with the previous code can also be reached using a slightly different syntax.

```
var animal = {
    family: "Unnamed",
    noise: "Silent",
    legs: 4,

    makeNoise: function() {
        console.log("The noise of " + this.family + " is " + this.noise);
    }
};
```

This method to create objects is called an *object initializer*. It can be useful to dynamically create anonymous objects and, for instance, return several values from a function; however, it doesn't offer the flexibility provided by other object-oriented languages, because the definition of the object here isn't easily reusable.

Using a Proper Constructor

The animal we have created obviously isn't very lively yet. Let's remedy this. To make our object structure reusable, we need to add a constructor using a Function object.

ECMAScript doesn't have actual classes but uses constructors that let you allocate the object and initialize its properties. The following code does just that:

```
/* Constructor */
var Animal = function() {
    /* Properties */

    this.family = "Unnamed";
    this.noise = "Silent";
    this.legs = 4;

    /* Method */
    this.makeNoise = function() {
        console.log("The noise of " + this.family + " is " + this.noise + ".");
    }
}
```

This allows you to get an instance of `Animal`, using the `new` keyword again.

```
/* Create a first instance of Animal */
var animal1 = new Animal();
animal1.family = "Mussel";

/* Create a new instance of Animal */
var animal2 = new Animal();
animal2.family = "Plankton";

animal1.makeNoise();
animal2.makeNoise();

--- result ---
> The noise of Mussel is Silent.
> The noise of Plankton is Silent.
```

This means we can use our object as many times as needed with totally independent instances, each holding their own properties. Still, this is not optimal, because the syntax used to declare each method forces the engine to instantiate a new `Function` object for the `makeNoise()` method for every instance rather than using a reference to the object. This means that more memory will be used, which could be a problem if the object is used intensively.

Better Performance with Prototype

There is a property introduced by ECMAScript that solves this reinstantiation issue, named `prototype`. Every constructor has this property available to implement inheritance and shared properties. Hence, we can further better our object:

```
/* Constructor */
var Animal = function() {
    this.family = "Unnamed";
    this.noise = "Silent";
    this.legs = 4;
}

/* A more efficient way to define a method */
```

```
Animal.prototype.makeNoise = function() {
    console.log("The noise of " + this.family + " is " + this.noise + ".");
}
```

The defined method will be shared by all instances of the Animal object and will be instantiated only once. This is true for all properties defined this way.

> **WARNING:** This is an important notion: all properties defined using prototype will be shared by all instances of the object. Hence, modifying the value of a property will impact all instances.

Of course, this syntax uses more code; therefore, you should always seek a good balance between concise code and memory usage. Still, referring to the Function object instead of instantiating makes a great difference in performance, because allotting memory is a very greedy operation. Safari's Web Inspector should be of some help to evaluate this, as shown in Chapter 3.

Implementing Inheritance

Although JavaScript is an object-oriented language, it isn't based on the class concept, like C++ or Java, for instance. Instead, it relies on constructors and prototypes, and each constructor has a prototype property available to it. The engine implicitly sets the value of this property to a reference that points to an instance of Object, which implies that it inherits from Object. This instance will be shared by all instances of your object, which is the reason why all methods defined using prototype will also be shared, because they extend prototype.

Prototype-Based Inheritance

To implement prototype-based inheritance for your own objects, you simply need to redefine prototype so that it inherits from your object instead of Object. Thus, to further specify your animals, you could use the following code:

```
/* Constructor */
var Dog = function() {
    this.family = "Dog";
    this.noise = "Woof!";
};

/* Dog will inherit from Animal */
Dog.prototype = new Animal;

/* Add a new method to Dog */
Dog.prototype.showLegs = function() {
    console.log("The " + this.family + " has " + this.legs + " legs.");
}
```

We define a new object called Dog, whose default properties are changed using the constructor to actually fit with a dog. Other properties are already defined through the

Animal constructor, as illustrated in our next block of code. The previous script starts with a instantiation of `Animal` that is associated with the `prototype` property of the Dog object when the code is evaluated. The call to the constructor of Dog will occur only after this initialization, using the `new` keyword.

```
var dog = new Dog();
dog.makeNoise();
dog.showLegs();
```

```
--- result ---
> The noise of Dog is Woof!.
> The Dog has 4 legs.
```

Here the `legs` property is present, although it hasn't been defined in the constructor of Dog, and the `makeNoise()` method returns a string with the appropriate values for `family` and `noise`. Proof is made that Dog inherits from Animal.

Shared Properties

However desirable limiting memory usage and function instance multiplication may be, you could learn the hard way that, using inheritance, all properties from the inherited object (arrays, anonymous objects, and so on) are also defined using this principle and thus are shared by all instances of your object. You could, for instance, add an array to your initial object to hold all of the eye color values for your animals.

```
var Animal = function() {
...
    this.eyeColor = [];
}
```

You would then create two dogs with their own eye color:

```
var dog1 = new Dog();
dog1.eyeColor.push("brown", "brown");

var dog2 = new Dog();
dog2.eyeColor.push("blue", "brown");
console.log(dog1.eyeColor);
console.log(dog2.eyeColor);
```

```
--- result ---
> ["brown", "brown", "blue", "brown"]
> ["brown", "brown", "blue", "brown"]
```

And, as you can see, you would have two dogs, each with no less than four eyes. This can be remedied by defining an `initialize()` method, which should be used to initialize sensitive properties. Doing just this will return more appropriate information.

```
var Animal = function() {
...
    this.initialize();
}

Animal.prototype.initialize = function() {
    this.eyeColor = [];
```

```
}
var Dog = function() {
    ...
    this.initialize();
}

--- result ---
> ["brown", "brown"]
> ["blue", "brown"]
```

This convenient method prevents the inheriting object from gathering what its parent contains and initializes. Reinitializing properties directly from the constructor of Dog is possible but would harm the maintainability of your code, because you would have to change Dog every time you altered the definition of Animal. However, redefining a property in an inheriting object doesn't mean that its initial value is lost, as shown with the following example:

```
Animal.prototype.initialize = function() {
    this.eyeColor = ["initial value"];
}
...
console.log(dog1.eyesColor);
delete dog1.eyesColor;          // Delete the property created with initialize()
console.log(dog1.eyesColor);    // Return the property from Animal
console.log(dog2.eyesColor);    // Other instances are not affected

--- result ---
> ["brown", "brown"]
> ["initial value"]
> ["blue", "brown"]
```

The object dog1 is instantiated, which creates a new eyeColor property on the prototype. This way, the previous code will return the correct value for the eye color of our first dog. Then, we empty this property using the delete operator. With the next access to the property, the scripting engine will move up the prototype hierarchy until it finds a property with the same name and returns the value of this property, if any. This is why we get the content of the array as defined for the Animal object.

Generally, this initialization issue isn't encountered with properties with a more primitive type such as Boolean or Number, because the most common technique is to redefine values directly on the property. On the contrary, it is common to use methods to populate an array (such as push() or unshift()) or to scan it (such as pop() or shift()); hence, you would be working directly on the shared instance of the Array object, instead of working on the property.

The Prototype Chain

ECMAScript introduces the *prototype chain* concept. The prototype property allows you, as indicated earlier, to move up the chain of the original properties of inherited objects. This is what the engine does when it calls a method. Thus, calling dog.makeNoise(), the engine checks whether Dog has this method; if this is not the case, it will move up the chain until it finds the called method—or not. This specificity can be used to call methods of the base object. For this, you simply have to get the base prototype and call the method with the correct execution context.

```
var Dog = function() {
    this._base = this.constructor.prototype;
...
}

Dog.prototype.makeNoise = function() {
    console.log("Modified Version...");
    this._base.makeNoise.call(this);
}

var dog = new Dog();
dog.makeNoise();

--- result ---
> Modified Version...
> The noise of Dog is Woof!.
```

We use the internal `constructor` property to access the prototype in order not to depend on the initial object. We could have used, for the value of _base, `Animal.prototype`. The _base property is used to call `makeNoise()` through the `call()` method of the object `Function`. This method will let you specify the execution context and thus use the values from the current object properties, not those of the base object.

The Execution Context

Programming with JavaScript, the execution context is a crucial notion. It is what determines what is accessible and what isn't at the moment some code is executed and functions are accessed. The `call()` method of the `Function` object takes at least an execution context as a first parameter; you can then add a comma-separated list of other parameters that will be passed to the called function.

Using the call() and apply() Methods

One problem is that you may not always know exactly how many parameters you might need to pass to your function when you call it. Moreover, fixing parameters explicitly for the `call()` method doesn't favor maintainability and code reusability. Here's an example:

```
Animal.prototype.initialize = function() {
...
    this.colors = [];
}

Animal.prototype.setColors = function(color1, color2) {
    this.colors.splice(0, this.eyesColor.length);
    this.colors.push(color1);
    this.colors.push(color2);
```

```
}

Dog.prototype.setColors = function(color1, color2) {
    console.log("Adding colors: " + color1 + ", " + color2);
    this._base.setColors.call(this, color1, color2);
}

dog.setColors("white", "maroon");
```

Here, it is clear that this process isn't very flexible, because only two colors can be attributed to an animal. This could be addressed simply by using a variable number of parameters that would be processed in a loop using the `arguments` property, as illustrated here:

```
Animal.prototype.setColors = function() {
    this.colors.splice(0, this.eyesColor.length);

    for (var i = 0; i < arguments.length; i++) {
        this.colors.push(arguments[i]);
    }
}
```

To solve the problem met with the `setColors()` function of the object inheriting from `Animal`, you can use the `apply()` method of the `Function` object. This method takes the execution context as a parameter, like when using `call()`, and takes arguments, unlike `call()`, as an array, instead of a list. Hence, our code can be optimized.

```
Animal.prototype.setColors = function() {
    this.colors.splice(0, this.eyeColor.length);
    this.colors.push.apply(this.colors, arguments);
}

Dog.prototype.setColors = function() {
    console.log("Adding colors: " + arguments.join(", "));
    this._base.setColors.apply(this, arguments);
}
```

Because we know which type of argument the function expects, we needn't list these in the function declaration; the only unknown element is the number of arguments. With the `setColor()` method of the `Animal` object, we use `apply()` on the `push()` method, which initially takes a list of elements to add to an array. In this case, the context needn't be modified but has to be specified, so we use `this.colors` to keep the correct context.

Then, to simplify the call of the base method from within `Dog`, we replace `call()` with `apply()`, to make the number of arguments totally unimportant. You will therefore be able to call any method from the base object whatever the signature of the function.

The `apply()` method should come to great use developing web applications as soon as the application relies on lists whose lengths vary dynamically. For instance, this method can be used to handle an array of objects holding data in order to display a list of e-mails and to let the user show more messages using a More button, like in the iPhone Mail application. In this case, `apply()` would let you save a loop by simply adding the objects to the list with the `push()` method of the `Array` object.

This is more efficient, because the process is handled natively by the scripting engine and doesn't have to be interpreted in a loop.

Taking Care of the Execution Context

This is all rather simple, but it may sometimes be difficult to identify where a piece of code is going wrong, especially when using a reference to a method. For instance, using the first definition of Dog, you could expect that funcRef() would return the same string as seen previously.

```
var funcRef = dog.makeNoise;
funcRef();
```

```
--- result ---
> The noise of undefined is undefined
```

On the contrary, here, the properties are not available, so their return value is undefined. This is because the reference was taken on the function makeNoise(). Although makeNoise() is referred to through an instance of Dog, it has no relation with any context. In this case, dog.makeNoise is a reference to an instance of the function.

Calling dog.makeNoise(), the context is fixed by the dog object. Because the method is called with dog and the context is the caller of the function, this refers to the instance of Dog, and the result is as expected.

On the other side, when defining funcRef, dog was used only to access the reference to the instance of the function. After that, the engine moves out of the context (dog) to execute the next instruction. Thus, when we actually call funcRef(), the *calling context* is set to the default context, the global window object. This is easily verified, as shown here:

```
...
var family = "Bird";
funcRef();
```

```
--- result ---
> The noise of Bird is undefined
```

This kind of issue comes up often when you're building web applications, because you will often rely on a reference to define event handlers and timers. Using addEventListener(), the context is always that of the object to which the listener is attached to; managing setTimeout() and setInterval(), which are methods of the window object, the context will be window itself.

Setting the Proper Context with Handlers and Callbacks

In Chapter 7, we have created a spinner with the canvas and JavaScript. In the functions we used, you may have noted that we put the value of this into the variable that and then encapsulated the call in an anonymous function. This technique lets you use the right context and thus allows you to correctly execute methods with the right instance. Here is the relevant part of the code, the `animate()` method of the `BigSpinner` object:

```
BigSpinner.prototype.animate = function() {
    /* Already running? exit... */
    if (this.timer) {
        return;
    }

    /* The execution context (this) will be the window object with setInterval()
       Save the correct context in "that" variable and run the timer */
    var that = this;
    this.timer = window.setInterval(function() {
        that.draw();
    }, 100);
}
```

The variable that is local. Still, because it is referenced within the timer, it will be kept in memory, and its range will be valid until the timer is canceled with the `clearInterval()` method. This is the most common way to call a method by reference. To make the syntax of such a technique easier in your code, you can extend the native `Function` object with a new method that will bind an execution to a specific context. Note that all native objects can be extended. You should also notice that we test for the existence of such a method; this is because it is planned for with the fifth version of the ECMAScript specification. Our version is simplified.

```
if (!Function.prototype.bind) {
    Function.prototype.bind = function(ctx) {
        var that = this;

        return function() {
            that.apply(ctx, arguments);
        }
    }
}
```

However convenient this may be, be aware that every time you call this function, the `Function` object will be instantiated anew. Therefore, if you need to use this reference several times, consider associating it to a variable or a property in order not to take up too much memory. Also take into account that saving the reference is necessary to remove an event listener. In the following code, you wouldn't obtain the expected result, because two different instances are passed to the `addEventListener()` and `removeEventListener()` methods.

```
/* Listen to "load" event */
document.body.addEventListener("click", some.method.bind(someParameter), false);

/* Try to remove listener, but nothing happens */
document.body.removeEventListener("click", some.method.bind(someParameter), false);
```

Instead, you should do as follows, which will work:

```
/* Get a reference */
var ref = some.method.bind(some);
```

```
/* Listen to "load" event */
document.body.addEventListener("click", ref, false);

/* The listener can be found and removed */
document.body.removeEventListener("click", ref, false);
```

Here, the references in the listener methods are to the same instance, and the second method will find the method used in the first. This of course is important, especially when repeatedly adding and removing listeners for animations, as we saw in our previous chapter about CSS transitions. Indeed, as long as a listener hasn't been removed, the instance of the object is still being referenced, the listener is still working, and the memory load and CPU load will continuously grow, as more and more code is executed for a same event.

Accessing Properties and Methods

As illustrated in this chapter, it is easy to access a property with commands with the form object.property. The same is true for methods, because these are properties that reference an instance of the Function object. All these properties are actually stored as key/value pairs in a hash table. Hence, they are accessible using the object["property"] syntax, which is especially useful, for instance, when setting properties for a character in a role-playing game. This is similar to the DOM setAttribute() method.

```
var Character = function(name) {
    this.patronym = name || "The Unknown";

    this.characteristics = {
        stamina: 10,
        mana: 10,
        skill: 10,
        health: 100
    };
}

Character.prototype.setCharacteristic = function(prop, value) {
    if (this.characteristics.hasOwnProperty(prop)) {
        if (value >= 0 && value <= 250) {
            this.characteristics[prop] = value;
        }
    }
}

Character.prototype.showCharacteristics = function() {
    console.log("Characteristics of " + this.patronym + ":");
    for (var prop in this.characteristics) {
        console.log("=>" + prop + ": " + this.characteristics[prop]);
    }
}

var paladin = new Character("Danis");
paladin.setCharacteristic("health", 200);
paladin.setCharacteristic("mana", 0);
```

```
paladin.showCharacteristics();

--- result ---
> Characteristics of Danis:
> => stamina: 10
> => mana: 0
> => skill: 10
> => health: 200
```

To prevent our characteristics object from artificially growing, we check that the requested property exists when setCharacteristic() is called. Besides, we check that the value is within a reasonable interval. Checking that properties exist also prevents errors due to letter case, because properties are always case sensitive.

In our example, we have used the hash table syntax to iterate through our properties using the for...in statement and to display their values. Be careful, however; because our example properties are displayed in the same order as they were declared in, this won't necessarily happen. Never expect a specific order when scanning the properties of an object.

Defining Getters and Setters

In our previous example, we have used a method to set the values for several properties, which is quite similar to using a setter in other object-oriented programming languages. JavaScript will also let you define getters and setters, also called *accessors*, though this is of limited use, because unlike some more complex languages, you won't be able to define object properties other than *public* ones. There is no native way to define private properties meant only for use within one specific object. Therefore, whereas programming with other languages you would try to protect access to some variables to make your code easier to maintain, it is common with JavaScript to leave variables of an object instance available to the client code.

Programming in JavaScript, you should dissociate elements from an existing object to use them as properties rather than use a method. Accessors will also allow for control over the access and over the associable values by a property. For instance, if you wanted to create an object that would count the time elapsed during the execution of a function to compare one technique to another, you could expose the conversion from milliseconds to seconds using a property created with a getter.

```
/* Object definition */
var Timing = function() {
    this.elapsed = 0;
}

Timing.prototype.test = function(iter, func) {
    var time = new Date();

    for (var i = 0; i < iter; i++) {
        func();
    }
    this.elapsed = new Date() - time;
}
```

```
Timing.prototype.__defineGetter__("seconds",
    function() { return this.elapsed / 1000; });

/* Using the object... */
var timer = new Timing();

/* Test Math.floor() speed */
timer.test(1000000, function() { var a = Math.floor(10.6) });
console.log(timer.seconds);

/* Test shorter/faster way */
timer.test(1000000, function() { var a = (10.6 << 0) });
console.log(timer.seconds);

--- result ---
> 0.035
> 0.011
```

We have a read-only property that lets us get the elapsed time in seconds using the __defineGetter__ method. This method takes the name of the property to create as a first parameter and a function to call as a second parameter. This, however, only allows you to read the value. To be able to write to the property, you also need to define a setter. You should define such a function like a getter, only passing a value to the associated function.

```
Timing.prototype.__defineSetter__("reset",
    function(value) {
        if (value === true) {
            this.elapsed = 0
        }
    });
```

Accessors can be added either to an object, as shown here, or dynamically to an instance. You can also use them directly with object initializers, using the get and set keywords to prefix the relevant property.

```
var something = {
    prop: "value",
    get someProp() { return this.prop },
    set someProp(value)  { this.prop = value }
};
```

This can be useful in some cases, but keep in mind that these accessors are slower to execute than a method that would do the same thing—which in turn would still be slower than a regular property. Note that although these accessors are not standards, they are supported by Mobile Safari and by many other browsers. Therefore, they may be of more use for very large JavaScript applications where strong control over properties guarantees that the code is correctly executed.

Code Isolation and Libraries

It is often desirable to isolate code as much as possible from other scripts in a web page or site to avoid conflicts when using a third-party snippet or when providing libraries to other web applications. This can be done resorting to the *scope chain*. The scope chain defines the environment, bound to the execution context, where a function is executed. In other words, it is a list of objects that are scanned when evaluating a property. Every call to a function pushes new elements on this chain.

Isolating Your Code

Isolating code is rather straightforward to implement: you just have to enclose your function in parentheses to force evaluation and then launch execution as with any function reference.

```
(function() {
    /* Your code here */
})();
```

Anything declared within this function will be pushed to the scope chain and won't be accessible from functions external to it, because its context will be bound to this function. Thus, there is no risk of overwriting external properties, as long as you use the var keyword to force the definition of a new variable. Not using this keyword would result in a search against the scope chain that could move up to a corresponding declaration outside the function.

```
var variable1 = "This is external variable 1.";
var variable2 = "This is external variable 2.";

function someFunc() {
    console.log("External someFunc() called.");
}

(function() {
    var variable0 = "Not accessible from external code.";
    var variable1 = "This is internal variable 1.";
    variable2 = "This is bad... replaced external variable 2.";

    function someFunc() {
        console.log("Internal someFunc() called.");
        console.log("Am I in 'window' context: " + (this == window));
    }

    /* Trace starts here... */
    someFunc();
    window.someFunc();
})();

/* ...and continues here */
console.log(variable0);
console.log(variable1);
console.log(variable2);
someFunc();

--- result ---
> Internal someFunc() called.
> Am I in 'window' context: true
> External someFunc() called.
```

```
x ReferenceError: Can't find variable: variable0
> This is external variable 1.
> This is bad... replaced external variable 2.
> External someFunc() called.
```

In the previous code, we define two external variables and a global function named someFunc; then, we write some code that is isolated and executed immediately. You will have noticed that the second internal variable doesn't overwrite its external counterpart, because it is defined using the var keyword. On the contrary, for the last variable, no keyword is used—the engine hence looks for a property with this name in the scope chain and, finding one, will set a new value for it. Finally, someFunc() is not overwritten, because its definition is equivalent to the following:

```
var someFunc = function() { ... }
```

Therefore, it will be pushed to the scope chain and found on the stack whenever someFunc() is called. Of course, you can also call the someFunc() method previously defined by specifying the object to which it is attached—window in our example. The var keyword works differently outside a function and binds variables and functions as properties of the global object.

Creating a Library

Now, let's consider that our isolated function may return something, like an object initializer; then, you would be defining a static object with private variables and functions.

```
var MyStatic = (function() {
    var localVariable = "LOCAL";

    var public = {
            someProp: "PUBLIC",
            someMethod: function() {
                console.log(localVariable);
            }
    };

    localVariable += " " + public.someProp;

    return public;
})();

MyStatic.someMethod();

--- result ---
LOCAL PUBLIC
```

Using an object initializer as with public in our example, we actually create an instance of Function. Thus, that is equivalent to the following:

```
var public = new function() {
    this.someProp = "PUBLIC";
    ...
}
```

When a function is defined within another function and a reference is made to this Function object, a *closure* is created. Thus, functions and variables outside public but used in these methods are referenced inside the closure and so will be stored as long as the closure remains valid. Such variables are a kind of private property to the public object, because they are accessible only by this object. We already met closures in a previous example, defining the bind() function.

This technique is used in many libraries and web application frameworks like jQuery, iUI, or WebApp.Net to isolate the library core as much as possible while still allowing for interaction with client code.

Enhancing Your Spinner Animation

You should now have a pretty firm grasp of what JavaScript OOP is. We are now going to use some of the principles presented earlier to make the BigSpinner object from Chapter 7 better. The new object will let you create different spinners by concentrating on the animation rendering. Of course, some of the code will be taken as is from the original object.

First, rename the BigSpinner object to CanvasAnimator, and apply the following changes:

```
/* Base object to be inherited */

var CanvasAnimator = function() {
    /* Default dimensions */
    this.width = this.width || 37;
    this.height = this.height || 37;

    this._base = CanvasAnimator.prototype;
}

CanvasAnimator.prototype.init = function(id, color, shadow) {
    /* Initialize the canvas and save the context */
    this.context = document.getCSSCanvasContext("2d", id, this.width, this.height);

    /* Animation variables */
    this.step = 0;
    this.timer = null;

}

CanvasAnimator.prototype.stop = function() {
...
        this.context.clearRect(0, 0, this.width, this.height);
...
}

CanvasAnimator.prototype.animate = function() { ... }

/* Abstract method */
CanvasAnimator.prototype.draw = null;
```

The changes brought to the original code are minor here. In this object, we only put what will be common to any spinner and define one abstract method that we set to null to force its definition from the object that will inherit CanvasAnimator. For our first spinner, we are going to use the methods from BigSpinner that draw the canvas context and fix the dimensions using the new width and height properties.

```
/* The new BigSpinner object */
var BigSpinner = new Function();

/* Inherit from BaseSpinner */
BigSpinner.prototype = new CanvasAnimator;

BigSpinner.prototype.init = function(id, color, shadow) {
    /* Call the base method */
    this._base.init.apply(this, arguments);

    /* Line style for the spinner */
    this.context.lineWidth = 3;
    this.context.lineCap = "round";
    this.context.strokeStyle = color;

    /* Define a shadow for the spinner */
    if (shadow) {
        this.context.shadowOffsetX = 1;
        this.context.shadowOffsetY = 1;
        this.context.shadowBlur = 1;
        this.context.shadowColor = shadow;
    }
}

BigSpinner.prototype.draw = function() {
    /* Clear the canvas */
    this.context.clearRect(0, 0, this.width, this.height);
...
}

BigSpinner.prototype.drawLine = function(i) { ... }
```

Coding JavaScript, there is no notion of abstract classes, in other words, incomplete implementations that will be finalized using an inheriting class. Still, this is what we try to achieve. The only missing method is draw(), which is moved to our inheriting objects in order to define our different spinners. We also override the init() method to prepare the canvas context. CanvasAnimator, the base object, only plays the animation drawing frames through the draw() method. All that is left to do is to create your own animations.

Summary

Although JavaScript OOP is more limited than other languages, with this application, you have proof that it can make your code notably more flexible and usable.

Always keep in mind that objects, like methods, should as much as possible focus on doing one thing or as much as possible pertain to one area of action. Also, always ponder the respective assets of inheritance or composition when defining what your objects are and what they hold. The object doesn't make everything, and design and architecture are more important because they are what will determine how flexible, maintainable, and easy to extend your applications will be.

## Chapter 11

Cross-Document Communication

There are many cases where integrating external content into a web page can really make a difference to its richness. It is no secret that the Web isn't as static as it initially was, and including pieces from other pages, importing raw data, RSS feeds, or so-called widgets has become a norm as found on Netvibes or iGoogle (shown in Figure 11–1), where content and tools from several sources are appropriately brought together in a single page to supply users with a kind of synthesis of their interests.

Figure 11–1. *iGoogle lets you create your own unique page by grouping external content*

This can be quite easily done by handling XML or JSON feeds (preferred for back-end and front-end treatment, respectively), but the easiest way to include a page into another is to virtually create a new page inside your page with an `iframe`. In many cases, you are likely to choose the latter method. Fetching feeds can be a lot of work, because you have to handle both getting the feed to parse or store it and handling its layout in your pages in the first place.

Because the `<iframe>` tag acts as a raw inclusion of a page into another one, you will just have to indicate the source URL and let the magic operate. This cuts out most of the maintenance work, leaving it to the site you load the page from. What's more, it takes care of security issues that arise when using untrusted or unreliable code, because no communication is possible between the `<iframe>` tag and the host page.

However, communication between part of your pages will quite often be desirable, either to add functionality, to operate tweaks on the imported content, or to gather specific information from the external document. Traditionally, this is possible only one way, when the page first loads, by passing data such as color or other styling information to the `iframe` source query string.

One of the most annoying problems using iframes arguably is that because your main document has no idea of the external document, there is no straightforward manner to determine which height should be allotted to the `<iframe>`. This often results in the appearance of scrollbars or in truncated content. Although specifically this is not a problem on the iPhone, as you will soon see, it could often be useful if the content of the frame could communicate this kind of information to the parent document or if, for instance, it could send a message to notify that its content has been successfully loaded to trigger some process in the main document. This is all possible now thanks to the new Cross-Document Messaging API.

Cross-Document Communication Limitations

For years, communication between pages from different domains—or even different subdomains—has been prevented because of security reasons and privacy considerations. Letting any page access any other freely can lead to uncontrollable attacks and the spreading of malicious programs.

The limitation also protects intellectual property, to some extent. Practically, you cannot apply styles to the included content, nor can you access it with scripting languages. Therefore, a request as basic as the following code will return an exception:

```
<!DOCTYPE html>
<html>
<head>
    <title>Quick Sample</title>
</head>

<body>
    <iframe src="http://www.apress.com/"></iframe>
    <script>
```

```
    window.addEventListener("load", function() {
        var frame = document.getElementsByTagName("iframe")[0];
        alert(frame.contentWindow.document.title);
    }, false);

    </script>
</body>
</html>
```

The exception simply occurs because, as far as your page is concerned, the conentWindow frame object has no document property.

> **NOTE:** This code will not yield an exception if you try to load the iframe inside a page accessed using a file:// URL scheme, because in this case, the security context is completely different. Therefore, always test your pages in real-life conditions to avoid delusions when putting your web applications online.

Up to now, there was no easy way out of this trap. If your conflict involved different domain prefixes on a single domain, you probably would have moved the relevant files from one place to another to make the problem disappear altogether, but if you were coping with multiple sites, the only solutions available would have been both mind-twisting and awkward to maintain.

Communication, the HTML5 Way

HTML5 introduces an API that is meant to allow communication between documents whatever their source domain while preventing cross-site scripting attacks as much as possible. It may seem a dream; the following sections detail how it works.

The Cross-Document Messaging API

The API itself is quite straightforward. It simply introduces the MessageEvent object and a method used to send messages that can be applied to a window object. Table 11–1 presents the main properties for the event object as it is sent to a remote document. This event cannot be canceled, it doesn't bubble, and it has no default behavior.

Table 11–1. *Main Properties of the* MessageEvent *Object*

Property	Description
event.data	The data that is sent with the postMessage() method.
event.origin	The origin of the message.
event.source	The source window.

The MessageEvent object is sent to the destination window with the postMessage() method. The parameters currently supported by Mobile Safari, listed in Table 11–2, are *all* required.

Table 11–2. *Parameters for the* postMessage() *Method*

Parameter	Description
message	The message that will be accessed in the target window with the data property of the event object
targetOrigin	The target to which you accept to deliver the message

The targetOrigin parameter can be defined under three forms, either an absolute URL, a / to indicate the same origin, or the * wildcard, indicating that no origin check will be performed.

If the value of targetOrigin doesn't match the actual origin of the target window, the message is ignored, for security reasons. If the targetOrigin parameter is not defined, a SYNTAX_ERR exception will be thrown.

Data Type Support and Handling

The API specifies that several data types should be supported by the data property. Unfortunately, only the string format is currently supported in Mobile Safari as of OS 3.2.

Nonetheless, there are quite effortless workarounds to handle several other types. For instance, the Number, Boolean, or Date objects have a convenient toString() method that will return appropriate values and allow for further processing—including reconversion to objects. Do remember, though, that because the elements passed as parameter will be plain strings, you won't be able to access any of their initial properties, as made clear in the following example:

```
var o = { someProperty: 'someValue' };
```

The preceding will appear in the data property as [object Object], a 15-character string. This requires that you pay attention, of course, to the elements that you pass as parameters to the postMessage() method but also that you take extra care of checking the data you receive.

Mobile Safari's implementation of the API yet isn't much more restrictive than the API itself. The Cross-Document Messaging API doesn't intend that native DOM objects should be handled by the postMessage() method. Therefore, you should never be able to access objects through the document.getElementById() method or get information about the page structure.

Security Considerations

The HTML5 specification indicates several stages of the process where developers should be particularly vigilant when using the method and recommends good practices. This is because using cross-document messaging can easily lead to vulnerability to scripting attacks that ultimately would affect the end user.

The main stage where developers should be careful is when receiving a message. First, you should verify the origin of the message and process it only if the source is trusted and expected to communicate at the specific moment in the specific context of the operation. You have to be able to rely on the code from the source, because security weaknesses in it could expose your site to attacks without the source site even being aware of it. Then, you should confront the communicated data to the expected data format.

Again, if the data you receive is different from what you were asking for without your noticing it, you are exposed to cross-site scripting attacks. Finally, you should never use the wildcard for the `targetOrigin` parameter when handling sensitive data, such as user information, because there is no way to verify recipients.

Case Study

To make the Cross-Document Messaging API more concrete, we are going to build a small widgets-based web application where a document on the domain `www.example1.local` is going to gather widget information from the `<iframe>` it contains, which loads a document from `www.example2.local`. You can easily set up this example on your computer following the instructions in Chapter 2 about the development environment.

Note that following these instructions, your files will be hosted in the same directories; however, the domain and the directory structure are two completely different realities, so you could actually call the same file for the main document and the `iframe` source, as long as you use different domains or subdomains.

The Main Document

If you've created a Komodo Edit project template as introduced in Chapter 4, you need to change the following bold elements in the *index.html* file:

```
<!DOCTYPE html>
<html>
<head>
    <title>Messaging Example</title>
    <meta name="viewport" content="initial-scale=1.0;
        maximum-scale=1.0; user-scalable=no">

    <link rel="stylesheet" href="styles/main.css">
    <script src="scripts/main.js"></script>
```

```
        <style>
                .group-wrapper p iframe {
                    width: 100%;
                    height: 1px;
                    border: 0;
                }

                .header-wrapper .header-button {
                    background-color: #2070e9;
                }

                .widget h2 {
                    -webkit-border-top-left-radius: 8px;
                    -webkit-border-top-right-radius: 8px;
                    background-color: #c5ccd3;
                    border: 1px solid #a9abae;
                    border-bottom: 0;
                    margin: 0;
                    color: gray;
                    font-size: 14px;
                    line-height: 25px;
                    padding: 0 10px;
                }

                .widget p {
                    margin-top: 0;
                    border-top: 0;
                    -webkit-border-top-left-radius: 0;
                    -webkit-border-top-right-radius: 0;
                }
        </style>
    </head>

    <body>
        <div class="view">
            <div class="header-wrapper">
                <h1>Messaging</h1>
                <button class="header-button" onclick="sendMessageToFrame()">Send</button>
            </div>

            <div class="group-wrapper">
                <div class="widget">
                    <h2>Loading Widget...</h2>
                    <p><iframe src="http://www.example2.local/calculator.html">
                        </iframe></p>
                </div>
            </div>
        </div>
    </body>
</html>
```

Because style is not the point in this example, we have kept it as simple as possible.
Therefore, we shall leave the styles in the <head> area of the page, rather than include
them from an external style sheet.

The Hosted Document

The following is the *calculator.html* file to be included in the main document through an `<iframe>` tag representing a widget. Because it needs to be a proper HTML document, do not forget to create a validating HTML structure (for example, with a `doctype` declaration). However, because its purpose is only to supply content for the main document, you needn't use additional markup for the content area or use a specific external style sheet.

```
<!DOCTYPE html>
<html>
<head>
    <title>Calculator</title>

    <style>
        body {
            font-family: helvetica;
            font-size: 14px;
            margin: 0;
        }

        p { margin: 0; }
    </style>
</head>

<body>

    <p>Hello, I'm a calculator widget.<br>
        Click "Send" to request the widget title.</p>

</body>
</html>
```

Things are getting into shape here, as you can see in Figure 11–2. You will notice that the `<iframe>` has taken an appropriate height, so its contents fit in. We will explain this behavior later in this chapter. But for now, the next step is to do some API magic and make the title above the `<iframe>` adapt to the actual content of the `iframe`.

Figure 11–2. *The initial document, without custom widget name*

Let's Send a Message

We are going to assume that the hosted document will be able to answer a request from our main document by returning a title relevant to its own content. The following is the code that we need to do that, using the API. Add it to the head of the main document.

```
<script>

    /* Register for the answer */
    window.addEventListener("message", handleFrameMessage, false);

    /* Send a message to the iframe */
    function sendMessageToFrame() {
        var frame = document.getElementsByTagName("iframe")[0];
        frame.contentWindow.postMessage("getFrameTitle", "http://www.example2.local");
    }

    /* Expects a string under the form "title:frame document title" */
    function handleFrameMessage(e) {
        if (e.origin == "http://www.example2.local") {
            if (e.data && e.data.indexOf("title:") == 0) {
                var h2 = document.getElementsByTagName("h2")[0];
                h2.textContent = e.data.substr(6);
            }
        }
    }

</script>
```

First, we have registered to be notified of message events. Then, we add a button in the header so that we can manually send our message with the sendMessageToFrame() function. Of course, we could have used the onload event of the body to trigger the message immediately after the document has loaded.

Handling the Response

The last step happens on the <iframe>document side. We want the document loaded in the inline frame to answer the message of the main document by sending the contents of its <title> tag. The following code, put in the <head> of the hosted document, should do:

```
<script>
    window.addEventListener("message", handleParentMessage, false);

    function handleParentMessage(e) {
        if (e.origin == "http://www.example1.local") {
            if (e.data == "getFrameTitle") {
                e.source.postMessage("title:" + document.title, e.origin);
            }
        }
    }
</script>
```

We add a new event handler to launch the handleParentMessage() function when we receive a message. Note how the checking process is done: first, we check whether the message is coming from the right domain; then, we check that the received message is in the expected format (in our example, we check for an exact string). Only after this security checking will we send a message with the requested data. Then, similar checking will be taken on by the hosting page before replacing the <h2> title with the one sent by the inline frame (see Figure 11–3).

The response will be caught using the handleFrameMessage() function. Note how we use the textContent property in the main document handling function, rather than the more common innerHTML. This is an extra security action, because innerHTML will write out all the content of the variable as it is received, while textContext will encode special characters into proper HTML entities.

Figure 11–3. *The title has been changed using the API*

Of course, you must also never get the target origin parameter wrong, or you will get an error as shown in Figure 11–4 and no data because the message will be ignored.

Figure 11–4. *An incorrect origin value will raise an exception*

Most importantly, you should neglect none of the security steps we have introduced. If you want to add more, all the better. The end user himself obviously cannot react to cross-site scripting attacks, so you are responsible for the security of your pages, especially when you are involving other sites.

So, let's repeat it: when working with cross-document messaging, always make sure, at the least, that the message you receive is from the right document or site, that its content is in the right format and holds appropriate data, and that you don't leave space for scripting.

Specific Mobile Safari Behavior with <iframe>

Frames in HTML5 have been dropped. You are no longer supposed to use the `<frameset>`, `<frame>`, and `<noframes>` tags. There are several reasons for this.

First, they tend to participate in bad user experience, while not bringing many advantages to web pages. Furthermore, they are usually very bad for visibility for search engines and are very badly supported by screen readers.

Yet, the <iframe> tag remains part of the language, although it has disappeared from the XHTML Strict specification. However, it should be resorted to only when absolutely necessary, especially in Mobile Safari, because <iframe> content requires a two-finger gesture to be panned (a rather uneasy one—try it). If you can display this content without it needing to be scrolled, the drawbacks will be fewer. For this, you need the size of the inline frame to adapt to the size of the browsing context it nests.

The use of iframes in Mobile Safari can result in strange rendering, because scrollbars as such do not exist. Therefore, if your content goes beyond the limits of the frame window, it will simply appear truncated, which can be unclear to the user.

However, Mobile Safari handles iframes differently from desktop browsers. By specifying both a width and a height for your <iframe>, you will trigger an iOS-specific behavior: the frame will adapt to the size of its content (see Figure 11–5).

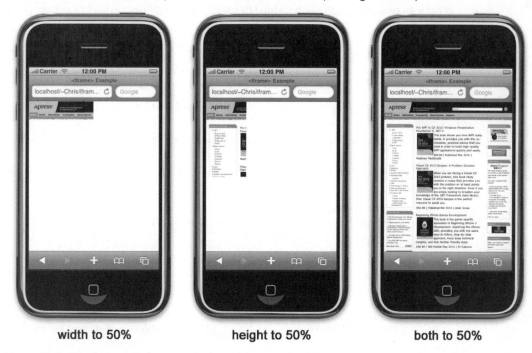

| width to 50% | height to 50% | both to 50% |

Figure 11–5. *If both dimensions are set, the frame is expanded to fit its contents*

This is why we have set the height of our frame to 1px in the main document of the previous case study. Do note that this behavior will not be triggered if the width or height is set to 0. Also, the reverse action will not apply. If you determine a width or height greater than that of the content, the frame will not be made smaller.

Working with Proper Windows

Inline frames are a way to cope with external content with a fully active browsing context and a child browsing context. However, there are cases where it would be desirable to create an auxiliary browsing context instead, in the form of a second window, either because the external content doesn't visually fit into the design of your page or because you would like to launch a stand-alone widget that could still communicate with the host document.

> **NOTE:** This of course is possible in Mobile Safari. However, if you are creating a web application meant to run in stand-alone mode, opening a new window in such a way would result in changing that window—without actually opening Safari—at loss of the main document. Therefore, the execution context could be lost.

The following is an example of how to open a new browsing context in a separate window and how to establish communication between the main document and the second one.

To begin, modify the case study by adding this code to your *index.html* file:

```
<script>
    var win;        // Global variable to work later on the window

    function openChildWindow() {
        if (!win) {
            win = window.open('http://www.example2.local/calculator.html', "childWin");
        }
        return false;
    }

    function sendMessageToWindow() {
        win.postMessage("getFrameTitle", "http://www.example2.local");
    }
...

</script>
...
        <div class="header-wrapper">
            <h1>Messaging</h1>
            <button class="header-button" onclick="openChildWindow()">Window</button>
        </div>
        <div class="group-wrapper">
```

```
            <h2>Loading Widget...</h2>
            <p>No iframe here.<br>Click the "Window" button.</p>
        </div>
    </div>
...
```

Because the pop-up blocker usually is turned on by default, we bind the opening of the new window to an action by the user using a button and an `onclick` handler. Also, it is better to open the auxiliary browsing context only once the main document is fully loaded to make synchronizing the windows together more reliable.

Only the `childWin` window can know when it has been fully loaded, and the window from which it has been opened has limited control over it. The only actions the main window can operate on its auxiliary context is to close it or change its location.

Next, modify the `handleFrameMessage()` function so you can get a "page loaded" notification, and then ask for the title information you want:

```
function handleFrameMessage(e) {
    if (e.origin == "http://www.example2.local") {
        if (e.data == "loaded") {
            sendMessageToWindow();

        } else if (e.data && e.data.indexOf("title:") == 0) {
...
        }
    }
}
```

The next step is to modify code inside the child window so that it indicates when its content is loaded.

Notify the Page Is Loaded

You want the child window to notify its parent window when it is ready for communication. Conveniently, auxilary browsing contexts have a object that keeps the memory of their parent browsing context.

Therefore, they can communicate both with the context from which it was opened and with the top-level browsing context of that opener. Here is the code that you need in the head of the *calculator.html* file for the newly opened window:

```
...
function contentLoaded() {
    if (window.opener) {
        window.opener.postMessage("loaded", "*");
    }
}
...
<body onload="contentLoaded()">
```

The `opener` property of the `window` object keeps record of the opening context for further processing. It will return a `WindowProxy` object related to its parent window, if the latter has one and is still available.

Still, be careful, because there is no way to check the domain of the window referred to by the `window.opener` object; therefore, be careful not to send private information to it. In our example, you simply notify of document loading state. Once both documents are ready, they can communicate with the `postMessage()` method, as we have seen previously.

Note that this load notification method works with windows but could also be used with inline frames, using the properties covered in the next section.

Properties of the Window Object

The `opener`, `top`, and `parent` properties initially are part of the DOM Level 0; that is, they are DOM properties first introduced by user agents themselves.

HTML5 makes them part of the web specifications, which means you will soon be able to use them more reliably to determine the position of browsing contexts within the parents/children hierarchy. Figure 11–6 shows different relationships possible between browsing contexts.

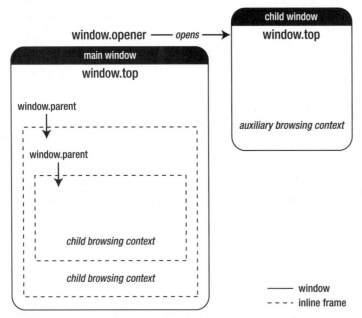

Figure 11–6. *Relationships between browsing contexts*

The `opener` is relative to the browsing context from which the child window was opened. When a new browsing context is created from a `<iframe>`, it can refer to its parent using the usual property from the `DOMWindow` object. Hence, you would simply have to replace `window.opener` with `window.parent`.

```
...
    function contentLoaded() {
        /* Do not post a message to self */
        if (window.parent && window.parent != window) {
            window.parent.postMessage("loaded", "*");
        }
    }
...
```

Remember to always check, as is done in our example, that `parent` doesn't refer to the current window, because `parent` and `top` are the same as `window` when the browsing context is the top level.

Encapsulating the API to Ease Communication

Up to now, in the examples, you have handled only one widget, with code specific to one host page, one widget, and one external source. Of course, as in any development process, it would be better to create code that can handle multiple elements to avoid creating processes over and over again. Here, what you want to do is create one process that could initiate communication for any widget of the kind.

With this aim in mind, we are going to gather all the functionality we have previously implemented into two objects: one for the host document, which will send requests to create titles, and one for the widgets, which will relieve the content providers from any specific implementation on the source side, except the use of the object and a few specific functions. This will enhance maintainability on both sides.

An Object for the Host Document

In a new *host.js* file, we are going to create our object for the document that will hold the widgets. As stated earlier, we want to make it possible to load several widgets with a communication process that is mainly automatic while still addressing security concerns.

```
var Communicator = function(element) {
    var widget = Communicator.widgetFromElement(element);
    this.title = widget.getElementsByTagName("h2")[0];
    this.iframe = widget.getElementsByTagName("iframe")[0];

    /* Force same origin if the domain cannot be extracted */
    var match = this.iframe.src.match(/^(https?:\/\/.+?)\/.*$/);
    this.domain = (match) ? match[1] : "/";
}

Communicator.prototype.setTitle = function(title) {
    if (!title) {
        this.iframe.contentWindow.postMessage("getFrameTitle", this.domain);
    } else {
        this.title.lastChild.textContent = title;
    }
}
```

As a parameter, the constructor takes a widget and gathers the HTMLHeadingElement and HTMLIFrameElement objects that are to be modified in the widget. The domain is gathered directly from the src attribute of the <iframe> element and will be used to secure the communication. This is done, as shown earlier, by validating the origin of the message.

The setTitle() method allows you to set a title for the widget either by giving it directly a new title directly or by getting it from the widget itself, using the postMessage() method.

Finally, we need a global process to receive messages and distribute them among the relevant widgets. To not overload the browser with too many listeners, we define one global listener that will listen for messages from widgets.

```
/* Static part of the Communicator object */

Communicator.listen = function() {
    window.addEventListener("message", Communicator.handleMessages, false);
}

Communicator.handleMessages = function(e) {
    var iframe = Communicator.containerFromSource(e.source);

    if (iframe) {
        /* When the widget is loaded,
            append a new property to the iframe element */
        if (e.data == "loaded") {
            iframe._com = new Communicator(iframe);
            iframe._com.setTitle("Loaded!");

        /* Handle messages and dispatch request to proper object */
        } else if (iframe._com) {
            if (e.data.indexOf("title:") == 0) {
                iframe._com.setTitle(e.data.substr(6));
            }
        }
    }
}
```

The first method is used for initialization and triggers the listening for messages. It is the only function explicitly called by the client code and will be launched immediately, without waiting for the load event, so as not to miss any messages from the widgets. This is done because the browser downloads elements moving down the document tree before it is completely loaded.

The second method is the handler that receives notifications. Its first action is to look for an <frame> that fits with the message source, and then it checks the type of the received message. If it is a "loaded" message, it instantiates a new Communicator object that will in turn be attached to the widget HTMLIFrameElement, appending to it a new _com property to make it easy to find and use later. For other message types, it will call the relevant method on the previously instantiated Communicator object, in our case, setTitle().

```
Communicator.containerFromSource = function(source) {
    var widgets = document.getElementsByClassName("widget");
    for (var i = 0; i < widgets.length; i++) {
        var iframe = widgets[i].getElementsByTagName("iframe")[0];
```

```
            if (iframe.contentWindow == source) {
                return iframe;
            }
        }
    }
}

Communicator.widgetFromElement = function(o) {
    return (o && o.className != "widget") ?
        Communicator.widgetFromElement(o.parentNode) : o;
}
```

Finally, we use two convenient methods that, respectively, allow you to search for a widget container (an `<iframe>`) or find a "widget" bloc using one of its children.

An Object for the Widget

The `Widget` object will let the widgets send information to their host and execute actions the host asks for. In our example, this is quite simple because the action will only show a title above each widget. In a new *widget.js* file, you need to add the following code:

```
var Widget = function(allowed) {
    this.allowed = allowed || [];
}

Widget.prototype.loaded = function() {
    /* The wildcard is not a problem here,
        there is no sensitive data sent to the parent window */
    window.parent.postMessage("loaded", "*");

    /* Prepare message handling */
    var that = this;
    window.addEventListener("message", function(e) {
        that.handleParentMessage(e);
    }, false);
}

Widget.prototype.isAllowed = function(origin) {
    for (var i = 0; i < this.allowed.length; i++) {
        if (origin == this.allowed[i]) {
            return true;
        }
    }
    return false;
}

Widget.prototype.handleParentMessage = function(e) {
    if (this.isAllowed(e.origin)) {
        if (e.data == "getFrameTitle") {
            e.source.postMessage("title:" + this.getTitle(), e.origin);
        }
    }
}
```

Again, the elements here have been used in previous examples. Our primary concern is security, so we pass a list of trusted sources to the constructor. This way, if the widget is available to several partners using the API defined here, there will only be an array to fill. If the origin of the widget doesn't match an entry of the array, the widget can be deactivated, and different content can be loaded instead.

The loaded() method is called by the widget with the load event to make sure communication between the host and the widget will happen as expected. It sends the "loaded" message to the host that will instantiate the Communicator object required for the communication process. The messages are handled by the handleParentMessage() function, which will first test for a valid request by checking the origin and then send the title for the document. Last, we need the widget-specific part:

```
Widget.prototype.getTitle = function() {
    return document.title;
}
```

Using this small API, all the partner has to do is implement this method to return the document title. It is used in handleParentMessage(). Thus, adding a new action is as simple as adding a handler to this function and adding the appropriate method to the object prototype.

The Host Document and the Widgets

To make this effective, we need to call our new scripts in our main document. From the *index.html* file we created previously in this chapter, remove the inline scripts that handled messages, and add the following code:

```
<head>
...
    <script src="scripts/main.js"></script>
    <script src="scripts/host.js"></script>
    <script>
        Communicator.listen();
    </script>
    <style>
        h2 a {
            float: right;
            color: inherit;
            text-decoration: none;
        }
...
</head>
```

Then, add two widget calls after the first one to make use of the new code:

```
...
    <div class="widget">
        <h2><a href="#" onclick="return getTitle(this)">&raquo;Title</a>
            <span>Loading Widget...</span></h2>
        <p><iframe src="http://www.example2.local/calculator.html"></iframe></p>
    </div>

    <div class="widget">
        <h2><a href="#" onclick="return getTitle(this)">&raquo;Title</a>
            <span>Loading Widget...</span></h2>
```

```
        <p><iframe src="http://www.example2.local/game.html"></iframe></p>
    </div>

    <div class="widget">
        <h2><a href="#" onclick="return getTitle(this)">&raquo;Title</a>
            <span>Loading Widget...</span></h2>
        <p><iframe src="http://www.example2.local/weather.html"></iframe></p>
    </div>
...
```

To make the process of gathering titles from the Title links more straightforward, you can use a function that is a shortcut to the `Communicator` object bound to each frame:

```
function getTitle(o) {
    var widget = Communicator.widgetFromElement(o);
    var iframe = widget.getElementsByTagName("iframe")[0];
    iframe._com.setTitle();

    return false;     // To cancel the click event
}
```

Finally, change the widget file, *calculator.html*, by removing the initial scripts and adding the following:

```
...
    </style>
    <script src="scripts/widget.js"></script>
    <script>
        function contentLoaded() {
            var allowed = ["http://www.example1.local"];
            new Widget(allowed).loaded();
        }
    </script>
</head>
<body onload="contentLoaded()">
```

You instantiate a new `Widget` object without relating it to a variable. Still, there is no risk of it being deleted by the garbage collector, because one of its methods is referred to in an event listener.

The last step is to actually create more widgets. Because the document is quite simple, all you need to do is change the `<title>` and the content of the `<p>` element in each document. Now, refreshing the host document in a browser, you should see something similar to Figure 11–7.

You can trigger the title request by clicking the Title link on the right of the widget title. The point here was to illustrate how requests using the messaging API can be encapsulated.

Figure 11–7. *Several widgets can be loaded and communicate with the host document without requiring specific scripts*

Relaxing Subdomain Communication

When handling subdomain communication, we evoked the possibility to simply change the location of one of the files to make both documents be called on the same domain. This of course, when it can be done, is a rather annoying and potentially problematic thing to do because it may harm the initial architecture. After all, if two documents were on different subdomains, there probably was a reason. There actually is a more elegant way to handle subdomain communication. It has drawbacks, but it is a reliable method.

Changing the Domain

DOM Level 1 allows you to redefine the domain for documents sharing the same suffix. The relevant property initially returns the host name of the server from which the page is served; it can also be assigned the domain suffix to allow communication between frames with the same top-level domain.

For instance, using the files from the previous case study, if you are working with *calculator.html* on `someplace.example1.local` instead of `www.example2.local`, you could set both documents to have a `domain` property `example1.local`, and communication will be enabled. This makes it possible not to resort to the Cross-Document Messaging API when not strictly necessary, thus letting you access the title directly using less code.

```
document.domain = "example1.local";
```

Here is what your main document code would look like:

```
...
    function getFrameTitle() {
        var frame = document.getElementsByTagName("iframe")[0];
        var h2 = document.getElementsByTagName("h2")[0];
        h2.textContent = frame.contentWindow.document.title;
    }
...
<body onload="getFrameTitle()">
```

Not only is the code made much simpler, but this method also allows you to directly read the entire DOM of the child document as if it were the same browsing context. Furthermore, no more code is needed in the child document, apart from the domain change.

Security

Using the latter method, you yet once again have to pay extra attention to security issues. The first thing to be careful about is the type of hosting you are using. If your pages are on a shared hosting, using the same top-level domain for all hosted sites (as is done, for instance, for people.wordpress.com, computers.wordpress.com, and so on), the obvious risk is that any other site using the domain could find a way to access your site in the same manner, especially by building a page to affect yours specifically (which actually some people do get into doing).

The Last Message

The Cross-Document Messaging API introduced by HTML5 opens a whole new range of opportunities for developers to build better web sites and applications. Indeed, because the Web grows ever more dynamic and mixed-source content becomes an inevitable way to make richer content and better service, being able to do more with alien content is a great step forward.

However, the causes for restrictions applied to iframes in HTML4 and previous are still to be taken into account. Communicating with alien content necessarily implies risks that this content could have harmful consequences—even when there was no such intention on your fellow developer's side.

Therefore, do be careful to always double- and triple-check any content or message that is embedded or called from sites you do not have a hand on. Security on the Web is a collective effort in which you too need to participate.

## Chapter 12

Ajax and Dynamic Content

Although inline frames can be an appropriate way to load external content into your web pages, they are not as flexible as much modern functionality would require. Building web applications, you will generally try to provide a specific answer to some request of the user, so it is likely that you will need to dynamically load external content on actions of the user or resort to server-side scripting to process user input.

This would traditionally require that you use multiple forms and load a new page every time the user has completed a significant piece of information, which of course violates a number of principles that we have presented in earlier chapters. Because the experience for the user should be made as seamless as possible, imposing daunting forms, regularly loading new pages without being confident that connectivity will be steady, and ultimately breaking the impression of users that they are within a proper application should by all means be avoided.

For some years now, Asynchronous JavaScript and XML (Ajax) has been widely accepted as the appropriate solution to provide functionality in such a manner. The principle of Ajax is that JavaScript can let you perform HTTP client functionality after your page has loaded. This is done using a specific API, maintained by the W3C, based on the XMLHttpRequest object.

Building an HTTP Request

The XMLHttpRequest object allows client scripts to perform HTTP functionality. This means you can perform actions that you traditionally would have accessed by loading a new page without leaving the current page and by loading external content into the current document. This typically is done asynchronously, although the object supports synchronous requests; the strength of asynchronous requests is that they do not depend on the global page-loading process, and because requests are executed in the background, they will not affect the rest of the page activity, be it simple rendering or the execution of other scripts.

Requests Using the XMLHttpRequest Object

The process to use the XMLHttpRequest object is pretty straightforward. All versions of Mobile Safari have an implementation that complies to the W3C standard. The following is the most basic way to do this:

```
function ajaxHandler() {
    /* Test state of the request and handle response */
}

var ajax = new XMLHttpRequest();
ajax.onreadystatechange = ajaxHandler;
ajax.open("GET", "file.xml");
ajax.send();
```

There are four steps to execute a typical Ajax request. First, you need to create a new XMLHttpRequest instance; then, you will open a connection using the open() method and, finally, send the request and process the response from the server, if any.

The open() Method

The purpose of the open() method basically is to set parameters and options for the request you want to perform. The two parameters in our example—the request method and URL—are mandatory. Other optional parameters should be passed as follows:

ajax.open(*method, url, async, login, password*);

The async parameter lets you specify whether the request should be run asynchronously. If this is set to false, the engine will complete the request before executing any other script. The default value is true, which is your best choice for most requests, because a synchronous request can often give the impression that the web application has frozen.

The two other parameters will let you pass a user name and password if needed to access the server pointed to in the url parameter.

The browser should check for the validity of the request. For instance, if the method is either CONNECT, TRACE, or TRACK, a SECURITY_ERR exception will be raised.

Sending Requests Using GET or POST

The differences between GET and POST requests using the XMLHttpRequest object are the same as with regular HTML forms. POST requests have the advantage that you can pass larger amounts of data, using more diverse formats. Another appreciable characteristic of all POST requests is that user agents shouldn't resort to cached data to display content.

However, although passing data with a GET request is very straightforward—you simply need to add a query string to the URL in the call to open()—passing data when using the POST method is a different process. The data passed with the request should be the parameter to the send() method, but first, you will have to tell the server that you are submitting data with you request; this is done by setting a custom Content-Type header:

```
var data = "firstname=John&lastname=Doe";

/* Pass data using GET... */
ajax.open("GET", "script.php?" + data);
ajax.send();

/* ... or using POST */
ajax.open("POST", "script.php");
ajax.setRequestHeader("Content-Type", "application/x-www-form-urlencoded");
ajax.send(data);
```

Handling the Request State

Naturally, you will need to define a function to process whatever data you would gather from your request; in the previous example, this function is called ajaxHandler(). In this example, we listen for the readystatechange event attached to the XMLHttpRequest object using the onreadystatechange property. Be aware that this is called every time the request state changes, which should be four times for each request. Of course, you could also use the traditional addEventListener() method:

```
ajax.addEventListener("readystatechange", ajaxHandler, false);
```

From the handler function, you can access the current state using the readyState property. Table 12–1 presents the possible values.

Table 12–1. *Possible States of the* XMLHttpRequest readystate *Attribute*

Constant	Description
ajax.UNSENT (0)	The object has been constructed, but nothing else has happened.
ajax.OPENED (1)	The open() method has been run successfully.
ajax.HEADERS_RECEIVED (2)	All headers have been received.
ajax.LOADING (3)	The response from the server is being received (in most cases, this means an external document is being loaded).
ajax.DONE (4)	Either all external data transfer has completed or an error has occurred.

When a new XMLHttpRequest object is instantiated, its readyState property is set to UNSENT. This is changed to OPENED when the open() method of the object has been successfully called. Once headers have been received, the property is set to HEADERS_RECEIVED, and the loading of the remote document begins (LOADING). Once all operations of the request have completed, the state is set to DONE.

The readyState property should be used to check that you can safely use the data that you requested. For instance, you can abort the request to prevent the response body from being loaded when the received content doesn't come in the expected format. This could be done by checking values for the response HTTP header using the getResponseHeader() method.

```
ajax.onreadystatechange = ajaxhandler;
...
function ajaxHandler() {
    if (this.readyState > this.HEADERS_RECEIVED) {
        if (this.getResponseHeader("Content-Type") != "text/xml") {
            this.abort();
        }
    }
}
```

This will also save some bytes to load for the user. Note that whatever happens during the process, the readyState property will end with the value DONE.

Handling Progress Events

In addition to the onreadystatechange event, Mobile Safari supports many events specific to the XMLHttpRequest object Level 2. Table 12–2 lists these events with their use.

Table 12–2. *Events Available for the* XMLHttpRequest *Object*

Event	Description
onreadystatechange	The readyState has changed during the HTTP request.
loadstart	The request has begun.
progress	The data is being received. This event can be sent several times for one request, depending on the time the request takes to complete.
load	The request has completed successfully.
abort	The request was interrupted, for instance through the abort() method.
error	An error has occurred during the request; for instance, an attempt was made to send a cross-origin request, if the remote page was not found (HTTP 404).

All these events, except the onreadystatechange event, return an XMLHttpRequestProgressEvent object that will let you provide feedback to the user while data is being downloaded.

You can see whether the download time is computable from the lengthComputable property and then evaluate the loading time with the loaded and total properties.

```
ajax.addEventListener("progress", progressHandler, false);

function progressHandler(e) {
    if (e.lengthComputable && e.total != 0) {
        var progress = 100 * e.loaded / e.total;
        /* Do something with progress value */
    } else {
        /* Not supported or not computable, do something else... */
    }
}
```

The progress is computable in most cases; still, you should always build an alternative in case it is not—as planned for in the previous example.

Checking the Response

However, this is not enough to be sure the data is really available, because it only indicates the state of the request. You should also check the status property available after the headers have been received. This property returns the HTTP status code 200 if the operation completed correctly and an error code otherwise—generally 404, meaning the requested document could not be found, or 500, if the server returns a fatal error. Note that redirection (for instance, codes 301 or 302) is automatically handled, so you will not have to worry about that.

There are also two cases when the HTTP status code is set to the specific value 0: when an unauthorized cross-origin request is attempted or when the request is performed from a file with the file:// URL scheme.

Once these verifications have been made, you will want to gather the data returned by the server. This comes in either of two formats: an XML document or plain-text content. Depending on the format, it will be stored in the responseXML or in the responseText properties of the XMLHttpRequest instance.

Gathering data through an HTTP request, especially on mobile devices, is prone to return errors. Therefore, you should check the state of your requests at all of these stages. This can be done by adding verifications to the ajaxHandler() function. Because the send() method can be called only if the readyState value is set to OPENED, we will also move it inside a conditional statement.

```
function ajaxHandler() {
    switch (this.readyState) {
        /* When possible, send the request */
        case this.OPENED:
            this.send();
            break;

        /* Test if the loading process has end */
        case this.DONE:
            if (this.status != 200) {
                console.log("An error occurred.");

            } else {
                /* Code to run if the response body is in XML format */
```

```
            if (this.responseXML) {
                console.log("XML response received.");

            /* Code to run if the body entity is of another format */
            } else if (this.responseText) {
                console.log(("Plain text response received.");
            } else {
                console.log("No data received.");
            }
        }
        break;
    }
}
```

Processing this way, the document will be accepted only if the response appears to be valid. Because the `responseXML` property is a `Document` object, you will be able to traverse it as you would an HTML document. The `responseText` property, on the other side, can be processed in various ways.

Handling Return Formats

Three main options are available to you for the format of the information you load using Ajax: XML, JSON and HTML. Every format has its fervent advocates, but it ultimately comes down to how you need to gather data and what you need to do with it. The fact that XML actually is the *X* in Ajax shouldn't misguide you, because this is only for historical reasons.

> **NOTE:** The `responseText` property can hold any other text data, such as SRT subtitles that we have used in Chapter 8. These could be processed in a similar way to dynamically add subtitles to a video.

Most Common Return Formats

The most obvious and straightforward solution to simply display data on the page from the perspective of the front-end developer probably is to gather already formatted HTML from the server, because such data will seamlessly integrate into the destination page, will be directly rendered by the browser without any kind of parsing and will be easily styled with CSS.

```html
<!-- publications.html -->
<ul id="books">
    <li>
        <em>Oliver Twist</em>
        <span><b>DICKENS</b>, Charles</span>
        <span>1838</span>
    </li>
    <li>
        <em>The Picture of Dorian Gray</em>
        <span><b>WILDE</b>, Oscar</span>
```

```
        <span>1890</span>
    </li>
</ul>
```

You can simply inject this snippet into your document as it is, using the `innerHTML` property, as shown here:

```
<section id="publications"></section>

<script>

var ajax = new XMLHttpRequest();
ajax.onreadystatechange = ajaxHandler;
ajax.open("GET", "publications.html");
ajax.send();

function ajaxHandler() {
    if (this.readyState == this.DONE && this.status == 200) {
        document.getElementById("publications").innerHTML = this.responseText;
    }
}

</script>
```

However, requesting HTML from the server will typically be less flexible, primarily because the back-end developer may not be the same person as the front-end developer but also because, unlike the two other formats, the descriptive nature of HTML is rather loose.

Parsing XML for Use in HTML Documents

The XML alternative is the most verbose option, not only because its formatting is based on tags but also because processing it requires a lot of code. When receiving a response in XML format, you can either convert the data to HTML to insert into your page by parsing the XML with JavaScript or develop specific style sheets to convert the XML to HTML using XSLT. Both solutions are pretty heavy to set up. Here is a sample XML file and two examples of how it can be rendered to look like the HTML shown earlier:

```
<?xml version="1.0" encoding="utf-8" ?>
<!-- publications.xml -->
<publications>
    <books>
        <book title="Oliver Twist">
            <author>
                <lastname>DICKENS</lastname>
                <firstname>Charles</firstname>
            </author>
            <year>1838</year>
        </book>
        <book title="The Picture of Dorian Gray">
            <author>
                <lastname>WILDE</lastname>
                <firstname>Oscar</firstname>
            </author>
```

```
            <year>1890</year>
        </book>
    </books>
</publications>
```

Parsing the DOM with JavaScript

The following is the ajaxHandler() function, which uses the W3C Selectors API Level 1 to parse the XML code and store it in the html variable after transformation:

```
...
ajax.open("GET", "publications.xml");
...
function ajaxHandler() {
    if (!(this.readyState == this.DONE && this.status == 200)) {
        return;
    }

    var input = this.responseXML.documentElement;
    var books = input.querySelectorAll("books book");

    var html = '<ul id="books">';
    for (var i = 0; i < books.length; i++) {
        html += "<li>" +
        "<em>" + books[i].getAttribute("title") + "</em>\n" +
        "<span><b>" + books[i].querySelector("author lastname").textContent + "</b>, " +
                    books[i].querySelector("author firstname").textContent +
        "</span>\n" +
        "<span>" + books[i].getElementsByTagName("year")[0].textContent + "</span>";
    }
    html += "</ul>";

    document.getElementById("publications").innerHTML = html;
}
```

As with our HTML example, the markup held in the html variable is then inserted into the HTML document with the innerHTML property. This method of course is heavier to process, because the HTML markup is generated directly on the client.

Using XML Style Sheet Transformations

Our second alternative is to parse the XML with XLST. XLST is supported by Mobile Safari 2.0 and newer, so you can confidently use it to process XML. It is a very appropriate language to convert XML into HTML, and it is extremely powerful because it uses XPath to gather information from nodes.

You'd start by creating a new document named *publications.xsl*, with the following code:

```
<?xml version="1.0" encoding="utf-8" ?>
<xsl:stylesheet version="1.0" xmlns:xsl="http://www.w3.org/1999/XSL/Transform">
    <xsl:template match="/">
        <ul id="books">
        <xsl:for-each select="//books/book">
            <li>
```

```
                <em><xsl:value-of select="@title" /></em>
                <span><b><xsl:value-of select="author/lastname" /></b>,
                    <xsl:value-of select="author/firstname" /></span>
                <span><xsl:value-of select="year" /></span>
            </li>
        </xsl:for-each>
        </ul>
    <xsl:template>
</xsl:stylesheet>
```

To use this style sheet, you would need to call the file from your XML as follows:

```
<?xml version="1.0" encoding="utf-8" ?>
<?xml-stylesheet type="text/xsl" href="publications.xsl" ?>
...
```

Unfortunately, doing this from an XML HTTP request, the XLST style sheet will simply not be downloaded—and thus not be applied. Therefore, we need to parse the XML document to check for style sheets and download any that are found.

```
function findStylesheet(xml) {
    var nodes = xml.childNodes;
    for (var i = 0; i < nodes.length; i++) {
        if (nodes[i].nodeType == xml.PROCESSING_INSTRUCTION_NODE &&
            nodes[i].nodeName == "xml-stylesheet") {

            return /href="(.+?)"/.exec(nodes[i].nodeValue)[1];
        }
    }
}
```

Of course, we also need to modify our response handler, because it now needs to trigger the download of another file:

```
function ajaxHandler() {
    if (this.readyState == this.DONE && this.status == 200) {
        var xml = this.responseXML;
        var fss = findStylesheet(xml);

        /* Send a request for the stylesheet */
        var xsl = new XMLHttpRequest();
        xsl.onreadystatechange = function() {
            if (this.readyState == this.DONE && this.status == 200) {
                var processor = new XSLTProcessor();
                processor.importStylesheet(this.responseXML);
                var doc = processor.transformToFragment(xml, document);
                document.getElementById("publications").appendChild(doc);
            }
        }
        xsl.open("GET", fss);
        xsl.send();
    }
}
```

We use the `transformToFragment()` method of the `XSLTProcessor` object, which takes an XML object and the document that will hold the fragment as parameters, to apply our style sheet. Because the `doc` variable then holds a document fragment instead of a string, we can insert it using the `appendChild()` method.

Although this method is rich and useful, it is not very flexible, because you will need to check for errors on two HTTP requests. A more flexible process would be to convert the data into HTML on the server.

Specificities When Parsing JSON

Parsing JSON-formatted data with JavaScript, as one can imagine when comparing it to the previous examples, is very similar to parsing XML. However, you will have noticed the close connection between JSON notation and JavaScript syntax.

```
{
    "publications": {
        "books": [
            {   "title":   "Oliver Twist",
                "author": { "lastname": "DICKENS", "firstname": "Charles" },
                "year":    "1838"
            },
            {   "title":   "The Picture of Dorian Gray",
                "author": { "lastname": "WILDE", "firstname": "Oscar" },
                "year":    "1890"
            }
        ]
    }
}
```

JSON stands for JavaScript Object Notation and can be transformed into a proper JavaScript object using the native eval() function. This means that following the same path as with our XML parsing script, our code would look like this:

```
...
ajax.open("GET", "publications.json");
...
function ajaxHandler() {
    if (!(this.readyState == this.DONE && this.status == 200)) {
        return;
    }

    var json = eval ('(' + this.responseText + ')');
    var books = json.publications.books;

    var html = '<ul id="books">';
    for (var i = 0; i < books.length; i++) {
        html += "<li>" +
            "<em>" + books[i].title + "</em>\n" +
            "<span><b>" + books[i].author.lastname + "</b>, " +
                        books[i].author.firstname +
            "</span>\n" +
            "<span>" + books[i].year + "</span>";
    }
    html += "</ul>";

    document.getElementById("publications").innerHTML = html;
}
```

Whereas JSON notation can be confusing to read with the multiple square and curly brackets, the JavaScript code to parse it is made clear by the common roots of JSON and JavaScript. This doubles the advantage it has over XML for file sizes. Be careful not to forget the parentheses around the JSON literal, which are mandatory to avoid the object literal being confused with a block.

JSON Security Considerations

Yet, because JSON closely resembles JavaScript, you must be careful with the code you evaluate, because actual scripts within JSON data would, of course, be run. However, because the syntax for JSON is a stricter version of JavaScript literal notation, you can quite easily eliminate most security risks by checking the format of the code you receive against the one you expect using regular expressions. Unquoted, only a bunch of expressions are allowed in JSON format (among which are numbers, boolean, and null); therefore, you can easily isolate what isn't acceptable data. Properties and values need to be wrapped in quotes, and quotes inside these should be escaped. This means you can easily build a reusable function to check the JSON data you receive.

The following validation script is based on that of the MooTools compact JavaScript framework:

```
function getJSON(s) {
    var check = s.replace(/\\./g, '').replace(/"[^"\\]*"/g, '');
    var regexp = /^[,:{}\[\]\s\d\.\-+eEfalr-un]*$/;

    if (regexp.test(check)) {
        try {
            return eval('(' + s + ')');
        } catch(e) {
            /* Ignore */
        }
    }
    return null;
}

function ajaxHandler() {
...
    var json = getJSON(this.responseText);
...
}
```

The first line of this function removes all escape characters and then all quoted values. At this stage, no backslash or quotation mark—which could be used in a script injection attempt—should remain. On the resulting "bare-bones" string, we use a regular expression representing the normal syntax of a JSON object in the test() method to check whether no unexpected character remains; we then return the resulting object using eval(). Using this small function, you can be pretty sure that no actual script is hiding within the JSON data you receive and add the evaluated object to access its data.

Client-Side Rendering Using Returned Data

When handling sensitive data from your own site, it is quite obvious that most rendering should be done on the server. However, when handling highly dynamic content or when the data you need to render your page comes as a feed or more generally from external sites, it can be useful to operate the rendering on the client. For such purposes, the easiest format, as mentioned earlier, is JSON, because its manipulation with JavaScript is very straightforward.

Handling Template Variables

A popular way to handle JSON is to build a template available to a script that will identify specific keywords to be replaced by dynamic content, using the global RegExp object. A similar system is used in the Prototype JavaScript library. A template could look something like this:

```
var template = "<h2>#{title}</h2><p>#{content}</p>";
```

This template could be populated using data in the following form:

```
var json = { "title": "Some title", "content": "Some cool content coming..." };
```

Here is the function to apply the relevant modifications:

```
function applyTemplate(template, data) {
    var item, regexp = /#\{(\w+)\}/g;
    var index = 0;

    while (item = regexp.exec(template)) {
        var pattern = new RegExp(item[0], "g");
        template = template.replace(pattern, data[item[1]]);

        var last = regexp.lastIndex;
        regexp.lastIndex = index;
        index = last;
    }

    return template;
}

var formatted = applyTemplate(template, json);
console.log(formatted);

--- result ---
> <h2>Some title</h2><p>Some cool content coming...</p>
```

Using the global search identifier g, our regular expression searches the whole document for all substrings beginning with #{, ending with }, and holding one or more word characters (represented by \w). The exec() method of the RegExp object returns an array whose first entry is the string found; we use this string to perform a new regular expression search on the template and replace it with the relevant data from the json variable. The subsequent entries list the captured patterns.

The lastIndex property stores the index position of the last occurrence found in the template to know where to continue the search from; in order not to miss any occurrences, we change the value of lastIndex to the previous search position using the index variable, which is then used as a starting point for the next exec() call. This prevents errors because of changes to the template length after a replacement has taken place but could also be used to apply recursive changes to the template.

Formatting Variables

Replacing a template item by some value is useful but sometimes isn't enough. Because JSON doesn't have specific date formats, you could typically want to format date elements before displaying them. To illustrate how this can be done, we are going to build a formatter that will be called when necessary to transform timestamps. The following is our modified template and JSON object:

```
var template = "<h2>#{title}</h2><p>#{content}</p>\n<time>#{dateFormatted}</time>";
var json = {
    "title": "Some title",
    "content": "Some cool content coming...",
    timestamp: 207698400000                         /* Aug 1st, 1976 */
}

function applyTemplate(template, data, formatters) {
...
    var value = undefined;
    if (item[1].substr(-9) == "Formatted") {
        var property = item[1].substr(0, item[1].length - 9);

        var func = formatters[property];
        if (typeof func == "function") {
            value = func(data[property], data);
        }
    } else {
        value = data[item[1]];
    }
    template = template.replace(pattern, value);
...
}

function formatDate(value, data) {
    var date = new Date(data.timestamp);
    return date.getFullYear();
}

var formatters = { "date": formatDate };
var formatted = applyTemplate(template, json, formatters);
console.log(formatted);

--- result ---
> <h2>Some title</h2><p>Some cool content coming...</p>
  <time>1976</time>
```

The formatters properties don't necessarily have to match a property from the JSON object; in such a case, value will be set to undefined. Otherwise, it will hold the value of the corresponding JSON property to make its formatting easier. Whatever the case, the data parameter will hold all the data required to build complex schemes, taking several properties into account.

Cross-Origin Communication

The most frustrating part of Ajax probably is the same-origin restriction, which notably prevents accessing content from another domain name. Although it unfortunately isn't possible to use the domain property of the Document object, as done in Chapter 11, to bypass this restriction, several workarounds are available to you.

Using Proxies

To perform a cross-origin XMLHttpRequest, you can send the request to a proxy. A proxy is a server used as an intermediate between a client and another server. The advantage of such a process for cross-site communication is that servers, unlike the Ajax request, will not be limited by the same-origin rule. Thus, rather than querying a distant site— which would return an error—you would let your own server do the work, simply passing it the relevant data for your query:

```
ajax.open("GET", "proxy.php?url=" +
    encodeURIComponent("http://www.example2.local/file.xml"));
```

In this example, the request is initiated from www.example1.local and needs data from www.example2.local. To create the *proxy.php* script, we are going to use PHP together with the cURL API, which is widely available, solid, and rather easy to understand and use.

```php
<?php

if ($url = $_GET['url']) {

    # Process the request using the cURL API.
    if ($curl = curl_init($url)) {
        curl_setopt($curl, CURLOPT_FOLLOWLOCATION, 1);
        curl_setopt($curl, CURLOPT_RETURNTRANSFER, 1);
        $data = curl_exec($curl);

        # Read the response information
        $code = curl_getinfo($curl, CURLINFO_HTTP_CODE);
        $type = curl_getinfo($curl, CURLINFO_CONTENT_TYPE);

        # Return the content and quit.
        if ($code == 200) {
            header("Content-Type: $type", true, $code);
            exit($data);
        }
    }
}
```

```
# If there is no valid content, we send a HTTP 500 error response.
header('Content-Type: text/plain', true, 500);
echo 'UNEXPECTED RESPONSE';

?>
```

Our PHP script expects a url parameter to be passed in the query string. If this entry is found, a new cURL session is initialized using the curl_init() function, and the request options are set. CUROPT_FOLLOWLOCATION will apply HTTP redirections, if any, while the CURLOPT_RETURNTRANSFER constant will let us store the result of our request in the $data variable using the curl_exec() function.

Once the request has been executed, we gather the HTTP status code with the curl_getinfo() function, together with the content type, which will allow you to return the expected header. If no error occurs, the content is sent back with the initial content type; otherwise, an HTTP 500 error code is returned.

The use we have made of the API is rather simple here, but the options available to you using cURL are numerous and can be finely tailored to your needs. Although the process is very straightforward, you should be especially careful when you send the header, because your client-side script may check the value of the status property ($code in the PHP file) to halt its execution. Nevertheless, the result is that, seamlessly, your Ajax request is done on the same domain, while still gathering data from a remote server.

Because server-side scripting is generally faster than client-side scripting (especially because client-side scripting performances partly depend on the device), it is a good idea to run whatever security checking or preliminary processing you need to do directly on the server. Don't forget that, as with any request to a site that isn't maintained by you, there is a risk that the returned data isn't what you expect.

The JSONP Way

If you would rather not use proxies or an Ajax request and the data you expect from your request is formatted as JSON, there is a simpler method—although it is one that implies greater security risks—namely, JSONP. JSONP stands for JSON with Padding. The idea behind this method is that data returned in JSON format needs to be evaluated and is meant to be processed and used, and this should be done without cluttering your code. To achieve this, the server should return not only the requested data in JSON format but also the call to the function that is going to process it. Thus, when the response is received, it will automatically be processed appropriately.

Let's start with the server-side script. We are going to use the json_encode() PHP function to generate JSON-formatted data from an array. Here are the contents of the *json.php* file that you can add to your server.

```
<?php

$json = json_encode(requestData());
```

```php
# We have a callback, process a JSONP behavior
if ($callback = $_GET['callback']) {
    header('Content-Type: text/javascript');
    echo "$callback($json);";

# No callback, send a classic JSON content
} else {
    header('Content-Type: application/json');
    echo $json;
}

# Request data from database or whatever...
function requestData() {
    return array(
        'firstname' => 'John',
        'lastname' => 'Doe'
    );
}

?>
```

The script expects a callback to be passed as a parameter that will process the JSON data on the client. If the parameter isn't set, the script simply returns the raw JSON-formatted data. This allows you to use this file for both requests using JSONP and proxies.

On the client side, you would define a function holding what needs to be done with the data in your client document. This is equivalent to the handler function used in our Ajax requests. It will be run when the <script> tag is added to the document.

```html
<script>
    function useJSON(data) {
        /* Do something with the data */
    }
</script>
```

You need to notify the server that this function is to be run when the data is sent. To achieve this, you would simply pass the relevant function in a query string when calling the remote file like any other external script.

```html
<script src="http://www.example2.com/json.php?callback=useJSON"></script>
```

When this <script> tag is evaluated, it would result in something similar to this:

```javascript
useJSON({"firstname":"John","lastname":"Doe"});
```

With this method, you needn't define complicated methods to handle the moment when data is made available: the JSON-formatted data can be evaluated in your function, and the relevant information can used in your page directly. This is obviously useful when a page is likely to receive different kinds of information, with different processing for each, because you can tightly relate specific functions to specific data.

The Cross-Origin Resource Sharing

As you can see, there are quite a few efficient methods that will let you gather data from distant pages, including documents from different domains. However, the most efficient method to perform cross-origin requests is to use the new Cross-Origin Resource Sharing (CORS) specification, maintained by the Web Applications Working Group. The specification, supported on Mobile Safari, lets you define a set of HTTP headers on the server side that will be read by the client application to check whether the request is authorized. We are going to see how this can be used to perform GET and POST requests.

> **NOTE:** For more complex HTTP requests such as DELETE or PUT, you can refer to the specification details at www.w3.org/TR/cors/.

Of course, the downside of this method is that it requires that you have some control over the server configuration and over the server-side scripts that will return the headers, or it requires that the site from which you want to retrieve information implements this specification.

The following is an example of the most basic use of this kind of authorization, using PHP:

```php
<?php

header("Access-Control-Allow-Origin: *");

?><xml>Data Sample</xml>
```

As with our proxy example, if this script is hosted at www.example1.local and the request is sent from www.example2.local, the request will be correctly executed, and the expected data will be received by the client. The Access-Control-Allow-Origin header is set to *, which acts as a wildcard for all origins.

Of course, you can limit the authorization to some selected origins by explicitly setting a URL, which is a better practice where security is concerned.

```
Access-Control-Allow-Origin: http://www.example2.local
```

Note that Mobile Safari doesn't allow you to set several URLs using this header, but the specification requires that the browser should send an Origin header indicating the source of the request. Therefore, the server-side script will be able to keep a list of authorized domains and return the relevant header when the request comes from one of these.

```php
<?php

$whitelist = Array('http://www.example2.local', 'http://www.domain.other');

foreach ($whitelist as $origin) {
    if ($_SERVER["HTTP_ORIGIN"] == $origin) {
        header("Access-Control-Allow-Origin: $origin");
        break;
    }
}
```

```
}
```

```
?><xml>Data Sample</xml>
```

In this example, we read the value of the HTTP_ORIGIN server variable corresponding with PHP to the client-side header Origin. Then, if the header value is recognized in the array of authorized origins, the authorization is sent. Otherwise, no extra header is added, and the request will fail.

Real-Life Example: Display Twitter Trends

Many sites nowadays make content available that you can use to enrich or spice up your applications. Remote data even comes more and more frequently with specifically developed APIs to help developers integrate them in many manners into their sites. Naturally enough, this information is often given in XML and JSON formats.

Twitter, the microblogging web service, is one of those sites. A growing number of APIs are made available to developers to follow popular topics or perform searches against user posts. Thus, building an application that would keep users informed of what topics are most discussed on Twitter is quite easy.

The Twitter Trends Feed

In our example, we are going to display the current most trendy topics, because the data to process is the shortest. For this specific query, the only available format is JSON.

The URL where you can fetch the JSON data is http://api.twitter.com/1/trends.json.

```
{
  "as_of": "Tue, 07 Sep 2010 9:10:11 +0000"
  "trends":
      [ { "url": "http://search.twitter.com/search?q=Apress", "name": "New Book!" } ],
}
```

Looking at this location, you will see that it holds a JSON object containing a trends property, with a series of url/name pairs. The previous is an example limited to the first trend.

Fetching and Rendering Data

With this JSON data, we are going to build an updatable list of popular topics, mostly using elements from the web application template we built in previous chapters. First, let's see the markup:

```
...
    <div class="header-wrapper">
...
        <button class="header-button" onclick="init()">Get</button>
    </div>

    <div class="group-wrapper">
        <h2>Twitter Trends</h2>

        <ul id="trends" class="template">
            <li><a href="#{url}">#{name}</a></li>
        </ul>
    </div>
...
```

Of course, we don't want to display this list without content; therefore, we add a rule in the head of our document to hide the list by default.

```
<style>
    .template { display: none; }
</style>
```

As you can see, a function call is attached to the button onclick event. The init() function creates a new XMLHttpRequest object and sends a request to Twitter's web site. Here, we use the proxy explained earlier in this chapter; the code for *proxy.php* is exactly the same as previously.

```
function init() {
    var xml = new XMLHttpRequest();
    xml.onreadystatechange = showTrends;
    xml.open("get", "proxy.php?url=" +
        encodeURIComponent("http://api.twitter.com/1/trends.json"));
    xml.send();
}

function buttonState() {
    var but = document.querySelector("button.header-button");
    but.disabled = true;
}
```

Likewise, the getJSON() function used in showTrends() is the one used earlier to check that our JSON object is safe.

```
function showTrends() {
    if (this.readyState == this.DONE && this.status == 200) {
        var txt = this.responseText;
        var json = getJSON(txt);

        if (json) {
            renderTrends(json);
            buttonState();
        }
    }
}
```

Finally, once we have gathered and checked the JSON from Twitter's site, we can insert the data into our template:

```
function renderTrends(feed) {
    var list = document.getElementById("trends");
    var template = list.innerHTML;
    var trends = feed.trends;
    var html = "";

    for (var n = 0; n < trends.length; n++) {
        html += applyTemplate(template, trends[n]);
    }

    appendContent(list, html);
}

function appendContent(list, html) {
    var dummy = document.createElement("div");
    dummy.innerHTML = html;

    list.innerHTML = "";
    while(dummy.hasChildNodes()) {
        list.appendChild(dummy.firstChild);
    }
    list.className = null;

}
```

Figure 12–1 shows the resulting page populated with the trends gathered from the JSON feed.

Figure 12–1. *Latest Twitter trends*

You may think that it would have been easier to run `list.innerHTML = html`; however, a rendering problem prevents Mobile Safari from applying styles correctly to the list elements if done so. Therefore, we add the content of the `html` variable to a dummy element and then move each node from the dummy element to the list. Surprisingly, this method is twice as fast as the `innerHTML` method one could have initially expected.

Be Kind to the Waiting User

As stated several times already, HTTP response times can be irregular on mobile devices, as are loading times depending on the quality of the connection the user currently has access to. Therefore, particularly for Ajax-based web applications, you should always provide visual feedback to your user during loading and processing times.

Adding Visual Feedback

To do this, you again can rely on the `readyState` property by adding a condition to the function used earlier. You could, for instance, use a spinner as a background for the element that should receive the content. This has the advantage of being lightweight and flexible. Here, we use the `BigSpinner` object created in Chapter 7.

```
var spinner = new BigSpinner();

function init() {
    spinner.init("spinner", "white");
...
}

function showTrends() {
    if (this.readyState == this.OPENED) {
        buttonState(true);

    } else if (this.readyState == this.DONE && this.status == 200) {
...
        buttonState(false);
    }
}

function buttonState(loading) {
    var but = document.querySelector("button.header-button");

    if (loading) {
        but.disabled = true;
        but.className += " spinning";
        spinner.animate();
    } else {
        but.className = but.className.replace(" spinning", "");
        spinner.stop();
    }
}
```

The new `buttonState()` function adds a `.spinning` class to the button to display the spinner. For the spinner to be shown in the button, you need to add a `<span>` surrounding the button text.

```
<button class="header-button" onclick="init()"><span>Get</span></button>
```

The final step is to add the relevant style into the *main.css* file so that it can easily be used in other projects. You can see the resulting button in Figure 12–2.

```
.header-wrapper .header-button.spinning span {
    color: transparent;
    text-shadow: none;
    background: -webkit-canvas(spinner) center center no-repeat;
    -webkit-background-size: auto 22px;
    padding: 4px;
    margin: -4px;
}
```

Figure 12–2. *The spinning button*

The CSS class `.spinning` hides the button text by setting its color to transparent and changes its background using the `-webkit-canvas()` function. Because the spinner is a little too big, we resize it using the `background-size` property so that it perfectly fits inside our button.

Handling Excessive Waiting Times

Additionally, you should plan for possible errors or excessive waiting times. Setting a timer for this is the most straightforward solution; depending on the kind of content you need to load, you may want to adapt the value for a "reasonable" wait.

```
var timerID;

function checkTime(msecs, ajax) {
    timerID = window.setTimeout(function() {
        ajax.abort();
        alert("The server is taking too long to respond... \n ↵
            Try reloading this page.");
    }, msecs);
}

function showTrends() {
    if (this.readyState == this.OPENED) {
        checkTime(1000, this);
...
    } else if (this.readyState == this.DONE && this.status == 200) {
        window.clearTimeout(timerID);
...
    }
}
```

Especially when everything doesn't depend solely on yourself, you cannot be sure that your application will run without any problem. Handling possible errors is an extra guarantee of a good user experience.

Summary

Building web applications shouldn't be considered an insular task. The richness of the Web nowadays partly depends on interaction between web sites, and you can seriously benefit from external sources and numerous third-party feeds and APIs to build better applications. You now have the tools to take full advantage of elements that have allowed the success of the Web 2.0 era and that should be fundamental for upcoming changes in the way people consume web content.

Master these thoroughly, take them further, and always remember that, regarding the use of external content, there is no absolute best solution. A format or technique will be more appropriate for some project, and another may be far better for another—not to mention that all are not necessarily available in all cases.

## Chapter 13

Using Touch and Gesture Events

The iPhone, iPad, and iPod touch, like many portable devices nowadays, uses the finger as the only pointing device. Apple's devices even support several simultaneous contact points, which, along with a simple, intuitive graphical interface, makes their use fluid, efficient, and overall pleasing for the user. As we have explained in earlier chapters, this entails a close, almost intimate connection between the user and the device. This particular relationship favors realistic designs; for instance, building a poker game application, you can allow your user to virtually "throw" cards on a table with a simple flick of the finger, adding to the real-life impression.

Since version 2.0 of the OS, you can use the Multi-Touch API with Mobile Safari to bring interaction between the user and your web applications a major step further. In this chapter, we are going to explain how to implement functionality from this API to catch touch events and how to interpret most any user movement and, ultimately, use this to build a simple handwriting recognition web application.

How to Handle Events

To catch events using JavaScript, developers are used to attributes such as `onclick`—normalized in the HTML5 specification—directly on an element or the DOM `addEventListener()` method, sometimes without really understanding how listeners are to be organized or what capturing events implies. A thorough understanding of this is crucial to efficiently work with events.

Calling Priority of Handlers

Not taking the capture into account, there is no actual priority among handlers; they are simply called in the order of their definition. Hence, event attributes within the HTML markup are generally interpreted before scripts, and code introduced using attributes will be executed first when an event occurs, as easily shown with the following example:

```
<div onclick="console.log('attribute')">Click Me</div>

<script>

    var div = document.getElementsByTagName("div")[0];
    div.addEventListener("click", function() { console.log("listener") }, false);

</script>
```

```
--- result ---
> attribute
> listener
```

Nevertheless, if a new click event is defined using *element*.onclick in a script, the onclick attribute will be overwritten, the previous handler will be removed, and a new handler will be created:

```
<div onclick="console.log('attribute')">Click Me</div>

<script>

    var div = document.getElementsByTagName("div")[0];
    div.addEventListener("click", function() { console.log("listener") }, false);
    div.onclick = function() { console.log("property") };

</script>
```

```
--- result ---
> listener
> property
```

Attributes basically allow you to define only one handler at a time. This doesn't mean you cannot preserve a previous attribute-defined handler when defining a new handler. Here is one method to do this:

```
/* First, we read the handler from the onclick attribute */
var old = div.onclick;

/* Next, we group all relevant functions in a global handler */
div.onclick = function() {
    old();
    console.log("property");
};
```

```
--- result ---
> listener
> attribute
> property
```

Obviously, this method isn't very flexible, and it entails that all your handlers are triggered only when the global handler is called. Using the addEventListener() and removeEventListener() methods should be preferred in most cases.

The Capture Stage

The third parameter to the addEventListener() method specifies whether you want to add a listener only for the capture stage, which means it won't be triggered during the target and bubbling stages. The capture stage is the process by which an event can be handled by parents to the target before being allotted to the target itself.

```
<div>0<div>1<div>2<div>3<div>4
    <div>5</div>
</div></div></div></div></div>

<script>

    var div = document.getElementsByTagName("div");

    div[0].addEventListener("click", handleEvent, false);
    div[1].addEventListener("click", handleEvent, false);
    div[2].addEventListener("click", handleEvent, false);
    div[3].addEventListener("click", handleEvent, false);
    div[4].addEventListener("click", handleEvent, false);
    div[5].addEventListener("click", handleEvent, false);

    function handleEvent(event) {
        console.log("(" + event.eventPhase + ") " + this.firstChild.nodeValue);
    }

</script>
```

In this piece of code, each <div> is the parent of the next <div>. Therefore, every click on a number will reach the direct target (target phase) and then move up the DOM tree to the top-level ancestor (bubbling phase). For instance, clicking 4 will cause 4, 3, 2, 1, 0 to be logged to the console. Naturally, ancestors will receive the event only if a listener exists.

To precisely identify the event target, you can rely on two properties of the Event object. The target property holds the actual target of the event; clicking 4 in the previous example, it would return a reference to the element holding the string "4". The currentTarget property is a reference to the object receiving the event during the bubbling phase or the capture phase. In a handler such as the one defined earlier, this and currentTarget are equal; if our handler had been bound to an object, on the contrary, this would refer to that object. Moreover, you can simply determine the phase relative to the received event using the eventPhase property, whose possible values are presented in Table 13–1.

Table 13–1. *Constants Use for the Different Event Phases*

Constant	Description
event.CAPTURING_PHASE (1)	The current event phase is the capture phase.
event.AT_TARGET (2)	The current event phase is the target phase.
event.BUBBLING_PHASE (3)	The current event phase is the bubbling phase.

Now, if you change the third parameter of the first listener from false to true, the order of the log will change, because the event will be in capture phase first. The console will display 0, 4, 3, 2, 1. Capture handlers are always added to the top of the call stack.

Control Over Event Propagation

If you want to precisely control every click within your web application—as, for instance, we have done in Chapter 4 to maintain the application in full-screen mode—you need to use capture (set the third parameter to true). Capture, for instance, could let you prevent the user from tapping some elements if the user is not logged in. The stopPropagation() method of the Event object allows you to prevent the propagation of the event at any chosen moment. This way, try modifying our previous handler as follows:

```
div[0].addEventListener("click", handleEvent, true);
...
function handleEvent(event) {
    console.log("(" + event.eventPhase + ") " + this.firstChild.nodeValue);

    if (event.eventPhase == event.CAPTURING_PHASE) {
        event.stopPropagation();
    }
}
```

Only the value 0 will be logged to the console, corresponding to the text of the first <div>, because propagation for any child <div> is halted directly during the capture phase. This doesn't mean that listeners defined with the same currentTarget and at the same phase won't be called, but using this method implies that there is no guarantee that your handler will be triggered, because the process can be interrupted at any moment by another handler at a higher level.

Preventing Default Behavior

It is also often desirable to locally prevent the default behavior of the browser to some event, typically changing the URL when a link or submit button is tapped or preventing gesture effects using the touchstart event. This can be done using the preventDefault() method, assuming that the event can be canceled. You can check this by reading the cancelable property of the Event object. Note that this method has the advantage of not stopping propagation.

Handlers and Object Methods

There are cases where you will need to use a handler based on an object method, and you will have to restore the calling context, as shown in Chapter 10, and encapsulate the method in a new Function object. This of course implies more memory usage. To address this issue, since DOM Level 2, you can use the handleEvent() method from the EventListener interface. To benefit from the advantages of this method, you should simply use the this keyword or any other instance of an object implementing the function in place of what generally would be a Function object as a parameter to the addEventListener() method.

```
someObject.addEventListener("click", this, false);
```

Proceeding this way, the scripting engine will seek a handleEvent() method attached to this and will call the method passing the Event-derived object (MouseEvent, TouchEvent...) with all its properties to it. The keyword this can be used when the handleEvent() is at the window level or when it is directly under an object definition. In other cases, you will need to pass an object instance, as shown here:

```
<div>Click Me</div>

<script>

    /* A sample objet */
    var Example = function(name) {
        this.name = name;
    }

    Example.prototype.handleEvent = function(event) {
        switch (event.type) {
            case "mousedown":
            case "mouseup":
                this[event.type + "Handler"](event);
        }
    }

    Example.prototype.mousedownHandler = function(event) {
        console.log("The 'mousedown' handler was called with " + this.name + ".");
    }

    Example.prototype.mouseupHandler = function(event) {
        console.log("The 'mouseup' handler was called with " + this.name + ".");
    }

    /* Create 2 objects and use them as event handlers */
    var div = document.getElementsByTagName("div")[0];
    var obj1 = new Example("Object 1");
    var obj2 = new Example("Object 2");

    div.addEventListener("mousedown", obj1, false);
    div.addEventListener("mouseup", obj2, false);

</script>
```

```
--- result ---
> The 'mousedown' handler was called with Object 1.
> The 'mouseup' handler was called with Object 2.
```

In this code, the handling of events is deferred to two instances of Example. As you can see, the execution context is maintained, and each event triggers a log using the expected value for name. To make maintenance easier, the subhandler has been externalized to specific methods called using the ability of JavaScript to provide object properties through a hash table. Of course, if the code you use is short, you could use switch...case directly without any additional method.

Classic Events with Mobile Safari

Although Apple portable devices have no support for external pointing devices, the events usually related to a mouse are supported by Mobile Safari. This, however, is of limited usefulness because they are simply faked and may react differently than what would be expected in a desktop environment.

Behavior of Mouse Events

Although the mouse events are triggered, they are sent only once the user has released finger pressure. Moreover, all events are sent at the same time, meaning that, for instance, a typical series of events such as mouseover, mousemove, mousedown, mouseup, and click would all be sent simultaneously, in this precise order, once the last event ended. The mouseout event will be sent only if the user points at a new element that tracks mouse events and a mouseover event has been previously recorded. Finally, the mousemove event will be sent once the finger pressure ends, meaning you won't be able to track movement as you would with a proper mouse event.

These events are all part of the default touchstart event behavior. Because touch events, as we shall see, are always sent before regular mouse events, it is possible to prevent the sending of a mouse event using the preventDefault() method, introduced earlier in this chapter, on the touchstart event. This will let you define differentiated behaviors for Mobile Safari and classic device browsers.

Scrolling Information

Another event that can come in handy is the scroll event. This can be used, for instance, to simulate a CSS position:fixed rule, because this is not supported on the iPhone. On desktop browsers, this event is sent repeatedly as the scrollbar position changes, whereas on Mobile Safari, the event will be sent only when the finger of the user leaves the screen surface. This all shows the necessity for specific events to implement interaction with the user. Appropriate touch events have been available since iOS version 2.0.

Multi-Touch Events

The superior efficiency of touch events over mouse events on portable devices by Apple is by no means a necessity, and other portable device manufacturers have preferred to implement mouse events more precisely. However, the favor given to touch events, and more precisely Multi-Touch events using several simultaneous touch points, on the iPhone, iPod touch, and iPad is a base for a fluid, natural, and efficient navigation experience.

New Interaction Processes

Fingers act as several mice plugged into the terminal; each one can "jump" from one point to another, whereas a mouse can move only along the desktop potentially triggering a mousemove event. Besides, mice *usually* have several different buttons whose click you can identify using the button property of the MouseEvent object. Using touch events, a tap naturally can have but one state.

There basically are three states for a touch event. Every touch event starts with a touchstart event and ends with a touchend event, possibly passing by a touchmove event in between. Unlike a mousemove, touchmove is triggered after a touchstart event and will take every new contact point into account, whatever the number of fingers used (though the limit appears to be 11 simultaneous contact points), until a touchend event is sent.

Handling Multi-Touch Events

Touch events should be listened for similarly to any other event, using the addEventListener() and removeEventListener() methods. Always be careful, however, not to carelessly prevent some gestures necessary to the browsing process, such as panning. An example as simple as the one presented here would prevent the user from panning to uncover parts of the page outside the viewport or showing a hidden address bar:

```
document.addEventListener("touchstart", function(event) {
  event.preventDefault();
}, false);
```

iOS has several predefined Multi-Touch gestures, such as pinch (to zoom) or rotate. Most can be overridden using touch events. We shall soon get into more detail about gestures.

> **WARNING:** As a rule of thumb, always be extremely careful when modifying the default behavior of the browser and OS interface. The user has habits and expectations, which when changed or disappointed can severely harm the quality of the user experience.

Unlimited Touch Points

The limit to the number of simultaneous events you can catch should logically never be a drawback in your developing process, because you can comfortably handle one event per finger. Each finger position can be gathered using the new TouchEvent object and its touches property. This property provides a TouchList holding a Touch object for each contact point, regardless of the event target. Whenever a new finger press is received, a new touchstart event is triggered, and the list is updated with a new Touch object. There are two other properties using the TouchList object: targetTouches, which holds all the Touch objects related to the target triggering the event, and changedTouches, which should be used as in the following example:

```html
<!DOCTYPE html>
<html>
<head>
    <title>Multi-Touch Demo</title>
    <meta name="viewport" content="width=device-width; initial-scale=1.0;
        maximum-scale=1.0; user-scalable=no">

    <style>

    div {
        -webkit-user-select: none;
        position: absolute;
        width: 44px;
        height: 44px;
        text-align: center;
        background-color: black;
        -webkit-border-radius: 22px;
    }

    div span {
        display: block;
        font: bold 9px/15px sans-serif;
        margin-top: -15px;
    }

    </style>

    <script>

    document.addEventListener("touchstart", handleTouch, false);
    document.addEventListener("touchmove", handleTouch, false);
    document.addEventListener("touchend", handleTouch, false);

    function handleTouch(event) {
        var touch  = event.changedTouches;

        for (var n = 0; n < touch.length; n++) {
            var id  = "i" + touch[n].identifier;
            var div = document.getElementById(id);
            if (!div) {
                div = document.createElement("div");
                div.innerHTML = "<span>" + id.substr(1) + "<span>";
                div.id = id;
```

```
                document.body.appendChild(div);
            }
        div.style.left    = (touch[n].pageX - 22) + "px";
        div.style.top     = (touch[n].pageY - 22) + "px";
        div.style.opacity = (event.type == "touchend") ? 0.05 : 1.0;
    }

    event.preventDefault();
}

    </script>
</head>
<body></body>
</html>
```

This code simply adds a disc-shaped <div> for every new contact point (Figure 13–1) that follows finger movement, in a kind of drag-and-drop style. To determine new contact points, we use the changedTouches property that holds all added or modified Touch objects that have triggered an event. This again happens independently from the initial object target, which allows you to delete only the relevant elements.

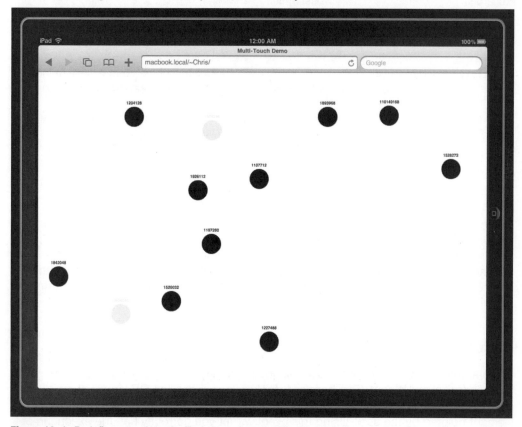

Figure 13–1. *Each finger touch on the iPad screen is materialized by a circle*

WARNING: From iOS version 3.2, the touch properties of the touchend event are unreliable, and touches and targetTouches will systematically remain empty. This implies that only the changedTarget property could let you appropriately handle the release of touches, but this will hold all current touches, making its use difficult, if not impossible. If you need to use this event, test it thoroughly on the iPad to avoid unpleasant surprises when your application goes online.

The Touch object has a identifier property holding a unique identifier for every instance. Because the order in which touches occur isn't fixed and the user can point fingers in one specific order and take them disorderly off the screen, we use this property to determine the previously created <div>. Because identifiers can be recycled and reused by the system, we do not delete previous discs; instead, we simply change its opacity to observe its movement when its identifier is recycled.

Table 13–2. *Properties of the* Touch *Object*

Properties	Description
touch.pageX and *touch*.pageY	Represent the position of the touch event relative to the full page.
touch.clientX and *touch*.clientY	Should represent the position of the event relative to the client area but returns the same values as pageX and pageY.
touch.screenX and *touch*.screenY	Should represent the event position relative to the screen but returns the same values as pageX and pageY. Values are adjusted, however, to the scale of the viewport.
touch.identifier	The unique identifier to the Touch instance.
touch.target	The target of the event for this touch.

Table 13–2 describes all properties available to the Touch object. As you can see, although the object holds three distinct properties to accurately position the event depending on your needs, all return the same value. Also take note that, although the TouchEvent object has a pageX property and a pageY property, these will always return 0, forcing you to always rely on the properties of the Touch object itself.

Cancelled Touch Events

The operating system can halt a touch sequence at any moment, in which case a touchcancel event is sent. This happens, for instance, when the OS launches an internal event, like with a long press that will initiate a copy/paste operation, selecting the element pointed by the user. Using this event will let you correctly halt the execution of your code, because any current or pending operation will not resume.

A Page View Built with Touch and Transform

In classic web pages, it is common to associate events with changes to the markup, to show a drop-down menu for instance. With Mobile Safari, you can take advantage of fluid CSS transitions when elements are moved. In the following example, we are going to implement drag-and-drop functionality using Multi-Touch events and transitions to achieve a result similar to the behavior of the iPhone photo album application. In Cocoa Touch, you would do this using the `UIPageView` object.

What We Are Going to Do

In an album, though there are generally several pictures or photographs, it is not necessary to create a placeholder for each, because only one image is focused at a time. When the user moves an image to the right or to the left, part of the next or previous image is uncovered. This means that we need only three areas where images will be displayed, as shown in Figure 13–2.

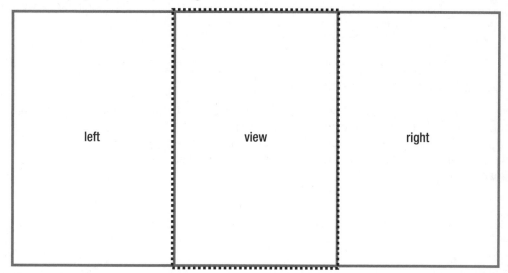

Figure 13–2. *Template for the page view*

With each movement to the right, the node holding the picture at the left will be moved to the focus area, and the area at the right will be shifted to the left of the focus area (and reversely for the left). After each movement, the placeholders from the hidden areas will need to be updated to display the relevant new picture.

The Container

We want to create the three necessary areas dynamically in order to make handling the page view easier. All we will need to do is define a container (with the class `.pageview-wrapper`) with its dimensions. Here are the styles necessary to set up our areas:

```css
.pageview-wrapper {
    position: relative;
    overflow: hidden;
}

.pageview-wrapper div {
    position: absolute;
    top: 0;
    left: 0;
    width: 100%;
    height: 100%;
}

.pageview-group div {
    border: solid 5px black;
    -webkit-box-sizing: border-box;
}

.pageview-group div:first-child { left: -100%; }
.pageview-group div:last-child  { left: +100%; }
```

Our three areas are absolutely positioned to make it easier to lay them out, and we have grouped them inside one container (`.pageview-group`) so that they do not need to be moved independently and less code is required. So that the areas are visible even if no image is displayed, we add a border to our areas. From there, let's simply set dimensions for our container:

```css
html, body {
        margin: 0;
        height: 100%;
}

.box {
    width: 100%;
    height: 100%;
    background-color: lightgrey;
}
```

In our example, we have given the container a relative width for it to take all the available space on the device used for testing. You can, of course, set any dimensions to fit your needs.

The definition of the container in the HTML markup is very straightforward:

```html
<div class="box pageview-wrapper"></div>
```

For now, this all only displays a gray rectangle. The group and the areas will be added when the PageView object we are going to create will be initialized.

Bring Elements and Interaction

The PageView object created here will add the elements necessary to add pagination in our container and handle user-initiated events related to the movement of the picture areas.

```
var PageView = function(target) {
    this.target = target;
    this.state = this.WAITING;

    /* Initialization phase */
    this.createElements();
    this.registerEvents();
}

/* The PageView is waiting for a user action */
PageView.prototype.__defineGetter__("WAITING",   function() { return 0 });

/* The user is pointing to the PageView container */
PageView.prototype.__defineGetter__("ATTACHED",  function() { return 1 });

/* The user released the container and the PageView is moving to its new position */
PageView.prototype.__defineGetter__("DETACHING", function() { return 2 });
```

The container is passed to the constructor as a parameter, which is stored in the target property. The page view state is then set to WAITING using the constants defined in the getters. The constructor then calls the initialization methods.

```
PageView.prototype.createElements = function() {
    /* Create a pages group */
    this.group = document.createElement("div");
    this.group.className = "pageview-group";
    this.target.appendChild(this.group);

    /* Add the 3 pages */
    for (var n = 0; n < 3; n++) {
        var div = document.createElement("div");
        this.group.appendChild(div);
    }
}

PageView.prototype.registerEvents = function() {
    this.target.addEventListener("touchstart", this, false);
    this.target.addEventListener("touchmove", this, false);
    this.target.addEventListener("touchend", this, false);
}
```

The createElements() method creates the page group that will be moved when the user wants to change the focused picture. The three pages are added to this container, and the touch event listeners are attached to the main container. Because we pass this as a handler, we need to define a handleEvent() method, as explained earlier.

```
PageView.prototype.handleEvent = function(event) {
    switch (event.type) {
        case "touchstart":
        case "touchmove":
        case "touchend":
            var handler = event.type + "Handler";
```

```
            this[handler](event);
        }
    }
```

Each event is then directed to the relevant function.

```
PageView.prototype.touchstartHandler = function(event) {
    if (this.state == this.DETACHING) {
        return;
    }
    this.state = this.ATTACHED;
    this.origin = event.touches[0].pageX;
    event.preventDefault();
}
```

When the user touches the container of the PageView, the state is changed to ATTACHED, indicating that the object should catch user actions. The origin of the finger movement is registered, and the origin property will let us calculate the movement during the touchmove event.

To prevent any irrelevant behavior, we also cancel any default action of the browser.

```
PageView.prototype.touchmoveHandler = function(event) {
    if (this.state != this.ATTACHED) {
        return;
    }
    var distance = event.touches[0].pageX - this.origin;
    this.group.style.webkitTransform = "translate3d(" + distance + "px, 0, 0)";
}
```

When the user moves a finger along the screen, we adjust the position of the pages group to move it simultaneously. As explained in Chapter 9, the translateX() method is currently unreliable because it lacks fluidity. We rely on the translate3d() method that doesn't come with this issue.

When the user releases pressure, we need to activate the newly focused image. Because we do not want the page view to jump from one area to the other abruptly, we use CSS transitions. This way, the areas move smoothly to their new position. Using transitions requires that the entire control (time, easing function) is shifted to the style sheet to make the transition easier to maintain than with JavaScript hard-coded values.

```
.pageview-group {
    -webkit-transition: -webkit-transform 0.35s ease-out;
}
```

To prevent transitions during the touchmove event, it is necessary to modify the createElements() method to initialize the time with the value 0, which will keep the transition from occurring.

```
PageView.prototype.createElements = function() {
    /* Create a pages group */
    this.group = document.createElement("div");
    this.group.className = "pageview-group";
    this.group.style.webkitTransitionDuration = 0;
    this.target.appendChild(this.group);
...
}
```

Moreover, if you do not rasterize absolutely positioned elements globally, flickers may occur during the animation. The shift from one state to another can occasionally entail rendering approximations, especially with large elements. The difference is notable on the iPad. This can be done simply by adding the following CSS property to the elements to be animated.

> **NOTE:** When dealing with very large elements, if you don't need to make the verso of your element visible, setting the `backface-visibility` property to `hidden` will improve performance.

```css
.pageview-wrapper div {
    -webkit-transform: translate3d(0, 0, 0);
    position: absolute;
...
}
```

We can now define the handler for the touchend event:

```javascript
PageView.prototype.touchendHandler = function(event) {
    if (this.state == this.DETACHING) {
        return;
    }

    var matrix = new WebKitCSSMatrix(this.group.style.webkitTransform);
    if (matrix.e == 0) {
        this.state = this.WAITING;
    } else {
        var jump = this.target.offsetWidth;
        matrix.e = (matrix.e > 0) ? +jump : -jump;

        this.group.addEventListener("webkitTransitionEnd", this, false);
        this.group.style.webkitTransitionDuration = "";
        this.group.style.webkitTransform = matrix;
        this.state = this.DETACHING;
    }
}
```

The touchendHandler() method gathers data from the current matrix to determine whether a movement has occurred. If no movement has taken place, the object simply returns to its WAITING state; otherwise, the method determines the direction of the movement and alters the matrix in order to apply the translation in the correct direction by a distance equivalent to the width of the container. The duration of the translation defined in the style sheet is restored so that the animation is executed correctly and the state of the object is set to DETACHING. This tells the other methods that an animation is running so that no event should be listened for.

To terminate the movement, a listener is added for the transitionend event. We need to modify the handleEvent() method to take this into account:

```javascript
PageView.prototype.handleEvent = function(event) {
    switch (event.type) {
        case "webkitTransitionEnd":
            this.moveNodes();
```

```
        break;
      case "touchstart":
...
    }
}
```

Once the animation is complete, the moveNodes() method is called. This method too reads the matrix to determine the direction, and then it moves the nodes appropriately. Finally, the listener is deleted, and the group is reset to its initial state. The object state returns to WAITING, expecting a new action from the user.

```
PageView.prototype.moveNodes = function() {
    var matrix = new WebKitCSSMatrix(this.group.style.webkitTransform);
    var first = this.group.firstChild;

    if (matrix.e < 0) {
        this.group.appendChild(first);
    } else {
        var last = this.group.lastChild;
        this.group.insertBefore(last, first);
    }

    this.group.removeEventListener("webkitTransitionEnd", this, false);
    this.group.style.webkitTransitionDuration = 0;
    this.group.style.webkitTransform = "";
    this.state = this.WAITING;
}
```

All that is left to do is associate the object with the main container, which is done as simply as this:

```
var wrap = document.querySelector(".pageview-wrapper");
var view = new PageView(wrap);
```

As you can see, this code is really short and makes defining the transitions and dimensions very flexible, because all is handled from the style sheet. If you run this code now, you can already make the areas move from right to left and from left to right. This of course is not very satisfying, because, for the moment, nothing is displayed in the defined areas.

Creating Custom Events

To handle the rendering of our images in the different areas, we are going to create new events. The first one, PageChanged, will initialize the page view images. The other two, PageMovedLeft and PageMovedRight, will be sent when images are moved to the left or to the right. This is done by first creating a sendEvent() method, as follows:

```
PageView.prototype.sendEvent = function(dir) {
    /* Create a new Event instance */
    var type, event = document.createEvent("Event");

    /* Prepare the event type */
    if (dir > 0) {
        type = "PageMovedRight";
```

```
    } else if (dir < 0) {
        type = "PageMovedLeft";
    } else {
        type = "PageChanged";
    }

    /* Initialize the new event */
    var vendor = "book";
    event.initEvent(vendor + type, false, false);

    /* Add a 'pages' property to the Event object */
    var nodes = this.group.childNodes;
    event.pages = {
        left:  nodes[0],
        view:  nodes[1],
        right: nodes[2]
    };

    /* Dispatch the vent to the target */
    this.target.dispatchEvent(event);
}
```

The createEvent() method of the DOM DocumentEvent interface returns an instance of the object passed as a parameter. Here, we create a basic event by passing the string Event. We also could have passed MouseEvent, TouchEvent, and so on, to create instances of these events.

Every object implementing the Event interface has its own initialization method. For the Event object, that is initEvent(), which takes only three parameters. The MouseEvent initialization method, for instance, is notably longer. The initEvent() method has the following signature:

```
event.initEvent(eventType, canBubble, cancelable);
```

Our event cannot be canceled, because it is sent after the markup is built, and the group is moved: the default behavior cannot be canceled, because it has already been executed. The prefix book is added to our event type to ensure forward compatibility with native events. You could, of course, use event names from the DOM and thus simulate a click, for instance.

Once the Event object is initialized, we add a new pages property to it, which will let the handler access and modify the areas at any moment. The event is then sent to its target, the main container.

Now, we can call our new sendEvent() function. We simply change our constructor so that the client code initializes the content of our areas with the PageChanged event.

```
var PageView = function(target) {
...
    this.sendEvent();
}
```

Next, we need to notify the client code after the transition has completed. Therefore, we change the moveNodes() method to add a function call at the end of it.

```
PageView.prototype.moveNodes = function() {
```

```
...
    this.sendEvent(matrix.e);
}
```

The PageView object is now ready to send its own custom events to the client code.

Handling Custom Events

Without getting into too-lengthy development, we are simply going to change the background color of our areas. If you want to use this in an application with proper images, you could use the background positioning and sizing rules presented in Chapter 6 in order to use all the available space while keeping a relevant ratio.

The catching of custom events is handled exactly like that of native events. We are going to use the new CSS hsl() function in order to loop through colors seamlessly, without coping with the value of the color variable.

The first event to catch is PageChanged, which will indicate when to initialize the colors for the three areas.

```
var color = 0;

function makeColor(hue) {
    return "hsl(" + hue + ", 100%, 50%)";
}

wrap.addEventListener("bookPageChanged", function(e) {
    e.pages.left.style.backgroundColor = makeColor(color - 20);
    e.pages.view.style.backgroundColor = makeColor(color);
    e.pages.right.style.backgroundColor = makeColor(color + 20);
}, false);
```

Next, we want to shift colors progressively as the user moves areas from one side to the other.

```
wrap.addEventListener("bookPageMovedLeft", function(e) {
    color += 20;      // New active color
    e.pages.right.style.backgroundColor = makeColor(color + 20);
}, false);

wrap.addEventListener("bookPageMovedRight", function(e) {
    color -= 20;      // New active color
    e.pages.left.style.backgroundColor = makeColor(color - 20);
}, false);
```

What we do is simply increment and decrement the color variable and change the color of the opposite node appropriately depending on the direction. The listeners need to be added before the instantiation of the PageView object, or the PageChanged event will be sent before a listener is created to catch it. The event is sent from the constructor once the page view is initialized.

Working with Precomputed Gestures

To make the interpretation of classic iPhone gestures easier, Apple has added higher-level events that encapsulate TouchEvent and will let you focus only on these gestures. With GestureEvent, there is no TouchList data but only information relative to rotation and scale (pivot and pinch gestures).

> **NOTE:** The rotation and scale data are also available through the TouchEvent object. However, gesture events allow you to focus only on this information, whereas touch events will send constant updates because of the touchmove events, even if there is no actual gesture. You therefore have a choice between the two, knowing that GestureEvent is less resource hungry.

The scale and rotation properties of the GestureEvent object will let you access the state of their respective gestures through gesturestart. They initially are set to 1 (scale) and 0 (rotation) when the touchstart event is sent, and then they change as the user moves fingers on the screen.

> **NOTE:** With iOS 3.0, the values for scale and rotation are fallacious with the gestureend if the event occurs immediately after a gesturestart event. In such a case, you would receive a scale at 0 and an incorrect angle for the rotation. If you want to use gestureend, always check that the returned values are consistent; you can, for instance, test whether a gesturechange event has been sent.

These gestures require the use of two fingers. Thus, when the second finger reaches the screen surface, the gesturestart event is sent just before the touchstart event. Gesture events are always sent before the associated touch event. The same is therefore true when the user releases one of two fingers: the gestureend event is sent before the touchend event. Likewise, gesturechange is sent before touchmove.

The following example illustrates the use of these events:

```
<!DOCTYPE html>
<html>
<head>
    <title>Gesture Demo</title>
    <meta name="viewport" content="width=device-width;
        initial-scale=1.0; maximum-scale=1.0; user-scalable=0;">
    <style>

        body { margin-top: 50% }

        div {
            margin:-125px auto 0;
            text-align: center;
            color: white;
            font: bold 20px/250px sans-serif;
            width: 250px;
```

```
            background: rgba(0,0,255,0.5);
            border: solid 1px blue;
            -webkit-border-radius: 32px;
        }

    </style>
</head>

<body>
    <div>SQUARE</div>

    <script>

        var div = document.getElementsByTagName("div")[0];

        div.addEventListener("gesturestart", startHandler, false);
        div.addEventListener("gesturechange", changeHandler, false);

        function startHandler(event) {
            if (event.target != event.currentTarget) {
                return;
            }
            var computed = window.getComputedStyle(event.target);
            event.target._originalMatrix = ↲
                new WebKitCSSMatrix(computed.webkitTransform);
        }

        function changeHandler(event) {
            if (event.target != event.currentTarget) {
                return;
            }
            event.target.style.webkitTransform = event.target._originalMatrix ↲
                .scale(event.scale).rotate(event.rotation);
            event.preventDefault();
        }

    </script>
</body>
</html>
```

Unsurprisingly, we start by adding the appropriate handlers to catch events. As the
<div> element holds a text node, if a finger passes over it, two events will be sent for the
same gesture change: one for the main target and the other one for the content of the
<div>. To avoid uselessly applying the same transformation twice, we filter the target to
focus only on the main one.

To make sure the transformation is applied on top of the current state of the object, the
startHandler() function gathers the computed style of the target and stores it in the
_originalMatrix property, which is dynamically added to the target node.

From there, the new matrix can be calculated when the gesturechange event is sent,
using the scale() method from the CSSMatrix object, and the rotation can be applied
using rotate(). Because these methods don't alter the original matrix, each new
gesturechange event will entail a correct transformation of the scale and rotation

values, which will change together with the movements of the fingers of the user within a gesture session.

Finally, because the event can be canceled, to make sure the viewport doesn't move when the user performs gestures, we use `preventDefault()` on the event.

Create Your Own Gestures

Using gesture events is rich and makes interpreting the classic iOS gestures much easier, because the value to apply is already computed. However, this can be limited, because only two predefined gestures are available.

Interpreting gestures can quickly become a chore as soon as one wants to define each gesture independently. The popular swipe-to-delete gesture is rather simple to handle, because all you need to do is record the finger position between the `touchstart` and `touchend` events and check that the line between these points is roughly horizontal. You could even check the direction of the movement. However, trying to handle more complex movements, such as letter drawing or shape, is an utterly different story.

One Code, Many Strokes

We are going to build a system that allows, with only one piece of code, to recognize any stroke. This, if relevant to your web application, can make its use far more productive. The system implemented is inspired by libraries such as LibStroke or Xstroke (using C/C++ on Linux systems) and the Graffiti character recognition application formerly found on PalmOS (Figure 13–3), which has recently been ported to Android devices. Note that the iPhone already has a similar system to write Chinese characters.

Figure 13–3. *The Graffiti's help screen on PalmOS and the iPhone recognition interface*

The movements used on the iPhone generally don't use more than one finger, because other movements typically are already interpreted by gesture events, as shown earlier. Therefore, we are going to use touch events, taking into consideration only the first finger. The script will first register all the points where the finger passes and will then try to interpret the sequence.

The interpretation will be handled by projecting the movement against a 3x3 block grid, numbered from 1 to 9, that will let us extract a signature associated with a specific shape. As shown in Figure 13–4, the grid has no definite dimensions, and dimensions will be determined by the amplitude of the movement; the bounding box will adjust progressively as new points are added.

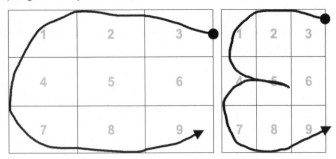

Figure 13–4. *The letters C and E, respectively, generate the signatures 3214789 and 321454789*

To make this more precise, it will be necessary to adjust some shapes. Indeed, if a shape is significantly larger in one direction, interpretation can be imprecise. In such cases, the grid will be adjusted in order to center the drawing by scaling the smallest span up (Figure 13–5).

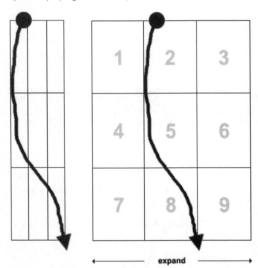

Figure 13–5. *A gesture that is exaggeratedly higher than wide needs to be adjusted*

Moreover, some characters—a plus sign, for instance—will most likely be traced with a pressure release at one or several stages. This is why we are going to store several contiguous sequences if they occur within a definite time length and sum them up to return the associated signature.

The Bounding Box Object

The bounding box is a simple rectangle that is built using the following definition:

```
var Rect = function() {
    var i = Infinity;
    this.coords = new WebKitPoint(+i, +i);
    this.extent = new WebKitPoint(-i, -i);
}

Rect.prototype.adjust = function(x, y) {
    if (x < this.coords.x) {
        this.coords.x = x;
    }
    if (x > this.extent.x) {
        this.extent.x = x;
    }
    if (y < this.coords.y) {
        this.coords.y = y;
    }
    if (y > this.extent.y) {
        this.extent.y = y;
    }
}

Rect.prototype.fit = function() {
    var w = (this.extent.x - this.coords.x + 1);
    var h = (this.extent.y - this.coords.y + 1);

    if ((w / h) > 4 || (h / w) > 4) {
        var ax = w < h ? w : 0;
        var ay = w < h ? 0 : h;

        this.coords.x -= ax;
        this.extent.x += ax;
        this.coords.y -= ay;
        this.extent.y += ay;
    }
}
```

To make this easier to read, we use the `WebKitPoint` object, which represents a point with x and y coordinates. The `adjust()` method allows you to adjust the bounding box appropriately as coordinates are passed to it when a finger strokes the screen. Finally, the `fit()` method adjusts the bounding box if it is at least four times as large in one direction.

Registering User Strokes

Strokes are recorded, and the signature is generated by the Recognizer object.

```
var Recognizer = function(element, interpreter) {
    this.element = element;
    this.element.addEventListener("touchstart", this, false);
    this.interpreter = interpreter;

    this.strokes = [];
    this.autoEndTimer = null;
    this.strokeSource = null;
}
```

As its first parameter, the constructor takes the object that will catch the touches. It can be either an HTML element with definite dimensions or the document object, which will let you catch all events of the device screen. The second parameter is a function that interprets the signatures.

Successive movements, which will be used to determine the final signature, are stored in the strokes array. To put an end to the figure and determine whether a stroke is part of the current sequence or starts a new one, we use a timer. The identifier for this timer is stored in autoEndTimer in order to keep control over it.

```
Recognizer.prototype.handleEvent = function(event) {
    var x = event.changedTouches[0].pageX;
    var y = event.changedTouches[0].pageY;
    var t = event.type;

    if (event.touches.length != 1) {
        t = "touchend";
    }

    switch (t) {
        case "touchstart":
            this.saveSource(event.touches[0].target);
            this.startStroke();
            this.savePoint(x, y);
            this.doAutoEnd();
            break;

        case "touchmove":
            this.savePoint(x, y);
            this.doAutoEnd();
            break;

        case "touchend":
            this.endStroke();
            this.savePoint(x, y);
            this.doAutoEnd();
            break;
    }

    event.preventDefault();
}
```

```
Recognizer.prototype.saveSource = function(node) {
    if (!this.strokeSource) {
        if (node.nodeType == node.TEXT_NODE) {
            node = node.parentNode;
        }
        this.strokeSource = node;
    }
}

Recognizer.prototype.startStroke = function() {
    this.strokes.push({
        points: [],
        bound : new Rect()
    });
    this.element.addEventListener("touchmove", this, false);
    this.element.addEventListener("touchend", this, false);
}
```

The recording starts with a touchstart event. We register new listeners to initiate a sequence only when this event is sent, which prevents the recording of initial points outside element.

A new object is pushed to the strokes array where all points and the bounding box will be stored. The bounding box is resized progressively as points are added, which saves a loop when the signature is processed. For every event, at least one point will be saved, and the autoEndTimer timer will be reinitialized.

```
Recognizer.prototype.savePoint = function(x, y) {
    var stroke = this.strokes[this.strokes.length - 1];
    stroke.points.push(new WebKitPoint(x, y));
    stroke.bound.adjust(x, y);
}

Recognizer.prototype.doAutoEnd = function() {
    if (this.autoEndTimer) {
        window.clearTimeout(this.autoEndTimer);
    }
    var that = this;
    this.autoEndTimer = window.setTimeout(function() {
        that.endStroke();
        that.finalizeStrokes();
    }, 500);
}
```

The user has 500ms to chain two gestures, which is long enough in most cases. Beyond this limit, the recording will be halted automatically, and listeners will be deleted, if any.

```
Recognizer.prototype.endStroke = function() {
    this.element.removeEventListener("touchmove", this, false);
    this.element.removeEventListener("touchend", this, false);
}
```

Once the sequence has come to an end, the finalizeStrokes() method is called to determine the signature.

```
Recognizer.prototype.finalizeStrokes = function() {
    var signature = [];
```

```
    for (var m = 0; m < this.strokes.length; m++) {
        var bound  = this.strokes[m].bound;
        var points = this.strokes[m].points;

        bound.fit();
        var w = (bound.extent.x - bound.coords.x + 1) / 3;
        var h = (bound.extent.y - bound.coords.y + 1) / 3;

        for (var n = 0; n < points.length - 1; n++) {
            var px = points[n].x - bound.coords.x;
            var py = points[n].y - bound.coords.y;
            var mx = px / w << 0;    // The bit shift operator allows
            var my = py / h << 0;    // very quick Math.floor()

            var value = my * 3 + mx + 1;
            if (value != signature[signature.length - 1]) {
                signature.push(value);
            }
        }
    }

    this.strokes = [];
    this.interpreter(signature.join(''), this.strokeSource);
    this.strokeSource = null;}
}
```

With each recorded stroke, the bounding box is adjusted if necessary, and the dimensions for the box grid are calculated. Then, points are adjusted to normalize their coordinates, and their position on the grid is estimated. If a new grid block is reached, we add it to the signature. Finally, the strokes array is emptied, and the interpreter is launched with the final signature as a parameter.

Using the Recognizer Object

From there, using the Recognizer object is very easy, because you simply need to instantiate the object and define an interpreter for the signature. We are going to use a list to receive the finger strokes and modify the text style of the list elements appropriately. For this example, we again build upon our web application template. Here are the changes to bring to *index.html*:

```html
<body onload="init()">
    <div class="view" style = "background: white">
...
        <div class="list-wrapper">
            <h2>Apress</h2>
            <ul>
                <li>Books</li>
                <li>Reviews</li>
                <li>Authors</li>
                <li>Contact</li>
            </ul>
        </div>
    </div>
```

```
<body>
```

Then, create a new JavaScript file named *strokes.js* holding the code for the Recognizer, along with the following:

```javascript
function interpreter(signature, source) {
    switch (signature) {
        case "456":    // 0--->
            sendEvent("SwipeRight", source);
            break;

        case "654":    // <---0
            sendEvent("SwipeLeft", source);
            break;

        default:
            console.log("Unknown stroke received " + signature);
    }
}

function sendEvent(type, target) {
    var vendor = "book";
    var event = document.createEvent("Event");

    event.initEvent(vendor + type, true, false);
    target.dispatchEvent(event);
}
```

As expected, the interpreter receives the signature together with the origin of the stroke. The signature is then interpreted, and an event is sent to the origin, setting the second parameter of initEvent() to true and thus allowing bubbling. You then need only instantiate the object and prepare the listeners whose handlers will modify the styles of the list elements.

```javascript
function init() {
    var ul = document.getElementsByTagName("ul")[0];
    var rs = new Recognizer(ul, interpreter);

    /* Change the text color on right-to-left swipe event */
    ul.addEventListener("bookSwipeLeft", function(event) {
        var style = event.target.style;
        style.color = style.color ? "" : "red";
    }, false);

    /* Change the text weight on left-to-right swipe event */
    ul.addEventListener("bookSwipeRight", function(event) {
        var style = event.target.style;
        style.fontWeight = style.fontWeight ? "" : "bold";
    }, false);
}
```

The new events sent are a right-to-left swipe and its left-to-right counterpart. Each stroke switches the text from black to red or from normal weight to bold, as shown in Figure 13–6. Because bubbling is activated for events, it isn't necessary to add an independent handler for every list element. The event will reach the list item and move up to the parent, to which the listener is attached. This allows you to concentrate the handler treatment.

Figure 13–6. *The swipe movement changes the text style*

Improve Accuracy

As you can see, implementing new gesture events is rather simple. Nonetheless, accuracy strongly depends on the stroke initiated by the user and may dwindle especially when dealing with diagonals. Diagonals will typically span over several columns and rows, thus multiplying possible paths for a single stroke. An interesting way to handle this would be to resort to regular expressions in the interpretation phase to limit the number of successive comparisons required to determine what the stroke was. This will speed your application up also because the regular expressions engine is executed natively, unlike custom tests that will grow more complicated as strokes grow more complex.

Another approach is to work with directions rather than a grid, seeking to determine the orientation of strokes rather than trying to position points. This method is used in many applications such as Firefox's FireGestures extension and has proven very accurate and efficient.

Summary

The unique relationship established by touch between the user and the device should be totally taken into account when developing your applications. Not only can the correct use and handling of touches and gestures let you greatly enhance user experience: with a bit of imagination, you can also bring new functionality and make your applications stand out in the Web crowd.

This all requires that you fully understand how these events work and how users are likely to use their device and react to the interface of your applications. More than ever, the best way to go further with touch and gesture events is to experience your own applications and experiments.

## Chapter 14

Location-Aware Web Applications

The App Store offers a myriad of applications that bring users services based on where they are at some particular moment, such as Where by uLocate, a multilocation-based services aggregator, or Foursquare, which offers a new way to discover your city.

By crossing information from growing spatial-related databases with the approximate position of the user, you get to suggest the perfect place to eat homemade chili con carne, customize the user experience by giving the impression you actually know about the user, give the relevant afternoon's weather, or show a map with the appropriate directions to any address. Since its very first release, the iPhone has featured ways to locate the user on a world map. Even though it didn't primarily ship with an Assisted Global Positioning System (A-GPS) chip, it used a hybrid algorithm to determine its position: by synthesizing data from triangulation—via cell towers, a method widely used in cell phones—and using information gathered from the network through the Wi-Fi Positioning System (WPS), it could return its location within reasonable time.

Triangulation became more efficient as the number of cell towers increased but never yielded results with an accuracy better than 100 meters; deducing position from network information could be very precise and fast but still depended on the network's density. The solution was good in most cases, but there was still room for improvement.

> **NOTE:** Geolocation on all devices is pretty tough on the battery's life, so always keep this in mind, and use these features only when required for the end user. For instance, prefer caching data rather than requesting a new position on every page load.

Moreover, the system in use made this feature available only to native iPhone applications using the Core Location API. iOS 3.0 brings the exciting possibility to access geographical data directly with JavaScript, thanks to a new API accessible to Mobile Safari. This chapter will get you going with this new, rich tool available to you.

The Geolocation API

The implementation for this API is based on a W3C specification. It allows you to determine the geographic position of the host device using the previously named sources and is very easy to start using. All the API methods are accessible with the `navigator.geolocation` object, and they let you easily request the user's position, either once or repeatedly, tracking the user's movement (if any).

Privacy Considerations

Granting access to such information about users without them knowing should always be controlled to some extent. To respect the end user's privacy, iOS will always ask for a user's permission before sending any information about their position, as in the Maps and Camera applications (see Figure 14–1).

Figure 14–1. *All iPhone applications ask for the user's authorization before sending location data*

Setup Considerations

Before testing the API on your own device, make sure the location service is active. You will find it in the Settings application, under the General submenu. It would be even "cleaner" to reset previously granted geolocation request authorizations, to work on a tabula rasa, for instance. This is achieved by navigating to **Settings ➤ General ➤ Reset ➤ Reset geolocation alerts**.

Also, when debugging on a desktop browser, don't forget to check for the actual availability of the API—this will save you precious time debugging code that simply cannot be interpreted. This is done simply with the following code that checks for the Geolocation object:

```
If (window.navigator.geolocation) {
    /* The API is available */
} else {
    /* Fallback message */
}
```

Likewise, targeting Mobile Safari, not all your users will have the latest version of the browser—especially on older versions of the iPod touch, for which the relevant update is either sold for a cost or not available at all. Generally speaking, proceeding this way will make your application available in better conditions to more users, and planning for errors will help you offer a better user experience.

Getting the Current Position

The most obvious and probably most common use of the API will be to ask for the user's present position. As stated earlier, you will use the Geolocation object, and you will access the getCurrentPosition() method.

```
window.navigator.geolocation.getCurrentPosition(
    function(position) {
        /* do something with the position object data */
    }
);
```

Because every request takes some time, which could quickly freeze the user's device, all requests are asynchronous. You will need to pass a callback function as a parameter to be called when data becomes available, as illustrated earlier.

Longitude, Latitude, and More

When the request is successful, the callback is called using the position parameter, which contains data about the user's location. This object makes eight properties available, as shown in Table 14–1.

Table 14–1. *Properties of the Position Object*

Property	Description
position.timestamp	Time at which the location information was determined (milliseconds).
position.coords.accuracy	The accuracy of the latitude/longitude information returned (meters; the lower, the better).
position.coords.latitude	The user's current latitude (decimal degrees).
position.coords.longitude	The user's current longitude (decimal degrees).
position.coords.altitudeAccuracy	The accuracy of the altitude information returned (meters). This is often set to null.
position.coords.altitude	The user's current altitude (meters). The same restrictions apply.
position.coords.heading	The direction in which the user is heading (decimal degrees). This is often set to null.
position.coords.speed	The user's current speed. The same restrictions apply (meters/second).

With varying performance and precision and as long as no error occurs (for example, the user refuses the request), the first method properties will return a value whatever device is used, be it an older iPhone, an iPod touch, or an iPad. However, as you can see, not all data is necessarily available. Heading and speed, for instance, obviously require that several location points have been recorded with a sufficient accuracy and therefore need tracking to return values, as we will soon explain. Depending on the device that is used—and the location technique it uses—not all data can be made available.

Besides, because using GPS usually takes time before satellites are reached, this location method will often be deferred by the device, causing performance to increase but returning less accurate data. It will be resorted to for tracking, because the request for position information is repeated, leaving enough time for GPS acquisition.

When testing your web application, you will often have to proceed outdoors, especially when relying on GPS precision, because GPS hardly works—if at all—indoors.

Therefore, whether you are expecting information from the basic properties or from the more advanced ones, you should always handle possible errors and approximation.

Handling Errors from Requests

Luckily enough, the getCurrentPosition() takes another optional parameter that gives you access to code and description for the occurring error. This gives you some latitude to understand and then handle the error. Here's an example of how to do this:

```
/* Request the user's position */
window.navigator.geolocation.getCurrentPosition(successCallback, failureCallback);

function successCallback(position) {
    /* Do something with the position object data */
}
function failureCallback(error) {
    /* Do something with the error object */
}
```

There are two properties to the error object, as shown in Table 14–2.

Table 14–2. *Properties of the Error Object*

Property	Description
error.code	One of the following error codes:
	error.UNKNOWN_ERROR (0)
	error.PERMISSION_DENIED (1)
	error.POSITION_UNAVAILABLE (2)
	error.TIMEOUT (3)
error.message	A message describing what happened.

Whereas the error.code property yields persistent error codes, the error.message property may be quite different depending on the device running the function.

Obviously, a single error code may cover several real-life errors. For instance, PERMISSION_DENIED is returned when the user refuses the request but also when the geolocation service on the device is disabled. However, the error message should shed light on the code, which is why both properties are useful together. Please note that indeed the error.message property is meant only for debugging purposes; it is by no means supposed to be seen on the user's end.

> **WARNING:** If an exception occurs within your success callback function, the failure callback function will be called with an UNKNOWN_ERROR code. Always double-check whether the error you are getting really is a location error or comes from your own code.

Accuracy, Timeout, and Cached Location

The W3C specification provides three options to refine your request, using an object-type parameter along with your callbacks. You can specify how long your request may take to succeed, how long the position yielded may have been cached before the request, and whether to require extra accuracy. These options are invoked as follows:

```
window.navigator.geolocation.getCurrentPosition(successCallback, failureCallback, {
    timeout: 0,
    maximumAge: 60000,
    enableHighAccuracy: false
});
```

There are many cases where there's no need to require an updated position of the user. For an application returning a list of trendy restaurants based on a user's location, chances are the user will often be in the same bounds. In such cases, you may want to use cached data from the user's device.

The maximumAge option tells the device to look for this kind of data before trying to determine the user's actual position and allows you to set an age limit for this data. As we have seen previously, another advantage of this solution is that it decreases the drain on the battery.

The default value for maximumAge is 0, meaning the device will try to return an updated value for each request; if set to Infinity, the user agent will necessarily return a cached value, if any. If none exists, it will acquire a new position.

The timeout attribute forces a time limit in milliseconds for the location acquisition to complete. The default value is Infinity which lets you imagine how the timeout option can be useful when developing an application. If not specified, the application will run until the terminal returns the requested information, even if this information is for some reason not available. Specifying a value for timeout, a TIMEOUT error will be sent to the error callback when the limit is reached.

In the previous example, if no value for the position is cached, the function's failure callback will be called immediately. Please note that whatever time the user takes to grant access to their position information is not taken into account.

Combining these options can make your application more responsive. However, when you do need this extra precision, the third option, enableHighAccuracy, tells the API to get the closest answer possible to the user's actual location. This option by default is set to false.

Keep in mind that users usually care about hyper-local information, so you may want to try to offer accurate positioning. The accuracy will increase as you poll for location. This can be helped by using the tracking functionality of the API. As a last resort, if the location is not available, you can rely on a text field so that users can specify their city or ZIP code, which is often the last acceptable level of precision.

Putting the User on a Map with Google Maps

To make the use of the data returned by the location API, we are going to make an example where the user is situated on a map using Google Maps.

Google Maps comes with a rich API that is used, among others, by the MapKit framework from Cocoa Touch in native applications. It will bring the same functionality to you as the Maps application on the iPhone. Its assets include that it is free, doesn't require preliminary registration, and is quite easy to use with JavaScript.

Showing the Map

Let's start with the beginning: displaying the map. What our web application is going to do is let the user show a position on a satellite view, with the level of precision represented by a circle.

Begin by creating a new project based on your web application template, and modify the *index.html* file as follows:

```
...
    <title>Geolocation Example</title>
...
<body>
    <div class="view">
        <div id="map"></div>

        <div class="header-wrapper">
            <h1>Geolocation</h1>
        </div>
    </div>
</body>
```

The `<div>` identified as map is the area that will hold the map. We want it to take up the available space, with a translucent header overlapping. Here are the styles to achieve this:

```
<head>
...
    <style>

        .header-wrapper {
            background-color: rgba(0,0,0,0.65);
            position: absolute;
            top: 0;
            width: 100%;
        }

        .view { height: 100%; }

        #map { min-height: 100%; }

    </style>
</head>
```

Now, we can call the Google Maps API to render the map inside our container. The sensor parameter tells the API if the device has location functionality; we set this to true.

```
<head>
...
    </style>
    <script src="http://maps.google.com/maps/api/js?sensor=true"></script>
    <script>
        var ns = google.maps; // Namespace
        var map;

        function init() {
            var latlng = new ns.LatLng(0, 0);
            var options = {
                zoom: 2,
                center: latlng,
                disableDefaultUI: true,
                scaleControl: true,
                mapTypeId: ns.MapTypeId.SATELLITE
            };

            map = new ns.Map(document.getElementById("map"), options);
        }

    </script>
</head>
<body onload="init()">
```

Because we are going to use the methods of the Map object, we store it inside the global variable map. Once the page has loaded, we call the init() function; this initializes the map by giving it a base location, the intersection of the equator, and the Greenwich meridian (0,0).

Because for now we cannot tell where the user is, we set the zoom factor to 2, which in the Google Maps API represents a 2000km scale. In satellite view, the zoom can range from 0 (10.000km) to 22 (2m). There is no particular step between the values: each one represents a scale determined in the API. Besides, all are not always available, depending on the map type.

The center property positions the map with the location passed in the parameters in the middle of the area. You will be able to modify this later using the setCenter() method of the Map object.

In order not to show useless controls on the map, we pass the disableDefaultUI property set to true as a parameter. This means controls to change the map type or the scaling slider won't appear. However, we are going to show the current scale in the bottom-left area of the map, which is hidden by default, by setting the scaleControl to true.

Next, we instantiate a new Map object to which we pass the element where the SATELLITE mode map will be rendered and the parameters listed earlier. Other available display modes are listed in Table 14–3.

Table 14–3. *Available Map Display Modes*

Constant	Description
HYBRID	Displays a transparent layer of major streets on a satellite view.
ROADMAP	Displays a street map.
SATELLITE	Displays a satellite view.
TERRAIN	Displays a map with shaded relief and terrain along with roads.

This parameter is mandatory, because there is no default value. You can already load this code to see the intermediate result and change the value for the map type to test what is available to you. The map rendered is shown in Figure 14–2.

Figure 14–2. *A full-screen view of the world*

Because Google Maps is fully adapted to Mobile Safari, you can use the same touch controls as with the native Maps application—double-tap, pinch to zoom, and so on.

Centering the Map on the Location of the User

Now that your map is correctly displayed, you can position the user on the map using the Geolocation API. To do this, we will add a button to the header of your application and add some code to launch the location request.

```
...
    <style>

        .header-wrapper .header-button {
            background-color: #2070e9;
        }
...
    </style>
...

        <div class="header-wrapper">
            <h1>Geolocation</h1>
            <button class="header-button" onclick="locate()" disabled>Locate</button>
        </div>
```

By default, the button we add is disabled so that the user cannot ask for their location before the map is initialized. Here is the JavaScript that will add functionality to your button:

```
function button(active) {
    document.getElementsByTagName("button")[0].disabled = !active;
}

function locate() {
    button(false);
    window.navigator.geolocation.getCurrentPosition(successCallback, failureCallback);
}
```

And we modify the `init()` function to activate our button:

```
function init() {
...
    button(true);
}
```

Finally, let's add callbacks to process the data returned by getCurrentLocation() and handle possible errors:

```
function successCallback(position) {
    var latlng = new ns.LatLng(position.coords.latitude, position.coords.longitude);
    map.setCenter(latlng);
    map.setZoom(17);
    button(true);
}

function failureCallback(error) {
    switch (error.code) {
        case error.PERMISSION_DENIED:
            alert("Positioning failed. Please check that the location service ↵
                is on and that you have accepted location for the application.");
            break;

        case error.TIMEOUT:
        case error.POSITION_UNAVAILABLE:
            alert("Positioning failed. This often occurs when you are indoors.");
            break;

        default:
            alert("Unexpected error occurred.");
```

```
    }
    button(true);
}
```

If the request succeeds, after creating a new LatLng object using the coordinates found
by the device, we change the alignment of the map so that it is centered on the position
of the user, and we set the zoom value to 17 (50m in satellite view) with setZoom(). If an
error occurs, we inform the user as accurately as possible to help find a solution, and we
reactivate the button.

Marking the Position of the User

The map now focuses on where the user is, but this is obviously frustrating for the user,
who would rather know his exact position, not only an area. The Google Maps API
allows you to add various types of data to your maps, such as markers. For our
example, we are going to create a custom marker using a canvas; here is the function
that will let us create different colored bullets without resorting to any image:

```
var bullet = document.createElement("canvas");

function createBullet(color) {
    /* Always clear the canvas */
    bullet.width = 16;
    bullet.height = 16;

    /* Get the drawing context */
    var ctx = bullet.getContext("2d");

    /* Create a gradient using the color argument */
    var main = ctx.createRadialGradient(5, 6, 1, 0.5, 6, 20);
    main.addColorStop(0, color);
    main.addColorStop(1, "white");

    /* Create the shiny effect */
    var shine = ctx.createRadialGradient(5, 6, 0.5, 5, 6, 40);
    shine.addColorStop(0, "white");
    shine.addColorStop(0.038, "black");
    shine.addColorStop(1, "white");

    /* Set the drawing styles */
    ctx.strokeStyle = color;
    ctx.fillStyle = main;
    ctx.lineWidth = 2;

    /* Draw the bullet */
    ctx.beginPath();
    ctx.arc(8, 8, 7, 0, Math.PI * 2, false);
    ctx.stroke();
    ctx.fill();

    /* Then apply the shiny effect */
    ctx.save();
    ctx.globalCompositeOperation = "lighter";
    ctx.fillStyle = shine;
```

```
    ctx.fill();
    ctx.restore();

    /* Bolder stroke */
    ctx.strokeStyle = "rgba(0,0,0,0.25)";
    ctx.stroke();

    return bullet.toDataURL();
}
```

The name says it all: the createBullet() function creates a bullet with the expected color and returns the content of the canvas using the toDataURL() method. The resulting image can then be used for your markers.

```
var markerBullet;

function drawMarker(latlng, color) {
    if (markerBullet) {
        markerBullet.setPosition(latlng);
    } else {
        markerBullet = new ns.Marker({
            position: latlng,
            map: map,
            icon: createBullet(color),
            zIndex: 1,
        });
    }
}
```

Because it is likely that several spots may be successively indicated and we do not want to create a new canvas for each one, we save the first instance of our marker and change only its position.

The constructor of the Marker object takes the LatLng object for the position, the map to which the position should be attached, and the icon to represent the position that we create using createBullet().

```
function successCallback(position) {
    ...
    drawMarker(latlng, "#0072f9");    // A blue marker
}
```

From there, every time the web application receives a new position, it will be marked with a blue bullet.

Showing Accuracy

There is still one piece of information that we want to display, and that is the accuracy. Because the position returned by the location API can be more or less precise depending on the position of the user and the positioning method internally used (WPS, GPS, and so on), the user may find it useful to know how accurate the indicated position is. In our web application, we are going to represent it visually using another object from the Google Maps API, namely, Circle. Because it is closely related to the position, we modify the drawMarker() function.

```
var markerBullet, markerCircle;

function drawMarker(latlng, accuracy, color) {
...
    if (markerCircle) {
        markerCircle.setCenter(latlng);
    } else {
        markerCircle = new ns.Circle( {
            center: latlng,
            radius: accuracy,
            map: map,

            fillColor: color,
            fillOpacity: 0.25,
            strokeColor: color,
            strokeOpacity: 0.65,
            strokeWeight: 2,
            zIndex:0
        });
    }
}
```

Following the same principle as for the marker, we resort to only one instance of the Circle object. It too is initialized with the LatLng and Map objects. The radius is set in meters and will be set by the value returned by the Geolocation API. In addition to these parameters, you can define colors for the fill and stroke of your indicator, as well as its opacity. As done earlier, you now simply have to modify your success callback to take accuracy into account.

```
function successCallback(position) {
...
    drawMarker(latlng, position.coords.accuracy, "#0072f9");    // A blue marker
}
```

This will bring the user a satisfying positioning service, displaying not only their position but also the accuracy of the positioning, as shown in Figure 14–3.

Figure 14–3. *The user position is displayed on the map along with the accuracy*

With the Google Maps API, you can go much further, from using itineraries defined on the Google servers to showing information with the Street View mode. Because there is a lot to discover and use for impressive applications, we invite you to study the online documentation at http://code.google.com/apis/maps/.

Tracking the User's Position

You have learned how to request the user's position and how to display this information on a map, and you now should have a pretty clear idea of how to do this most efficiently depending on the applications you are planning for this data.

Let's now concentrate on another feature of the Geolocation API: the ability to track changes in a device's situation. By keeping up with a user's location, you will be able to respond to events as they occur, for instance in an itinerary application or in conjunction with some geotagging utility.

Registering for Updates

This functionality is accessed with the watchPosition() method. This method is used in the same manner as getCurrentPosition(), with the same parameters. However, whereas the latter sends a position and ends, the former will send a position and run again.

The `watchPosition()` method also returns a unique identifier, which in time can be used to stop the tracking. The easiest way to call this function is as follows:

```
var watchId = window.navigator.geolocation.watchPosition(successCallback);
```

The repeated request will come to an end when the `clearWatch()` function is called with the relevant ID as a parameter:

```
window.navigator.geolocation.clearWatch(watchId);
```

It seems a reasonable choice to leave this option always available to the end user, who should always have control over their device and usually will know why they launched the application and thus when to stop it.

Nonetheless, `clearWatch()` can also be triggered on some specific event depending on the use of `watchPosition()`, for instance when the user reaches the requested destination with an itinerary application.

Specific Behavior of the Watcher

Because `watchPosition()` is an iterative function, it is useful to understand what happens when the user quits the application without calling the `clearWatch()` function, when the device runs out of battery, or whatever else.

When the user returns to the launcher, if there is enough room to cache the application's state, the function will be temporarily suspended and will resume when the browser is launched again. If an error occurs, the update attempt will continue, and the API will call the failure callback.

You can check this behavior using the following code:

```
window.navigator.geolocation.watchPosition(successCallback, failureCallback);

function successCallback(position) {
    var msg = 'Position: ' + ↵
        position.coords.longitude + ', ' + ↵
        position.coords.latitude;
    console.info(msg + '\nAt ' + (new Date()).toTimeString());
}

function failureCallback(error) {
    var err = error.message + ' (' + error.code + ')';
    console.error(err + '\nAt ' + (new Date()).toTimeString());
}
```

Load a page running this code, quit Mobile Safari, and activate or deactivate the geolocation service. You will see that the position update goes on, meaning neither errors nor quitting an application stops the API's operation.

If the user denies access to the geolocation service, the API will continue sending error messages, although no second chance will be given to the user to change his answer to the request. However, in this case, after the user has quit Mobile Safari and restarted it, the authorization pop-up will appear again; under these circumstances, it is understandable that the API keeps the polling active in this way.

Being aware of this special behavior, the developer should anticipate it by building appropriate callbacks to inform the user of a problem with tracking or stop the tracking with the clearWatch() method after a defined number of attempts.

Watching Position on Google Maps

To illustrate this tracking possibility, we are going to modify the previous Google Maps example to take tracking into account, first by binding the following code to our button:

```
var firstRun, trackerID, failedCount = 0;

function swapAction() {
    var button = document.getElementsByTagName("button")[0];

    if (trackerID == undefined) {
        trackerID = window.navigator.geolocation.watchPosition(
            successCallback, failureCallback);

        button.textContent = "Stop";
        button.style.backgroundColor = "#c6323d";    // Turn to red
        firstRun = true;
    } else {
        window.navigator.geolocation.clearWatch(trackerID);
        trackerID = undefined;
        button.textContent = "Track";
        button.style.backgroundColor = "";
    }
}
```

It is important here to let the user stop the tracking whenever he wants, because tracking can be hard on the battery life of the device, because the user will want to stop if he stops moving, and because, depending on the location method used, the data returned by the tracking may not be satisfying. To do this, we are going to change the Track button into a Stop button when tracking is occurring. The swapAction() function will be used altogether for this, for the stop action itself and to halt the tracking if an error occurs.

Then, we slightly alter the successCallback() function.

```
function successCallback(position) {
    var latlng = new ns.LatLng(position.coords.latitude, position.coords.longitude);
    map.panTo(latlng);

    if (firstRun) {
        map.setZoom(17);
        firstRun = false;
    }
    ...
    failedCount = 0;
}
```

Here, we replace setCenter() with panTo(). The advantage of the panTo() function over setCenter() is that it slides to a new position rather than jumping to it. Besides, we zoom for only the first position; this way, if the user changes the zoom factor, his choice will not be discarded when his position changes.

Because our request has been successful in this case, we set the error counter to 0. On the other side, the failure callback needs slightly more work.

```
function failureCallback(error) {
    /* Stop the tracking after 100 errors */
    if (error.code != error.PERMISSION_DENIED) {
        failedCount++;
        if (failedCount < 100) {
            return;
        }
    }

    failedCount = 0;
    swapAction();

    switch (error.code) {
...
    }
    button(true);
}
```

Reception may not always be optimal, which means that location may not succeed with every attempt, but most likely it will succeed enough to send satisfying data. Therefore, we cannot throw an error to the user with every failure, nor can we halt the tracking on the first failure. Because several calls can be performed every second, we fix a limit to the number of failures at 100, which should approximately mean a 30- to 60-second wait before an error message is sent to the user. After that, the process will be halted.

From Data to Math

The Geolocation API provides you with useful methods to get static data but no helper function to process this data and truly "draw" it in space. Here are a few calculations that may be handy in your workflow. We are going to explain these formulas to some extent so you can understand what is happening; nevertheless, as long as you know what result they yield, you can just copy the snippets and use them in your code.

Distance Between Two Points

If you are going to take your user from one point to another, it is likely that the distance to go will be welcome information. Because you have already learned to find the coordinates of the current and prospective positions of the user, this is rather easily deduced.

Latitude and longitude lines cross each other throughout the map, forming a more or less regular grid. For now we will consider it regular so we can calculate any distance between two points with some elementary mathematical rules.

Provided that one latitude degree (ϕ) roughly represents 69 miles and one longitude degree (λ) spans approximately 53 miles, we apply the Pythagorean theorem: our distance is the hypotenuse of an imaginary triangle following the latitude and longitude "sides." The following formula returns the distance in miles between two given points:

$$distance = \sqrt{(69\Delta\phi)^2 + (53\Delta\lambda)^2}$$

And here is how the formula translates to JavaScript:

```
function computeDistance(p1, p2) {
    var lat1 = p1.coords.latitude;
    var lat2 = p2.coords.latitude;
    var lng1 = p1.coords.longitude;
    var lng2 = p2.coords.longitude;

    return Math.sqrt( Math.pow(69 * (lat2 - lat1), 2) ↵
        + Math.pow(53 * (lng2 - lng1), 2) );
}
```

This will often be your best choice to determine a distance. However, it is an approximation. Indeed, because the earth is an oblate spheroid, latitude and longitude are arcs, not straight lines, meaning the distance between two points will vary depending where you are on the globe, especially for longitude degrees. A longitude degree's length gets smaller as you get closer to either pole.

Sharper Distance Between Two Points

Several methods using spherical geometry can be used to calculate exact distances on curvy lines. Without superfluous detail, here is how to use the Haversine formula to determine the distance between the two points *a* and *b*:

$$distance = r2\sin^{-1}\left(\sqrt{hav(\Delta\phi) + cos\phi_a cos\phi_b hav(\Delta\lambda)}\right)$$

where

$$hav(\theta) = \sin^2\left(\frac{\theta}{2}\right)$$

This is the JavaScript implementation of this formula (3959 being the earth's mean radius, *r*, in miles):

```
function computeDistance(p1, p2) {
    var lat1 = toRad(p1.coords.latitude);
    var lat2 = toRad(p2.coords.latitude);
    var lng1 = toRad(p1.coords.longitude);
    var lng2 = toRad(p2.coords.longitude);

    var deltaLat = (lat2 - lat1);
```

```
    var deltaLng = (lng2 - lng1);

    var calc = Math.pow(Math.sin(deltaLat / 2) , 2) + ↵
            Math.cos(lat1) * Math.cos(lat2) * Math.pow(Math.sin(deltaLng / 2) , 2);

    return 3959 * 2 * Math.asin(Math.sqrt(calc));
}

/* Convert degree to radian */
function toRad(deg) {
    return deg * Math.PI / 180;
}
```

Although this method is quite precise, it is more complex and may take about three times longer to calculate. Again, when you do not need such precision, the first formula is the one to use.

The Direction to Take

Using two points, as for distances, it is possible to calculate the direction to take, called *bearing*. This can be easily mistaken with heading, a value available from the API, but they are two distinct notions. Heading is the direction currently taken by the user while moving; bearing is the direction to take, regardless of any idea of movement. In other words, the bearing is the angle between a line connecting two points and a longitude line and can be determined as such:

$$bearing = tan^{-1}\left(\frac{cos\phi_b sin\Delta\lambda}{cos\phi_a sin\phi_b - sin\phi_a cos\phi_b cos\Delta\lambda}\right)$$

This translates to the following, using JavaScript:

```
function computeBearing(p1, p2) {
    var lat1 = toRad(p1.coords.latitude);
    var lat2 = toRad(p2.coords.latitude);
    var lng1 = toRad(p1.coords.longitude);
    var lng2 = toRad(p2.coords.longitude);

    var deltaLng = (lng2 - lng1);

    var y = Math.cos(lat2) * Math.sin(deltaLng);
    var x = Math.cos(lat1) * Math.sin(lat2) - ↵
                Math.sin(lat1) * Math.cos(lat2) * Math.cos(deltaLng);

    return (toDeg(Math.atan2(y, x)) + 360) % 360;
}

/* Convert radian  to degree */
function toDeg(rad) {
    return rad * 180 / Math.PI;
}
```

To optimize our code, we use Math.atan2() rather than Math.atan() to simplify formulation; it has the advantage of taking into account the signs of both values and places the angle in correct quadrant. However, because `atan2()` returns a value ranging from -180 to +180, we need to normalize the angle to range from 0 to 360 degrees.

Building a Compass Web App

In the following section, we are going to use some of the elements introduced in this book to build a compass web application from scratch. Canvas will be used to draw the elements of our compass, while more lightweight (and thus less choppy) CSS animations will be used to bring it to life.

> **NOTE:** For this real-life example, we recommend you do your testing outdoors to increase the probability of gathering more precise coordinates (with the use of A-GPS). Also be careful that your application will not work from the simulator, because the API will only return Apple's location in California. However, in iPad mode, the API will use information from the network and will at least work for polling.

This application is going to use the data returned by the Geolocation API functions we have previously been through; therefore, building it can also be a convenient way to actually test the accurateness of the data in various situations to build better applications downhill.

Figure 14–4 shows all the graphic elements of the compass that we are going to build using the Canvas API. This will give us great control over the rendering while keeping the weight of required files lower than with regular images.

| compass frame | dial graduations | bearing needle | heading needle | dial shine |

Figure 14–4. *The constitutive elements of our compass*

Because canvas elements are quite consuming of CPU time—they are not drawn on the hardware—it would be too heavy to draw the animations directly using the API, especially dealing with complex elements. Therefore, to move the needles and the dial of the compass, we are going to resort to CSS transitions presented in Chapter 9.

Create the Mobile Elements

As a beginning, we are going to build all the mobile elements from the compass. Although these are going to be drawn using the Canvas API, we will use the elements as images to simplify the code. First comes the object that will hold the functions to create elements. Create a new file named *compass.js*, and add the following:

```
var Compass = function(size) {
    this.dialGraduations = new Image();
    this.bearingNeedle   = new Image();
    this.headingNeedle   = new Image();
    this.dialShine       = new Image();

    this.builder = document.createElement("canvas");
    this.setSize(size);
}
```

The canvas and the images are created dynamically so that our object is independent from the code from which it is used. You will simply need to specify the node where the compass elements should be added. The constructor takes the size of the expected canvas as a parameter. This is first defined as a 140 by 140 pixel frame that will then be scaled using the scale() method. Because we are going to use only vector graphics for rendering, quality loss will be no problem.

```
Compass.prototype.setSize = function(size) {
    /* Original size of the canvas = 140x140 */
    var scale = size / 140;
    this.builder.width  = 140 * scale;
    this.builder.height = 140 * scale;

    this.context = this.builder.getContext("2d");
    this.context.scale(scale, scale);
    this.context.translate(70, 70);
}

Compass.prototype.clear = function() {
    this.context.clearRect(-70, -70, 140, 140);
}

Compass.prototype.render = function(node) {
    this.clear();
    this.drawDialGraduations();
    this.dialGraduations.src = this.builder.toDataURL();

    this.clear();
    this.drawBearingNeedle();
    this.bearingNeedle.src = this.builder.toDataURL();

    this.clear();
    this.drawHeadingNeedle();
    this.headingNeedle.src = this.builder.toDataURL();

    this.clear();
    this.drawDialShine();
    this.dialShine.src = this.builder.toDataURL();

    /* Append nodes to the document */
    node.appendChild(this.dialGraduations);
    node.appendChild(this.bearingNeedle);
    node.appendChild(this.headingNeedle);
    node.appendChild(this.dialShine);
}
```

Each element has its own creation method. At each stage, we empty the canvas and call the relevant method to create an element. Then, the canvas is transformed into a data URL in order to be passed to an image, and it is added to the node passed as a parameter to the main function.

The Graduations

All elements are drawn using vector graphics, and the dial is the part that requires the most code, while still remaining quite simple.

> **NOTE:** In this operation, we are cheating a little, because the text API is not supported yet as of iOS 3.2 but will be in the next major version of the OS. To give our compass more style and give an illustration of the text API, we are using it all the same.

```
Compass.prototype.drawDialGraduations = function() {
    var ctx = this.context;
    ctx.save();

    ctx.beginPath();

    ctx.strokeStyle = "white";
    ctx.arc(0, 0, 15, 0, Math.PI * 2, false);
    ctx.stroke();

    /* Draw cardinal points */
    ctx.fillStyle = "white";
    ctx.textAlign = "center";
    ctx.lineWidth = 0.75;

    for (var n = 0; n < 4; n++) {
        /* Letter place holder */
        ctx.save();
        ctx.beginPath();
        ctx.arc(0, -34, 7, 0, Math.PI * 2, false);
        ctx.fillStyle = "rgba(0, 0, 128, 0.3)";
        ctx.fill();
        ctx.restore();

        /* Cardinal letter */
        ctx.font = "bold 9px Georgia";
        ctx.fillText("NESW".substr(n, 1), 0, -31);

        /*  Inner arrow */
        ctx.beginPath();
        ctx.moveTo(-3, -15);
        ctx.lineTo(0, -30);
        ctx.lineTo(3, -15);
        ctx.fill();

        /* Graduation */
        ctx.beginPath();
```

```
        ctx.moveTo(0, -42);
        ctx.lineTo(0, -39);
        ctx.stroke();

        /* Next letter... */
        ctx.rotate(90 * Math.PI / 180);
    }

    ctx.rotate(45 * Math.PI / 180);
    for (var n = 0; n < 4; n++) {
        /*  Smaller cardinal letters */
        ctx.font = "bold 5px Georgia";
        ctx.fillText("NESESWNW".substr(n * 2, 2), 0, -34);

        /*  Smaller inner arrow */
        ctx.beginPath();
        ctx.moveTo(-2,-15);
        ctx.lineTo(0, -25);
        ctx.lineTo(2, -15);
        ctx.fill();

        /* Smaller graduation */
        ctx.beginPath();
        ctx.moveTo(0,42);
        ctx.lineTo(0,40);
        ctx.stroke();

        /* Next smaller letters... */
        ctx.rotate(90 * Math.PI / 180);
    }

    /* Graduations */
    ctx.globalAlpha = 0.75;
    for (var n = 0; n < 360 / 5; n++) {
        ctx.beginPath();
        ctx.moveTo(0,42);
        ctx.lineTo(0,41);
        ctx.stroke();
        ctx.rotate(5 * Math.PI / 180);
    }

    ctx.restore();
}
```

First we draw the central circle, and the four cardinal points with the corresponding arrows pointing outward. With each iteration, we operate a 90-degree rotation to draw the next point. Once the four cardinal points have been drawn, we add secondary graduations using the same process. Finally, we draw graduations every five degrees. Using the save() and restore() methods prevents altering the state of the canvas for following drawings.

The Needles

The code for the bearing needle is much shorter. It is slightly translucent and drops a shadow on its background so that it is visible while not drawing too much attention.

```
Compass.prototype.drawBearingNeedle = function() {
    var ctx = this.context;
    ctx.save();

    ctx.shadowColor = "rgba(0, 0, 0, 0.3)";
    ctx.shadowOffsetX = 2;
    ctx.shadowOffsetY = 1;
    ctx.shadowBlur = 2;

    ctx.fillStyle = "rgba(0, 0, 128, 0.75)";
    ctx.strokeStyle = "white";

    ctx.beginPath();
    ctx.moveTo(-7, 0);
    ctx.lineTo(0, -38);
    ctx.lineTo(7, 0);
    ctx.lineTo(0, 18);
    ctx.closePath();
    ctx.fill();
    ctx.stroke();

    ctx.restore();
}
```

Once the shadow configuration has been defined, we draw the outline and the fill of the needle using only one path.

The heading needle is a little more complex. Although it uses the same shadow configuration as the bearing needle, its shape and details take several elements to build.

```
Compass.prototype.drawHeadingNeedle = function() {
    var ctx = this.context;
    ctx.save();

    ctx.shadowColor = "rgba(0, 0, 0, 0.3)";
    ctx.shadowOffsetX = 2;
    ctx.shadowOffsetY = 1;
    ctx.shadowBlur = 2;

    /* White part */
    ctx.beginPath();
    ctx.moveTo(-5, 0);
    ctx.lineTo(0, 40);
    ctx.lineTo(5, 0);
    ctx.fillStyle = "white";
    ctx.fill();

    /* Red part */
    ctx.beginPath();
    ctx.moveTo(-5, 0);
    ctx.lineTo(0, -40);
    ctx.lineTo(5, 0);
```

```
ctx.fillStyle = "red";
ctx.fill();

/* Emboss effect */
ctx.beginPath();
ctx.moveTo(5, 0);
ctx.lineTo(0, -43);
ctx.lineTo(0, 43);
ctx.fillStyle = "rgba(0, 0, 0, 0.2)";
ctx.fill();

/* Screw */
ctx.beginPath();
ctx.arc(0, 0, 3, 0 ,Math.PI * 2, false);
ctx.fillStyle = "white";
ctx.fill();
ctx.stroke();

    ctx.restore();
}
```

Every part of this needle is drawn using a separate path, and an emboss effect is added using a black translucent path, superimposed on the white and red parts. Finally, we draw the pinhead by which the needles are fixed to the compass dial.

The Dial Shine

The final part of the compass is not mobile but needs to be drawn all the same, because it will be shown above all the compass elements.

```
Compass.prototype.drawDialShine = function() {
    var ctx = this.context;
    ctx.save();

    var shine = ctx.createLinearGradient(0, -60, 0, 20);
    shine.addColorStop(0, "white");
    shine.addColorStop(1, "rgba(255, 255, 255, 0)");

    ctx.lineWidth = 0.25;
    ctx.strokeStyle = "rgba(255,255,255,0.55)";
    ctx.fillStyle = shine;

    ctx.beginPath();
    ctx.arc(0, 0, 42, Math.PI, Math.PI * 2, false);
    ctx.quadraticCurveTo(0, -17, -43, 0);
    ctx.fill();
    ctx.stroke();

    ctx.restore();
}
```

Using paths again, we draw half a circle, and using a Bézier curve, we draw the inner curve, as shown in Figure 14–4. The quadratic curve has only one control point, which greatly simplifies positioning of the arc. The fill is applied using the gradient defined in the shine variable.

Render the Compass

Now, we can draw the missing part of the compass, namely, the frame, which unlike our other elements will be used directly as a canvas element. To do this, we use the render() method, which calls dedicated drawing methods after the mobile parts have been created.

```
Compass.prototype.render = function(node) {
...
    this.dialShine.src = this.context.canvas.toDataURL();

    this.clear();
    this.drawCompassFrame();
    this.drawDialBackground();
    this.drawDirectionArrow();

    /* Append nodes to the document */
    node.appendChild(this.builder);
...
}
```

The first method draws the compass frame.

```
Compass.prototype.drawCompassFrame = function() {
    var ctx = this.context;
    ctx.save();

    var frame = this.context.createRadialGradient(0, 0, 0, 0, 0, 56);
    frame.addColorStop(0.85, "#e7ba5a");
    frame.addColorStop(0.9, "#fcd97c");
    frame.addColorStop(1, "#e7ba5a");

    ctx.beginPath();
    ctx.arc(0, 0, 56, 0, Math.PI * 2, false);
    ctx.strokeStyle = "#444";

    ctx.save();
        ctx.shadowColor = "rgba(0, 0, 0, 0.75)";
        ctx.shadowOffsetX = 1;
        ctx.shadowOffsetY = 1;
        ctx.shadowBlur = 4;
        ctx.stroke();
        ctx.fillStyle = frame;
        ctx.fill();
    ctx.restore();

    /* Shiny effect */
    ctx.beginPath();
    ctx.fillStyle = "rgba(255, 255, 255, 0.4)";
    ctx.arc(2, 2, 48, 0, Math.PI * 2, false);
    ctx.fill();

    ctx.beginPath();
    ctx.fillStyle = "rgba(0, 0, 0, 0.1)";
    ctx.arc(-2, -2, 48, 0, Math.PI * 2, false);
    ctx.fill();

    ctx.restore();
}
```

The frame is built from a disc that uses the golden radial gradient frame, which mimics depth. To make the effect even more realistic, we add two semitranslucent discs on top of this.

```
Compass.prototype.drawDialBackground = function() {
    var ctx = this.context;
    ctx.save();

    var back = this.context.createLinearGradient(-50, -50, 50, 50);
    back.addColorStop(0, "#122a91");
    back.addColorStop(1, "#61a1f4");

    ctx.beginPath();
    ctx.fillStyle = back;
    ctx.arc(0, 0, 43, 0, Math.PI * 2, false);
    ctx.fill();
    ctx.stroke();

    ctx.beginPath();
    ctx.fillStyle = "white";
    ctx.moveTo(-1, -38);
    ctx.lineTo(0, -41);
    ctx.lineTo(1, -38);
    ctx.fill();

    ctx.restore();
}
```

The dial background uses only a blue gradient-filled disc. A small arrow is added to the upper part of the dial that shows the current direction, which should make the position on graduations more readable.

```
Compass.prototype.drawDirectionArrow = function() {
    var ctx = this.context;
    ctx.save();
    ctx.translate(0, -59);

    ctx.strokeStyle = "rgba(0, 0, 0, 0.25)";

    ctx.beginPath();
    ctx.moveTo(-10, 0);
    ctx.lineTo(0, -10);
    ctx.lineTo(10, 0);
    ctx.stroke();

    ctx.strokeStyle = "rgba(255, 255, 255, 0.25)";

    ctx.beginPath();
    ctx.moveTo(-10, 0);
    ctx.lineTo(10, 0);
    ctx.stroke();

    ctx.restore();
}
```

The last element to be added to the compass is another arrow, which will indicate the direction where the user is heading. This arrow will not move: it only gives a constant indication of which way the user is pointing in order to make the compass more readable.

Add Elements to the Document

The document to which we add our compass elements is based on the web application template created in Chapter 4. Simply modify the *index.html* file as follows:

```
<body onload="init()">
    <div class="view">
        <div class="header-wrapper">
            <h1>Heading</h1>
        </div>

        <div id="compass"><div></div></div>
    </div>
</body>
```

To make the presentation of the page more appropriate and attractive, add the following styles to a new *compass.css* style sheet. They add a brown gradient background and a translucent header.

```
.view {
    background: -webkit-gradient(radial,
        0 0, 0, 0 0, 300,
        from(#a98), to(#654));
}

.header-wrapper { background-color: transparent; }
```

For all our elements to fit appropriately together in the available space, also add the following rules to your style sheet:

```
#compass div {
    position: relative;
    margin: 0 auto;
    top: 10px;
}

#compass canvas {
    display: block;
    margin: 0 auto;
}

#compass img {
    position: absolute;
    top: 0;
    left: 0;
}
```

To complete the first part of our compass building, you will have to add to the *compass.js* file the code to initialize the compass.

```
const COMPASS_SIZE = 220;

var compass = new Compass(COMPASS_SIZE);

function init() {
    var target = document.querySelector("#compass div");
    target.style.width = COMPASS_SIZE + "px";
    compass.render(target);
}
```

Next, we want to add the code necessary to gather, process, and display the positioning data.

Prepare the Document to Receive Location Data

To explain the method used to calculate distance and bearing, we are going to calculate the distance of the user from Apple's headquarter and the direction that should be taken to go there. In addition, we will also display the position of the user (longitude and latitude). The following elements are added to the HTML document:

...

```
    <div id="compass"><div></div></div>

    <div class="list-wrapper">
        <div id="location">latitude | longitude</div>
        <ul>
            <li><span>0</span>Distance to Apple's Headquarter</li>
            <li><span>0</span>Bearing</li>
            <li><span>0</span>Current Speed</li>
            <li><span>0</span>Location Accuracy</li>
        </ul>
    </div>
```

...

The following style rules will make our fields stick to the bottom of the screen:

```
.list-wrapper {
    position: absolute;
    width: 100%;
    bottom: 0;
    border-top: solid 1px black;
}

#location {
    position: absolute;
    bottom: 140px;
    font-size: 10px;
    color: white;
    text-shadow: rgba(0,0,0,0.7) 0 -1px 0;
    width: 100%;
    text-align: center;
}

.list-wrapper li {
    font-size: 12px;
    line-height: 1;
```

```
}
.list-wrapper li span { float: right; }
```

The header and the list items will be updated from the callback to the `watchPosition()` method.

Use Location Data

The heading (the direction the user is taking) is available only when the user is moving and the precision of the data gathered by the device is great enough, because we need two points to determine this piece of information. As previously, we are going to use tracking. Here is how the initialization function should be modified:

```
function init() {
...
    window.navigator.geolocation.watchPosition(successCallback,
        null, { enableHighAccuracy: true });
}
```

As stated earlier, the data available needs to be accurate enough for the API to determine the heading. For that, we force the enableHighAccuracy parameter to `true` to make sure the A-GPS is activated if available. Everything else happens in the `successCallback()` function shown here:

```
var appleLocation = {
    coords: {
        latitude : 37.331689,
        longitude: -122.030731
    }
}

function successCallback(position) {
    /* Append location information */
    var loc = document.getElementById("location");
    loc.textContent = position.coords.latitude + " | " + position.coords.longitude;

    /* Read and compute data */
    var heading  = position.coords.heading || 0;
    var accuracy = position.coords.accuracy;
    var speed    = position.coords.speed;

    var bearing  = computeBearing(position, appleLocation);
    var distance = computeDistance(position, appleLocation);

    /* Show current formatted heading */
    var header = document.querySelector(".header-wrapper h1");
    header.innerHTML = getAngleString(heading);

    var list = document.querySelectorAll("li span");
    list[0].textContent = round(distance, 3) + "mi";
    list[1].innerHTML   = getAngleString(bearing);
    list[2].textContent = round(speed, 2) + "m/s";
    list[3].textContent = round(accuracy, 2) + "m";
}
```

First, we display the current position of the user inside the location container. Then, we read the values for heading, accuracy and speed, and we calculate the bearing and the distance using the appleLocation position. Our data is then added to the header (heading) and to the list (all other elements).

The callback uses two utility functions that let us format the angle by indicating the position on the compass rose (four cardinal points with four intermediate positions) and round off the floating-point values with a precision passed as a parameter.

```
function getAngleString(angle) {
    var position = ((angle + 45 / 2) / 45 | 0) % 8 * 2;
    return (angle * 10 | 0) / 10 + "&deg;" + ("N NEE SES SWW NW".substr(position, 2));
}

function round(value, prec) {
    prec = Math.pow(10, prec);
    return ((value || 0) * prec << 0) / prec;
}
```

At this stage, if you launch the web application, the data will appear where expected, but no element of the compass will move. The final step is to translate information into a visual change to the compass.

Animate the Compass

To animate the transition from one state of the needles and dial graduations to another, we are going to use CSS animations, as presented in Chapter 9. On a regular compass, the dial itself doesn't move: the holder takes the compass, waits for the needle to point north, and then turns the compass to know which way he is turning. In order not to make users repeatedly turn their device around, we are going to make the dial turn— slightly off-time from the heading needle to produce a realistic effect. Likewise, the bearing needle will move more slowly to make the compass more readable.

The animation of the elements does not take much code. Simply add the following to your *compass.css* file:

```
#compass img {
...
    -webkit-transform-origin: 50% 50%;
    -webkit-transform: rotate(0);
    -webkit-transition-property: -webkit-transform;
    -webkit-transition-timing-function: ease-out;
}
```

This, of course, only handles the animation itself. The states of the elements are handled with JavaScript. The rotation can occur only if heading data is available. This is checked in the following code:

```
function successCallback(position) {
...
    if (position.coords.heading != null) {
        compass.setHeading(heading);
        compass.setBearing(bearing - position.coords.heading);
    }
```

```
}
```

The bearing should adjusted relatively to the heading so that the needle points in the right direction relatively to the direction of the user. Therefore, we subtract the angle of the heading to the angle of the bearing. Here are the relevant functions:

```
Compass.prototype.setBearing = function(deg) {
    this.rotate(this.bearingNeedle, deg);
}

Compass.prototype.setHeading = function(deg) {
    this.rotate(this.headingNeedle, -deg);
    this.rotate(this.dialGraduations, -deg);
}
```

Our three elements are going to move off-time. The duration of the animations is defined using the following code, which should be added to the constructor of the Compass object:

```
var Compass = function(size) {
...
    this.dialShine      = new Image();

    this.dialGraduations.style.webkitTransitionDuration = "2s";
    this.bearingNeedle.style.webkitTransitionDuration   = "5s";
    this.headingNeedle.style.webkitTransitionDuration   = "3s";
...
}
```

The rotate() method is somewhat more complicated, because there are chances that a new heading value will be received before the animation has completed. In such a case, it is necessary to begin the next rotation from the current position of the animation so that the element doesn't jump from one position to another. To do this, we resort to the CSSMatrix object.

```
Compass.prototype.rotate = function(item, deg) {
    var gs = window.getComputedStyle(item);
    var mx = new WebKitCSSMatrix(gs.webkitTransform);

    var current = toDeg(Math.acos(mx.a));
    /* Adjust quadrant */
    if (mx.b < 0) {
        current = 360 - current;
    }
    var delta = deg - current;
    item.style.webkitTransform = mx.rotate(delta);
}
```

First, we read the current matrix, which reflects the position of the transition. This will let us deduce the angle currently applied to the element. Then, we apply a clockwise rotation using the 2D matrix.

$$rotation = \begin{bmatrix} cos\theta & sin\theta & 0 \\ -sin\theta & cos\theta & 0 \\ 0 & 0 & 1 \end{bmatrix}$$

Using this matrix and a little trigonometry, we can evaluate the current angle by reading the arccosine of the first element (mx.a) of the matrix and position the angle on the correct quadrant based on the sign of the sine (mx.b). The new angle to apply can then be calculated by subtracting the desired angle from the current angle. The rotate() method allows you to simply apply the new angle and resume the animation to its new position. Figure 14–5 shows the final result.

Figure 14–5. *The compass and data relative to the user's position*

Prevent Staggering Needles

Because the position is sent several times a second, a new value for the heading can be sent while the rendering engine is still handling the rotation matrix. In such a case, there is a risk that the current position be considered as the initial position (before rotation), which will cause the needles to jump from one point to another. To prevent this behavior and not let the engine run useless calculations, we are going to temporize the reading of received data.

```
var prevTime = 0;

function successCallback(position) {
    if ((new Date() - prevTime) < 1500) {
        return;
    }
    prevTime = new Date().getTime();
...
}
```

This way, the data will be read every second and a half only, leaving the rendering engine sufficient time to apply the current matrix during the transition and actually produce the expected effect.

Summary

The Geolocation API allows you to get useful data and build new types of applications and opens a path for innovative developing on modern devices. Because the API is an implementation of a W3C specification, applications built for the iPhone, iPod touch, or iPad could soon be used on all modern browsers.

Quite practically, Apple has made this API available on Mobile Safari before bringing it to the desktop version. Likewise, it is an excellent move to get familiar with this API, because localized services are very likely to become more and more popular—entailing a new expectation for users. The most intelligent use of this API may well be to use it to add value to location-unspecific applications, as an extra service for the user. So, jump in and go further with this opportunity.

## Chapter 15

A Better Handling of Client-Side Data Storage

For years, when data needed to be stored on the client to enhance a page or actually allow it to work properly, developers could rely only on cookies. Although this has worked well for various applications, cookies have limitations that make them somewhat unfit for developing complex functionality. Size limits are not a problem when storing an identifier or some information from a session—such as shopping cart data—but they easily become impossible to handle when dealing with more complex tasks, such as calendar synchronization.

This doesn't mean client-side storage isn't a profitable practice: limiting the amount of data transitioning between the client and the server naturally makes a page more responsive, thus making for a better user experience. However, when dealing with cookies, this is only partly true, because cookies are sent with every request (be it the download of an image, a style sheet, or whatever else), uselessly making each sent element heavier during the transfer.

In this chapter, you will dive into the new client-side storage options available to developers through JavaScript APIs and learn how to handle offline mode correctly using new features from HTML5.

Different Storage Areas

To make client-side storage persistence more flexible and work beyond the limitations imposed by cookies, it is now possible to rely on the Web Storage API, maintained by the WHATWG. This specification defines a new `Storage` interface implemented by the new `localStorage` and `sessionStorage` properties of the `window` object.

Among the advantages of this storage mode over cookies is a size limit of 5MB instead of 4KB; this limit is applicable to the fully qualified domain name (FQDN). Once this quota has been reached, you will no longer be able to store data to the client, and a `QUOTA_EXCEEDED_ERR` will be sent (Figure 15–1).

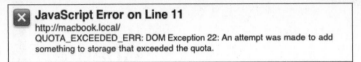

Figure 15–1. *An error is sent upon attempt to store data beyond the maximum limit*

One could say that the sessionStorage property is analogous to session cookies, which are available across browsing contexts and are deleted when the user quits the browsing application. However, the meaning of *session* in this case is slightly different whether you are talking about cookies or the sessionStorage property. The localStorage property behaves more or less like a cookie that would never expire, meaning data stored using this property will be persistent until it is deleted with a script or on an action by the user. Both properties work much like cookies, except that there is no path implication to access the stored data as with cookies but instead an origin rule based on the scheme/host/port tuple.

How to Use New Storage Capabilities

Data storage using the Web Storage API, as when creating cookies, relies on key/value pairs. The key can be defined as any valid string—including an empty string. The value, in the current implementation of the API in Mobile Safari, can also only be a valid string. Consequently, if you try to store an object, the stored data will be the object after its toString() method has been called. Because, according to the specification, you should be able to store many kinds of objects as clones (not as references), chances are storing objects should be a feature soon available.

This limitation on types applies to all objects, including numeric values. If for instance you want to use a key to store a counter, don't forget to convert the data retrieved back to a Number object before incrementing or decrementing it, or the string will simply be concatenated with 1. Also, because strings are stored using UTF-16, a character takes two bytes, thus taking more space; therefore, to store a Date object for instance, you should rather store the value of the getTime() method than that returned by toString().

These limitations, however, are trivial compared to the process to set or retrieve values with cookies. Such basic operations are extremely straightforward with the Web Storage API. The API provides specific methods to insert, read, or delete values.

```
/* Write data */
window.localStorage.setItem("myKey", "myValue");
window.localStorage.setItem("anotherKey", "myOtherValue");

/* Read data */
var value1 = window.localStorage.getItem("myKey");
var value2 = window.localStorage.getItem("anotherKey");

/* Delete data */
window.localStorage.removeItem("myKey");
```

All keys are easily accessed independently, because you can browse stored data as you would an object. The following code does the same as the previous code:

```
/* Write data */
window.localStorage.myKey = "myValue";
window.localStorage.anotherKey = "myOtherValue";

/* Read data */
var value1 = window.localStorage.myKey;        // "myValue"
var value2 = window.localStorage.anotherKey;  // "myOtherValue"

/* Delete data */
delete window.localStorage.myKey;
```

To work with the `Storage` object as a whole, you can also rely on two useful methods: the `clear()` method, which will reset the object by deleting all pairs, and the `key()` method, which will allow you to target a key by index rather than by name.

```
for (var i = 0; i < window.localStorage.length; i++) {
    console.log(i + ": " + window.localStorage.key(i));
}
```

```
--- result ---
0: myKey
1: anotherKey
```

As often with key/value pair collections, the order in which keys appear isn't predictable; it should, however, remain constant as long as no key has been modified.

Specific Behavior of sessionStorage

A session cookie is valid in whatever the window or tab the user is browsing in until the user quits the browser. This means, for instance, that whatever items a user would have put in the online shopping cart will be kept in memory if the user opens a new document in their current window, opens the same site in a different window, or closes the tab where the online store site was open.

The drawback in this solution is that a user wanting to browse the same shopping site with two different carts—in order to use different credit cards or be delivered to two different addresses or whatever else—would need to shop in two different browsers (for instance, Safari and Firefox) or complete the first session, close the browser, and then move on to the second session.

The `sessionStorage` object works differently. Whereas cookies are related to a browser session and the `localStorage` object creates a unique instance of the `Storage` object for one origin, `sessionStorage` creates an instance of the `Storage` object for each browsing context, which is inherited by any browsing context created by the initial one. This means that a frame (child browsing context) will have access to the same `sessionStorage` object as its host document; yet, if a new window (auxiliary browsing context) is opened from the parent window, this new browsing context will have access to a copy of the initial `Storage` object, which will then be altered independently from the first object.

Using Mobile Safari, this is true only for windows opened by a script. Indeed, a window opened because of a `target` attribute will be considered as opened after a deliberate action by the user. This means when a user opens a new window or tab, it will be attributed a new empty `sessionStorage` object. Of course, the content of the object will be accessible only from the same origin. You can refer to Chapter 11 for more detail about browsing contexts.

Being Notified of Storage Area Modification

Every time a storage area is modified, a `storage` event is raised, which cannot be canceled and doesn't bubble. It can be caught like any other event from the `DOMWindow` object.

```
window.addEventListener("storage", function(event) {
    /* do something with the StorageEvent object */
}, false);
```

This event is sent to all documents using the modified storage area, except the document from which the area was altered. This means that no event will be fired if only the document from which the storage area is modified uses the storage area. On the contrary, if this document holds an `<iframe>`, whether the storage area is modified from the `<iframe>` or from the main document, the other browsing context will be notified.

The `storage` event allows you to control modifications, for instance allowing only changes originating from the main document. However, you should be careful not to provoke infinite event exchange, for instance by setting each browsing context to refuse modifications by another. That the `storage` event is not sent to the document where the action took place also is a step to prevent this.

Table 15–1 lists the properties of the `StorageEvent` object passed as a parameter to the handler. Note that where the working draft specifies a `url` property, the WebKit implementation uses the `uri` property.

Table 15–1. *Properties of the* `StorageEvent` *Object*

Property	Description
event.storageArea	The storage area that has been modified.
event.key	The key whose value has been added, modified, or removed from the Storage object.
event.oldValue	The value associated with the key before modification.
event.newValue	The value associated with the key after modification.
event.uri	The address of the document from which the modification was run.

When using the `setItem()` and `removeItem()` methods, the property values `key`, `oldValue`, and `newValue` are set as shown in Table 15–1. On the other side, using `clear()`, all three properties will be set to `null`, letting you easily identify when this method is called to change item values. In all cases, the `storageArea` and `uri` properties will be set, letting you identify the origin of the event.

Security and Privacy Considerations

As when working with cookies or cross-document communication, you will run into restrictions that originate in security risks. First, although the size limit on the `Storage` object is far less restrictive than that of cookies, it is set in order to prevent denial-of-service attacks.

Access to a storage area is limited to the scheme/host/port tuple, and it is currently not possible to relax the access to storage using the `domain` property of the `Document` object, accessible with DOM Level 1, which is a limitation compared to cookies but also makes this kind of storage more secure, especially if you use a shared host name.

Last, when the stored data is very sensitive, you should limit the usage of storage areas to secure areas relying on SSL—or its successor TLS—thus giving access to the data only if a valid certificate is given, validating the origin of requests. This is critical to protect user privacy.

Caching Ajax Requests

One interesting application of local storage is to cache data from Ajax requests. Of course, you can use HTTP caching, but this is less reliable.

The Base Document

To illustrate how you can cache data from Ajax requests, we are going to syndicate a RSS feed from Apple and display it appropriately for users. We again build upon our web application template, applying the following changes to the body:

```
<body onload="init()">
    <div class="view">
        <div class="header-wrapper">

        <h1>Apple's RSS Feed</h1>

        </div>

        <div class="list-wrapper">
            <h2>Latest News</h2>
            <ul id="feed" class="template">
                <li><a href="#{link}">
                    <span>#{title}</span><small>#{dateFormatted}
                        #{contentFormatted}</small>
                </a></li>
            </ul>
        </div>
    </div>
</body>
```

If you have been through Chapter 12, you will notice that we are going to use the client-side rendering method used to process content loaded using Ajax. You can refer to Chapter 12 if you need further detail on this method and to get the functions required for this example.

We need to initialize the request to gather content from the feed. This is done with the following code:

```
/* Apple's news feed */
var feedUrl = "http://images.apple.com/main/rss/hotnews/hotnews.rss";

function init() {
    refresh();
}

function refresh() {
    var xml = new XMLHttpRequest();
    xml.onreadystatechange = showFeed;
    xml.open("get", "proxy.php?url=" + encodeURIComponent(feedUrl));
    xml.send();
}

function showFeed() {
    if (this.readyState == this.DONE && this.status == 200) {
        processFeed(this.responseXML);
    }
}

function processFeed(xml) {
    var arr = [];
    var all = xml.getElementsByTagName("item");
    var list = document.getElementById("feed");

    /* Compute resulting HTML */
    var html = "";
    for (var i = 0; i < all.length; i++) {
        var data = {
            title:      getText(all[i], "title"),
            content:    getText(all[i], "description"),
            date:       new Date(getText(all[i], "pubDate")),
            link:       getText(all[i], "link")
        };
        html += applyTemplate(list.innerHTML, data);
    }

    /* Append content to the document */
    appendContent(list, html);
}

function getText(node, name) {
    var item = node.getElementsByTagName(name);
    return item.length && item[0].hasChildNodes() ?
        item[0].firstChild.nodeValue : null;
}
```

Because we gather XML, we need to turn the markup into an object for use in our template. This is done with the processFeed() method. Luckily, RSS feeds are simple

enough, and this operation doesn't require too much code. We then use the getText()
method to make reading the text nodes easier.

Our template has two formatted values; we therefore need to add the two relevant
formatters to display the expected values in the template.

```
var formatters = {
    "date": formatDate,
    "content": formatContent
};
function formatDate(value, data) {
    if (typeof value == "string") {
        value = new Date(value);
    }
    return ("0" + value.getDate()).substr(-2) + "/" +
           ("0" + (value.getMonth() + 1)).substr(-2) + " -- ";
}
function formatContent(value, data) {
    return value.replace(/<.+?>/g, "").substr(0, 200) + "...";
}
function processFeed(xml) {
...
        html += applyTemplate(list.innerHTML, data, formatters);
...
}
```

Our first step will end with an addition to the *main.css* file, which will give the specific
styles to our list items.

```
.group-wrapper ul li a,
.list-wrapper ul li a {
...
}

.group-wrapper ul li a:active,
.list-wrapper ul li a:active {
...
}

.group-wrapper ul li a:active *,
.list-wrapper ul li a:active * {
...
}

.list-wrapper ul li a {
    margin: -10px;
    text-decoration: none;
    color: inherit;
}

.list-wrapper ul li a span {
    display: block;
    margin-right: 24px;
    overflow: hidden;
    text-overflow: ellipsis;
    white-space: nowrap;
```

```
}
.list-wrapper ul li a small {
    display: block;
    margin-right: 24px;
    font-size: 13px;
    line-height: 15px;
    height: 30px;
    overflow: hidden;
    color: gray;
}
```

Now, if you load the HTML file into a browser, you will see that the feed is loaded and appropriately displayed, as shown in Figure 15–2.

Figure 15–2. *The Apple feed is loaded using Ajax and rendered on the client*

This is a rather common way to display a feed. Unless you use HTTP caching, the user will see an up-to-date feed every time he refreshes the page. Now, we are going to take this further by loading the feed from cache by default and leaving the choice to the user of when to refresh the display. Using this method, your application would load faster and give enhanced control to the user—a win-win system.

Adding Caching Capabilities

To let the user decide when to refresh the list, we will first create the appropriate button. Let's add a Refresh button to our header, as follows:

```
...
        <div class="header-wrapper">
            <h1>Apple's RSS Feed</h1>
            <button class="header-button" onclick="refresh()">
                <span>Refresh</span>
            </button>
        </div>
...
```

As in Chapter 12, the `<span>` will be used to hide the text and display a spinner while the content is loading. The function used to refresh the feed is the one used earlier. However, when the `processFeed()` function is called a second time, the template will no longer be readable from the markup, because the HTML content has already been modified: it needs to be saved beforehand. This is best done with `sessionStorage`, because the template needn't be stored beyond the session (the template will be available again for a new session), and you may moreover want to change your template at some stage—which could cause errors. This is how the function is modified:

```
function processFeed(xml) {
...
    var list = document.getElementById("feed");
    if (window.sessionStorage.template == undefined) {
        window.sessionStorage.template = list.innerHTML;
    }
...
        html += applyTemplate(window.sessionStorage.template, data, formatters);
...
}
```

To activate the spinner, you will need the `BigSpinner` object, created in Chapter 7. Add it to your code, and use it as follows:

```
var spinner = new BigSpinner();

function init() {
    spinner.init("spinner", "white");
...
}

function refresh() {
...
    buttonState(true);
}

function showFeed() {
    if (this.readyState == this.DONE && this.status == 200) {
        processFeed(this.responseXML);
        buttonState(false);
    }
}

function buttonState(loading) {
    var but = document.querySelector("button.header-button");

    if (loading) {
        but.disabled = true;
```

```
        but.className += " spinning";
        spinner.animate();
    } else {
        but.disabled = false;
        but.className = but.className.replace(" spinning", "");
        spinner.stop();
    }
}
```

Now, while the feed list is loading, the user will be informed of the application activity.

A first level of cache thus relies on sessionStorage. The second cache level, using localStorage, will store the XML data and a loaded time to determine whether to send the Ajax request.

```
function showFeed() {
    if (this.readyState == this.DONE && this.status == 200) {
        /* The date will be serialized as string */
        window.localStorage.feedDate = new Date();
        window.localStorage.feedXML = this.responseText;
        processFeed(this.responseXML);
        buttonState(false);
    }
}
```

Because it isn't possible to store anything else than strings, we store the XML as text using responseText. This will be transformed to XML later using the DOMParser object. We also record the date to calculate the cache Time To Live (TTL).

Our cache is now ready for use. This is handled from the refresh() method.

```
function refresh() {
    var last = new Date(window.localStorage.feedDate || 0);
    var ttl  = new Date() - 1000 * 60 * 60 * 1;

    if (last <= ttl) {
...
    } else {
        var xml = (new DOMParser()).parseFromString( ↵
            window.localStorage.feedXML, "text/xml");
        processFeed(xml);
    }
}
```

The date is serialized as a string, which can be easily reversed by passing the resulting string to the constructor of the Date object. This way, we can calculate the time elapsed since the last cache was stored and allow the Ajax request to run only if this time is more than one hour ago. Otherwise, we use the parseFromString() method of the DOMParser object to convert our text to an XML document.

> **NOTE:** The DOMParser object is actually part of no standard but is implemented in some way on most browsers including Mobile Safari, so you can safely rely on it.

Currently, when the user clicks the Refresh button, the script will use the cache if that seems reasonable or load the content anew otherwise.

Sending Client Data to the Server

One issue with cookies is that they are automatically sent with every request to the server—needlessly increasing data transfer sizes—which of course is an especially bad thing when working with unreliable connections.

Storage area data isn't sent this way. However, you may actually need to send data from a storage area to the server, for instance when a user validates a cart. To do this, you can catch the check-out form validation event and add information necessary to process the shopping cart. Supposing our product IDs have been stored under the products key, we could use code similar to this:

```
<script>

    /* Sample content */
    window.sessionStorage.products = "3,5,9,100";

    function appendData(form) {
        var products = form.elements["products"];
        products.value = window.sessionStorage.products || "";
    }

</script>

<form method="get" action="checkout.php" onsubmit="appendData(this)">
    <input type="hidden" name="products">
    <input type="submit" value="Checkout">
</form>
```

When the form is submitted, the value of the products input is updated with the values from the sessionStorage (if any), and the form is submitted with the relevant data.

When several properties from the storage area have to be passed to the form, it is possible to iterate through the elements of the form to check whether a property is available for each element. Hence, by using the same names for the storage area properties and the form fields, you can easily create a generic function to facilitate data exchange.

```
function exchangeData(form) {
    var all = form.elements;

    for (var i = 0; i < all.length; i++) {
        var data = window.sessionStorage.getItem(all[i].name);
        if (data) {
            all[i].value = data;
        }
    }
}
```

This function is basic. Of course, to be functional in real-life cases, the script should, for instance, handle different input types, such as check boxes, whose value shouldn't be changed but should be checked or unchecked.

You could also use a similar method directly on classic links:

```
<script>

    function appendData(link) {
        var url = link.href;
        link.search += (link.search ? "&" : "") + "products=" +
            encodeURIComponent(window.sessionStorage.products);
    }

</script>

<a href="checkout.php" onclick="appendData(this)">Checkout</a>
```

This method yields the same results as the previous. By modifying the Location object of the link passed as a parameter to the appendData() function, we add the data to the query string. The server-side script will have the necessary data available to process the user cart.

SQL Local Database

The Storage API, like cookies, offers a useful way to handle rather simple data. However, there is another alternative to store data on the client when needs are more specific. The Web Database specification, which is maintained by an entity of the W3C, will let you take client side storage further.

Although this API is more complex to use than the Storage API, the handling of data is made more flexible, for instance with the use of powerful sorting, more advanced possibilities as for data structure, and easier update processes. Moreover, more data types are available for storage.

Data stored using the Database API can be queried using Structured Query Language (SQL), a language used by most relational database management systems (RDBMSs), like mySQL, SQL Server, or Oracle. The SQL dialect implemented in all browsers to date is based on a subset of SQLite 3.6.19.

> **NOTE:** The functioning of RDBMSs and how to use SQL is beyond the range of this book. Quite a few commands will be used and explained in our examples, but you can find thorough information in the SQLite documentation at www.sqlite.org.

This API can be used in your web applications, because it is already implemented in WebKit browsers. However, the current implementation of the API functions is a mix of synchronous and asynchronous versions. In other words, for now opening the database will be a synchronous operation, while querying it will be done asynchronously.

Opening the Database

With a classic DBMS, a new database is generally created with the SQL command
CREATE DATABASE. In the case of web databases, in order to protect data integrity when
the schema changes and limit errors, the database creation is done with the
openDatabase() function from the WindowDatabase interface. No actual SQL command
related to the creation or modification of the database itself is available.

```
var db = window.openDatabase("Apress", "1.0", "Apress Storage Demo", 10 * 1024 * 1024);
```

The first parameter sets the physical name for the databases that will be used to store
data on the disk. The second should be used to specify a version for the database. This
is useful, because it will prevent the client code from using a database that has evolved
and from attempting to add data that might cause errors, thus making the web
application unstable. If an error occurs on the version number, an INVALID_STATE_ERR
fatal exception will be sent. The third parameter sets the logical name for the database,
which will be used by the browser to display messages.

Finally, the size of the database is given in bytes, which again defaults to 5MB. Fixing a
value lower than the default will not actually reduce the maximum size of the database;
however, fixing a limit higher than this default (as in our example), the user is sent a
message inquiring whether the space required by the current operation should be
allotted, as shown in Figure 15–3.

Figure 15–3. *A message is sent when the estimated amount of data exceeds the default maximum*

If the user refuses the request, the openDatabase() function will return null. If the operation is successful, the function will return a Database object allowing you to query the data of the database. If the database doesn't exist when the function is executed, it will be created. In this case, in recent versions of WebKit, you can pass a callback function as the final parameter that will let you interact with the database after creation. However, this feature isn't implemented yet in Mobile Safari, so you will need to initiate the database by other means.

```
var globalDB = window.openDatabase("Apress", "1.0", ↵
                                    "Apress Storage Demo", 1 * 1024 * 1024);
checkDatabase(globalDB);

function checkDatabase(db) {
    /* Transaction created */
    db.transaction(
        function(tran) {
            tran.executeSql("SELECT 1 FROM News LIMIT 1");
        },

        /* Failed? The database should not be initialized */
        function() {
            initDatabase(db);
        },

        /* Success? The database is already initialized */
        function() {
            /* Start database jobs */
        }
    );
}

function initDatabase(db) {

    /* Create the database schema using the 'db' Database object */

}
```

The checkDatabase() function attempts to execute a simple request on the expected data model with the transaction() method (that takes three parameters) and the executeSql() method, which we will see later. We intentionally limit the result to one row in order for the query to be executed quickly, avoiding the retrieval of a potentially heavy result set. If the query succeeds, we can assume that the database schema has already been created. At this point, because we have asked for a specific version, the job can begin, because we know that the schema is correct. Otherwise, an error is raised, and we call the schema creation function.

Creating Tables

Once you have a Database object available to you, you can use transactions, as shown previously, to modify the contents of the database. A transaction lets you group one or several queries, which are generally interdependent. If one query fails, all will be canceled. Just like you can't create a database using the CREATE DATABASE command directly, you cannot use the BEGIN TRANSACTION, ROLLBACK, or COMMIT command without throwing an error. These are encapsulated inside methods from the API, and you should use the transaction() method of the Database object to execute read/write operations. This method takes a callback function as parameter, which will be passed a SQLTransaction when it is called.

The first step to work with a database is to create tables that will hold the data. As previously, we are going to store news from an RSS feed, so we will need two tables: one holding the information source and one holding the news from each feed.

```
function initDatabase(db) {
    db.transaction(function(transaction) {
        createSchema(transaction);
    });
}

function createSchema(tran) {
    var schema = [
        "CREATE TABLE Source (" +
        "    SourceID     INTEGER NOT NULL PRIMARY KEY AUTOINCREMENT," +
        "    Name         VARCHAR(100) NOT NULL," +
        "    URL          VARCHAR(100) NOT NULL," +
        "    LastUpdated  DATETIME NULL" +
        ")",

        "CREATE TABLE News (" +
        "    NewsID     INTEGER NOT NULL PRIMARY KEY AUTOINCREMENT," +
        "    SourceID   INTEGER NOT NULL," +
        "    GUID       CHAR(32)," +
        "    Title      VARCHAR(200) NOT NULL," +
        "    Content    TEXT NOT NULL," +
        "    Date       DATETIME NOT NULL," +
        "    TargetURL  VARCHAR(100) NOT NULL," +
        "    FOREIGN KEY (SourceID) REFERENCES Source(SourceID)" +
        ")"
    ];

    executeSequence(tran, schema);
}
```

NOTE: Although we have specified limits for fields such as CHAR or VARCHAR, these are not yet taken into account by the current implementation of web SQL, and these types are simply considered as regular strings. The same is true for DATETIME field types. However, this is necessary to guarantee forward compatibility.

```
function executeSequence(tran, list) {
    var i = -1;

    /* Transaction created */
    (function recursive(tran) {
      if (++i < list.length) {
          tran.executeSql(list[i], null, recursive);
      }
    })(tran);
}
```

The initialization of transactions is asynchronous, which means the scripting engine will immediately move to the following statement after the call to `transaction()`, without waiting for the callback to be executed. However, as a transaction produces a global lock on the database, transactions most probably will be called one after the other. This asynchronous behavior allows for more flexibility from the point of view of the user, because the web application will not be paralyzed during heavy operations.

The `executeSql()` method, unsurprisingly, lets you run SQL statements. Like the `transaction()` method, this function works asynchronously. However, one request can take longer than another, which can cause errors when, as in our example, queries depend on the success of previous queries. In our example, the second request holds a reference to the table created by the first request in order to guarantee the referential integrity of data. Therefore, rather than looping through our queries, we define a recursive function that will iterate through the list of requests and execute the next only when the previous has completed.

As you can see in this example, the `executeSql()` function takes several parameters. The following is its signature:

```
transaction.executeSql(command, parameters, successCallback, failureCallback);

function successCallback(transaction, resultSet) { ... }
function failureCallback(transaction, error)     { ... }
```

The first parameter is the SQL query to be executed. Then, an array of parameters should be passed to secure the query—which we will explain shortly. The two final parameters are callback functions. In our example, we use the first parameter to execute the next query every time a query is successful. It receives the current transaction as the first parameter and, if any, the result of the just-completed query as the second parameter. The failure callback receives a `SQLError` as its second parameter, which will let you handle the problem. Because an error isn't necessarily fatal, you can also resume the transaction from the failure callback. Such a case will be treated separately in a subsequent section.

Adding Data to Tables

Our database is now ready to hold data. First, we are going to populate the `Source` table, using the `INSERT` instruction. This still happens within the database initialization phase.

```
function initFeedList(tran) {
    var sql  = ["INSERT INTO Source (Name, URL) VALUES(?, ?)"];

    var data = [
        ["New York Times", "http://www.nytimes.com/services/xml/rss/nyt/HomePage.xml"],
        ["Financial Times", "http://www.ft.com/rss/world/us"]
    ];

    executeSequence(tran, sql, data);
}
```

Here, we use parametrized queries. In a query, a parameter is represented by a question mark, and for each question mark there needs to be an entry in the array passed as a parameter to executeSql(). This technique will not only save you the cumbersome building of long strings, it is above all a solid protection against SQL injection attacks. We will get into more detail about this in the upcoming section about security.

Because queries are run asynchronously, we need to chain the calls using callbacks. Moreover, because creating tables and inserting initial data is an atomic and sequential operation, the same transaction has to be used so that, if an error should occur, all operations are canceled. Therefore, we pass a reference to initFeedList() to the createSchema() function, which will be called after the tables have been created.

```
function initDatabase(db) {
    db.transaction(function(transaction) {
        createSchema(transaction, initFeedList);
    });
}
```

To make parametrized queries usable, we need to improve the executeSequence() method in order to pass the parameters. Also, because a query can be used several times for a same data set, we add the possibility to loop through a set of queries for a set of given parameters.

```
function createSchema(tran, next) {
...
    executeSequence(tran, schema, null, next);
}

function executeSequence(tran, list, params, next) {
    params = params || [];
    var max = Math.max(list.length, params.length);
    var i   = -1;

    (function recursive(tran) {
        if (++i < max) {
            tran.executeSql(list[i % list.length], params[i], recursive);

        /* Sequence completed */
        } else if (next) {
            next(tran);
        }
    })(tran);
}
```

We calculate the utmost size between the list and the params parameters to go through a sufficient number of iterations to use all available data. Then, to execute the following instructions set, we test for the next parameter, and if it is set, we execute the function referred to. This way, the insertion will occur after the tables are created and never during their creation.

Querying Data from the Tables

Our database is now fully initialized. To fill the News table, we are going to fetch data from the Source table and send Ajax requests to gather data.

```
function checkDatabase(db) {
...
    function() {
        /* Start database jobs */
        refresh(db);
    });
...
}

function initDatabase(db) {
    db.transaction(function(transaction) {
        createSchema(transaction, initFeedList);
    }, null, function() {
        refresh(db);
    });
}

function refresh(db) {
    /* Always display the previous content */
    processFeed(db);

    /* Then try to refresh the News table */
    db.transaction(function (tran) {
        tran.executeSql("SELECT SourceID, URL, LastUpdated FROM Source", null,
            function(tran, res) {
                for (var i = 0; i < res.rows.length; i++) {
                    var row  = res.rows.item(i);
                    var last = row.LastUpdated || new Date(0);
                    var ttl  = new Date() - 1000 * 60 * 10;    // 10 minutes
                    /* If the feed needs update */
                    if (last <= ttl) {
                        loadFeed(row.URL, db, row.SourceID);
                    }
                }
            }
        );
    });
}
```

First, we add the relevant calls to the refresh() function from the success callback of the checking transaction. Then, using the new transaction created in refresh(), we read the data returned by the query from the SQLResultSet object, which holds all the rows resulting from the query inside the rows property. This property is a list of type SQLResultSetRowList whose elements are accessible only through the item() method. Table 15–2 gives detail for the ResultSet object properties.

Table 15-2. *Properties of the* SQLResultSet *Object*

Property	Description
result.insertId	When data is inserted into a table that has a field of type AUTOINCREMENT, this property holds the value of the last generated identity. If no such field is set, it holds the row number of the inserted line. If there is no insertion, trying to access this property will raise a INVALID_ACCESS_ERR exception.
result.rowsAffected	Returns the number of lines that have been modified by a query, or 0 if nothing was altered (for instance, if the query was a SELECT statement).
result.rows	A list of lines returned by the query.

Every column is accessible by name, like an object property, with the same case as when it was created in the table. The length property will let you know how many lines are in the result set.

Updating Data

Once the last update time has been checked, if needed, we launch the Ajax requests to retrieve the data that we will then extract from the RSS feed.

```
function loadFeed(url, db, id) {
    var xml = new XMLHttpRequest();
    xml.onreadystatechange = function() {
        feedLoaded(this, db, id);
    }
    xml.open("get", "proxy.php?url=" + encodeURIComponent(url));
    xml.send();
}

function feedLoaded(xhr, db, id) {
    if (xhr.readyState == xhr.DONE && xhr.status == 200) {
        updateFeed(xhr.responseXML, db, id);
    }
}

function updateFeed(xml, db, id) {
    db.transaction(function (tran) {
        tran.executeSql("UPDATE Source SET LastUpdated = ? WHERE SourceID = ?",
            [new Date(), id]);

        var all = xml.getElementsByTagName("item");
        for (var i = 0; i < all.length; i++) {
            var params = [];

            params.push(getText(all[i], "title"));
            params.push(getText(all[i], "description"));
            params.push(new Date(getText(all[i], "pubDate")));
            params.push(getText(all[i], "link"));
            params.push(id);
```

```
            params.push(getText(all[i], "guid"));

            upsertNews(tran, params);
        }
    });
}

function upsertNews(tran, params) {
    var len  = params.length;
    var guid = params[len - 1];
    var id   = params[len - 2];

    tran.executeSql(
        "SELECT NewsID FROM News WHERE SourceID = ? AND GUID = ?", [id, guid],

        function(tran, res) {
            var sql = (res.rows.length == 0) ?
                "INSERT INTO News (Title, Content, Date, TargetURL, SourceID, GUID) " +
                "    VALUES(?, ?, ?, ?, ?, ?)"
                :
                "UPDATE News SET " +
                "    Title = ?, Content = ?, Date = ?, TargetURL = ? " +
                "WHERE SourceID = ? AND GUID = ?";
            tran.executeSql(sql, params);
        }
    );
}
```

The loadFeed() function launches the Ajax requests one after another, without delaying
for the previous request to complete. Then, after each response from the server, we
immediately browse the XML with the processFeed() function. At this stage, the
LastUpdated field is changed in the Source table, and for each news entry from the feed,
we add entries in the relevant table. Here, there is no need to synchronize the line
updating, because the order in which this operation is done is unimportant. Therefore, a
bulk insert is good enough, and we will be able to order the news later with a request
such as SELECT...ORDER BY.

If you are familiar with DBMSs, you may be used to running some kind of custom UPSERT
(UPdate or inSERT). When dealing with the Web Database API, there is no stored
procedure to do this, and there is no conditional statement applicable in the SQL
language. The only way to perform such an operation is to chain a SELECT command to
determine whether data is available with an UPDATE (if data is available) or an INSERT (if
not). Our key here for the selection is the SourceID/GUID couple, because although a
GUID is supposed to be unique globally, it is really unique only at the level of its source.

> **NOTE:** For UPDATE operations, we could have used the NewsID returned by the SELECT
> operation. However, using the same parameters array makes the code simpler.

Our News table now holds information from our two feeds. If you test this on Desktop
Safari, it is possible to use the Storage section of the Web Inspector introduced in
Chapter 3 to read the data stored in the database, simply by clicking the Apress

database from the left pane and running a request from the built-in command prompt, as shown in Figure 15–4.

```
> SELECT Title, Date, Name
    FROM News
    INNER JOIN Source
        ON News.SourceID = Source.SourceID
    ORDER BY Date DESC
```

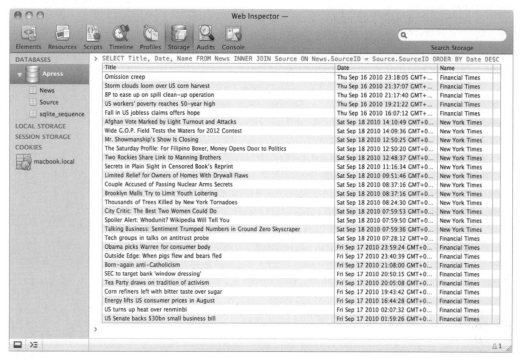

Figure 15–4. *The news list resulting from a SQL query in Desktop Safari's Web Inspector*

You can now modify the Web Storage example to use the database rather than cache.

Using Database in Place of Storage

To use Web Database rather than Web Storage for our sample application, you simply need to modify the init() function and add a success handler to the updateFeed() function to gather data after each feed has been updated.

```
function init() {
    spinner.init("spinner", "white");
    checkDatabase(globalDB);
}

function updateFeed(xml, db, id) {
    db.transaction(function (tran) {
...
    }, null, function() {
```

```
            processFeed(db);
    });
}
```

Then, you would adapt processFeed() so that the data is no longer gathered from localStorage but is retrieved from the client database.

```
function processFeed(db) {
    db.transaction(function (tran) {
        tran.executeSql("\
            SELECT Title AS title, Content AS content, \
                Date AS date, TargetURL AS link \
            FROM News ORDER BY Date DESC \
            LIMIT 10", null, processFeedCallback
        );
    });
}

function processFeedCallback(tran, res) {
    var all = res.rows;
    var list = document.getElementById("feed");
    if (sessionStorage.template == undefined) {
        sessionStorage.template = list.innerHTML;
    }

    /* Compute resulting HTML */
    var html = "";
    for (var i = 0; i < all.length; i++) {
        var data = all.item(i);
        html += applyTemplate(sessionStorage.template, data, formatters);
    }

    /* Append content to the document */
    appendContent(list, html);
}
```

To maintain the same rendering logic as when reading data directly from the feed, we use an alias on the columns so that property names are consistent with the template. Naturally, we keep the template cache, because several successive calls can be run after the update of each feed.

You could also add another feed to the Source table and check the resulting data using the Web Inspector.

Handling Transaction and Query Errors

As indicated previously, the transaction() method can also take a failure and success callback, just like the executeSql() method. Here is the callback signature:

```
database.transaction(initCallback, errorCallback, successCallback);

function initCallback(transaction) { ... }
function failureCallback(error)    { ... }
function successCallback()         { ... }
```

The first function is a failure callback that will receive a SQLError object, with a message property holding the reason of the failure (thoroughly described) and a code property holding the corresponding error code. Table 15–3 lists the possible error codes common to SQL transactions and requests using executeSql(), with their meanings. Unlike other APIs implemented in Mobile Safari, the specification constants are currently not available, and error codes don't exactly match; therefore, you can only use the numerical codes. The second function is a success callback that doesn't take any parameter.

Table 15–3. *Error Codes Applicable to Transactions and Queries*

Constant	Description
error.UNKNOWN_ERR (0)	An unknown error, unrelated to the database, has been raised. Generally, this is caused by an error in a callback.
error.DATABASE_ERR (1)	An error related to the database has occurred. This is sent, for instance, in the case of syntax errors or when a table or field name isn't found.
error.VERSION_ERR (2)	The requested version number isn't the same as the database version. This error will be used when the database schema should be updated.
error.TOO_LARGE_ERR (3)	The result set for the query is too large to be returned. To avoid this error, you should resort to the LIMIT and OFFSET instructions, for instance, to paginate the results.
error.QUOTA_ERR (4)	The space allocated to the database has been outgrown. This also occurs when the request for the database to grow is refused by the user.
error.TIMEOUT_ERR (5)	The lock for a transaction wasn't obtained within a reasonable time. This is generally sent when another transaction is taking too long to execute, preventing a normal behavior of the database.
error.CONSTRAINT_ERR (6)	A foreign key violation has occurred. This would happen, for instance, if you tried to insert a line in News for a sourceID that doesn't exist.

Both can be useful, for instance, to trace the behavior of the API and bring the user relevant information when an error occurs, inviting to try again. We can modify our function to build a more precise response regarding the relevancy of initializing the database.

```
function checkDatabase(db) {
    ...
        /* Failed? The database should not be initialized */
        function(error) {
            if (error.code == 1) {      // Unknown table
                initDatabase(db);
```

```
        } else {
            alert("An error occurred:\n" + error.message);
        }
    },
    ...
}
```

Both of these methods will be called after the execution of the transaction contents—here, the calls to executeSql(). If a request fails, the execution will be halted, and the whole transaction will be rolled back, and the database will return to its state prior to the transaction operations. If all requests succeed, the transaction will be committed, and the database will be updated.

However, it is possible to continue the transaction after an error from within a SQL command. The failure callback of the executeSql() method can return a value indicating if the error is fatal and if it is possible to resume the transaction. The value false will allow you to continue the transaction, while the value true will halt it. If no value is returned, true will be implied. The upsertNews() function could be changed to implement this.

```
function upsertNews(tran, params) {
...
    tran.executeSql(
...
            tran.executeSql(sql, params, null, function() {
                /* Do not stop transaction on error */
                return false;
            });
...
    );
}
```

Proceeding this way, if an update of insert fails, whatever the reason, other requests will not be affected and will continue updating the table.

Maintaining Coherent Access with Versioning

During a database life cycle, there always comes a time when it is necessary to evolve. Of course, you can apply tests similar to those used previously and check whether a table is available on initialization and attempt to create one if not, but this would dilute the schema maintenance logic throughout the code. Moreover, if the structure of an existing table should change, it is preferable to control the database version on a higher level and apply necessary modifications.

We have seen that the openDatabase() method takes a parameter allowing you to ask for a specific version for the database. If, when the function is called, the version stored in the browser doesn't match, an INVALID_STATE_ERR exception is raised. This DOM exception isn't very explicit and will not let you determine whether the error is a version problem. To handle version evolution, you will need to pass an empty string as a version parameter and read the version property of the Database object.

> **WARNING:** In Mobile Safari, the value of the `version` property will be modified only if the user closes all open browser windows on the domain holding the database. Thus, even after the version has changed, the former schema version will still appear, executing the migration code again. For such cases, remember to add a verification querying, for instance, the new schema.

With the value of this property, you can use the asynchronous `changeVersion()` method to evolve the database schema. Here is its signature:

```
database.changeVersion(oldVersion, newVersion, ↵
                       changeCallback, errorCallback, successCallback);
```

Each callback receives parameters equivalent to those of the `transaction()` method. Thus, the first will receive a `SQLTransaction` object allowing you to execute modification queries, and the second will receive a `SQLError` object. You can use them as shown here:

```
var globalDB = window.openDatabase("Apress", "", ↵
                                   "Apress Storage Demo", 1 * 1024 * 1024);

if (globalDB.version == "1.0") {
    /* Do database evolution job to new version */
    globalDB.changeVersion("1.0", "1.2", ↵
                           changeCallback, errorCallback, successCallback);

} else if (globalDB.version == "1.2") {
    /* Always check the schema if the expected version is correct */
    checkDatabase(globalDB);

} else {
    throw("Unexpected database version number.");
}

function changeCallback(tran) {
    tran.executeSql("ALTER TABLE Source RENAME TO Feed");
}

function errorCallback(err) {
    alert("An error occurred:\n" + err.message);
}

function successCallback() {
    alert("Database successfully updated to version 1.2!");
    refresh(globalDB);
}
```

Once the update has completed, of course, you will no longer have access to the former version of the database. The version number, to the scripting engine, is no more than a string; therefore, there is no actual version evolution, simply a version change. If the `oldVersion` parameter doesn't match the current database version, a `VERSION_ERR` exception will be raised.

Deleting the Database

Creating a database is very simple. However, suppressing a database can prove trickier. Dropping a database cannot be done from JavaScript, and the SQL command DROP DATABASE isn't available either. Deleting a database, luckily, is possible, but only on an action by the user. This obviously is very handy in the development stage.

With Desktop Safari

On Desktop Safari and most WebKit-based browsers, deleting a database can be done from the preferences panel. Go to **Safari ➤ Preferences...** and select the Security tab. The window shown in Figure 15–5 should appear.

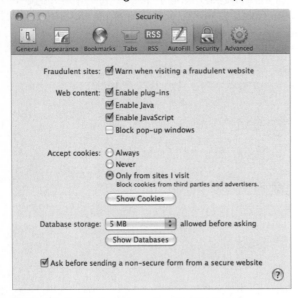

Figure 15–5. *The security panel on Desktop Safari*

Here, click the Show Databases button at the bottom of the screen to trigger a list of databases. You can then simply remove any of them using the Remove button. This way, you can test your code as many times as you need on a clean basis.

With Mobile Safari

In Mobile Safari, once a database has been created, a new menu item appears in the browser preferences, as shown in Figure 15–6. From there, it is possible to access a list of databases from the Settings application, under **Safari ➤ Database**.

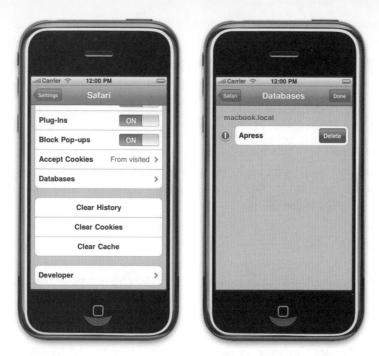

Figure 15–6. *Database preferences in Mobile Safari*

Simply tap the Edit button in the upper-right side of the screen, and select the database to delete. The options here are less rich than on the Desktop version; for instance, it is not possible to set an initial size for a database.

Security Again

For security reasons, the same limitations for Web Storage apply to web databases, namely, a strict limit on the scheme/host/port tuple. Accessing data between subdomains is possible using the HTML5 Cross-Document Messaging API, as explained in Chapter 11.

You should be careful with Web Database storage when storing critical data, such as user passwords or personal information. Nonreversible encryption such as MD5 should be preferred, because reversible encrypting would imply that the encryption key would be somewhere in the code. Of course, because Mobile Safari has no Web Inspector, you could legitimately think that your database is safe, but because a web application can be viewed in any browser, you should apply security measures taking the greater risk into account.

One security risk to be extra careful with when using web databases is SQL injection, which should make you very careful when building your queries. This kind of attack is frequent when coping with concatenated queries, where single quotes in a variable are not escaped, which allows for other queries to be inserted. This is especially easily done as requests will be readable from the client. Here is an example where a user enters his name, which is passed in the query:

```
var name = "'; DELETE FROM Source --";
var sql  = "SELECT * FROM Source WHERE Name='" + name + "' AND URL IS NOT NULL";
```

The semicolon is an instruction separator, and the double hyphen (--) begins a comment. Hence, this code should be interpreted as follows—emptying the Source table:

```
SELECT * FROM Source WHERE Name=''; DELETE FROM Source --' AND URL IS NOT NULL;
```

The first step to prevent this of course is to escape all single quotes inside user input by replacing them with two single quotes (''), but it is preferable to use the secured version of executeSql(), passing an array of parameters.

```
var sql  = "SELECT * FROM Source WHERE Name=? AND URL IS NOT NULL";
transaction.executeSql(sql, [name]);
```

This way, as previously seen, the scripting engine will replace every question mark with the relevant value from the table automatically, and no injection will be possible. Always double-check your code for this and thoroughly think your queries through before moving them online, both for selection and for parameter lists.

Offline Web Application Cache

In addition to new storage possibilities, you can also make all or part of your web application available offline by storing resources in your users' devices thanks to new caching possibilities brought by HTML5. This can take your web applications another step closer to a native application experience, because, depending on the use they make of your applications, users could see no difference between online and offline usage. Also, this allows for shorter load times in all circumstances. This specification is supported in Mobile Safari with iOS 2.1 and newer.

How Does It Work?

When your pages are first loaded inside the browser, an attached manifest document will be loaded holding information on how to handle resources from your application. This way, on subsequent connections to the application, the relevant files would be expectedly cached and would not be loaded from the server.

Once the manifest file has been read, no file set for caching will be checked on the server or loaded anew unless the manifest file has been changed. The manifest file is compared byte to byte, meaning that a change in the modification date will not force reevaluation. Neither changes on the server for other files nor HTTP headers indicating a more recent version will trigger a new download by the browser.

However, always remember that when the cache is renewed, the new version of the files will not be used by the client until the web application has been refreshed, in a way similar to updates on a desktop computer. Therefore, it can be desirable to be able to notify the user when new versions of files are available. This can be done using a specific API that will let you control cache and receive notifications during file updates. We will cover the relevant events in an upcoming section.

The Manifest File

Basically, the manifest file will let you list files to be cached together with rules on how to handle the web application elements. It bears the special `.manifest` extension and is a simple UTF-8 encoded file, necessarily served with the `text/cache-manifest` content type to be interpreted by the browser. You can use a byte order mark (BOM) to sign the file. Be careful that most servers for now do not send this MIME type with their default configuration, which is mandatory for the manifest to work.

> **NOTE:** Naturally, running local tests for this file isn't easy, because you cannot cut the connection to the server. The only way to run local tests is to load your application, stop the local server, and check what is displayed then by reloading the web application. Also note that the manifest file is not shown in the Resource Viewer section of Safari's Web Inspector, which doesn't help checking if it has been loaded.

Using the following *cache.manifest* file, we can simply cache the web application example developed in this chapter to make it available offline or when the user suffers from bad connection speeds.

```
CACHE MANIFEST
index.html
styles/main.css
scripts/main.js
```

The `CACHE MANIFEST` line is required as the first line in the file and should have no extra space or line feed. It acts as a file signature that identifies the file as the cache manifest to the browser. The URLs can be either absolute or relative, but be careful that relative paths are relative to the directory where the manifest is hosted. Therefore, for the sake of consistency, it is a good practice to place the manifest file in the same directory as the HTML file it is called from.

> **NOTE:** Although the file from which the manifest is called is automatically cached, following the specification, we add it to the manifest too.

The manifest will be used in the document from which it is included. It should be called using the new `manifest` attribute on the `<html>` tag. As with any other attribute allowing to pull remote files, it can take both relative and absolute paths.

```
<html manifest="cache.manifest">
...
```

This is the simplest possible definition of a manifest file, which will let you store elements on the device without having to download them with every page load. You can simply list resources to cache, but it is also possible to more precisely determine how the cache should be handled.

The CACHE Sections

The files to be cached can be defined in a specific section of the manifest file resorting to the CACHE directive. You can define several sections in a similar way, which can be useful to order your file indications. You can also make your file more easily readable by humans by adding comments, as illustrated here:

```
CACHE MANIFEST

# Our cached resources

CACHE:
index.html
styles/main.css
scripts/main.js
```

Any kind of file can be registered for caching, even images or server-side scripts. Of course, server-side scripts will be stored after their execution, so be careful when using this feature. This is possible because the cache application not only stores data but also stores resource metadata, such as HTTP headers.

The NETWORK Sections

The use of a manifest file makes the web application work in offline mode, which means that files not listed in the manifest file will not be downloaded, even if the device is connected to a network. This behavior can be changed from the NETWORK section. In this section, you can specify resources that should be downloaded from the server if a network is available, which will be especially useful for dynamic elements of your applications.

The section simply holds an online white list, similarly to what is found under the CACHE section. However, this section functions differently: each URL is a prefix match pattern. Thus, you will be able to target all resources from a given directory by listing only this directory. Be careful not to uselessly list the same prefix several times.

In our previous example, using only a CACHE section in our manifest file would keep our web application from working, because the proxy used to gather the RSS feed could not be accessed. To change this, we simply add the following to our manifest:

```
NETWORK:
proxy.php
```

Our proxy uses the url parameter from the query string to know which feed should be downloaded, but as proxy.php is a prefix, authorization to access the full URL is given by the browser.

You can also use the * wildcard to allow access to all resources. This naturally is taken into account for resources not listed under the CACHE section, which has precedence over other sections. Of course, this makes writing your manifest file much easier and reduces the risks of forgetting files and ending up with a partially functional application.

The FALLBACK Sections

For cases where the network is necessary to fetch a resource that is not cached but no network is available, it is possible to define one or several fallback sections.

Under these sections, lines are built by space- or tab-separated element couples. The first element is a fallback namespace defining a prefix match pattern that will let you target a set of resources from some URL, as done under the NETWORK section. All resources matching this namespace will be cached, and if the resource listed as the second element is not available, this will be used instead.

To observe the behavior of this section, we are going to specify a static RSS feed (*default.xml*) as the default, for cases where the network is not available.

```
<?xml version="1.0" encoding="UTF-8" ?>
<rss version="2.0">
<channel>
    <title>Offline Application Cache</title>
    <description />
    <link>http://www.apress.com/</link>

    <item>
        <title>Fallback Element</title>
        <description>This is a fallback resource cached to be used
                when the network is not available.</description>
        <link>http://www.apress.com/</link>
        <guid>http://www.apress.com/guid/</guid>
        <pubDate>Mon, 01 Aug 2011 00:00:00 +0000</pubDate>
    </item>
</channel>
</rss>
```

The relevant files will be listed in the manifest as follows:

```
FALLBACK:
proxy.php    default.xml
```

Thus, when the network is unavailable, the RSS file will be used in place of the proxy call, and the only available element will be added for every feed to be gathered. You can use this section not only for unavailable networks but also to handle any other missing file problem, such as HTTP 404 errors.

Beware, however, that the browser will not necessarily use the most specific prefix to use the relevant resource; hence, the declaration order is important. In the following example, the first line will be used for all fallbacks, because it will match all resources, including those that would be matched by the second line.

```
FALLBACK:
./          any.html
proxy.php   default.xml
```

In such a case, you should specify the most specific prefixes first, moving down to the less specific. Also consider thinking a well-organized directory structure to make the process easier. This will probably be beneficial for your directory structure anyway.

Controlling the Cache with JavaScript

HTML5 allows control over the cache based on a JavaScript API attached to an ApplicationCache object. Every page that has a manifest automatically has an instance of the ApplicationCache object attached to it; it can be accessed from the DOMWindow object.

```
var cache = window.applicationCache;
```

With this instance, you will be able to check the state of the cache, for instance by checking that the manifest file has been considered, reading its status property.

Table 15–4 shows all the possible states for the cache of the current page. If it is UNCACHED, your manifest file has not been loaded. In such a case, you should typically check that the content type is correct and that your file holds no errors.

Table 15–4. *applicationCache State Constants*

Constant	Description
cache.UNCACHED (0)	The document isn't cached.
cache.IDLE (1)	The document is available from cache and is the most recent. This is the state when the page is loaded for the first time, or the application has been reloaded after an update, and all resources have been loaded.
cache.CHECKING (2)	The document is available from cache and is checking for an update.
cache.DOWNLOADING (3)	The document is available from cache and is currently downloading updates or new resources.
cache.UPDATEREADY (4)	The document is available from cache and has finished downloading updates or new resources. These will be available on the next access to the application.
cache.OBSOLETE (5)	The document available from cache is obsolete, which means the manifest is no longer available. The browser receives an HTTP 404 (Not Found) status or a 410 status (Gone).

This can be used to check whether the browser has downloaded a new version and notify the user:

```
if (window.applicationCache.status == window.applicationCache.UPDATEREADY) {
    if (window.confirm("A new version is available.\nDo you want to use it now?")) {
        window.location.reload();
    }
}
```

This status will not necessarily be available straightaway. If you check this status while resources are loading, the sent state will be CHECKING. Therefore, it is useful to add listeners for the update and download processes, as we will soon see.

You can also control cache directly from the JavaScript, using the methods presented in Table 15–5.

Table 15–5. *Cache-Related Methods*

Method	Description
cache.update()	Force the verification and the update of cache, if the resources are available from the server. An INVALID_STATE_ERR exception will be sent if no cache is associated to the document.
cache.swapCache()	Activates new cache resources if available (UPDATEREADY). Throws an INVALID_STATE_ERR exception otherwise.

For instance, even if the status is set to IDLE and the manifest file has just been modified, a call to the update() method will force the cache to be reloaded. The status will then change to UPDATEREADY after the new resources have been downloaded. A call to swapCache() will force the new resources to be used, and the status will return to IDLE.

Of course, the current page will not be automatically updated, and you will have to wait for the next web application launch for the user to see the changes. However, you can also read the new resources using JavaScript. If the call to update() was successful and the downloading is complete, you can call an updated resource as follows:

```
/* Update an iframe */
var iframe = document.getElementById("myIframe");
iframe.src = iframe.src;

/* Update the first image of the document */
var image = document.images[0];
image.src = image.src;
```

You can also associate a newly cached resource:

```
image.src = "newlyCachedImage.png";
```

In Safari, surprisingly, the cache is available before the call to swapCache(), although this is meant to switch the application cache. Therefore, you should run such operations only after a swapCache() call, instead of simply after a call to update().

Reacting to Events Sent by the Application Cache

During the execution cycle of the application update, a number of events are sent to let the application know what is happening and react accordingly. These events are listed in Table 15–6.

Table 15–6. *Cache Update Events*

Event	Description
checking	The browser is attempting to download the manifest for the first time or is checking whether an update is available.
noupdate	The manifest hasn't been changed.
downloading	The download of resources listed in the manifest has begun, either to gather the resources for the first time or to update the cache.
progress	The browser is downloading the resources listed in the manifest.
cached	The resources listed in the manifest have all been downloaded, and the application is now available from cache. This is sent only on first download.
updateready	The resources form the cache have all been downloaded anew.
obsolete	The manifest is no longer available, and the server has sent a 404 or 410 status. The cache will be deleted the next time the application is launched.
error	The manifest has not been found or contains errors.

These events can be registered using the regular DOM method or using the ApplicationCache object properties.

```
window.applicationCache.addEventListener("updateready", doSomethingHandler, false);

/* or... */
window.applicationCache.onupdateready = doSomethingHandler;
```

The sequence of events necessarily begins with the checking event, because the document holds a reference to the manifest in the <html> tag.

Then, if the document has no application cache associated with it, and if the manifest contains no error, the downloading event will be triggered, followed by a series of progress events, until all listed resources have been fetched. The sequence will terminate with the cached event, indicating the application cache has been created and that the web application is now cached.

If the document already has an application cache associated with it and the browser hasn't detected any changes in the manifest, a noupdate event will be sent, and the sequence will halt immediately. Otherwise, the sequence will be the same as earlier but will finish with a updateready event instead of a cached event. In such a case, you can call the swapCache() method, as shown earlier.

If the manifest isn't accessible or the manifest contains errors (such as a signature problem, an unavailable resource...), the sequence will be interrupted with an error event. Still, if a cache exists and the manifest file isn't found, an obsolete event will be sent, and the cache will be deleted from the device.

The specifications plan for the progress event to be of ProgressEvent type, allowing you to follow the progress of the download. As illustrated in Chapter 12 dealing with Ajax, this type will let you determine whether the downloading is computable using the lengthComputable property and will then evaluate the loading time with the loaded and total properties.

For the moment, the progress event type is not supported on iOS, nor is it implemented in Desktop Safari. It will return a regular Event object. You can, yet, resort to this event using a callback, because there will be no warranty that the progress would be computable anyway.

Deleting Cache

Once a web application is cached, it is no longer possible to delete it. Indeed, the user emptying the browser cache will not affect the offline application cache. Thus, the only way users can delete the cache is to visit the site again, hopeful they will have an option to unload the application.

If your manifest is a dynamic file (a PHP script, for instance), it is possible to offer this option by setting a cookie that will be read by the manifest script in order to return a 404 error if the cache should be deleted.

```
<script>

function switchMode(online) {
    var now = new Date().getTime();
    var tenYears = 1000 * 60 * 60 * 24 * 365 * 10;
    var expires =  new Date(now + tenYears) * (online ? +1 : -1);
    document.cookie = "online=true; expires=" + expires;
}

</script>
...
        <div class="header-wrapper">
...

            <button onclick="switchMode(true)">No Cache</button>
        </div>
...
```

The PHP manifest could look something like this:

```
<?php
    $code = ($_COOKIE['online'] == 'true') ? 410 : 200;
    header('Content-type: text/cache-manifest', true, $code);

?>CACHE MANIFEST
```

When the user clicks the No Cache button, a new `online` cookie will be created with the boolean value `true`. The expiration date is set far enough in the future not to expire. When the manifest file is accessed again, the script will check for the cookie using the `$_COOKIE` hash table and will send a response relevant to the value of `online`. The web application will finally receive an `obsolete` event, as explained earlier.

Is the User Online?

Whether an offline application cache is associated with the current document or not, you can easily check the state of the network. This piece of information can be gathered from the `onLine` property of the `navigator` object. This way, it is possible to prevent downloading some elements from the JavaScript, such as the RSS feed used previously, if the network is not available, thus preventing access to the callback content.

```
function refresh(db) {
    /* Always display the previous content */
    processFeed(db);

    /* Do not try to download feeds if not online */
    if (!window.navigator.onLine) {
        return;
    }
    ...
}
```

In addition to this property, Mobile Safari has support for two new events; when the state of the network changes, either an `online` event (if the `onLine` property changes from `false` to `true`) or an `offline` event (the user is disconnected) is sent. This should let you fine-tune the loading and behavior of your application for the best user experience.

Summary

Naturally, you can dynamically generate your manifest file using PHP or any other server-side scripting language, similarly to what we did in Chapter 6 to generate a list of images for our Photos-like album. This opens a full range of possibilities to develop complex yet flexible applications.

Making your applications work both online and offline in a satisfying manner is a great step toward a native application–like experience, and the different storage APIs should let you customize your data behavior to most of what your application requires. Combine this with full-screen mode, a user interface, and behavior similar to that of iOS, and users will wonder why they ever went to the App Store.

Index

■Special Characters and Numbers

!important statement, 115
#coverflow container, 276
$_COOKIE hash table, 466
$_SERVER['DOCUMENT_ROOT'] variable, 24
$data variable, 357
% button, 59
%d format, 48
%f format, 48
%i format, 48
%o format, 48
%s format, 48
3D aspect, preserving with CSS, 265–266

■A

a command, Vi utility, 16, 25
AAC (MPEG-4 Advanced Audio Coding), 250
AAC-LC (Advanced Audio Coding - Low Complexity), 250
abort( ) method, 232, 346
Access-Control-Allow-Origin header, 359
accuracy, and gestures, 394–395
activate( ) method, 241
Adaptive Multi-Rate (AMR), 251
adaptive styles method, 152
ADC (Apple Developer Connection), 10–11
Add as Snippet context menu option, Komodo Edit utility, 5
Add port. option, 20
Add to home screen option, 77
Add web site context menu option, 26
addColorStop( ) method, 174
addEventListener( ) method, 285, 310–311, 345, 367–369, 371, 373

address bar, hiding web applications, 85–86
adjust( ) method, 389
adjustHeight( ) function, 86
adjustVideo( ) function, 229
AdLib framework, 69
ads, showing thoughtfully, 92–95
Advanced Audio Coding - Low Complexity (AAC-LC), 250
Advanced Packaging Tool (APT), 22
Advanced tab
    HandBrake, 253
    Safari, 30
advantages of web applications, 71–73
    App Store not necessary, 72–73
    cross-platform, 71–72
    hardware access for, 72
A-GPS (Assisted Global Positioning System), 397
Ajax, 343–365
    building HTTP request, 343–348
        events for, 346–347
        GET and POST requests for, 344–345
        HTTP status codes for, 347–348
        open( ) method for, 344
        request states for, 345–346
        and XMLHttpRequest object, 344
    client-side rendering using JSON, 354–356
        formatting variables, 355–356
        using template variables, 354–355
    cross-origin communication for, 356–360
        using CORS, 359–360
        using JSONP, 357–358
        using proxies, 356–357
    feedback during processing, 363–365
        and excessive waiting times, 364–365
        visual feedback, 363–364
    requests, caching, 435–440
        add caching capabilities, 438–440

base document, 435–438
return formats for, 348–353
and JSON security considerations, 353
parsing JSON, 352–353
parsing XML, 349–352
Twitter trends example, 360–363
feed for, 360
rendering data, 360–363
ajax.DONE (4) constant, 345
ajaxHandler( ) function, 345, 347, 350
ajax.HEADERS_RECEIVED (2) constant, 345
ajax.LOADING (3) constant, 345
ajax.OPENED (1) constant, 345
ajax.UNSENT (0) constant, 345
ALAC (Apple Lossless Audio Codec), 250
alert( ) method, 46
alignment
of box model for CSS, 161–162
of text, in <canvas> tag, 186–187
Allow a program through Windows Firewall option, Control Panel, 20
alpha channel, for colors with CSS, 135–136
AMR (Adaptive Multi-Rate), 251
Anamorphic combo box, HandBrake, 254
Animal constructor, 306
animate( ) method, 170, 172, 311
<animateTransform> tag, 209
animating compass, in compass web app, 427–429
animation-delay property, 283
animation-duration property, 283
animationend event, 285
animationiteration event, 285
animation-iteration-count property, 283, 285
animation-name property, 282–283
animationName property, 285
animation-name property, 285
animations, with CSS, 282–285
events for, 285
evolution curve, 284–285
key frames, 282–283
properties for, 283–284
starting and timing, 283
animationstart event, 285
animation-timing-function property, 284
Apache
on Mac OS, 14–15
virtual hosts for web server with, 24–25
Apache config file, 25
apache2 configuration file, 15

app header, buttons in, 150–152
App Store, and web applications, 72–73
appendChild( ) method, 351
appendData( ) function, 442
Apple Developer Connection (ADC), 10–11
Apple Lossless Audio Codec (ALAC), 250
apply( ) method, and execution context of JavaScript, 308–310
applySVGBackground( ) function, 204
APT (Advanced Packaging Tool), 22
apt-get command, 22
arcs, in <canvas> tag, 177–178
arcTo( ) method, 177
arguments property, 309
Assisted Global Positioning System (A-GPS), 397
async parameter, 344
atan2( ) method, 416
ATTACHED state, 380
audio
embedding in web apps, 224–225
supported formats, for media content in web apps, 250–251
audio codec option, HandBrake, 255
Audio tab, HandBrake, 255
<audio> tag, 219, 225, 233, 250
Audits pane, in Web Inspector, 61–63
AUTOINCREMENT field type, 448
autoplay attribute, 224
Average bitrate option, HandBrake, 254
Average column, 59

■B

<b> tag, 290, 292, 294
back face visibility, three-dimensional effects with CSS, 266–268
background-clip property, 126–127
background-color property, 84
background-image property, 205, 286
background-origin property, 125–126
background-repeat property, 175
backgrounds, with CSS, 124–135
background-clip property, 126–127
background-origin property, 125–126
clipping of, 128
multilayer, 134–135
photo gallery with, 130–133
sizing, 128–130
background-size property, 129–130, 202
_base property, 308

baseline, of text in <canvas> tag, 185–186
BEGIN TRANSACTION command, 444
beginPath( ) method, 176
bezierCurveTo( ) method, 178
big.css file, 114
.bigSpinner class, 171
bind( ) function, 317
black option, content attribute, 80
black-translucent option, content attribute, 80
<body> tag, 37
BOM (byte order mark), 459
border property, 154
border-image declaration, 146
border-image property, 288
border-radius property, 85
bounding box object, for gestures, 388–389
box model, for CSS, 158–162
    efficiency of, 158–159
    flexibility of, 160–161
    ordering of, 159–160
    packing and alignment of, 161–162
box shadows, with CSS, 148–149
box-align property, 161–162
box-direction property, 159–160
box-flex property, 161, 291
box-ordinal-group property, 159
box-orient property, 160
box-pack property, 161–162
box-shadow property, 147–148
box-sizing property, 143
breakpoints, for JavaScript debugging, 50–51
browsers, 6–7
    Firefox, 7
    Internet Explorer, 7
    Opera, 7
    and support for web standards, 8
    WebKit engine, 6–7
buffered property, 227
buildList( ) function, 242, 246
buttons, in app header, 150–152
buttonState( ) function, 364
byte order mark (BOM), 459
    Inetpubwwwroot directory, 21
    WindowsSystem32drivers\ directory, 24

◼C

CACHE sections, 460–461
cache.CHECKING (2) constant, 462

cached event, 464
cached location, in location-aware web
        applications, 402
cache.DOWNLOADING (3) constant, 462
cache.IDLE (1) constant, 462
cache.manifest file, 459
cache.OBSOLETE (5) constant, 462
cache.swapCache( ) method, 463
cache.UNCACHED (0) constant, 462
cache.update( ) method, 463
cache.UPDATEREADY (4) constant, 462
calcMode attribute, 209
calcPosition( ) method, 230
calculator.html file, 327, 339
call( ) method, and execution context of
        JavaScript, 308–310
Call Stack pane, for JavaScript debugging,
        53
callbacks, and execution context of
        JavaScript, 310–312
calling priority, of handlers, 367–368
callout, disabling with CSS, 120–121
Calls column, 59
cancelling Multi-Touch events, 376
canplay event, 232
canplaythrough event, 232
Canvas API, 171–175, 181, 189, 191, 201,
        208
<canvas> tag, 165–195
    clipping to drawing area, 188–189
    colors for, 174
    compositing and transparency for, 189–
        190
    getContext( ) method for, 167–172
    gradients for, 174–175
    manipulating pixels in, 191–195
    patterns for, 175
    saving and restoring states of, 183
    shadows in, 187–188
    shapes in, 175–181
        arcs, 177–178
        basics of, 172–173
        curves, 178–179
        line styles, 179–180
        native-style menus with, 180–181
    text in, 183–187
        alignment of, 186–187
        baseline of, 185–186
        drawing, 184–185
    transformations for, 181–183
captions keyword, 240

capture stage, and events for touch, 369–370

Cédille application, 212

center property, 404

changedTarget property, 376

changedTouches property, 374–375

changeVersion( ) method, 455

chapter type, 243

chapters, for media content in web apps, 243–247

chapters keyword, 240

CHAR field type, 445

checkBuffered( ) function, 229

checkDatabase( ) function, 444

checking event, 464

CHECKING state, 463

checkPlayed( ) function, 229

childWin window, 333

chown command, 22

<circle> tag, 197

class selector, 39

clear( ) method, 48, 433–434

clearInterval( ) method, 311

clearWatch( ) function, 411–412

clickHandler( ) function, 87

client-side data storage, 431–466
    offline web application cache, 458–466
        checking state of network, 466
        controlling with JavaScript, 462–463
        deleting, 465–466
        how it works, 458–459
        manifest file, 459–462
        reacting to events sent by, 464–465
    Web Database API, 442–458
        adding data to tables, 446–447
        creating tables, 444–446
        deleting database, 455–457
        handling transaction and query errors, 452–454
        maintaining coherent access with versioning, 454–455
        opening database, 442–444
        querying data from tables, 447–449
        security issues, 457–458
        updating data, 449–451
        using database in place of storage, 451–452
    Web Storage API, 431–442
        caching Ajax requests, 435–440
        notification of storage area modification, 434

security and privacy considerations, 435

sending client data to server, 441–442

sessionStorage, behavior of, 433–434

using, 432–433

client-side rendering, using JSON, 354–356
    formatting variables, 355–356
    using template variables, 354–355

clip( ) method, 188–189

clipping
    <canvas> tag, to drawing area, 188–189
    of backgrounds with CSS, 128

Clock application, 102–103

closePath( ) method, 176–177

clutter, avoiding, 96–97

CMSs (content management systems), 18

Cocoa Touch framework, 129

code isolation, in JavaScript, 314–317

code property, 452

colors
    for <canvas> tag, 174
    with CSS, 135–137
        alpha channel for, 135–136
        hsl( ) definitions, 136–137

color-stop( ) function, 140–142

color-stop(0, <color>) function, 140

color-stop(1, <color>) function, 140

column-gap property, 154

column-rule property, 154

columns layout, with CSS, 152–157
    column flow, 152–155
    magazine example, 155–157

column-width property, 155

COMMIT command, 444

Communication API, 322

compass web app, 416–430
    adding elements to document, 424–425
    animating compass, 427–429
    creating mobile elements, 416–418
    dial shine, 421
    graduations, 418–419
    needles, 420–421
    preparing document to receive location data, 425–426
    preventing staggering needles, 429–430
    rendering compass, 422–424
    using location data, 426–427

compass.css file, 424, 427

compass.js file, 417, 424

completed event, for CSS transitions, 274
compositing for <canvas> tag, 189–190
computed Style, 39
Computer Management option, Control Panel, 26
conext.arc(x, y, radius, startAngle, endAngle, anticlockwise) method, 176
CONNECT method, 344
console, logging to, 46–48
console.assert(condition) function, 47
console.count(name); function, 47
console.debug(format, .); function, 47
console.dir(object); function, 47
console.dirxml(node); function, 47
console.error(format, .); function, 47
console.groupEnd( ); function, 47
console.group(format, .); function, 47
console.info(format, .); function, 47
console.log( ) function, 47
console.log(format, .); function, 47
console.profile( ) function, 57
console.profileEnd( ) function, 57
console.profileEnd(name); function, 47
console.profile(name); function, 47
console.timeEnd(name); function, 47
console.time(name); function, 47
console.trace( ); function, 47
console.warn(format, .); function, 47
constructor property, 308
constructors, in JavaScript, 303–304
content attribute, 76, 80
content management systems (CMSs), 18
content.html file, 333
Content-Type header, 345
context.arcTo(cpx1, cpy1, cpx2, cpy2, radius) method, 176
context.beginPath( ) method, 176
context.bezierCurveTo(cp1x, cp1y, cp2x, cp2y, x, y) method, 176
context.closePath( ) method, 176
context.fill( ) method, 176
context.lineTo(x, y) method, 176
context.moveTo(x, y) method, 176
context.quadraticCurveTo(cpx, cpy, x, y) method, 176
context.rect(x, y, w, h) method, 176
context.stroke( ) method, 176
controls attribute, 225
Cookies pane, in Storage Inspector, 61

copy/paste function, disabling with CSS, 119–120
CORS (Cross-Origin Resource Sharing), cross-origin communication for Ajax using, 359–360
Cover Flow example, with CSS, 274–282
    animation for, 278–281
    flipping current cover, 280
    main document, 275–278
    preventing unexpected behavior, 281–282
coverflow.js file, 276
CREATE DATABASE command, 442, 444
Create template from project menu option, Komodo Edit utility, 88
createBullet( ) function, 408
createElement( ) method, 206, 224
createElementNS( ) function, 210
createElements( ) method, 379–380
createEvent( ) method, 383
createIcons( ) function, 295
createImageData( ) method, 195
createPattern( ) method, 175
createSchema( ) function, 447
createShadows( ) function, 295
cross-document communication, 321–341
    encapsulating API, 335–339
        implementing scripts, 338–339
        object for host document, 335–337
        object for widget, 337–338
    example of, 325–330
        handling response, 329–330
        hosted document, 327
        main document, 325–326
        sending message, 328–329
    with HTML5, 323–325
        API for, 323–324
        data type support, 324
        and security, 325
    limitations of, 322–323
    Mobile Safari behavior for, 330–331
    for subdomains, 340–341
        changing domain properties, 340–341
        and security, 341
    between windows, 332–335
        notifying page is loaded, 333–334
        properties of window object, 334–335
cross-document messaging API, 324, 340–341

cross-origin communication, for Ajax, 356–
        360
    using CORS, 359–360
    using JSONP, 357–358
    using proxies, 356–357
Cross-Origin Resource Sharing (CORS),
        359–360
cross-platform, web applications, 71–72
CSS, 117–163, 257–298
    animations, 282–285
        events for, 285
        evolution curve, 284–285
        key frames, 282–283
        properties for, 283–284
        starting and timing, 283
    backgrounds, 124–135
        background-clip property, 126–127
        background-origin property, 125–126
        clipping of, 128
        multilayer, 134–135
        photo gallery with, 130–133
        sizing, 128–130
    borders, 142–147
        drawn with images, 145–147
        rounded corners, 143–145
        sizing, 142–143
    box model, 158–162
        efficiency of, 158–159
        flexibility of, 160–161
        ordering of, 159–160
        packing and alignment of, 161–162
    buttons in app header with, 150–152
    colors, 135–137
        alpha channel for, 135–136
        hsl( ) definitions, 136–137
    columns layout, 152–157
        column flow, 152–155
        magazine example, 155–157
    combining with JavaScript, 268–270
        accessing current styles, 268
        native object to compute matrices,
            268–270
    Cover Flow example, 274–282
        animation for, 278–281
        flipping current cover, 280
        main document, 275–278
        preventing unexpected behavior,
            281–282
    disabling
        callout with, 120–121

        copy/paste functionalities with, 119–
            120
    gradients, 137–142
        color handling for, 140–142
        sizing, 139
        syntax for, 137–140
    selectors, 121–124
        overview, 121–122
        repetitive layout patterns with, 122–
            124
    shadows, 147–150
        box, 148–149
        example of, 150
        text, 149–150
    special effects with, 285–288
        masks, 287–288
        reflections, 286–287
    tab bar with masks example, 288–298
        icons for, 292–296
        images as icons, 297–298
        initial tab bar, 289–291
        placeholder for icons, 291–292
    targeting WebKit specifically, 162–163
    three-dimensional effects, 262–268
        back face visibility, 266–268
        functions for, 263
        preserving 3D aspect, 265–266
        setting perspective, 263–265
    transforming elements, 257–262
        custom transformations with
            matrices, 261–262
        distorting, 261
        and origin of transformation, 262
        rotating, 259–260
        scaling, 260
        support for, 258
        translating element coordinates, 260
    transitions, 270–274
        completed event, 274
        initiating, 271–272
        property for, 271
        timing function curve, 272–273
    user feedback with, 118–119
    in Web Inspector, 38–40
cubic-bezier( ) function, 273, 284
cURL API, 356
curl_exec( ) function, 357
curl_getinfo( ) function, 357
curl_init( ) function, 357
current position, in location-aware web
        applications, 399–402

accuracy, 402
cached location, 402
handling errors from requests, 401
longitude and latitude, 399–400
timeout, 402
currentTarget property, 369–370
currentTime property, 227, 233, 245
Curtis, Nick, 216
curves, in <canvas> tag, 178–179
Cut( ) function, 217

D

Dashcode, 5–6
data processing, in location-aware web
    applications, 413–416
    direction to take, 415–416
    distance between two points, 413–414
    sharper distance between two points,
      414–415
data property, 242
data type support, for cross-document
    communication with HTML5, 324
Databases pane, in Storage Inspector, 61
DATETIME field type, 445
Debug Console, Safari, 32–33
default behavior, preventing events for
    touch, 370
default option, content attribute, 80
defaultPlaybackRate property, 233
default.xml file, 461
__defineGetter__ method, 314
<defs> tag, 208
descriptions keyword, 240
design guidelines, for user experience, 105–
    109
    adaptability, 105–106
    using lists, 106–109
Desktop Safari, deleting database with, 456
DETACHING state, 381
Develop menu, for WebKit Developer tools,
    30–32
Develop option, Safari, 30
Developer Tools window, in Web Inspector,
    35–36
/Developer/Platforms/iPhoneSimulator.platfo
    rm/Developer/Applications/ folder,
    9
development environment, 13–63
    JavaScript debugging, 46–57
      and breakpoints, 50–51

Call Stack pane, 53
and exceptions, 54–55
interactive shell for, 48
logging to console, 46–48
Scope Variables pane, 54
stepping buttons for, 52
Watch Expressions pane, 53
Linux, 22
Mac OS, 14–16
    Apache on, 14–15
    PHP script engine for, 15–16
Web Inspector, 34–44
    Audits pane in, 61–63
    CSS in, 38–40
    Developer Tools window, 35–36
    Elements Inspector in, 37–38
    error notifications in, 36
    Metrics pane in, 40–43
    Profile tab in, 57–60
    Resources viewer, 44–46
    searching in, 43–44
    Storage Inspector in, 60–61
    Timeline tab in, 55–57
web server for applications, 13–14
    multiple hosts for, 23–24
    testing, 27–28
    virtual hosts for, 24–27
WebKit Developer tools, 29–34
    Develop menu, 30–32
    and Mobile Safari, 32–34
Windows, 16–22
    PHP script engine for, 17–20
    security settings for, 20–22
development tools, 3–11
    ADC, 10–11
    browsers, 6–7
      Firefox, 7
      Internet Explorer, 7
      Opera, 7
      WebKit engine for, 6–7
    source editors
      Dashcode, 5–6
      Komodo Edit, 3–5
    testing
      using real device, 10
      using simulator for iPhone and iPad,
        9–10
    and web standards, 8–9
device-height constant, 76
device-width constant, 76, 106

DHCP (Dynamic Host Configuration
        Protocol), 28
dial shine, in compass web app, 421
Disable Caches option, Safari Develop
        menu, 32
disableDefaultUI property, 404
display, table-cell rule, 115
displayName property, 53
distance between two points, in location-
        aware web applications, 413–415
distorting elements, with CSS, 261
<div> element, 133, 386
DocumentEvent interface, DOM, 383
document.getElementById( ) method, 324
dog.makeNoise( ) method, 307, 310
DOM, parsing with JavaScript, 350
DOMContentLoaded event, 45
DOMWindow navigator.platform property,
        225
downloading event, 464
draw( ) method, 318
drawImage( ) method, 192–193, 295
drawing area, clipping <canvas> tag to,
        188–189
drawMarker( ) function, 409
DROP DATABASE command, 455
dummy element, 363
duration property, 227, 233
durationchange event, 232
Dynamic Host Configuration Protocol
        (DHCP), 28

▮E

ease keyword, 273
ease-in keyword, 273
ease-in-our keyword, 273
ease-out keyword, 273
Edit Breakpoint. context menu option, 51
Edit button, 457
edition mode, Vi utility, 25
elapsedTime property, 274, 285
element coordinates, for CSS, 260
Elements Inspector, in Web Inspector, 37–
        38
Elements tab, 37
email type, 100
<embed> tag, 224
embedding
        audio in web apps, 224–225
        video in web apps, 220–224

getting video info, 221–222
        placeholder for, 222–223
        playing, 222–223
emptied event, 232
Enable Vi emulation option, Komodo Edit
        utility, 16
enableHighAccuracy option, 402
encoding media, for web apps, 251–256
        using HandBrake, 253–256
        using QuickTime Player, 251–253
end( ) method, 226
ended event, 232–233
error event, 346, 464
error notifications, in Web Inspector, 36
error.code property, 401
error.CONSTRAINT_ERR (6) constant, 453
error.DATABASE_ERR (1) constant, 453
error.message property, 401
error.QUOTA_ERR (4) constant, 453
errors, in location-aware web applications,
        401
error.TIMEOUT_ERR (5) constant, 453
error.TOO_LARGE_ERR (3) constant, 453
error.UNKNOWN_ERR (0) constant, 453
error.VERSION_ERR (2) constant, 453
esc command, Vi utility, 16
/etc/ directory, 23–24
eval( ) function, 352–353
Event Listeners pane, for Metrics pane, 42–
        43
event.AT_TARGET (2) constant, 370
event.BUBBLING_PHASE (3) constant, 370
event.CAPTURING_PHASE (1) constant, 370
event.data property, 323–324
event.key property, 434
EventListener interface, 371
event.newValue property, 434
event.oldValue property, 434
event.origin property, 323
eventPhase property, 369
events
        for Ajax HTTP request, 346–347
        for animations with CSS, 285
        for media content in web apps, 232–233
        for Mobile Safari, 372
        for touch, 367–372
                calling priority of handlers, 367–368
                and capture stage, 369–370
                handlers based on object methods,
                        371–372
                preventing default behavior, 370

propagation of, 370
event.source property, 323
event.storageArea property, 434
event.target property, 274
event.uri property, 434
evolution curve, for animations with CSS, 284–285
exceptions, for JavaScript debugging, 54–55
Exceptions button, 20
exec( ) method, 354–355
Execute Script. menu option, 217
executeSequence( ) method, 447
executeSql( ) method, 444, 446, 452–454, 458
execution context, of JavaScript, 308–312
    apply( ) method, 308–310
    call( ) method, 308–310
    and funcRef( ) method, 310
    handlers and callbacks, 310–312
export dialog box, 214
ext command, 22
extract( ) method, 238
eyeColor property, 307

F

FALLBACK sections, manifest file, 461–462
feedback during processing, using Ajax, 363–365
    and excessive waiting times, 364–365
    visual feedback, 363–364
file, // URL scheme, 323
fill( ) method, 176
fillStyle property, 175
finalizeStrokes( ) method, 391
Firebug Lite tool, 63
Firebug tool, 63
Firefox browser, 7
fit( ) method, 389
.flip class, 280
font window, 214
<font> tag, 213–214
FontForge tool, 213–214, 216
FontMetrics property, 185
fonts, preinstalled and downloadable, 211–218
for.in statement, 313
formats, for Ajax returned data, 348–353
    and JSON security considerations, 353
    parsing JSON, 352–353

parsing XML, 349–352
formatTime( ) function, 230
FQDN (fully qualified domain name), 431
<frame> tag, 330
<frameset> tag, 330
frameworks
    Cocoa Touch, 129
    MooTools, 353
    PastryKit, 69
from( ) function, 140
from(<color>) function, 140
full-screen, for stand-alone mode, 79–81
fully qualified domain name (FQDN), 431
funcRef( ) method, and execution context of JavaScript, 310
function curve, timing of for CSS transitions, 272–273
function keyword, 302
functions, for three-dimensional effects with CSS, 263
Functions column, 59

G

<g> tag, 208–209
gallery.css file, 132
General submenu, Settings application, 398
Generate( ) function, 217
Generate Fonts. menu option, 214
geolocation API, 397–399
    privacy considerations, 398
    setup considerations, 398–399
gesturechange event, 385–386
gestureend event, 385
gestures
    creating, 387–395
        and accuracy, 394–395
        bounding box object for, 388–389
        one piece of code for, 388–395
        registering user strokes, 389–392
        using recognizer object, 392–393
    precomputed, 384–386
gesturestart event, 385
GET request, for Ajax HTTP request, 344–345
getComputedStyle( ) method, 268
getContext( ) method, for <canvas> tag, 167–172
getCSSCanvasContext( ) method, 168
getCurrentLocation( ) method, 406
getCurrentPosition( ) method, 399, 401, 410

getElementById( ) function, 59
getFilteredIndex( ) method, 241
getImageData( ) method, 194
getJSON( ) function, 361
getMatrix( ) function, 279
getResponseHeader( ) method, 346
getSVG( ) function, 205
getSVGDocument( ) method, 207
getters and setters, in JavaScript, 313–314
getText( ) method, 436
getTime( ) method, 432
globalAlpha property, 190
globalCompositeOperation property, 189–
    191
Google Maps
    putting user on map with, 403–410
        centering map on location of user,
        405–407
        marking position of user, 407–408
        showing accuracy, 408–410
        showing map, 403–405
    watching users's position on, 412–413
Google Maps API, 407
Gradient Editor tool, 141
gradients
    for <canvas> tag, 174–175
    with CSS, 137–142
        color handling for, 140–142
        sizing, 139
        syntax for, 137–140
graduations, in compass web app, 418–419
Graffiti application, 387
graphical user interface (GUI), 67
.group-wrapper, 108
GUI (graphical user interface), 67

H

<h1> heading, 44
HandBrake, encoding media for web apps
    using, 253–256
handleAsyncState( ) function, 238
handleChapter( ) method, 245
handleEvent( ) method, 371, 379, 381
handleFrameMessage( ) function, 329, 333
handleParentMessage( ) function, 329, 338
handlers
    events for touch
        based on object methods, 371–372
        calling priority of, 367–368

and execution context of JavaScript,
    310–312
hash property, 206
Haversine formula, 414
HE-AAC (High Efficiency Advanced Audio
    Coding), 250
<head> tag, 75, 326
header-button class, 152
height attribute, 196, 210, 221, 224, 260
height property, 76, 221, 318
Hewitt, Joe, 70
hide( ) function, 93
hiding address bar, web applications, 85–86
High Efficiency Advanced Audio Coding
    (HE-AAC), 250
hosts.js file, 335
href attribute, 80, 210
hsl( ) definitions, colors with CSS, 136–137
hsl( ) function, 136, 384
html variable, 350, 363
<html> tag, 459, 464
HTML5
    cross-document communication with,
    323–325
        API for, 323–324
        data type support, 324
        and security, 325
    web standards for, 8
HTMLAudioElement interface, 224
HTMLMediaElement interface, 226–227
HTTP status codes, for Ajax HTTP request,
    347–348
HTTP_ORIGIN variable, 360
HYBRID constant, 405

I

i button, Safari, 30
<i> tag, 290, 292, 294
icon, for stand-alone mode, 77–78
id attribute, 166
id selector, 39
IDE (integrated development environment), 3
<iframe> tag, 196
IIS (Internet Information Services), 16, 20
IIS Manager view, 26
iLBC (Internet Low Bitrate Codec), 251
images directory, 130–131
<img> tag, 167, 197–199, 205, 260
Inbound Rules option, Control Panel, 21
incrementCounter( ) function, 53

index_code.php file, 131
INDEX_SIZE_ERR exception, 226–227, 245
index.html file, 82, 130, 325, 332, 338, 403, 424
index.php file, 130
inheritance, in JavaScript, 305–308
    prototype chain, 307–308
    prototype-based, 305–306
    shared properties, 306–307
init( ) method, 170, 277, 318, 404, 406, 451
initChevron( ) function, 203
initEvent( ) method, 383, 393
initFeedList( ) method, 447
initialize( ) method, 306
Initial-scale property, 76
initTabBarIcons( ) function, 294, 297
innerHTML method, 363
innerHTML property, 41, 329, 350
input elements, 101
input types, and user experience, 100–101
INSERT instruction, 446
Inspect Element context menu option, Safari, 30, 37
inspect(object); function, 47
install option, apt-get command, 22
Install PHP button, 17
integrated development environment (IDE), 3
interactive shell, for JavaScript debugging, 48
Internet & Wireless section, Apple menu, 14
Internet Explorer, 7
Internet Information Service Manager option, 26
Internet Information Services (IIS), 16, 20
Internet Information Services Manager administrative tool, 20
Internet Low Bitrate Codec (iLBC), 251
INVALID_ACCESS_ERR exception, 448
INVALID_STATE_ERR exception, 245, 443, 454, 463
iOS Dashboard style, 149
ipconfig command, 22
iPhone & iPod Touch profile option, HandBrake, 253
iPhoneOS, UI for web apps, 109–110
item( ) method, 448
iUI framework, 70

code isolation, 314–317
combining with CSS, 268–270
    accessing current styles, 268
    native object to compute matrices, 268–270
controlling offline web application cache with, 462–463
debugging, 46–57
    and breakpoints, 50–51
    Call Stack pane, 53
    and exceptions, 54–55
    interactive shell for, 48
    logging to console, 46–48
    Scope Variables pane, 54
    stepping buttons for, 52
    Watch Expressions pane, 53
execution context of, 308–312
    apply( ) method, 308–310
    call( ) method, 308–310
    and funcRef( ) method, 310
    handlers and callbacks, 310–312
getters and setters in, 313–314
inheritance in, 305–308
    prototype chain, 307–308
    prototype-based, 305–306
    shared properties, 306–307
libraries in, creating, 316–317
methods in, accessing, 312–313
object-oriented programming with, 302–305
    constructors in, 303–304
    objects in, 302–303
    prototypes in, 304–305
procedural model of, 301–302
properties in, accessing, 312–313
spinner animation example, 317–319
web standards for, 8–9
JavaScript API, 166–167
jQTouch framework, 70
jQuery library, 70
JSON
    client-side rendering using, 354–356
        formatting variables, 355–356
        using template variables, 354–355
    parsing, 352–353
    security considerations for, 353
json_encode( ) function, 357
JSONP, cross-origin communication for Ajax using, 357–358
json.php file, 357

J

JavaScript, 301–319

K

key( ) method, 433
key frames, for animations with CSS, 282–283
kind attribute, 240
Komodo Edit, 3–5, 16, 27

L

label attribute, 233
language, auto-selection, 239–240
lastIndex property, 355
latitude, 399–400
length property, 226, 449
lengthComputable property, 346, 465
<li> element, 123
libraries, creating in JavaScript, 316–317
/Library/Webserver/Documents/ folder, 15
limitations, of cross-document communication, 322–323
line styles, in <canvas> tag, 179–180
linear keyword, 273
Linear PCM (linear pulse-code modulation), 250
<link> tag, 36, 39, 78–79, 87, 114
Linux, 22
lists, and user experience, 106–109
Live Preview option, HandBrake, 256
load( ) method, 247–248
load event, 45, 346
loaded( ) method, 338
loaded property, 346
loadeddata event, 232
loadedmetadata event, 222, 232, 247
loadFeed( ) function, 450
loadImage( ) function, 133
Loading timeline, 55
loadResource( ) method, 238
loadstart event, 346
local( ) function, 214
Local Storage pane, in Storage Inspector, 61
localStorage property, 431–432
location-aware web applications, 397–430
    building compass web app, 416–430
        adding elements to document, 424–425
        animating compass, 427–429
        creating mobile elements, 416–418
        dial shine, 421

graduations, 418–419
needles, 420–421
preparing document to receive location data, 425–426
preventing staggering needles, 429–430
rendering compass, 422–424
using location data, 426–427
geolocation API, 397–399
    privacy considerations, 398
    setup considerations, 398–399
getting current position, 399–402
    accuracy, 402
    cached location, 402
    handling errors from requests, 401
    longitude and latitude, 399–400
    timeout, 402
processing data, 413–416
    direction to take, 415–416
    distance between two points, 413–414
    sharper distance between two points, 414–415
putting user on map with Google Maps, 403–410
    centering map on location of user, 405–407
    marking position of user, 407–408
    showing accuracy, 408–410
    showing map, 403–405
tracking user's position, 410–413
    registering for updates, 410–411
    specific behavior of watcher, 411–412
    watching position on Google Maps, 412–413
logging to console, JavaScript debugging, 46–48
longitude, 399–400
loop attribute, 233

M

Mac OS, 14–16
    Apache on, 14–15
    PHP script engine for, 15–16
magazine.html file, 155
magnifying glass tool, 43
mailto, URL scheme, 110
main view, 45

main.css file, 83, 118, 150, 180, 203, 290, 364, 437
main.js file, 86–87, 118, 180
makeNoise( ) method, 304, 306, 308, 310
Manage security settings, for Windows firewall option, 20
Manager administrative tool, Internet Information Services, 20
Manager option, Internet Information Service, 26
manifest attribute, <html> tag, 459
manifest file, 459–462
    CACHE sections, 460
    FALLBACK sections, 461–462
    NETWORK sections, 460–461
map variable, 404
MapKit framework, 403
masks, with CSS, 287–288
Math.atan( ) method, 415
Math.atan2( ) method, 415
matrices
    combining CSS with JavaScript, native object to compute, 268–270
    custom transformations with, 261–262
matrix( ) function, 257, 261, 268–270
matrix3d( ) function, 263, 268–270
matrix.inverse( ) method, 269
matrix.multiply(matrix) method, 269
matrix.rotateAxisAngle(x, y, z, angle) method, 270
matrix.rotate(x, y, z) method, 269
matrix.scale(x, y, z) method, 269
matrix.setMatrixValue(newMatrix) method, 269
matrix.toString( ) method, 270
matrix.translate(x, y, z) method, 269
maximumAge option, 402
maximum-scale property, 76
maxWidth parameter, 184
measureText( ) method, 184–186
media attribute, 87, 114
media content in web apps, 219–256
    audio formats supported, 250–251
    chapters for, 243–247
    embedding audio, 224–225
    embedding video, 220–224
        getting video info, 221–222
        placeholder for, 222–223
        playing, 222–223
    encoding for, 251–256
        using HandBrake, 253–256

using QuickTime Player, 251–253
    events supported for, 232–233
    playing automatically, 247–248
    ranges for, 227–232
    reasonable amounts of, 225
    subtitles for, 234–243
        displaying, 234–238
        language auto-selection, 239–240
        methods for, 240–243
    video formats supported, 248–250
media.HAVE_CURRENT_DATA (2) constant, 245
media.HAVE_ENOUGH_DATA (4) constant, 245
media.HAVE_FUTURE_DATA (3) constant, 245
media.HAVE_METADATA (1) constant, 245
media.HAVE_NOTHING (0) constant, 245
message parameter, postMessage( ) method, 324
messaging API, 339
metadata keyword, 240
methods
    in JavaScript, accessing, 312–313
    for subtitles, for media content in web apps, 240–243
metrics
    of Mobile Safari, 74
    of viewport, 75–76
Metrics pane, in Web Inspector, 40–43
    Event Listeners pane for, 42–43
    Properties pane for, 41–42
minimum-scale property, 76
MMS (Multimedia Messaging Services), 251
Mobile Safari
    behavior for cross-document communication, 330–331
    deleting database with, 456–457
    and web applications, 73–75
        and app considerations for, 75
        is full-featured, 73–74
        metrics of, 74
    and WebKit Developer tools, 32–34
Mobile Safari resize algorithm, 129
Model-View-Controller (MVC), 6
MooTools framework, 353
More button, 309
mouse events, for Mobile Safari, 372
moveNodes( ) method, 382–383
moveSlides( ) function, 279
moveTo( ) method, 177

MP3 (MPEG-1 audio layer 3), 250
MPEG-4 Advanced Audio Coding (AAC), 250
multilayer, backgrounds with CSS, 134–135
Multimedia Messaging Services (MMS), 251
multiple hosts, for web server, 23–24
    Unix system, 23
    Windows system, 24
multitasking user experience, 91
Multi-Touch events, 373–376
    cancelling, 376
    handling, 373
    overview, 373
    unlimited touch points for, 374–376
MVC (Model-View-Controller), 6
myTimer( ) function, 49–50, 53–54, 59

N

Nakano, Tomoaki, 212
native-style features in web apps, menus
        with <canvas> tag, 180–181
navigation, and user experience, 91–92
navigator.language property, 233
navigator.userAgent property, 225
needles, in compass web app
    overview, 420–421
    preventing staggering needles, 429–430
NETWORK sections, manifest file, 460–461
networkState property, 247–248
new _com property, 336
new keyword, 303–304, 306
New Live Folder menu option, Komodo Edit
        utility, 130
New project from template menu option,
        Komodo Edit utility, 88
New Project menu option, Komodo Edit
        utility, 82
New Rule option, Control Panel, 21
No Cache button, 466
<noframes> tag, 330
no-repeat rule, 202
noupdate event, 464
number type, 100

O

<object> tag, 196–197, 199, 205–206
object-oriented programming, with
        JavaScript, 302–305

constructors in, 303–304
    objects in, 302–303
    prototypes in, 304–305
objects, in JavaScript, 302–303
obsolete event, 464, 466
offline web application cache, 458–466
    checking state of network, 466
    controlling with JavaScript, 462–463
    deleting, 465–466
    how it works, 458–459
    manifest file, 459–462
        CACHE sections, 460
        FALLBACK sections, 461–462
        NETWORK sections, 460–461
    reacting to events sent by, 464–465
offsetHeight property, DOM, 221
offsetWidth property, DOM, 221
onclick attribute, 368
onLine property, 466
onreadystatechange event, 346
onreadystatechange property, 345
open( ) method, for Ajax HTTP request, 344
Open File. menu option, QuickTime Player, 251
openDatabase( ) function, 442–443, 454
OpenType Font (OTF), 213
Opera, 7
option menu, 40
ordering of box model, for CSS, 159–160
origin property, 380
_originalMatrix property, 386
OTF (OpenType Font), 213
Output Settings, HandBrake, 255
overflow property, 276

P

<p> tag, 44, 122, 339
packing of box model, for CSS, 161–162
page view state, 379
PageChanged event, 382–384
PageMovedLeft event, 382
PageMovedRight event, 382
pageview-group container, 378
pageview-wrapper class, 378
pageX property, 376
pageY property, 376
panTo( ) function, 413
parse( ) method, 238, 240, 242
parseFromString( ) method, 440
PastryKit framework, 69

patterns, for <canvas> tag, 175
pause( ) method, 245
pause event, 232
paused property, 245
perspective, three-dimensional effects with CSS, 263–265
perspective( ) function, 263
phone element, 101
photo gallery, with CSS, 130–133
PHP file template, Komodo Edit utility, 27
PHP script engine
    for Mac OS, 15–16
    for Windows, 17–20
PHP5 module, 16
Picture Settings button, HandBrake, 254
Picture tab, HandBrake, 254
pixels, and <canvas> tag, 191–195
placeholder, for video in web apps, 222–223
play( ) method, 223–225, 232, 246–247
playbackRate property, 233
played container, 230
played property, 227
playing media content, in web apps automatically, 247–248
<polygon> element, 201
<polyline> element, 201
position, fixed rule, 372
position property, 40, 258
position.coords.accuracy property, 400
position.coords.altitude property, 400
position.coords.altitudeAccuracy property, 400
position.coords.heading property, 400
position.coords.latitude property, 400
position.coords.longitude property, 400
position.coords.speed property, 400
position.timestamp property, 400
POST request, for Ajax HTTP request, 344–345
poster attribute, <video> tag, 222, 253
postMessage( ) method, 324, 334, 336
precomposed option, 78
Preferences window, Safari, 30
prepareFlipCurrent( ) function, 280
prepareFlipSide( ) function, 280
preventDefault( ) method, 370, 372, 386
preventing default behavior, events for touch, 370
Preview in browser menu option, Komodo Edit utility, 83
Preview Window button, HandBrake, 256

print function, 47
privacy considerations, geolocation API, 398
procedural model, of JavaScript, 301–302
processFeed( ) function, 436, 439, 450–451
products key, 441
Profile tab
    Developer Tools window, 35
    in Web Inspector, 57–60
Profiles icon, 57
progress event, 346, 464–465
ProgressEvent type, 465
Project menu, Komodo Edit utility, 88
propagation, of events for touch, 370
properties
    for animations with CSS, 283–284
    in JavaScript
        accessing, 312–313
        shared, 306–307
Properties pane, for Metrics pane, 41–42
propertyName property, 274
prototypes, in JavaScript, 304–305
    chain of, 307–308
    prototype-based inheritance, 305–306
proxies, cross-origin communication for Ajax using, 356–357
proxy.php script, 356, 361
push( ) method, 309
putImageData( ) method, 195

Q

quadraticCurveTo( ) method, 178
Quality section, HandBrake, 254
querySelector( ) method, 93
QuickTime Player, encoding media for web apps using, 251–253

R

ranges, for media content in web apps, 227–232
ratechange event, 232–233
readyState property, 238, 245, 345–346
recognizer object, for gestures, 392–393
Record button, 57
<rect> tag, 197
reflections, with CSS, 286–287
refresh( ) function, 440, 448
Refresh button, 438, 440
rel attribute, 78

Reload button, 59
removeEventListener( ) method, 311, 368, 373
removeItem( ) methods, 434
render( ) method, 422
Rendering timeline, 55
request method, 344
resize algorithm, Mobile Safari, 129
Resources viewer, in Web Inspector, 44–46
responseText property, 238, 347–348
responseXML property, 347
responsiveness, and user experience, 103–105
    handling taps, 105
    handling wait times, 103–104
restore( ) method, 183, 189, 419
restoring states, of <canvas> tag, 183
result.insertId property, 448
result.rows property, 449
result.rowsAffected property, 448
return formats, for Ajax, 348–353
    and JSON security considerations, 353
    parsing JSON, 352–353
    parsing XML, 349–352
reveal( ) function, 93
rgb( ) function, 135, 205
ROADMAP constant, 405
ROLLBACK command, 444
rotate( ) method, 182, 257, 259, 386, 428–429
rotate3d( ) function, 263
rotateX( ) function, 263
rotateY( ) function, 263
rotateZ( ) function, 263
rotating elements, with CSS, 259–260
Run ActiveX Control option, 18
Run Add-on option, 18

S

Safari, deleting database with, 456–457
SATELLITE constant, 405
save( ) method, 183, 189, 419
Save For Web. menu option, QuickTime Player, 251
saving states, of <canvas> tag, 183
scale( ) method, 257, 260, 386, 417
scaleX( ) method, 260
scaleY( ) method, 260
scaling elements, with CSS, 260

Scope Variables pane, for JavaScript debugging, 54
screen orientation, handling changes of, 86–87
<script> tag, 36, 49, 358
Scripting timeline, 55
scripting window, 217
scripts directory, 86–87
Scripts tab, 49
scripts/gallery.js file, 132
scrolling events, for Mobile Safari, 372
scrollTop( ) method, 86
SDK (Software Development Kit), 9
search type, 100
searching in Web Inspector, 43–44
security
    and cross-document communication
        with HTML5, 325
        for subdomains, 341
    Windows, settings for, 20–22
Security Center option, Control Panel window, 20
Security tab, 456
SECURITY_ERR exception, 191, 344
seekable property, 227
seeked event, 232–233
seeking property, 232–233
Select( ) function, 217
SELECT command, 450
SELECT statement, 448
<select> tag, 110, 242
selectors, and CSS, 121–124
    overview, 121–122
    repetitive layout patterns with, 122–124
Self column, 59
send( ) method, 345, 347
sendEvent( ) method, 382–383
sendMessageToFrame( ) function, 329
sensor parameter, 404
Services and Applications section, 26
Session Storage pane, in Storage Inspector, 61
sessionStorage, behavior of, 433–434
setAttribute( ) method, 208, 312
setAttributeNS( ) function, 210
setCenter( ) method, 404, 413
setCharacteristic( ) method, 313
setColor( ) method, 309
setInterval( ) method, 310
setItem( ) method, 434
setters and getters, in JavaScript, 313–314

setTimeout( ) method, 310
Settings application, 398, 456
setTitle( ) method, 336
setTransformation( ) method, 270
setup( ) function, 238, 242, 247
setZoom( ) method, 407
shadowBlur property, 188
shadowColor property, 187
shadowOffsetY property, 188
shadows
    in <canvas> tag, 187–188
    with CSS, 147–150
        box, 148–149
        example of, 150
        text, 149–150
shapes, in <canvas> tag, 175–181
    arcs, 177–178
    basics of, 172–173
    curves, 178–179
    line styles, 179–180
    native-style menus with, 180–181
shared properties, inheritance in JavaScript,
    306–307
shine variable, 421
shouldDisplay( ) method, 238
shouldStop property, 245
Show Databases button, 456
Show Develop menu in menu bar option,
    Safari, 30
Show Error Console option, Safari Develop
    menu, 31
Show Web Inspector option, Safari Develop
    menu, 31
showImages( ) function, 133
showTrends( ) method, 361
simplicity of user experience
    adapting text size, 99
    allowing space for touch, 98
    avoiding clutter, 96–97
    avoiding multiplying steps, 102
    and input types, 100–101
    limiting user-supplied information, 101–
        102
    user interface concerns, 97–98
simulator for iPhone and iPad
    testing using, 9–10
    vs. using real device, 10
Size view, 45
sizing
    of backgrounds with CSS, 128–130
    of gradients with CSS, 139

skew( ) method, 257, 261, 270
skewX( ) method, 261
skewY( ) method, 261
slide( ) function, 278–279, 282
.slide class, 279
SMIL (Synchronized Multimedia Integration
    Language), 195, 207
Snippet Editor menu, Safari, 31
Software Development Kit (SDK), 9
someFunc( ) function, 316
source editors
    Dashcode, 5–6
    Komodo Edit, 3–5
Source table, 446, 458
space, allowing for taps, 98
special effects, with CSS, 285–288
    masks, 287–288
    reflections, 286–287
spinner animation example, and JavaScript,
    317–319
.spinning class, 364
splash screen, for stand-alone mode, 79
SQLResultSetRowList list type, 448
src attribute, 196
staggering needles, preventing, 429–430
stand-alone mode, for web applications, 77–
    81
    icon for, 77–78
    running app full-screen, 79–81
    splash screen for, 79
    status bar for, 80
start( ) method, 226
Start Page, Komodo Edit utility, 4
startHandler( ) function, 386
starting for animations, with CSS, 283
startTime property, 227
startup.png file, 83
states, of <canvas> tag, 183
status bar, and stand-alone mode, 80
status property, 357
stepping buttons, for JavaScript debugging,
    52
stop( ) method, 172
Stop button, 412
stopPropagation( ) method, 370
Storage Inspector, in Web Inspector, 60–61
    Cookies pane in, 61
    Databases pane in, 61
    Local Storage pane in, 61
    Session Storage pane in, 61
Storage interface, 431

storageArea property, 434
Street View mode, 410
stroke( ) method, 176, 189
strokes.js file, 392
strokeStyle property, 175
<strong> tag, 44
style attribute, 39
style property, 268
<style> tag, 39
styles directory, 114, 132
Styles pane, 41
styles.css style sheet, 107
subdomains, cross-document
        communication for, 340–341
    changing domain properties, 340–341
    and security, 341
subtitles, for media content in web apps,
        234–243
    displaying, 234–238
    language auto-selection, 239–240
    methods for, 240–243
subtitles keyword, 240
successCallback( ) function, 412, 426
sudo command, 22
supported formats, for media content in web
        apps
    audio, 250–251
    video, 248–250
<svg> tag, 196, 214
svgLoaded( ) function, 206
swapAction( ) function, 412
swapCache( ) method, 463, 465
Synchronized Multimedia Integration
        Language (SMIL), 195, 207
syntax, for gradients with CSS, 137–140
SYNTAX_ERR exception, 324
System Preferences, Apple menu, 14

■T

tab bar with masks example, with CSS,
        288–298
    icons for, 292–296
    images as icons, 297–298
    initial tab bar, 289–291
    placeholder for icons, 291–292
table property, 114
tables
    adding data to, 446–447
    creating, 444–446
    querying data from, 447–449

Tabs & Sidebars menu, Komodo Edit utility,
        4
taps
    allowing space for, 98
    responsiveness of, and user experience,
        105
:target pseudoclass, 289, 291–292
:target pseudoselector, 75
:target pseudoselector, CSS, 75
targetOrigin parameter, postMessage( )
        method, 324–325
targetTouches property, 374, 376
tel, URL scheme, 110
tel type, 100
Template folder, 88
template variables, client-side rendering
        using JSON, 354–355
Terminal window, 15–16, 22, 24
TERRAIN constant, 405
test( ) method, 353
testing
    using real device, 10
    using simulator for iPhone and iPad, 9–
        10
    web server for applications, 27–28
text, in <canvas> tag, 183–187
    alignment of, 186–187
    baseline of, 185–186
    drawing, 184–185
Text API, 183, 418
text shadows, with CSS, 149–150
text size, adapting, 99
textAlign property, 186
textBaseline property, 185–186
textContent property, 329
text-shadow property, 147, 149–150
text-stroke-color property, 150
text-stroke-width property, 150
this keyword, 303
three-dimensional effects, with CSS, 262–
        268
    back face visibility, 266–268
    functions for, 263
    preserving 3D aspect, 265–266
    setting perspective, 263–265
Time To Live (TTL), 440
Timed Text Markup Language (TTML), 234
Timeline tab, in Web Inspector, 55–57
timeout, in location-aware web applications,
        402
TIMEOUT type error, 402

timeupdate event, 222, 232, 238, 245
timing
    for animations with CSS, 283
    function curve, for CSS transitions, 272–
        273
Title link, 339
<title> element, 329, 339
TLD (top-level domain), 23
to( ) function, 140
to(<color>) function, 140
toDataURL( ) method, 172, 408
top-level domain (TLD), 23
toString( ) method, 303, 324, 432
Total column, 59
total property, 346
touch
    allowing space for, 98
    events for, 367–372
        calling priority of handlers, 367–368
        and capture stage, 369–370
        handlers based on object methods,
            371–372
        preventing default behavior, 370
        propagation of, 370
    events with Mobile Safari, 372
        mouse events, 372
        scrolling, 372
    Multi-Touch events, 373–376
        cancelling, 376
        handling, 373
        overview, 373
        unlimited touch points for, 374–376
    page view example with, 377–384
        container for, 378
        creating custom events, 382–383
        elements for, 378–382
        handling custom events, 384
        overview, 377
touchcancel event, 376
touch.clientX property, 376
touch.clientY property, 376
touchend event, 373, 376, 381
touchendHandler( ) method, 381
touches property, 374, 376
touch.identifier property, 376
touchmove event, 373
touch.pageX property, 376
touch.pageY property, 376
touch.screenX property, 376
touch.screenY property, 376
touchstart event, 373–374, 385, 391

touch.target property, 376
TRACE method, 344
Track button, 412
TRACK method, 344
<track> tag, 233–234, 237, 239
tracking user's position, in location-aware
        web applications, 410–413
    registering for updates, 410–411
    specific behavior of watcher, 411–412
    watching position on Google Maps, 412–
        413
transaction( ) method, 444–446, 452, 455
transform( ) method, 182, 270
transform attribute, 201
transform property, 257–258
transformations, for <canvas> tag, 181–183
transforming elements, with CSS, 257–262
    custom transformations with matrices,
        261–262
    distorting, 261
    and origin of transformation, 262
    rotating, 259–260
    scaling, 260
    support for, 258
    translating element coordinates, 260
transform-origin property, 262
transform-style property, 266
transform-timing-function keywords, 273
transformToFragment( ) method, 351
transition-delay property, 271
transitionend event, 274, 381
TransitionEvent type, 274
transitions, with CSS, 270–274
    completed event, 274
    initiating, 271–272
    property for, 271
    timing function curve, 272–273
translate( ) method, 182, 257, 260, 279
translate3d( ) method, 272, 380
translateX( ) method, 260, 380
translateY( ) method, 260
translating element coordinates, for CSS,
        260
transparency, and <canvas> tag, 189–190
TrueType Font (TTF), 213
try.catch statement, 55
TTF (TrueType Font), 213
TTL (Time To Live), 440
TTML (Timed Text Markup Language), 234
Twitter trends example, using Ajax, 360–363
    feed for, 360

rendering data, 360–363
Typefaces application, 212

U

UNCACHED state, 462
Unix, multiple hosts for web server with, 23
update( ) method, 463
UPDATE operation, 450
updateFeed( ) function, 451
updateready event, 464
updates, for web applications, 73
updateTime( ) function, 230
updatetime event, 230
upsertNews( ) function, 454
uri property, 434
url( ) function, 214
url parameter, 344, 460
url type, 100
<use> tag, 209–210
user experience, 89–116
    and app focus, 102
    design guidelines for, 105–109
        adaptability, 105–106
        using lists, 106–109
    giving users control, 95
    iPad user interface, 110–115
        considerations for, 110–112
        targeting for, 113–115
    iPhoneOS user interface, 109–110
    and multitasking, 91
    and navigation, 91–92
    responsiveness, 103–105
        handling taps, 105
        handling wait times, 103–104
    showing ads thoughtfully, 92–95
    simplicity of
        adapting text size, 99
        allowing space for touch, 98
        avoiding clutter, 96–97
        avoiding multiplying steps, 102
        and input types, 100–101
        limiting user-supplied information,
            101–102
        user interface concerns, 97–98
user feedback, with CSS, 118–119
user strokes, registering for gestures, 389–
    392
user-scalable property, 76
/Users/username/Sites/ folder, 14
.useSpinner class, 171

V

v parameter, 221
var keyword, 315
VARCHAR field type, 445
vector graphics, 195–211
    animation of, 207–210
    bugs with, 210–211
    coordinates system for, 196–199
    drawing shapes with, 200–201
    interoperability of, 201–207
    using in documents, 196
version property, 454
VERSION_ERR exception, 455
Vi utility, 16, 23–25
video
    embedding in web apps, 220–224
        getting video info, 221–222
        placeholder for, 222–223
        playing, 222–223
    supported formats for media content in
        web apps, 248–250
Video Codec option, HandBrake, 255
Video tab, HandBrake, 254–255
<video> tag, 219, 221, 223, 225, 233, 239,
    253
video.css style sheet, 228
video.js file, 229, 238
View and create firewall rules section,
    Control Panel, 21
.view container, 107
View menu, Komodo Edit utility, 82
.view rule, 84
viewBox attribute, 198–199
viewport, metrics of, 75–76
viewport meta tag, 76
virtual hosts, for web server, 24–27
    with Apache, 24–25
    on Windows, 26–27
visual feedback, during processing, 363–364
volume property, 233
volumechange event, 232–233

W

W3C (World Wide Web Consortium), 8, 74
W3C WebApps Working Group (WWAWG),
    61
wait times
    feedback during processing, using Ajax,
        364–365

and user experience, 103–104

waiting event, 232

WAITING state, 381–382

Watch Expressions pane, for JavaScript
   debugging, 53

watchPosition( ) method, 411, 426

Web App Template project, 82

web applications, 67–88
   advantages of, 71–73
      App Store not necessary, 72–73
      cross-platform, 71–72
      hardware access for, 72
      updates for, 73
   example project for, 81–87
      click handler for, 87
      document template for, 82–85
      handling screen orientation changes,
         86–87
      hiding address bar, 85–86
   and focus of app, 102
   iPhone revolution of, 67–70
   and Mobile Safari, 73–75
      and app considerations for, 75
      is full-featured, 73–74
      metrics of, 74
   not easier than native apps, 73
   overview, 70
   stand-alone mode for, 77–81
      icon for, 77–78
      running app full-screen, 79–81
      splash screen for, 79
      status bar for, 80
   viewport metrics, 75–76

Web Database API, 442–458
   adding data to tables, 446–447
   creating tables, 444–446
   deleting database, 455–457
      with Desktop Safari, 456
      with Mobile Safari, 456–457
   handling transaction and query errors,
      452–454
   opening database, 442–444
   querying data from tables, 447–449
   security issues, 457–458
   updating data, 449–451
   using database in place of storage, 451–
      452
   versioning, 454–455

Web Hypertext Application Technology
   Working Group (WHATWG), 74

Web Inspector, 34–44

Audits pane in, 61–63
CSS in, 38–40
Developer Tools window, 35–36
Elements Inspector in, 37–38
error notifications in, 36
Metrics pane in, 40–43
   Event Listeners pane for, 42–43
   Properties pane for, 41–42
Profile tab in, 57–60
Resources viewer, 44–46
searching in, 43–44
Storage Inspector in, 60–61
   Cookies pane in, 61
   Databases pane in, 61
   Local Storage pane in, 61
   Session Storage pane in, 61
Timeline tab in, 55–57

Web Optimized option, HandBrake, 255

Web PI (Web Platform Installer), 17

web server for applications, 13–14
   multiple hosts for, 23–24
   testing, 27–28
   virtual hosts for, 24–27
      with Apache, 24–25
      on Windows, 26–27

Web Sharing check box, Apple menu, 14

Web Sharing option, System Preferences,
   16

web standards, 8–9

Web Storage API, 431–442
   caching Ajax requests, 435–440
      add caching capabilities, 438–440
      base document, 435–438
   notification of storage area modification,
      434
   security and privacy considerations, 435
   sending client data to server, 441–442
   sessionStorage, behavior of, 433–434
   using, 432–433

WebKit Developer tools, 29–34
   Develop menu, 30–32
   and Mobile Safari, 32–34

WebKit engine, 6–7, 162–163

WebKit interpreter, Web Inspector window,
   36

webkit-canvas( ) function, 287, 294, 364

webkit-gradient( ) function, 84, 139

webkit-mask-box-image property, 288

webkit-tap-highlight-color property, 105,
   118

webkit-touch-callout property, 121

webkitTransform property, 268
webkit-transform-3d condition, 263
webkitTransitionEnd event, 274
webkit-user-select property, 119
WHATWG (Web Hypertext Application
        Technology Working Group), 74
widget.js file, 337
width attribute, 196, 210, 221, 224, 260
width property, 76, 221, 318
Wi-Fi Positioning System (WPS), 397
window property, 302
window.location.hash method, JavaScript,
        75
window.navigator.language command, 240
window.navigator.standalone property, 79
window.orientation property, 87
Windows, 16–22
    PHP script engine for, 17–20
    security settings for, 20–22
    web server with
        multiple hosts for, 24
        virtual hosts for, 26–27
windows, cross-document communication
        between, 332–335
    notifying page is loaded, 333–334

properties of window object, 334–335
window.setTimeout( ) function, 86, 224
World Wide Web Consortium (W3C), 8, 74
WPS (Wi-Fi Positioning System), 397
:wq command, Vi utility, 16, 25
WWAWG (W3C WebApps Working Group),
        61

X, Y

xlink, herf attribute, 209
XLST, and Ajax returned data, 350–352
XML, Ajax return format, 349–352
    parsing DOM with JavaScript, 350
    using XLST, 350–352
XMLHttpRequest object, for Ajax HTTP
        request, 344
XMLHttpRequest readystate Attribute, 345

Z

zip element, 101
    zoom property, 149, 260